W9-BDZ-150

Norman E. Saul is professor of history at the University of Kansas. He received the B.A. in slavic studies at Indiana University, the M.A., Ph.D., and Certificate of the Russian Institute at Columbia University, and has also studied Russian history at the University of London and Leningrad State University. He worked on this volume as a Fulbright Research Scholar at the University of Helsinki. He is the author of *Russia and the Mediterranean, 1797-1807,* as well as articles in *The Russian Review, Soviet Studies,* and *William and Mary Quarterly,* among others.

SAILORS IN REVOLT

DK 265.35
B3
S28

SAILORS
IN REVOLT

The Russian Baltic Fleet in 1917

NORMAN E. SAUL

THE REGENTS PRESS OF KANSAS

Lawrence

FEB 1 7 1984

356041

© Copyright 1978 by The Regents Press of Kansas
Printed in the United States of America

Library of Congress Cataloging in Publication Data

Saul, Norman E.
Sailors in revolt.

Bibliography: p.
Includes index.
1. Russia—History—Revolution, 1917-1921—Naval
operations. 2. Russia (1923-   U.S.S.R.)-Voenno-
Morskoi Flot. Baltiiskii flot. I. Title.
DK265.35.B3S28   947.084'1   77-24915
ISBN 0-7006-0166-X

FOR

Alyssa, Kevin, and Julia

CONTENTS

LIST OF ILLUSTRATIONS

PREFACE

THE RUSSIAN REVOLUTION of 1917 is recognized as one of the most important events of the twentieth century. The bulk of the literature concerning the events in Russia is immense. Objective, scholarly appraisals of the period are few, however; and this has led to a weakness in the general accounts upon which students and the general public must depend for their information about the revolution. For example, one of the most obvious characteristics of the literature of the Russian Revolution is that so much of it is ideologically and intellectually oriented. This is because so many of those people who wrote memoirs or commentaries on the events were politically involved intellectuals. Relatively little is available, on the other hand, on the objectives of the rank-and-file participants in the event.

The sailors of the Russian Baltic fleet were among the most radical segments of the Russian population, committing the most violence in the February-March revolution, intensifying the opposition to the Provisional Government in northwest Russia during the summer of 1917, and actively supporting the Bolsheviks in October. Why? It is hoped that the attempt to find the answer to that question will not only tell the story of the fleet in 1917 but will also, from the perspectives of both outside and inside the Russian capital, provide insights into the revolution as a whole. Although the focus of the study is necessarily limited and little attempt is made to assess the role of other important components of the Russian population or of the Petrograd area—such as workers, peasants, the business community, garrison units—a continuity of action is intended in order to include not only 1917 but also the background and aftermath of the Bolshevik seizure of power.

Among the most important aspects of the revolution in the Baltic that will be analyzed are the interaction of war and revolution, the role of organization and indigenous leadership at the lower and middle echelons of the fleet, and the nature and degree of rank-and-file adherence to party programs. The peculiar circumstances and conditions of the fleet in 1917 were obviously of importance. To what extent did they shape the course of events in northwest Russia in 1917? The answer may show that the revolution was neither as accidental nor as fortuitous as some Western and émigré scholars have maintained, nor as determined and inevitable as Soviet commentators have asserted.

Although source material on the Baltic fleet is voluminous, thanks to a Soviet and émigré proclivity for writing memoirs and collecting documents, there are some severe limitations. Lack of opportunity to research Soviet archives has been a handicap, but one that has been mitigated by the Soviet documentary works and monographic studies based on those archives and by the ability to use Finnish archives that contain many of the original records of the fleet for that period. The greatest gap in the literature on the Baltic fleet is from the moderate and non-Bolshevik radical perspectives. So that while memoirs of Bolsheviks and émigré officers abound, fewer are available of the anarchists, the Left Socialist Revolutionaries, or the officers who stayed with the fleet beyond October of 1917.

My work on the revolution in the Russian Baltic fleet began in a graduate seminar at Columbia University under the direction of Professors Geroid T. Robinson and Oliver H. Radkey. Valuable assistance and encouragement came from Henry L. Roberts, Michael T. Florinsky, Alexander Dallin, and David Joravsky. Any researcher is indebted to the staffs of the archives and libraries where the material was collected. Special thanks are due to those of the institutions listed in the first section of the bibliography. My appreciation for expert assistance is due particularly to Captain Virkko of the War Archive in Helsinki, Harry Schwartz of the National Archives in Washington, Lev Magerovsky of Columbia University, and David Kirby of the School of Slavonic and East European Studies of the University of London. I wish to thank those who read the manuscript, especially my colleagues at the University of Kansas, Anna Cienciala, Heinrich Stammler, and John T. Alexander, for their helpful corrections and suggestions. Financial support necessary for the research and writing came from the Ford

Preface

Foundation, the United States Educational Foundation in Finland (Fulbright research fellowship), the American Council of Learned Societies, and the General Research Fund of the University of Kansas. My wife Mary Ann's advice and encouragement were vital in all aspects of the work.

For all cited extracts from the Public Records Office in London, copyright resides with the crown.

In general, I have followed the Library of Congress transliteration system, with slight modifications, in the text. Some names of individuals appear in the usual English spelling, for example, Kerensky and Trotsky, while place names are rendered in the form commonly in use at the time—for example, Helsingfors rather than Helsinki. All dates in the text are according to the official Russian calendar at the time, but the original date of a source is retained in the footnotes. For most of the reports of Western diplomats and attachés, there will be a "discrepancy" of thirteen days between the text and footnote references.

1

THE BALTIC FLEET BEFORE 1914

RUSSIA AT THE BEGINNING of the twentieth century offered a unique setting for revolution. Paradoxes and contradictions beset a country that was culturally abreast of the advanced Western powers but politically, socially, and economically quite far behind. A growing conflict, created to a large degree by the nineteenth-century technological revolution, between pressures for political and social change inside Russia and an international situation that required the maintenance of Great Power status produced a crisis that would be dramatically revealed in the Russo-Japanese War and the Revolution of 1905.

The accelerated modernization of Russia, which Peter the Great began at the end of the seventeenth century, always tended to emphasize military improvements for the basic security requirements of the Russian state—and to create and maintain an empire for which the personal glorification of rulers and officials and the need to demonstrate power in the European and world contexts played their part.

The history of the Baltic fleet provides a good example of Russia's almost desperate effort to maintain modern fighting forces and a Great-Power reputation. Created by Peter the Great both as a military necessity against Sweden in the Great Northern War (1700–1721) and as a symbol of Russia's entry into world affairs, the fleet defended the newly occupied coastline and rapidly became a modern instrument of war which was nearly on a par with the most advanced navies of the time. Much of the credit for this phenomenal naval development must go to the foreign officers and shipbuilders —mainly English, Scottish, and Dutch—who served the Russian navy

1

through much of the eighteenth century. Suffering neglect after Peter's death and handicapped by limited access to open sea, the fleet still became famous for explorations, especially in the Pacific, and provided important auxiliary services for Russia's European campaigns of the Seven Years' War. Catherine the Great revitalized the Baltic fleet for her ambitious expansion schemes and deployed a squadron to the Mediterranean in 1769–70, where it won an impressive victory over the Turks at Chesme. In the early Napoleonic Wars the navy, now divided into Black Sea and Baltic fleets, again played a major role in the Mediterranean, liberating the Ionian Islands from the French and patrolling the Italian coasts. The Russian navy, under the leadership of Admirals Apraksin, Greig, Elphinstone, Mordvinov, Ushakov, and Seniavin, established a respectable fighting record during its first hundred years, especially when one considers its natural handicaps of little merchant-marine foundation, few bases, and home waters that were frozen for several months each year.[1]

During the first half of the nineteenth century, the economic backwardness of Russia, compared with rival European powers, again became an important factor in both external and internal relations. But surprisingly, the navy nearly kept pace with the rapid technological changes of this period; at the Battle of Sinope, in 1853, the Russian fleet—ironclad and using modern artillery—annihilated its Turkish opponents and thereby contributed to the involvement of the French and British in a war against Russia. The Russian fleet, however, could not match the more maneuverable, steam-powered Western navies and therefore avoided battle with them, using the ships mainly as shore defenses or to block entrances to ports. Although Russia did not suffer a serious naval defeat in battle, the Crimean War demonstrated Russia's weakness both in the Black Sea and in the Baltic, where the fleet was placed on defense and made no effort to break the Allied naval blockade of Russia's Baltic ports.

After the Crimean War and paralleling internal reforms aimed at modernizing the government, a major naval rebuilding program was begun under the leadership of Grand Duke Constantine, minister of the navy, who, as brother of Tsar Alexander II, was one of the most influential advocates of technological advance. He was handicapped, however, by limited funds and the requirements of other duties of state; and during the last half of the century, especially after the remilitarization of the Black Sea began in 1870, the Baltic fleet suffered neglect in comparison with the Black Sea fleet and the new Pacific fleet, based at Vladivostok. It became a common practice in the Baltic fleet to maintain ships in service long after the period of their maximum potential, with the result that the fighting effectiveness of a fleet or squadron was often reduced to the capability of the worst vessel in it. Towards the end of the century, Russia, under French pressure to strengthen the military alliance (formed by 1894) against Germany, began again to concentrate on revitalizing the Baltic fleet. In 1904 there were enough new ships and trained crews to make it possible to send the fleet around Africa to the Pacific to fight Japan, but there were too many antiquated ships and poorly trained crews to ensure success.

The Battle of Tsushima, 14 May 1905, marks a major turning point in Russian naval history. Not only was a large part of the Baltic fleet destroyed, but also the morale of the navy as a whole was badly damaged. The Second Pacific Squadron, as it was called, lost nearly all of its ships and 4,500 men. This was the first major defeat (allowing for excuses for the "dastardly" surprise attack on the squadron at Port Arthur that began the war) in the two-hundred-year history of the navy. Considered by many in Russia as one of the best examples of the successful adaptation of Western technology, the Baltic fleet had been wrecked by the "Eastern" Japanese.

This naval disaster signaled Russian defeat more dramatically than anything that happened on the land side of the war could; after Tsushima, Russia was psychologically, if not actually militarily, beaten. It promoted dismay and demoralization at the upper levels of government, which may have hindered effective response to internal crises, while at the same time it demonstrated vulnerability and weakness to the revolutionary forces that had been growing in number and courage since the "Bloody Sunday" incident in January. The Battle of Tsushima was a definite contributory cause of the famous mutiny in June on the battleship *Potemkin*, which was a major landmark in Russian revolutionary history. The army, by contrast, remained basically loyal to the government in 1905, partly because no comparable portion of Russia's land forces suffered such a defeat as the Baltic fleet suffered at Tsushima.

THE REBUILDING OF THE FLEET

For the background to World War I and the Revolution of 1917, Tsushima meant most of all that the Baltic fleet would have to be rebuilt. After losses on such a scale, it was perhaps understandable that a construc-

3

tion program would eventually be inaugurated that would go well beyond the reasonable need for a fleet and would distort the rational use of Russia's defense budget.

But Tsushima was not the only cause of the increase in Russian naval expenditures that followed the war. Rapid technological changes and international rivalries sparked a naval armaments race that, in a few years' time, doubled the displacement tonnage of most classes of warships. Russia's largest battleship in the Russo-Japanese War, the 13,000-ton *Borodino*, was now outclassed by the new dreadnoughts, of which Britain and Germany were building several in the 25,000-ton range. In the interwar years a debate ensued over whether to enter this race, what kind of battle fleet to build, and in what area to concentrate—Baltic, Black Sea, or Pacific. The Naval General Staff, created in May 1906, produced one expansion plan, while the minister of the navy, Admiral A. A. Birilev, who resented the independent investigating powers of the new staff, proposed another. Both were opposed by army staff officers and by leading government officials such as Minister of Finance V. N. Kokovtsov and Grand Duke Nikolai Nikolaevich, who presided over the State Defense Council, for going far beyond the defensive role of a navy.[2] These plans, though based on carefully calculated costs, were quite unrealistic, for they would have required over 5,000 million rubles in new construction, which was equal to the entire Russian budget for two and one-half years.

Another construction plan, dubbed "the small program," which was submitted by a new naval minister, Admiral I. M. Dikov, in April 1907, called for the expenditure of only 870 million rubles over ten years (738 million for the Baltic) for new ships and base facilities. The State Defense Council continued to oppose the expanded mission of the Baltic fleet that was contained in the proposal: "to defend the Gulf of Finland, and, besides this, to act as a free naval force for supporting the interests of the empire in foreign waters."[3] Nicholas II refused to accept the council's verdict, however, and approved "the small program."

The tsar's personal dislike of Grand Duke Nikolai Nikolaevich and some of the generals, as well as the possibility that he entertained delusions of grandeur about playing a major role in world affairs, have been cited as reasons for his partiality to the navy. But it is also obvious that Nicholas II was very fond of ships. In peacetime the emperor often wore a naval uniform, and according to several sources, he spent his happiest days on one of the imperial yachts, surrounded by naval men.[4] If Nicholas I can be described as a colonel of a regiment, with each of his days a battle, then Nicholas II was a captain of a battleship, and each of his summers was a training cruise.

In actuality the proposed construction program of 1907 would have raised the Russian Baltic fleet to a level competitive with or superior to the German fleet that was normally stationed in the Baltic. This was an ambitious undertaking, considering the simultaneous naval building in Germany. The program involved, then, not only joining the armaments race by constructing dreadnoughts, but also building a host of new auxiliary ships (a main weakness in 1904-5), expanding port and base facilities, and revamping naval training programs.

Though Nicholas II's support did help in bolstering the ambitions of the naval authorities, particularly vis-à-vis the army, the tsar could no longer command the situation completely. This was partly because of Nicholas II's weakness, owing to family problems, and his natural limitations in political ability. But any tsar, even under the pre-1905 conditions of autocracy, would have had difficulty finding the revenue to finance such an enormous construction program in the already overtaxed and overindebted country. Moreover, Russia had changed since 1905: the imperial budget was now subject to public review and discussion in a new state institution, the Duma, whose authority in the field of finances was somewhat complex. In general, either the Duma—the "lower house"—or the more tractable State Council could approve budgets and vote increases in taxes, but both houses could discuss and debate these items. Though the Duma could be by-passed, as Prime Minister Stolypin demonstrated in changing the electoral laws in 1907, the government, at least after 1907, desired the cooperation and assistance of the elected Duma in carrying forth its programs. Naval construction, which constituted the single largest increase in state expenditure for this period, naturally generated considerable debate in the Duma.

The first and second Dumas were too divided, too much in opposition, and too short in duration to do much about the navy or anything else. But in the Third Duma, which lasted the full term of five years from 1907 to 1912, the appropriations for naval construction were among the most important topics of discussion. Radical and liberal delegates opposed the naval expansion on grounds of general principle (opposition to anything that would strengthen the military posture of the tsarist government) and on the more rational basis that Russia had no business trying to compete with the other Great Powers in the construction of a large navy. The Right and

5

Center groups that controlled the body favored strong military forces, but most members believed that the army should come first. This was particularly true of the Octobrists, the largest single party in the Duma, which was led by Alexander Guchkov. As a result the Duma refused to approve and finance the "small program" which had already received the tsar's blessings. What followed was a protracted and concentrated effort by the government under Stolypin to convince the Duma of the necessity for rebuilding the navy.[5]

The complexities of the maneuvering between the Duma and the government over naval construction programs are too involved to describe in detail here. Generally, the government was gradually able to persuade the leadership of the majority Right-Center bloc that a large navy was necessary in order to foster Russia's prestige and foreign policy, specifically to provide Russia with a demonstrable asset as a political ally. The Duma, however, wanted to tie any substantial concessions over naval funding to reforms of the navy, especially of the administrative and command structure, in what V. M. Purishkevich referred to openly in the Duma as "the Tsushima department."[6] The result was delay, debate, compromise, and more debate. As an emergency measure, to replace some of the capital losses in the Baltic fleet, the government proposed a bill in 1908 for the construction of four battleships of the dreadnought class at a cost of 30 million rubles each, with additional funds for the modernization of the naval shipyards that would be involved. The Third Duma again refused to sanction such a large expenditure without the promise of reform and a more detailed overall naval plan, but the State Council did give its approval after considerable prodding by Stolypin.

The Duma's reluctance to finance naval expansion was due not only to haunting memories of the navy's war record but also to fear of more naval mutinies—fear that increasing the fleet would only advance its revolutionary potential. As Purishkevich noted, "Every time that our Black Sea fleet departs for a cruise, I am afraid that in it will be another *Potemkin* and on that *Potemkin* [there will be] a Matiushenko [a leader of the mutiny of 1905]."[7]

Further development of a Baltic building program was delayed by the Bosnian crisis and by a new Turkish naval-expansion program. The latter caused the Foreign Ministry and the Duma to favor a concentration on the Black Sea fleet, and a major building program was finally approved for that area in 1911.[8] In the meantime, additional arguments were marshaled for enlarging the Baltic fleet, which the Naval Ministry and Nicholas II had

6

consistently favored. A plan to detach a portion of that fleet for more or less permanent duty in the Mediterranean, using French bases, was one of these arguments. The exposure of the political center and a major industrial area in the north to sea attack was also emphasized in support of Baltic construction, to which was added the claim that a large, active fleet would be capable of suppressing any revolutionary disturbance that might spring from the non-Russian Baltic littoral, where national consciousness was rapidly rising—in Riga, Revel, and Helsingfors—and it was no accident that expansion of bases in this area did accompany development of the fleet.[9]

But behind all of the pre–World War I debate was the growing predominance of Mahanism, the importance of sea power for national prestige. Leading the publicity effort was Nicholas Klado, Russia's foremost naval theorist and an ardent supporter of Mahan's doctrine of a large, active fleet.[10] He was backed by the editorial staff of the naval journal *Morskoi Sbornik*, the League for a Renewed Navy, and the Russian Naval Union, all of which carried on an intensive public campaign for the Naval Ministry. Most of the government and right-wing Duma leaders gradually became believers in this emphasis on the importance of the navy in the military spectrum, though they were also concerned about support for the army as well and were still insistent on naval reforms in order to make the implementation of a building program more effective. Pressure by the Duma to secure the appointment of a more-reformist naval minister was instrumental in the rise of Admiral Ivan Grigorovich to the post in 1911.[11] The new minister quickly proved to be the most adept of the tsar's officials in furthering the interests of his own department while at the same time maintaining imperial favor, one proof of which is the fact that he was the only prewar minister to keep his position until after the fall of the imperial government in 1917. His success was in glaring contrast to the failures of the minister of war, General Sukhomlinov.[12]

Within a few months of his appointment, Grigorovich secured the Duma's approval for "the program of urgent ship construction," a 420 million ruble building plan for the Baltic fleet that included four dreadnoughts and five light cruisers. Nicholas II signed it on 23 June 1912, which the tsar termed a day of great hopes for Russia, adding, "The navy must be reconstituted in a strength and power that will answer to the dignity and glory of Russia."[13] Although Admiral Grigorovich definitely deserves some of the credit for this success, improvements in Russian finances and increasing international tensions were also responsible.

How expensive it was for the Russian Empire to build a modern navy may be illustrated by the following statistics: on the eve of the war the navy absorbed 7 percent of the imperial budget, and the army 18 percent; but allotments to the navy rose 165 percent between 1909 and 1913, while the army budget rose only 22 percent. Of 352.2 million rubles actually spent on new naval construction in the seven prewar years (1908–14) about 250 million went to the Baltic fleet. According to data collected by one Soviet scholar, the average increase in naval expenditures of the Great Powers from 1907 to 1914 was 64.5 percent. Russia headed the list with an increase of 174 percent (Austria-Hungary, 143 percent; Italy, 79 percent; France, 67 percent; Germany, 62 percent; Britain, 48 percent; the United States, 39 percent; and Japan, 34 percent). Russia's total proposed naval expenditure for 1914— 246,111,003 rubles ($126,747,165)—was slightly more than Germany's and was surpassed only by those of Britain and the United States.[14]

By 1912 the now half-hearted and compromised efforts at naval reform put forward by the Duma concentrated upon the inefficiency and corruption of the state shipyards, which were notorious for being behind schedule and for exceeding anticipated budgets. These shipyards and the naval arsenals were slow to convert to twentieth-century business methods, and they remained, in comparison with those of most other countries, low in labor productivity and high in corruption. Considerable renovation and expansion were nonetheless necessary in order to build more and larger ships. The number of workers employed in the four largest Admiralty shipyards more than doubled between 1908 and 1914 to reach over 21,000.[15]

Private industries that were engaged in naval work expanded even faster. The Putilov Works—one of the largest heavy-machine building factories in Russia, located in St. Petersburg—had been producing ship parts and an occasional ship for many years, but only in 1908 did it organize a separate Shipbuilding Department. After the 1912 construction program was inaugurated, this section of the plant was enlarged, and on 1 January 1913 it officially became the Putilov Shipyards, covering 275 waterfront acres. After the completion of a new turbine factory in October, the Putilov Shipyards was one of the most modern in Europe, with two cruisers and eight destroyers under construction.[16] The awarding of government contracts to private firms followed a new policy of subsidizing industries that were in difficulty, though, considering the deplorable state of Russia's railroads by 1917, it would have been wiser for the government to spur the production of locomotives and rolling stock, of which the Putilov Works turned out only one-half its total capacity in the years before the war.

These factories were interlinked with state ones through a series of subcontracts, especially for technical equipment. In this area, corruption and conflict of interest were rampant: officials of the Naval Ministry received large "bonuses" of stock in private companies, and both active and retired naval officers obtained high salaries as consultants or directors of these firms. The degree of this activity, as well as the excessive profits of Russian and foreign businesses engaged in naval work, may have been exaggerated by Soviet historians, but there can be no doubt that naval work loomed large in the industrial activity of the Baltic ports.[17]

THE EFFECTS OF BALTIC NAVAL EXPANSION

The nature of Russian decision-making in regard to naval expansion—publicity about appropriations, delays, and the sudden passage and award of contracts—added to the industrial difficulties of the Baltic area. A foreign observer reported that in 1908 the naval section of the Putilov Works was operating with 4,500 laborers, half of the usual complement, and they were working only three days a week: "These works have suffered very severely from the strikes due to political and labor unrest. . . . The men whom I met at the various works saw little light ahead of them and have to content themselves with marking time till the political and financial skies begin to clear."[18] The same situation existed at the Obukhov Works, a few miles up the Neva from St. Petersburg, where all of the large guns for the fleet were made: "I enquired as to the class of workmen they had, and they said the men in the gunshops were the best and were good on the average, but they complained that they could not domesticate them, that is, they want to go home to their villages from time to time, with which they rarely lose touch." The average monthly wage for Russian shipyard workers in 1911 was 100 to 120 rubles ($51.50 to $61.50). But the new technical demands of the navy also increased the need for higher-paid foreign labor. Most of the employees in the gunsight shop of the Obukhov Works were Germans, under the direction of an Italian: "All the expert workmen are German or foreigners, with the exception of one Russian lad who is on one of the glass-grinding machines, the first native who has been able to work his way up successfully. The men in charge are willing to have Russians, but say that it is difficult to make careful, patient workmen of them."[19]

9

A special investigation initiated by the Duma found that because of the labor situation, the costs of materials, and general administrative inefficiency, it cost 40 percent more to build ships in Russia than to obtain them by direct foreign contracts. Nevertheless, the Duma, in approving the 1912 program, stipulated that the ships be built in Russian yards. An effort to do so only caused further delays in waiting for shipyard space to be expanded, and then it proved to be impossible. In order to save time and cut costs, much work was subcontracted abroad. Designs, especially, were often ordered from foreign firms, which also supplied their own naval engineers. But in any event, Russian private shipyards had interlocking agreements with other European companies, and some of them, Nobel-Lessner, for example, were wholly or partly owned by foreign capitalists.

In order to speed the commissioning of new warships of the latest design, the Naval Ministry also contracted indirectly with foreign firms for the construction of entire ships, mostly of small and medium size. Security and financial reasons, in addition to the pressures of Russian shipbuilding interests, naturally limited this possibility and interfered with other plans to buy existing warships from South American countries. Apparently to avoid a demonstration of political partiality, or simply to hedge bets, orders were placed with all major naval powers—France, Germany, England, and the United States. Two cruisers, for example—which were nearly ready for delivery, and were largely paid for, in German shipyards, when World War I began—became valuable additions to the German navy.[20] Even if it had been possible to complete the 1912 program, the Baltic fleet would have been severely dependent on a host of foreign companies for ongoing maintenance and replacement.

Worst of all, and despite the emergency situation that prevailed in the Baltic, a comprehensive long-term naval program was completed only in 1913. This program, had it been carried through, would have resulted in an impressively strong Russian Baltic fleet by 1930. By 1914, on the other hand, the actual results of the construction were an inadequate compromise and unrealized objectives. A few new large ships were in service but were not yet integrated into the fleet as a whole. For example, the pride of the fleet was the 23,000-ton dreadnought *Petropavlovsk*, which was laid down in 1908, launched in 1911, and commissioned in 1914 with a complement of 59 officers and 1,066 men. There was little opportunity for active training, since the mounting of guns was not finished until August; and then the ship was virtually immobilized by minefields. In 1917 its crew was one of the most radical in the navy.

Although six out of the eight fleet battleships were commissioned between 1906 and the beginning of the war, two of the new ones were of antiquated, pre-1904 design, and only three of the projected nine battle cruisers were completed during these years. Though some of the older ships had been modernized, this program had also fallen behind schedule. One of the older ships, the cruiser *Aurora*, spent an important part of the war and revolution undergoing extensive refitting in Petrograd. Around 80 percent of the destroyers, minelayers, patrol boats, and auxiliary ships that were active in 1917 entered service after 1905; but again, because of the large number of technical and strategic changes that were taking place in the interwar period, many of these were obsolete. Only one modern destroyer of the "Novik" type and a few competitive submarines were available. But the greatest handicap from the standpoint of battle performance was the number of ship designs and capabilities, with their accompanying armament; this necessitated the stockpiling and channeling of an unusually large variety of ordnance. At least the Naval Ministry and the General Staff were well aware of this problem, and influenced by studies of the Battle of Tsushima that revealed a much lower rate of fire for Russian gunners than for the Japanese, they were fairly successful in filling the naval ammunition depots. This was a sharp contrast to the situation in the army and was ironical, since the navy used little except mines during the war. The navy was also better equipped with small arms in comparison with the army, and when new Japanese rifles were brought into the country in 1916 and 1917, they were allocated to the navy first, probably because of the difficulties with regard both to retraining and to ammunition supply that might occur on the land fronts.

It should also be pointed out that while the Baltic fleet in many respects was deficient in equipment, the situation described above was to some extent unavoidable in a period of rapid technical changes and was present in all countries on the eve of World War I. What Russia especially lacked, in comparison with both its friends and foes, was the ability to remedy these defects once the war had started. Just to mention one other example of prewar short-sightedness, no one seems to have anticipated that the normal supply channel of fuel for the boilers of the Baltic fleet—anthracite coal from Britain—was likely to be cut off at the outset of a general European conflict.

Russia's greater unpreparedness for war in relation to other European powers is demonstrated by the almost total lack of coordination of strategic planning between the army and navy. This can be ascribed, at least in part, to tradition and to the rivalry during the interwar years between the Naval and War ministries for money and imperial favors, which engendered a simmering hostility down through the respective army and navy staffs. While the army, under French prodding, was developing an offensive strategy for northern Europe in an attempt to wreck the Schlieffen plan, which called for a concentration of German forces on the Western Front, the navy was evolving defensive plans for the Baltic fleet, a disharmony that was particularly odd in an age symbolized by a staff officer with an attaché case filled with plans.

THE PERSONNEL OF THE FLEET

But even the worst deficiencies in equipment and planning can be overcome, or at least mitigated, by the loyalty and bravery of well-trained officers and men in the units concerned. Unfortunately, the Baltic fleet contained too many men who fell short of the combat ideal. Correcting the physical causes and effects of Tsushima, on paper, was much easier than dealing with the causes and effects of the *Potemkin* mutiny, but the shadow of both hung over the Baltic fleet in the interwar years, and the causes and effects of both were interconnected.

The senior officers of the Baltic fleet were, on the whole, products of an earlier era—before Tsushima (and those who survived that battle could hardly be said to have gained much valuable command experience from it). For a long time, promotion on the basis more of age and connections than of merit prevailed in the fleet. Moreover, before 1905 the navy's officer corps, in contrast to that of the army, had remained largely a noble satrapy, a comfortable refuge for the younger sons of the middle nobility. The officer corps also tended to be hereditary and caste-like, with sons succeeding fathers, sometimes on the same ship. The complexion of the navy was changing, however, at the turn of the century, especially after 1907, as the result of a heavier than normal turnover in officers and of more liberal policies regarding admission to the Naval Cadet School.[21] Because of the relative rise of the middle class in Russia at the beginning of the twentieth century and because more complicated machinery required technically qualified personnel, a larger number of officers of nonnoble background entered the navy; and the change was producing strain and dissension among the officers. On the same ship there might be a commanding senior officer of aristocratic background, with little qualification for handling modern ships, and young lieutenants, recently graduated from technical schools, who were from urban, middle-class origins. This division, transcending technical abilities and age, included different world views—from the older generation's Pan-Slavism to the newer one's "Westernism."[22]

Admiral Nicholas von Essen, commander of the Baltic fleet from 1908 until his death in 1915, achieved a degree of successful working relations among the officers of the fleet. Respect for von Essen was widespread among the officers, because of his proven ability both as commander of a destroyer squadron before 1908 and as an active and steady commander in chief.[23] But this admiral does illustrate two other difficulties that existed in the officer corps. One was the large number of officers of non-Russian background. Though there is little evidence that this caused resentment among the Russian officers, it probably affected the ability of the fleet to form a solid esprit de corps, a patriotic fervor to defend "Mother Russia." Not that the Baltic fleet's German and Finno-Swedish officers were disloyal; on the contrary, they seemed to have bent over backward to demonstrate their devotion to the Russian crown. Non-Russian names seem to predominate among those commanders who had a reputation for being strict disciplinarians, while Russians stand out among those at the other end of the scale, those most sympathetic and responsive to their crews. Another divisive factor was the gulf between command and staff officers: many of the former, including von Essen, demonstrated an open dislike for the rapidly growing paper work involved in administration of the new fleet. The interwar separation of command and staff work that resulted from the creation of the Naval General Staff was reflected down through the unit structure of the Baltic fleet, creating what Admiral Grigorovich termed "a state within a state."[24]

The factions that existed among the officers were thus based on class and national backgrounds, but also on age and outlook; most of the newer officers, whether from the nobility or other classes, were oriented more toward technical and administrative work. Their greater reliance upon basic salary for support was possibly an additional factor that would have inclined them toward the security of staff jobs, and when placed in command positions, they would have been more likely to seek comfortable accommodations with their crews.

An American naval officer who visited a Russian squadron cruising in the Mediterranean during the winter of 1908-9 was informed by one of the officers that "the flag officer (Rear Admiral Litvinov) owed his promotion and present command entirely to the fact that he had been captain recently of the Imperial Yacht *Shtandart*." The visitor observed that none of the Russian officers

> cared to talk much about naval matters; in fact, that is what impresses me about the Russian naval officers, especially the older ones. They are still very sick over the war, the results of which, apparently, took the heart and spirit out of them. It will undoubtedly take some years for them to fully recover, and meanwhile, the apparent lack of spirit of the older officers cannot fail to have its effects on the younger officers eventually. . . . From my talks with the Commanding Officer, I could not see that the Division was engaged in any serious work, and was simply cruising in the old fashioned way, putting in the time as agreeably as possible.[25]

Though at least in part a reflection of Russian character as seen through American eyes, this report does provide a fairly objective outside view of life in the interwar fleet as well as proof of the existence of dissension within it. The proportion of young, technically oriented officers grew steadily after 1908, while the major commands remained in the hands of the older pre-Tsushima officers. Very few of the newer officers were able to gain command positions in the fleet prior to 1914, and then they were almost exclusively on small ships such as destroyers or patrol boats.

Still, it would be wrong to overemphasize the age division among the officers at this time, because it was a factor in almost all armed forces. The Russian bureaucracy, of which the navy was a part, tended to protect the interests of older commanders, while generational conflict was reinforced by the Russo-Japanese War, the Revolution of 1905, a new admission policy regarding cadets, and the naval-technological revolution. In comparison with that of the German navy in the same period, the Russian officer corps was lower in morale, esprit de corps, and command cohesion, factors that retarded assimilation into a unified body.[26] But the conflict lies much deeper, in the psychic clash of men and machines, with the world of Dostoevsky and Chekhov transported to the decks of a modern battleship, that peculiarly Russian ambivalence—one foot planted firmly in "Mother Russia" sentimentality and the other in the age of technology. A bridge in the form of a cult of militarism, which existed in Germany, was barely under construction in Russia.

A similar situation existed in the enlisted ranks. Many of the veteran seamen were conditioned to the discipline and traditions of the Imperial Navy, but they had been through a losing war and a tumultuous revolution. The new recruits, like the new officers, were influenced by the experience of revolution and the needs of technology. As a result of Tsushima and the expansion that followed, they formed a greater proportion of the cadre than before 1904. The normal separation between officers and men that exists in all navies, especially on larger ships, was naturally reinforced in Russia by class feelings and tradition. While some of the officers still tried to run their ships as preemancipation estates, their crews were not far removed from the condition of serfs.

Regarding the potential for mutiny or revolution, there is another important point to note about the background of the rank-and-file Baltic sailors: a majority came from nonpeasant origins. The "working class" character of the men of the Baltic fleet has been emphasized by many Soviet scholars. Statistics, confined to the 1914–16 wartime recruitments which constituted about half of the sailors of the Baltic fleet in 1917, indicate that only 25.4 percent were actually workers; the others were "semiproletarian" (26 percent) and peasant and petty bourgeois (48.6 percent).[27] Admitting the difficulty of determining class background from imperial records, even Marxist historians have problems with precise identification. Included in the petty-bourgeois classification, lumped together with the peasantry, are clerks, bakers, butchers, traders, and telegraphers. Most of the "workers" were hardly proletarian, having had only a few years of factory experience, and most were born in peasant villages. But some of the "peasants," on the other hand, may have had factory, transportation, or other work experience and were classified as "peasant" on the basis of the point of recruitment or by what they called themselves at the time.

A better idea of the origins of Baltic seamen can be obtained from a study of recruitment practice. According to a new policy that went into effect in the 1890s, assignments were made to the army and navy on the basis of qualifications at the annual recruitment in November. Up to 1897 the northern and central provinces, the most advanced in industry and trade, provided the draftees for the Baltic fleet. But the growing need in the navy for personnel with special skills forced an expansion of Baltic naval recruitment to other areas of the country.[28] An official naval manual stated:

There are appointed to the navy mechanics who have served in factories as locksmiths, turners, brass and iron boiler workers and smiths, as well as founders, pattern-makers, motorists, telegraphers, electric-light experts, fitters, and other specialists. To complete the number lacking after this, recruits are chosen preferably from inhabitants of localities near the sea coast or on navigable rivers, or the population of which, by their occupations, are the most suitable for naval service, as well as those who feel a calling to the naval service and express their wish to enter it.[29]

The results of the new recruitment policy were soon apparent. The literacy rate of recruits for the Baltic fleet jumped from 49 percent in 1897 to 75.5 percent in 1900.[30]

Quite clearly the navy received a special pick of draftees, which included a large portion of those with ship, factory, or trade experience. In some years of the early twentieth century, "workers" composed 60 percent of the navy's new inductees, while they seldom surpassed 2 percent of the army's.[31] Even the Black Sea fleet could obtain most of its manpower requirements from the ports and industrial cities of the Ukraine and the Crimea in peacetime, but in extraordinary wartime drafts, larger numbers of peasants, who constituted the great bulk of the population of the South, entered Black Sea service. In contrast with the situation in Germany, where a similar recruitment emphasis prevailed, the Russian "workers" came into service with very little, if any, trade-union discipline but with volatile strike experience. Traditionally the Russian army relied on special units, such as Cossacks, to set an example and to police other units if necessary. No such body existed in the navy. The potential for disturbance would thus obviously be greater in the Baltic fleet than in the army or in other fleet units as a result of its composition.

Special circumstances dictated, however, additional variances in recruitment for the Baltic fleet. A systematic adherence to the aforementioned policy of choosing the most qualified draftees from the northwest provinces for the fleet would have resulted in a sizable proportion of non-Russian, mainly Baltic, nationalities as sailors. To avoid this an unofficial quota system was employed to ensure a predominance of Slavs.[32] This practice only increased the chances of a Russian or Slavic worker in the area, no matter what his place of origin, of being drafted for the navy. For example, Pavel Dybenko, one of the Bolshevik leaders in the fleet in 1917, was originally from a peasant village in the Ukraine but was working as a longshoreman in Riga at the time of his induction in 1912. Generally, those who were recruited and trained in one of the two major areas—the Baltic and the Black seas—remained there. Exceptions were necessary in order to fill in losses, especially after Tsushima, and for disciplinary reasons. Geographic factors and tradition restricted the transfers of men from fleet to fleet and from ship to ship more than in most navies, but officers, on the other hand, were more frequently rotated. A sailor commonly would serve his entire term of service after training school on the same ship but under several different commanders.

Naval recruits who could not be identified as "workers" before induction would likely soon approximate this classification after entering the navy. In the years just before World War I a naval draftee would normally spend most of his first two years in training detachments, much of this time in the classroom. The emphasis on education was especially strong in the Baltic, since there was little else to do while bases were closed by ice. The course of instruction for mine men, a typical specialty, included the Russian language, arithmetic, geometry, physics, magnetism, electricity, ship tackle, shopwork, and torpedoes and explosive substances. The quality of instruction and training equipment impressed foreign observers, especially the amount of time spent in actual practice with the equipment in classroom situations.[33] Indeed, this was an area of the most successful reforms engineered by the Naval General Staff, but antiquated training ships and limited opportunity for sea practice were persistent handicaps.

The pay of enlisted men varied considerably, depending upon rank— from 9 rubles, 13 kopecks (approximately $5.00) a year for a new recruit (seaman second class) to 60 rubles, 90 kopecks for petty officers. A typical sailor in the second and third years would receive about 25 rubles base pay per year, plus 3 to 5 rubles per month for sea duty, the higher amount for service in foreign waters. Even with bonuses for meritorious performance and for reenlistments, remuneration in the navy was far less than that for a shipyard worker (100 rubles a month).[34] The low pay, the five-year term of service, crowded living quarters, scant opportunity for leave, and stiff discipline could easily arouse the hostility of the men.

An émigré Russian naval officer, reflecting on the causes of naval rebellion, listed two other special characteristics of sailors besides the high proportion that were from urban, worker backgrounds and their harsh conditions: visits to foreign ports and a special consciousness which was instilled by a combination of naval esprit de corps, skilled labor, and teamwork.[35]

Though calls to foreign ports sometimes introduced sailors to revolutionary ideas, they were not a major source of rebellious spirit in the navy. Visits were usually short; discipline and performance were at a maximum; and liberty from a ship was strictly controlled. Russian sailors abroad were usually more interested in having a good time than in absorbing revolutionary ideas. Though émigré radical agents did seek out sailors, especially in Danish and French ports, the Okhrana (political police) were usually right on their heels.

The second factor, though more elusive, did indeed play a part in fostering seaboard radicalism. Navy work was very compartmentalized, with teams functioning competitively while leadership qualities developed quickly. With many places in which to hide, or to hide things in, a spirit of rebellion could begin with one man, then infect his team, then the whole ship. Even when thoroughly radicalized in 1917, sailors would seldom forsake their uniforms or their ship. There was a certain pride about being "sailors of the *Slava*" or "Aur, oramen," and when sailors stormed the Winter Palace in October 1917 they did so as units, not as a mob. Indeed, there is evidence to suggest that those who cared the least for naval service also did not care for revolution and simply deserted both. Figures available for the manpower of the fleet indicate a surprisingly low desertion rate in 1917, especially considering the lack of control that prevailed.[36]

One of the best summations, though oversimplified, was made by Leon Trotsky:

> The very nature of their activities demands from sailors a greater degree of independence and resourcefulness, makes them more self-reliant than land soldiers. The antagonism between common sailors and the closed upper-class caste of naval officers is even deeper than it is in the army, where half the officers are plebians. Lastly, the disgrace of the Russo-Japanese war, the onus of which had been borne by the navy, destroyed any last vestige of respect the sailors might still have had for their grasping and cowardly captains and admirals.[37]

Because of the winter ice, sailors and officers of the Baltic fleet were confined to bases longer each year than those of any other large active fleet. While most of the officers lived ashore with families, the men were quartered on ships or in barracks and frequented dock areas of the base port, where contact with industrial workers and other lower-class elements of the population was possible. These bases were in or near major industrial centers—Kronstadt, near the capital city; Revel, in Estonia; Riga and Libau, the main ports of Latvia and Lithuania, respectively; and Helsingfors and Åbo (Turku), the largest cities of the Grand Duchy of Finland. But this feature is usual for all navies; what was unique for the Baltic fleet was the larger proportion of time spent in port and the greater interdependency of naval bases and industrial plants, especially after 1905. Government factories were often in close proximity to private ones. Kronstadt, for example, the old port town on Kotlin Island, about twenty miles from St. Petersburg, was under the jurisdiction of the navy for defense and administrative purposes, but it was also the site of a number of nongovernment industrial and commercial enterprises.

The interconnection of service men and workers in the factories was much greater in the navy than in the army. Artillery, the most complex item of equipment used by the army, was normally delivered in finished form to units that were many miles from the place of production. The launching of a ship in Russia initiated a period of a year or more when shipyard workers and a newly designated crew worked side by side in the heart of a port city while completing the installation and testing of equipment. Also, the ships of the Baltic fleet usually retained full crews while undergoing repairs; such was the situation of the famous cruiser *Aurora* in the winter of 1916–17, which was being remounted with new guns and engines at the Franco-Russian Works, adjacent to the Putilov Shipyards in the capital.

It should be clear from the above that the sailors of the Baltic fleet had much in common with the lower classes in the urban centers of northern Russia. This does not mean that a revolution in the Marxist sense was inevitable in the navy, but it does show that some conditions for such a revolution were present and that events that happened in the urban centers of northern Russia were bound to affect the fleet. And there were, of course, differences between workers and sailors. The living conditions of sailors were probably worse than those of workers—poor pay and hard work on steel ships (cold in winter, hot in summer) resembled prison conditions—but the monotony was broken by classroom instruction and by training cruises. The knowledge that this type of life was legally limited to the term of service probably strengthened the sailors' ability to endure, whereas the future, as reflected in workers' circumstances, could not appear very rosy.

Moreover, the 1902 code for naval servicemen prohibited attendance at public lectures and at any kind of public demonstrations or gatherings including "spectacles and concerts," riding inside streetcars or in first- and second-class coaches on the railway, and presence in any places habituated by the upper classes. Certain streets of Kronstadt, for example, were off-limits to sailors. To compensate for low pay the sailors were assured food and shelter, such as they were. Close quarters and the nature of duty aboard ship also normally meant tighter control and the maintenance of strict discipline, far greater than that in a Russian factory.

The status of the officers and men of the fleet merely provided the soil for revolutionary agitation. The seeds were not sown chiefly from abroad, or solely within the navy, but came from the development of a revolutionary movement in Russia as a whole; and in keeping with the elitist nature of Russian radicalism—a virtual monopoly of the intelligentsia—the first revolutionaries in the Baltic fleet came from the ranks of the noble officers.

THE REVOLUTIONARY MOVEMENT IN THE NAVY

Though naval "dissidents" can be found in the earliest Russian political movement, that of the Decembrists in the first quarter of the nineteenth century, the first genuinely revolutionary organization in the fleet dates from the 1870s and was directly connected with the radical offshoot of the populist movement—the People's Will—and its assault against the military bulwarks of the empire. By 1880 a Kronstadt "naval circle" was formed through the initiative of Andrei Zheliabov from Odessa, who was the "very soul" of the People's Will. The leader of the Kronstadt revolutionaries was Lieutenant Nikolai Sukhanov, who was already a member of the central committee of the group that focused its activities on the assassination of Alexander II. Sukhanov and several other naval officers—including A. P. Shtromberg, F. I. Zavalishin, and E. A. Serebriakov—concentrated their energies on the propaganda efforts of the People's Will, and it was on the hectograph in Sukhanov's apartment that the famous letter to Alexander III was printed for distribution following the successful assassination. By this time, March 1881, over one hundred officers and men of the Baltic fleet were members of the People's Will.[38]

After the arrest of Zheliabov and others most directly involved in the assassination of Alexander II, Sukhanov, along with Vera Figner, carried on the work of the central committee until December 1881, when Sukhanov himself was detained by the police. The trial of this revolutionary of the fleet received wide publicity, especially through the underground publication of his testimony and a poem, "The Decembrist," that he wrote in prison. Meanwhile, revolutionary activity in the fleet continued under the leadership of one of his associates, Lieutenant Aleksandr Butsevich, who formulated the first plan to bring the fleet to the assistance of an armed uprising in the capital. With the help of over one hundred fifty sympathetic officers he hoped to seize Kronstadt and two battleships, but before any attempt could be made, Butsevich in turn was arrested in June 1882. The involvement of the military officers in revolutionary activity naturally aroused the concern of the government of Alexander III, and a thorough screening of the armed forces netted the arrest of two hundred officers, most of whom were based at Kronstadt. This purge, however, did not bring an end to the revolutionary movement in the fleet. In fact, the agitation that began in 1880 was never fully eliminated until after the Kronstadt revolt of 1921. Several officers managed to preserve their secret affiliation with the People's Will, and one, L. F. Dobrotvorskii, rose to the rank of rear admiral. A few, such as Serebriakov, left the navy and went abroad to continue their propaganda activities.[39] And in 1884, at the height of the repression, the St. Petersburg chief of police reported: "It can be stated with almost complete certainty that a firm foundation is being prepared among the sailors of Kronstadt that in due course will provide the capability for disseminating criminal propaganda."[40]

Through the 1880s and 1890s the unequal contest persisted between the police and military authorities, on the one hand, and the revolutionaries on the other. In 1884 the Special Commission for the Prevention of the Distribution of Revolutionary Propaganda in the Army and Navy was created under the presidency of Grand Duke Nikolai Nikolaevich, the tsar's uncle. Arrests continued, but so did the seditious activity. One of the most successful and enduring of the circles in the fleet was that organized by Nikolai Shelgunov, a cadet in a Kronstadt naval school. Though adhering basically to the program of the People's Will, Shelgunov established contact with the Marxist circle of D. N. Blagoev in St. Petersburg, and through its influence he made the works of Marx, Engels, and Plekhanov known among the naval cadets.[41] Despite the fact that both Populist and Marxist leaders, most of whom were either exiled or imprisoned, recognized the importance of propaganda within the military bastions of autocracy, relatively little success was achieved in widening their footholds in the fleet until the very end of the century. But the government's skill in containing this activity in the fleet through police infiltration, confinements to compounds, reassignments, and increased use of disciplinary battalions only provoked more people to join radical circles.

By 1900, two additional developments heightened tensions in the fleet: the growth of unrest in the country as a whole, which had as its basic cause the oppressive living conditions of workers and peasants, and the maturing of the revolutionary movements in the form of better organization and firmer leadership. Measures that accelerated the pace of industrialization, the increased burden of taxation, and a rapid growth in population, combined with a stricter regime of law and order, extended the most common complaints of the sailors—poor food, low wages, and a police regime—to much of Russia. But the focal points of these grievances were in the industrial and port cities, where the organized revolutionary movements and their sympathizers were strongest. Another dynamic of the interplay between "conscious" revolutionaries and the "spontaneous" feelings of the masses was the intensifying competition between the old Populist movement that had revived in the form of the Socialist Revolutionary party and the new Marxist movement (the Social Democrats).

But how did revolutionary parties take advantage of the opportunities now present in Russia during a period of tight police suppression? The answer is found partly in the inefficiency of that police and also in the rapid growth of the intellectual communities in the larger cities; it was particularly in educational institutions that the ideas of Marxism and Populism were debated at the end of the century. Though free expression was limited by police surveillance in the classroom, discussion on the theoretical level was possible; but more important were the informal meetings of teachers and students and the circulation of both legal and illegal publications in the educated community as a whole. By 1900 this "unofficial society" had enlarged to include a diversity of creative groups and a host of specialized schools, such as the new St. Petersburg Polytechnical Institute, which were themselves natural results of the need for trained people to staff the new and more sophisticated industries. The expanded naval schools in the capital area were part of this development.

And many of those who were caught up in the revolutionary movements in this environment devoted their attention to reaching the broader masses, especially those close at hand—factory workers and the garrison soldiers and sailors. The products of a veritable craze for organization at this time provided the conduits for the dissemination and discussion of programs and literature. An important tactical question that all Russian revolutionaries discussed was how to translate mass discontent into revolution, not only by neutralizing the military forces that could prevent or suppress revolts, but also by securing arms for the masses and winning the allegiance of soldiers and sailors to their cause. Vladimir Lenin, emerging as a chief spokesman of the militant wing of the Russian Marxists, wrote from abroad in 1902, addressing himself especially to this question and calling for the dispatch of the "best revolutionaries" to the armed forces.[42] He was only one of several radicals whose opinions were read and discussed within educated circles.

By the end of 1902, three Social Democratic circles were active in the naval schools in Kronstadt, in the Mine, Artillery, and Guard-Marine schools. Propagandists, arriving from St. Petersburg, directed the members of these groups, which included sailor-cadets as well as workers in Kronstadt's factories and port.[43] When arrests broke up these circles, new ones quickly sprang up. Sevastopol, the main base and training center of the Black Sea fleet, also attracted Social Democratic activity. In 1904 the members of the circle there formed the Central Naval Executive Committee (Tsentralka) of the Russian Social Democratic Labor Party (RSDLP), a united (Menshevik and Bolshevik) group that included leaders of the future *Potemkin* mutiny. By that time, in Kronstadt there was a similar "central committee," the All-City Executive Committee of the RSDLP, which included ninety members from units of the fleet.[44]

Awareness of a sudden increase of revolutionary activity in the armed forces at the beginning of the twentieth century naturally stirred considerable alarm in the government. A conference of staff officers, under the chairmanship of the tsar, met in Moscow in February 1903 for the discussion of measures to tighten supervision and discipline. The "solution" for the factory workers—police-sponsored and -controlled trade unions—could not be applied in military units, though an expansion of enlisted men's messes was considered (effected only after the 1905 revolution). The policy resolved upon by Minister of the Interior von Plehve and Acting Naval Minister Admiral Fedor Avelan in the summer of 1903 was the isolation of naval units from the urban centers in which they were based.[45] Increased discipline, confinements to ships and bases, and other restrictions only encouraged hostility, as before; and complete isolation could never be effected, because naval units were dependent upon the bases, where there were large numbers of civilian workers.

But if it is true, as the above evidence suggests, that a revolutionary potential was building in the Russian navy that could not be adequately controlled, why was it that the first real outbreak occurred on the streets of St. Petersburg in January 1905 and why was it not until several months later, after the revolution was gaining momentum in other parts of Russia, that serious revolt took place in units of the fleet? The answer will help place the naval revolutionary activity in proper perspective. First of all, revolutionary ideas did not have a monopoly on propaganda within the fleet. Quite the contrary. Officers and priests were part of a massive official indoctrination machine that served the interests of the Russian state. For every sailor who was attracted to the revolutionary movement before 1905, at least fifty, probably more, were still within the grip of the official ideology, which stressed allegiance to established institutions. Loyalty to the flag, to the tsar, and to Mother Russia still had meaning for the great majority. Authority in the form of a chain of command as well as the training and drill that accompanied it provided the framework, the dam, to contain the pressures that might build up behind it. Sailors simply did not possess the freedom to go into the streets. The advent of war in January 1904, moreover, mobilized and strengthened that authority. The general excitement and expectations of victory reinforced morale and discipline in the naval units; significantly, it was only after the Battle of Tsushima, when defeat rather than victory was certain, that the dam burst.

THE REVOLUTION OF 1905 IN THE NAVY

A mutiny on a ship is a miniature revolution. As a self-contained unit, a ship can pass through the normal stages of revolution just like a separate city or country. Disaffection among the crew, poor command leadership, bad living conditions, a focal incident provide the immediate causes. The mutiny of the crew of the battleship *Potemkin* on the Black Sea is the best-known example of naval revolution in Russia before 1917. Whether the meat was as full of maggots or the officers as near-sighted as they were depicted in Sergei Eisenstein's brilliant film that commemorated the twentieth anniversary of the event is problematical. The general conditions in the Russian navy, aggravated by war, on a large hot ship on which officers and crew were demoralized by a major defeat and by contact with a large commercial-university city (Odessa), provided the situation for revolt. That a spontaneous breaking point could become a complete, successful revolution

24

in miniature was due primarily to the presence of leaders who, in the case of the *Potemkin*, were experienced sailors, sensitive to the prevailing conditions in Russia and aware of the growing mood of dissension and revolt along the Black Sea coast during May and June.

While the *Potemkin* was undergoing gunnery practice not far from Odessa on 14 June, torpedo boat *N267* arrived with supplies, including the infamous meat. Afanasii Matiushenko, a senior quartermaster who happened to be in charge of the armory and who was also the leader of a small group of Social Democrats, learned from the crew of the torpedo boat that a general strike had begun in Odessa on 12 June, followed by a day of rioting and disorder, during which the authorities had hesitated to use force. Encouraged by this news, Matiushenko seized upon the opportunity presented by the crew's dissatisfaction with the food and with the punishment being levied for insubordination to agitate for a general rebellion. Once control of the ship had been won, there was little hesitation about the next step—to sail to Odessa. What happened there has become a legend—the charge of the Cossacks down the long Richelieu steps, the bombardment of the city, the escape of the *Potemkin* across the Black Sea, and the temporary exile of the mutineers in Rumania.[46]

Revolutionary agitation had combined with the peculiar circumstances of a naval ship to produce one of the most striking examples of mutiny in naval history. What was most remarkable was the presence of dedicated revolutionaries as leaders who then attempted to bring a warship to the service of a wider revolution. Failure to implement this goal was due to a general weakness of revolutionary sentiment, not only in other ships and units along the Black Sea coast, but also among the majority of the crew of the *Potemkin*, who had been carried along by events and viewed the whole thing either as "getting even" or as a lark.

In the general literature on the Revolution of 1905, the dramatic events on the Black Sea coast have obscured the extent of disturbances in the Baltic fleet. What prevented an outbreak as dramatic as the one on the *Potemkin* from happening in the Baltic fleet was simply the fact that most of that fleet had sailed to the Pacific. With the exception of the new battleship *Slava*, only old training ships and small vessels remained, and these were kept close to port. A major demonstration over local conditions did occur in the Baltic, however, even before news of the *Potemkin* affair was known, on 15 June at the Alexander III Base at Libau. The disturbance was quickly suppressed; 139 were arrested, of whom 8 were sentenced to be

25

shot, 18 were sentenced to do hard labor for a total of 116 years, and the rest were given jail terms.[47]

The Baltic fleet—in a state of suspended agitation throughout the summer of 1905—was under a tight disciplinary regime, but was relatively calm, except for a spontaneous protest on the *Slava* at Revel on 4 July that resulted in 34 sailors being assigned to a disciplinary battalion.[48] The turmoil in Russia that reached a climax in the October general strike was bound to affect the fleet, however. After the proclamation of the October Manifesto on the seventeenth, excitement continued to rise, even though the strike ended on the twenty-first. The recently formed Soviet of Workers' Deputies continued to meet and to publish its newspaper, *Izvestiia*. While an air of new freedom spread around the capital and while radicals, including Bolsheviks, pressed for more, a strengthened police under General D. F. Trepov began to tighten controls. At immediate issue was the question of funeral marches and celebrations scheduled for Sunday, 23 October—how far to go on the side of the Soviet; how much to allow on the part of the police.[49]

In an atmosphere of exhiliaration on one side and of fear and danger on the other, a mass meeting of about five thousand sailors and soldiers gathered on Anchor Square in Kronstadt that day and drew up a petition demanding (1) designation as Russian citizens, with the right to assemble and decide their own affairs; (2) that the length of service be shortened; (3) salaries of at least six rubles a month; (4) better uniforms and food; (5) more free time, with no permission necessary to leave the fortress; (6) an unlimited access to liquor ("since sailors are not children"); and (7) the right to enter public places. These demands, except for the first, articulated typical service grievances, but the meeting also passed general resolutions calling for the abolition of class privileges and the establishment of freedom of religion, personal immunity, education in native languages, and freedom of speech, including the right to discuss any question openly with officers.[50]

When the Kronstadters received no satisfaction to these demands, unrest resumed on 26 October with a revolt by the Third Artillery Battalion. Though this was quickly quelled by local police, sailors from various ships and training units joined in to secure the release of those who were arrested, and a general uprising was soon under way. Loyal troops from St. Petersburg—battalions of the Pavlovsky and Preobrazhensky regiments—succeeded in reestablishing a semblance of order, and martial law was declared on the twenty-eighth. The facts that the sailors had not seized the ships and that they had failed to secure many arms rendered suppression rather easy. The presence of Father John of Kronstadt, a respected and influential priest, and a strategic distribution of vodka were also credited with helping to restore order to the base.[51]

Interesting aspects of the demi-revolt at Kronstadt are that it was clearly inspired by the heightened tensions in St. Petersburg and that it, in turn, contributed to persisting agitation in the capital and to a decision by the imperial government to use more severe repressive measures. Martial law at Kronstadt was quickly followed by a declaration of the same for Poland and by a session of the St. Petersburg Soviet, on 1 November, that protested both actions. After an impassioned speech by a Kronstadt sailor, who concluded, "Now they will shoot us. You alone can help,"[52] the Soviet passed a resolution declaring another general strike "to manifest its fraternal solidarity . . . with Kronstadt," which lasted a week.[53] Outcries in the rapidly developing and relatively free press produced a reaction to the Kronstadt events that forced the government to begin to curb the newly declared freedoms and, at the same time, to promise leniency to the Kronstadters who were under detention. Of the eighty-three who were formally arrested, only one was sentenced to hard labor; the others, to disciplinary battalions.[54]

In the meantime, spurred by events in Kronstadt and St. Petersburg, revolutionary agitation in the navy reached its zenith at Sevastopol, where a full-fledged revolt, led by Lieutenant Petr Shmidt and centered on the cruiser *Ochakov*, failed to win the support of the majority of sailors and was eventually suppressed by force on 28 November. The government was now using harsher measures to end the Moscow insurrection, and perhaps for that reason, punishment was more severe for the Sevastopol mutineers than for those of the Baltic. Four of the leaders, including Lieutenant Shmidt, were executed in March 1906, and thirty-two others received sentences of hard labor for life, while the remainder of the six thousand participants were given lighter sentences or were transferred to army units.[55]

REVOLUTIONARY ACTIVITY IN THE BALTIC FLEET AFTER 1905

The effects of military disaster and a revolutionary year were not easily removed from the Russian navy. While the Black Sea was the scene of the greatest disturbances in 1905, the next year witnessed a Baltic revolt on a larger scale.

The success of the government's measures to cope with the revolution (the October Manifesto and the use of armed forces), the exhaustion of the resources of the revolutionary movement, and a natural anticipatory wait-and-see attitude of much of the population regarding the new freedoms and institutions produced a brief period of calm in the winter and spring of 1906. Two developments set the background for the 1906 revolt in the Baltic fleet. One, affecting only the Baltic fleet, was the return of the survivors of the Battle of Tsushima, many of whom were wounded or dispirited after nearly two years at sea. The other was the dissolution of the First Duma on 9 July and the subsequent public protest by the radical wing of that body—the Viborg Appeal, which called for "passive resistance," particularly in the form of refusing to serve in the armed forces and to pay taxes. But many members of one of the radical parties, the Socialist Revolutionaries, wanted to go much farther and to provoke general revolt, believing that "Russia at present is a powder box, and Kronstadt is the torch that must light this box."[56]

Two incidents at the naval training base fueled the torch. A unit of dragoons had been sent to Kronstadt in May to reinforce the shore patrol. A campaign of terror resulted in a series of beatings of sailors and culminated in injuries to sailors from the cruiser *Gromoboi* who had been wounded at Vladivostok. A large part of the crew of that ship became aroused, and they obtained control of landing guns, which they proceeded to unload from the ship to fire at the dragoons. Officers eventually regained control and were able, through official complaints, to obtain the removal of the dragoons from the island. The other incident involved a Kronstadt infantry regiment on the firing range outside the town on 26 June. A boy who was selling kvas to the hot troops was ordered away by an officer, and when he failed to leave, the officer attacked and wounded him with his sword. As word of this outrage spread around the base, protests grew, demanding the removal and trial of the officer.

The Socialist Revolutionaries (SRs) quickly took advantage of the bad mood of the troops and sailors, and in an effort to rally all of the revolutionary forces for a major revolt, they organized an "Executive Committee," which consisted of five SRs and five Bolsheviks. Dmitri Manuilsky, the main Bolshevik spokesman at Kronstadt, joined this "contact" committee even though he opposed the revolt as premature. Soviet sources stress the "correctness" of the Bolshevik position; nevertheless, it is obvious that many of the sailors who were inclined toward social democracy participated in the SR-led events that followed.

28

The uprising began in the Sveaborg fortress complex at the entrance to Helsingfors Harbor on 18 July. Mine and artillery detachments under the leadership of an artillery officer and member of the SR party, Sergei Tsion, seized three of the islands, along with the heavy guns and ample ammunition. By prearranged signal—a telegram that said "Father ill"—Kronstadt and the remainder of the fleet was to be alerted and was to begin a simultaneous revolt; but for some reason the signals were changed, causing confusion. On 19 July the first division of artillery at Kronstadt was led in revolt by Fedor Onipko, a *trudovik* (member of a SR splinter labor group) former member of the Duma. They succeeded in capturing Fort Konstantin, which overlooked the port, but the guns could not be used on the land side. Though the second division of artillery and some of the naval mine detachments joined the revolt, little success was achieved at other key points such as the arsenal. The commander of the cruiser *Gromoboi*, under repair in dock, had been warned, and a detachment of rebels found the crew confined below deck, with armed officers above. Other ships that the SRs had counted on, such as the battleship *Slava*, were unprepared for revolt and actually participated in the bombardment of the rebels at Sveaborg.[57]

The most serious and potentially most damaging mutiny occurred on the old cruiser *Pamiat' Azova*, which had been a neutral bystander during the October uprising at Kronstadt the previous year. As the event was described by an officer assigned to this vessel, the wintering procedure—during which the crew and young officers lived on ship, senior officers lived at home, and the commander and executive officer alternated on board ship—allowed discipline to weaken. A revolutionary committee was formed on the ship early in 1906; it was led by Quartermaster First Class Nikolai Lobadin, whose prior reputation as a hard-working, nondrinking Old Believer had won him the respect of the crew. According to the officer, writing several years later, a sudden transformation had come over Lobadin as a result of the events of 1905, and he became a hard-drinking atheist and leader of a twelve-man revolutionary committee. At the beginning of the summer campaign, three hundred artillery students, also influenced by the revolutionary experiences of 1905, joined the regular crew of five hundred for a training cruise, which resulted in crowded conditions aboard ship. During a stop at Revel the ship was visited by the minister of the navy, Admiral Birilev, who received the traditional standing ovation from the crew.[58]

Shortly after this, however, on 19 July, during gunnery practice in Papovik Bay along the Finnish coast, the commander arrested Arsenii

Koptiukh, a civilian who was found hidden on the ship. Under the alias of Oskar Mines, Koptiukh was a central figure in the Revel Bolshevik organization, bringing to the ship the news of the Sveaborg revolt by disguising himself as a sailor on a supply vessel. After the Koptiukh-Mines arrest, Lobadin led a protest of the crew against the officers, which resulted in the killing of the commander and six other officers. Reports of the uprising at the naval base of Sveaborg contributed to the enthusiasm for revolt, and as on the *Potemkin* in 1905, control of the armory and of the electrical switchboard appeared to be the keys to success. The rebels then sailed for Revel with the intention of winning over the crews of other ships as well as the city itself. Before reaching port, however, they learned from a passing Finnish steamer that the Sveaborg revolt had been suppressed. This produced consternation among the crew; the artillery students separated and managed to take over in a counterrevolution, killing Lobadin and several other rebels. This brave action not only ended the worst mutiny in the history of the Baltic fleet, but also may have saved the ship, since Admiral Birilev had become so alarmed at the prospect that the revolt would spread to other ships that he had dispatched the battleship *Tsesarevich* from Helsingfors with orders to sink the cruiser if necessary. With the surviving officers in charge, the *Pamiat' Azova* anchored in Revel Harbor, where an unwarned Socialist Revolutionary welcoming committee, headed by A. I. Bunakov-Fundamenskii, was arrested.[59]

The *Pamiat' Azova* affair parallels the *Potemkin* mutiny of the previous year. The crew of a large ship that was on gunnery training revolted, under the leadership of committed revolutionaries, who were spurred to action by shore disturbances and were provided with an incident aboard ship. While the revolt on the *Pamiat' Azova* was led by Socialist Revolutionaries, whereas Social Democrats claimed credit for the one on the *Potemkin*, there is much more evidence of concerted planning on the Baltic in 1906 than on the Black Sea in 1905. The SRs had assigned agents to the main fleet bases in order to promote agitation and organize the revolt—Bunakov-Fundamenskii, to Revel; Onipko, to Kronstadt; and Tsion and Victor Chernov, to Helsingfors. Of the four, Tsion was the most successful; he became virtual commander of the large Sveaborg fortress at the entrance to the harbor for three days, and he managed to escape when collapse was imminent.[60] Ironically, all of these men would be on the other side after February 1917, trying to contain agitation in the fleet on behalf of the Provisional Government.

The revolt on the *Pamiat' Azova*, though it was much less publicized abroad, naturally had a greater effect on the Baltic fleet than the one on the *Potemkin* the year before, because of its location and because of the lengthy trials that followed. Of 98 sailors tried, 18 were sentenced to be shot; 15, to hard labor; 40, to various jail terms; and the remainder were released. Bunakov-Fundamenskii and two other Socialist Revolutionaries arrested at Revel were transferred to civil jurisdiction in St. Petersburg, where, in a widely publicized trial, a skillful defense obtained their acquittal.[61] The sailors and soldiers of Kronstadt received more severe sentences in secret military trials. Of over 1,800 arrested, 36 were executed, 228 were sentenced to hard labor, and 1,333 spent various terms in prison and disciplinary battalions.[62]

The Socialist Revolutionary effort to carry political revolution to the capital by starting with the Baltic fleet was too hastily organized and too poorly conceived to be successful. There was simply not enough time to coordinate these acts with worker strikes and demonstrations, and the authorities were already on guard and prepared with countermeasures. The Baltic revolt of 1906 was much less spontaneous than the one of 1905, but it did not prove SR dominance of the revolutionary movement in the fleet, only its ability to stir things up. The SRs did set an important precedent by looking to the fleet for revolutionary support, and the sacrifices, though they weakened the potential for rebellion for several years, furnished a host of grievances and a large number of sailor-martyrs.

Although all of the major bases of the fleet—Kronstadt, Sveaborg (Helsingfors), Revel, and Libau—were affected by unrest in 1905 or 1906, they were relatively quiet for the next few years. A severe repression of radical activities throughout Russia, and the induction of a large number of new recruits (12,000 in 1906 alone), who were at first more easily disciplined, rendered revolts less likely. Increased safeguards assumed the typically bureaucratic form of greater numbers of police. A new rank of *konduktor* (equivalent to warrant officer) was used to place agents on ships and in shore units of the fleet, and specially selected sailors were courted for reenlistment. The revolutionaries probably exaggerated the number of informers in the fleet; however, the *konduktory* and reenlistees, because of their strategic position between officers and seamen, put the sailors on the defensive and diminished the danger that dissension would reach the point of open rebellion.

Revolutionary activity did persist, however. Despite the drop in the number of Bolsheviks in St. Petersburg from 7,300 in 1907 to around 600 in early 1910 and despite the arrest of members of the Battle Organization of the party in March 1908, the Bolsheviks increased their efforts to win sailor converts.[63] Leading the agitation in the fleet from 1908 to 1912 were Ivan Glukhachenkov, Adolf Taimi, and Vladimir Zaitsev. Glukhachenkov, a worker at the Franco-Russian Works who was drafted in 1907, served on the student ship *Evropa*, where he organized a revolutionary circle in 1909. Taimi, an experienced Finnish Social Democrat, returned from exile in 1907 to be assigned by the party to Helsingfors, where he propagandized among the sailors while working in the military port. In 1909 he embarked on the steamer *Arturus* to concentrate on winning over Russian sailors who were being sent to Britain to bring home the newly constructed battle cruiser *Riurik*. Zaitsev, who had been a commercial seaman on the Volga River and Caspian Sea before 1904, became a Bolshevik while serving with the Black Sea fleet in 1904–5. He was both a professional sailor and a revolutionary when he was reassigned to the crew of another new cruiser, the *Admiral Makarov*, which was being built for Russia at the French port of Toulon in 1909.[64]

Much less is known about Socialist Revolutionary activity in the fleet in the interwar years, but it was probably even more widespread, if less organized, than that of the Bolsheviks. In 1910, SR circles existed on the cruiser *Riurik* and the battleship *Tsesarevich*. The Machine School at Kronstadt was known as a center of SR strength, and in 1911 the General Military Political Organization operated at the training base, under the leadership of a staff captain, Sokolovskii, to win converts in the schools and on the training ships.[65]

Most of the larger ships and training units of the Baltic fleet contained secret revolutionary circles by 1910, but the battleship *Slava* presented the first challenge to authority. The vessel was on a Mediterranean cruise in the summer of 1910, when it was unexpectedly forced to undergo extensive repairs at Toulon that lasted through the winter. Avgust Samson, a Latvian Social Democrat who had been active in the 1905 revolution, was serving on the *Slava* as a petty officer machinist, and he led a group of about fifty Bolsheviks. He is celebrated in Soviet histories for having taken the initiative to acquire, through the Latvian party organization, Lenin's Paris address, and to request literature directly from the Bolshevik leader. Lenin sent to Toulon a "Comrade Aleksei" with leaflets and personal greetings.[66]

The Socialist Revolutionaries were also making an impression on the *Slava* at Toulon. Dmitri Krasnolutskii, who had jumped ship in 1908 in

Alexandria, was living in the French port, and he supplied the Russian crew with SR newspapers. All of this activity could hardly escape the attention of the police, and French and Russian foreign agents cooperated in the arrest of nineteen troublemakers at the end of March 1911. Samson, however, avoided detection until the beginning of 1912.[67]

Extended cruises away from home base seem to have provided the best opportunities for agitation. Aleksandr Egorov was the leader of a group of Bolsheviks on the cruiser *Aurora* in 1910. He reported that revolutionary propaganda was spread throughout the summer campaign, with the effect that discipline had nearly broken down completely on the vessel by the time it returned from the summer cruise. After the commander, Captain Leskov, forwarded a special report on the morale of the crew, several of the most unreliable were transferred to other ships.[68] This action would seem to have had the result of improving discipline on one ship at the risk of endangering that on others.

The training ship *Dvina* (formerly the *Pamiat' Azova*) maintained its reputation for revolt during cruises with unruly trainees of the Student Mine Detachment in 1911 and 1912. The leaders of agitation were Ivan Sapozhnikov, a Bolshevik, and Vasilii Badin, an SR; but the police were there also, and many sailors were arrested. At his trial, in the "process of the 52," Sapozhnikov accused the chief prosecution witness of agitating among the sailors on the *Dvina* in order to obtain evidence for their arrest.[69]

The interplay of revolt and repression mounted in the years just prior to World War I. The shooting of a number of demonstrating strikers in the Lena gold mines in early April 1912 caused a heightening of tensions throughout Russia. Plans were again made for demonstrations and revolt in the Baltic ports, and as in 1906, Helsingfors took the lead. There the Bolsheviks established liaison with the sailors through Adolf Taimi, Aleksandr Shotman, and Isidor Vorobev (Aleksei Volkov), whose center of operations was the Russian Workers' House in the city. A "Revolutionary Committee," mostly Bolshevik but including at least one SR (Ermakov), sponsored meetings of sailors on shore, especially from the battleship *Tsesarevich* and the cruiser *Riurik*. Other SRs circulated among the sailors; though opposed by the Bolsheviks who wanted only to stage a demonstration, they planned to seize control of three battleships anchored in the harbor and to sail them to Kronstadt and Revel for the purpose of setting off a general uprising. Police, however, watched the joint planning session of 22 April, and on the day set for the uprising, 24 April, they made a number of key arrests both on board ships and among the shore-based radical groups. After the squadron sailed to Revel in May, SR agitation continued at more shore meetings of sailors. These resulted in the arrest of seventy-two more sailors, who were transported to St. Petersburg for imprisonment in the Peter and Paul Fortress.[70]

One important result of this nipped-in-the-bud revolt was the escape of Shotman and Vorobev abroad, where they made their way to Paris and obtained an interview with Lenin, posing as a delegation from Baltic workers and sailors. In a letter written to Maxim Gorky in August, Lenin remarked: "And in the Baltic fleet it is seething! I had a special delegation in Paris, sent by an assembly of sailors and Social Democrats. There is no organization—it simply makes you want to cry!! If you have officer connections, all the necessary forces at your disposal, you might get things started. The sailors are in a fighting mood, but can again lose everything for nothing." This Paris meeting, coming on top of the contact of the sailors of the *Slava* with Lenin, probably influenced his article "The Uprising in the Army and Navy," published in *Rabochaia Gazeta* on 30 July, in which he stressed that military revolts must be concerted with the risings of the worker and peasant masses.[71]

Meanwhile, each round of arrests meant trials and more publicity for the radical sailors. In the "process of the 59," several groups of potential rebels were judged by a secret military court in July 1912 in the compound of the Second Baltic Fleet Depot Troop at St. Petersburg. They represented all those who had been arrested since early 1911, including the 19 on the *Slava* at Toulon. News of the trial, however, leaked out and was published in *Pravda*, the Bolshevik newspaper. The United States naval attaché reported that of 65 originally accused, 3 committed suicide (or escaped?) while awaiting trial and 3 others were too ill to stand trial. Of the 59 remaining, 29 were acquitted; 11 were found guilty of "membership in a revolutionary society" and were given sentences of four to four and one-half years in prison; and the remainder were convicted of various degrees of complicity for disseminating revolutionary propaganda and were given terms in disciplinary battalions or naval jails.[72]

While this trial was going on, and prompted in part by the testimony collected at it, another round of arrests was made, chiefly on the large ships at Helsingfors and Revel. The result was another formal hearing in June 1913, the "process of the 52." Despite their secrecy, both trials received wide publicity at home and abroad. This resulted in pressures on the government,

Demonstrations in Helsingfors: Column marching past University of
Helsinki Library into Senate Square on 18 April 1917 (top); in Railroad
Station Square, 18 June 1917 (bottom)

Bolshevik leaders
in the fleet:

Pavel Dybenko

Fedor Raskolnikov

particularly in the form of political strikes in Baltic ports and outcries in French newspapers, that contributed to lightening the sentences. But these proceedings only represented the top of the disciplinary pyramid. An early Soviet source reported that 5,757 out of 45,000 men recruited during the period 1906–10 were punished for insubordination or for inciting unrest.[73] Some of those who were detained were later allowed to return to their units, but others were released only by the February Revolution.

The ongoing repression was obviously effective in preventing major revolts in the fleet in the years just before World War I, but it was not a cure. Instead, sores were allowed to fester by creating martyrs, by building up a reservoir of embittered men in the jails and disciplinary battalions, and by lowering the morale of the remaining sailors. Those who were removed to confinement were quickly replaced by new converts to radical ideas, such as Pavel Dybenko, who joined the Bolsheviks in June 1912 while a member of the Student Mine Detachment at Kronstadt; a few months later he became a leader of the party nucleus on the battleship *Imperator Pavel I.*[74] Stepan Lysenkov and Ilia Dudin were two more who performed yeoman duty in 1913 as liaison between Kronstadt and the Petersburg Committee of the Bolsheviks, the latter also managing to be assigned to the military prison in the capital, where he volunteered as a priest's assistant in order to establish contact with prisoners. And an active SR, who had deserted in 1911 and would later become a Bolshevik, Semen Pelikhov, returned to duty in 1913 under the general amnesty connected with the three-hundredth anniversary of the Romanov dynasty.[75]

By 1914 the centers of radical activity in the fleet were the shore-based depot and training units at Kronstadt, chiefly the First Baltic Fleet Depot Troop and the Student Mine Detachment, but these acted as feeders to the revolutionary circles that were still active on the larger ships. Party loyalties of the ordinary sailors continued to be ill defined, with most radical circles consisting of only a few Bolsheviks and SRs, the majority of sailors being simply sympathetic to the general idea of revolt. The minister of the navy believed in retrospect that if 1912 marked the real beginning of the revolution in the fleet, the summer of 1914 witnessed an increase in and maturing of socialist agitation, especially at the shipyards and bases.[76]

Despite delays in construction and a confused naval policy, Russia in 1914 possessed a fleet in the Baltic that had some of the outward appearances of strength, modernity, and expert training; but the ships and the shore units were served by officers and men who were badly divided among themselves

35

and had been infiltrated by small but dedicated cadres of revolutionaries. Russia was about to enter two wars—an outer one and an inner one.

2

THE FLEET GOES TO WAR

THE DECLARATION OF WAR was greeted by a burst of patriotism in the Baltic fleet, just as in the rest of Russia. Although the construction program was far from complete, the fleet had made a substantial recovery from its lowest level after Tsushima and was probably as well prepared for battle as any other major Russian military unit. On 1 August 1914 the active Baltic fleet consisted of four battleships, six heavy cruisers, three light cruisers, thirty-six old destroyers, one new destroyer (*Novik*), five submarines of the modern type, seven gunboats, four dispatch vessels, eleven minesweepers, six armored yachts, twenty transports, nine training ships, six minelayers, and a number of patrol and torpedo boats.[1] Several additional capital ships, including four dreadnoughts, were rushed to completion within the first year of war. Thanks to the costly building effort, the Russian government could be more confident regarding war against Germany in the Baltic area than one might have expected so soon after the Russo-Japanese debacle. And now, in a situation reminiscent of the early coalitions against Napoleon, in which the Russian navy played a substantial role, Russia was allied with the foremost naval power, Great Britain, whose squadrons were poised in the North Sea, at the other end of the Baltic. In fact, German fear that an eventually reconstructed Baltic fleet, in alliance with Great Britain, would tip the balance of naval power in that area may actually have been a contributory cause of the war.

THE DEFENSIVE POSTURE OF THE BALTIC FLEET

Even before actual hostilities began (during the period of mobilization), the Baltic fleet went into action, following well-rehearsed plans for laying defensive minefields in the Gulf of Finland and the Gulf of Riga and bringing shore-defense batteries to full strength.[2] The war, however, produced a major change in the strategic position of the fleet. For so long having enjoyed administrative and financial independence from the army, the fleet now became completely subordinate to the land forces for military operations. The chain of command extended from Supreme General Headquarters (Stavka) to the commander of the Northern Front to the commander of the Sixth Army, defending the capital region, to the commander of the Baltic fleet. The army staff allotted the fleet a complementary mission: naval forces were to be held in reserve until the army was on the offensive, then the fleet would sweep the enemy from the sea. This limited use of naval forces would not seem to have justified the building of a large surface fleet at great expense, but of course, the Russians were thinking mainly of the final, decisive engagement. This was a common fallacy of all of the participants: after expending so much on constructing capital ships, governments appeared reluctant to risk them in preliminary skirmishes. At least, the new command structure alleviated the problem of division of control between the Russian army and navy that had been notoriously bad in the recent past.

Since the Russian forces on the Northern Front never succeeded in mounting a sustained offensive, but, on the contrary, met disastrous defeat early in the war and fell back onto Russian territory to the northeast, the fleet remained largely in defensive reserve. Most efforts by navy commanders to secure permission for offensive raids against German shipping and naval patrols were vetoed by the tsar himself as a needless risk of expensive equipment. As early as 18 September, two operations officers—Alexander Kolchak and Prince Cherkasskii—sent an offensive battle plan to the fleet commander, which was immediately relayed to Stavka. There the chief of staff, General N. N. Ianushkevich, supported by the commander of the Sixth Army of the Northern Front, rejected the naval plan.[3] Other offensive projects were turned down, and in 1916 the commander of the Baltic fleet could sum up the mission of his command quite simply: "The fundamental, strategic picture is clear. The Baltic fleet is a continuation of the extreme flank of the army; the task of the Fleet is, as far as possible, to support the movements of the army, protecting it against envelopment by the German fleet."[4]

In the course of policing and strengthening minefields, small squadrons of the fleet actually did engage in small-scale offensive action, especially during the first year of war under the active leadership of Admiral von Essen; and in 1915 and 1916 the fleet inflicted heavy losses on the German navy during its probes of Russian sea defenses. As in the Atlantic, so also in the Baltic, great naval battles on the order of Sinope (1853) or Tsushima failed to materialize. They continued to be expected, however, and naval construction was advanced with even greater vigor during 1916 and 1917, when naval armaments factories were as busy as any in Russia.

A sustained emphasis on naval development increased the manpower of the fleet considerably during the war. In addition to large recruitments in 1914, 1915, and 1916, despite the fact that no replacements were necessary, the terms of enlistment of those who were in the navy at the beginning of the war were extended, and several classes of reserves were called up. The peacetime strength of 56,000 jumped to about 90,000, including officers and *konduktory*. For its mission of defending the Baltic shores the fleet was assigned supplementary infantry, artillery, and support units, bringing the total complement of the command to over 160,000 men,[5] a greater concentration of military force in Baltic ports than ever before.

As a rule, those reserves who were veterans of Baltic service returned to duty more "proletarian" than at the time of their original enlistment, because of the natural tendency for released sailors to seek urban employment (demobilization from the navy, unlike that from the army, always took place in or near industrial cities). For example, after Ivan Glukhachenkov, one of the Bolshevik activists among the sailors in the interwar years, was demobilized in 1912, he worked for two years at the Franco-Russian Works, maintaining contact with his sailor friends and providing liaison for the party; then he was reactivated in 1914 and was assigned to the Student Mine Detachment at Kronstadt as an instructor.[6]

But there were other categories of "reserves." A unique institution called the Russian Volunteer Fleet originated from patriotic fervor during the Russo-Turkish War of 1877–78. Initially financed by a combination of private donations and state funds, the Volunteer Fleet quickly became a moderately successful semipublic corporation. Its growing commercial fleet (twenty-one modern steamers in 1901) was entitled to exemptions from customs duties, a major advantage during an era of high tariffs, with the understanding that the ships and men would transfer automatically to military status at the commencement of war.[7] This was a fine idea for a country that had a relatively weak merchant marine, but there was one important drawback—a number of the ships were in foreign waters or ports when the war began and had no way of returning. A small increment of experienced seamen still was possible, though they lacked the discipline and esprit de corps of the regular navy.

Because of German dominance over most of the Baltic, the size and location of Russian minefields, and the accompanying security precautions, Russian commercial vessels of all types were unable to continue their accustomed schedules. Some of them were purchased or leased by the navy for conversion as minelayers or auxiliary vessels. For example, the *Ariadne*, one of the finest passenger ships in the Baltic and the flagship of the Finnish Steamship Company, was requisitioned for use as a hospital ship,[8] while other Russian and Finnish merchant vessels served simply as storage or barracks facilities. The presence of standby commercial crews and dockyard workers, who were not counted in the official complement of the fleet, sometimes made it difficult to distinguish the military from the nonmilitary components along the Baltic coast during the war.

Still another strange anomaly confused the wartime navy. Realizing that the fleet was not up to planned strength, but not considering the realities of the situation in the Baltic, the government purchased from Japan a number of old Russian ships that had been captured or salvaged by the Japanese after Tsushima. Officers and men were sent overland to Vladivostok to man the "Separate Baltic Detachment," which consisted of one battleship, two cruisers, and six destroyers. Though perhaps setting a war record for nautical miles logged on its long journey to European waters, the squadron was plagued with mishaps and could not enter the Baltic. Kept at a safe distance from the war and the revolution, this squadron was, nevertheless, an additional grievance factor in the Baltic, because of the long separation of the men from bases and from their friends and relatives and because of the widely known ludicrousness of the whole affair.

Wartime conscriptions usually furnish a host of stories about misplaced talents. The Russian draft may have been, in revolutionary perspective, too thorough and too rational—skilled workers to the navy, peasants to the army, was the general rule, which was employed even more vigorously than before the war. Many university students were commissioned as officers or were sent to cadet schools, with little concern that some were already socialists (everyone was patriotic in 1914!). One newly commissioned medical student, Anatolii Lamanov, presided over the radical Kronstadt Soviet through most of 1917, and one of the Bolshevik leaders in the fleet, Fedor Raskolnikov, attended the naval cadet school.

Other peculiarities of the war situation of the Baltic fleet soon became apparent. The only harbor that was large enough to accommodate the main part of the fleet on a more or less permanent basis and that could also provide it with both security and room for maneuverability, was Helsingfors. So the capital of the Grand Duchy of Finland became the main base of the Baltic fleet for the duration of the war. Because of the degree of autonomy that had been retained by the Finns through most of the nineteenth century and was restored after 1905, Finland bore some resemblance to a neutral country, and Helsingfors was somewhat like a foreign port. Recruitment did not apply to Finland, for example, and very few Finns volunteered to fight for the empire. Though there were large numbers of Finns in the civilian merchant marine, very few served in the ranks of the Baltic fleet. But Russia was responsible for the defense of the territory, so it stationed substantial land forces there. Because the prewar base program was incomplete and had not foreseen this situation anyway, the Sveaborg port and fortress complex, on a small archipelago at the entrance to Helsingfors Harbor, lacked adequate arrangements for extended docking of all of the ships; so the inactive commercial ports in the north and south harbors, adjacent to the city proper, were also used. Across Finnish territory, Russia maintained its most regular communications with the Allies—through neutral Sweden and Norway. Since the same route was used by spies and revolutionaries, the Baltic fleet was anchored practically on top of the "northern underground."[9]

To the south, Libau, one of the most modern and best-equipped bases, was hastily abandoned as being too vulnerable to German attack (and indeed it soon fell into German hands). While installations guarding the entrances to the Gulf of Riga were strengthened, these posts were too exposed to be used as ship bases. Revel, too, was believed to be dangerous for large ships (air attack was a constant but largely unwarranted fear), especially in winter, though it became the main permanent station for submarines and for destroyer squadrons. These factors placed an added burden on Finnish ports, especially by the winter of 1916–17. By this time, Hango and Åbo (Turku) were being used as advanced posts from which smaller ships guarded and policed the mine defenses of the Gulf of Finland and the Gulf of Bothnia.

But bases were not the only tactical problem that the Baltic fleet faced after the war began. In order to remove the blot of Tsushima, prewar planning had designed a fleet for offensive operations, and its deficiency in defensive capability soon became obvious. The small number of minelayers and minesweepers was quickly augmented by adapting old destroyers and fishing trawlers. Not so simply remedied was the shortage of submarines, of which the Baltic fleet possessed only eleven (five modern) in 1914. After a year of war their importance was recognized, and a massive construction program began in December 1915 for building seventy more; not many of them could be completed before 1917, however.[10]

At Russian urging, two British submarines ran the gauntlet into the Baltic in the fall of 1914 and reached the Gulf of Finland. The next year, two additional British subs squeezed through the German blockade, and at considerable expense, four more were delivered to the Baltic through inland waterways from Arkhangelsk. Constituted as a squadron of the Royal Navy attached to the Russian Baltic fleet, these submarines rendered valuable service for the duration of Russia's participation in the war.

One might have expected the presence of a squadron of the Royal Navy in Russian waters to provide a useful example of discipline and training for Russian seamen. But the submarines spent much of their time on patrol from forward stations and had minimal contact with the large bases. The squadron's fighting capability was widely known and praised; but rather than being instilled with a sense of discipline by example, the Russians probably became envious of the working relationships between British officers and crews, of their performance and spirit, that "jolly well-done" tradition for which the Royal Navy has always been so famous. That a small British submarine squadron could sink as much enemy tonnage as the whole Russian Baltic fleet must have been somewhat discouraging to the Russians, especially in view of the accidental sinking of their own submarines—such as diving with an open hatch—for which Russian submarines became notorious during the war.

During the long winters, the British had ample time to visit the main bases of the fleet, but invitations were surprisingly rare, perhaps because Russian officers were not anxious to have their commands "inspected" by the Royal Navy. Instead, the British officers rested in the Hotel Astoria in Petrograd or journeyed to other cities. In January and February 1916 they spent several weeks in Moscow. The British consul, R. H. Bruce Lockhart, described their visit as a complete success: "The Navy may have fallen on evil days, but my own experience of British naval officers abroad has been of the happiest. Far better than Army officers do they understand the gentle art of placating and impressing the foreigner. They can relax without loss

42

of dignity. There are few brass hats and few brass heads among them." Lockhart added that Commander Francis Cromie's speech to a group of intellectuals was the shortest and most impressive that he heard in Russia: "A tall, dark Byronesque figure with heavy eyebrows and side-whiskers, he faced his audience without a tremor. 'Ladies and Gentlemen,' he said, 'You are all artists—musicians, poets, novelists, painters, composers. You are creators. What you create will live long after you. We are only simple sailors. We destroy. But we can say truthfully that in this war we destroy in order that your works may live.'"[11] Such expressions of Western idealism no doubt were warmly received in sophisticated circles, but what would the reaction to such platitudes have been in the Russian Baltic fleet?

Though the contribution of the British submarine squadron to the allied war effort was positive, it added one more element to the heavy logistical strain in the Russian northwest. It must be remembered that the war brought Russia's Baltic trade virtually to an end (small ships continued to ply the Gulf of Bothnia). Almost the only activity in the ports was military, and the interruption of normal transport complicated the supply of the entire area. For example, the Baltic fleet, as well as the heavy industries of the region, were normally fueled with high-grade English and Welsh coal. Although a substantial quantity—around 70,000 tons—was stored in the naval coalyards at the start of the war, ships, especially large ones, rapidly depleted this stock.[12] Resupply from mines in the Ukraine proved to be difficult because of the priority of rail transport for the army; so that scarcity of fuel by the summer of 1916 was forcing the curtailment of patrols, especially by the large coal-burning ships. English coal might still have reached the Baltic through Arkhangelsk or even through Sweden, but Britain had little to spare for export during the war. Moreover, it was considered wiser to conserve scarce sea and rail transport for "more essential" war matériel.

But some of these problems posed obstacles that could be overcome, and the Russian Baltic fleet, until the end of 1916, did a creditable job of performing its assigned military missions. It was particularly in mining operations, in which special preparations had been made before the war by Admiral von Essen, that the fleet excelled. The original defensive minefields were strengthened and extended so that they proved a formidable defense when tested in 1915 and 1916 by the German northern squadrons at the entrances to the Gulf of Riga and the Gulf of Finland. Though Russian sea mines were the best and most effective used by any navy in the war, credit must also go to the regular ships of the line, such as the destroyer

Novik and the battleship *Slava*, which by their adroit maneuvers prevented a greatly superior German force from effectively sweeping the fields. In fact, because of the setbacks to the Russian army, the right sea flank was proving to be the strongest sector of the Northern Front. Of course, the most important factor of all was the concentration of German naval forces on the North Sea Front.

In the early part of the war the Russians also employed mines with great skill in offensive operations, playing havoc with German shipping routes around the Baltic by unexpectedly laying mines near their Baltic ports. Captain Alexander Kolchak, who was operations officer for mining at the beginning of the war, received the laurels for the success of these "commando" missions, which were carried out under his supervision, and he soon advanced to the rank of admiral.[13]

Considering the technical difficulties and real dangers inherent in mine warfare, Russian losses were minimal, the most significant occurring in the sinking of the cruiser *Pallada*, with its entire crew, during the third month of the war, and the loss of a few older destroyers in minefield defense. German ship casualties attributed to Russian mines, ships, and coastal batteries and to the British submarines in the Baltic were much heavier, especially in those craft that were damaged and thus forced to undergo costly and extensive repairs. German losses in the tentative offensive operations in 1914, chiefly of the cruiser *Magdeburg*, which ran aground off the coast of Finland, and in the larger-scale attacks of 1916, which were made possible by British naval concentration in the Mediterranean theater, produced a considerable dent in the German northern squadrons, which would meet their fullest test at Jutland afterwards. The loss of the *Magdeburg* and the retrieval of German signal-code books from it by Russian officers were, in fact, rather decisive events in the naval history of the war, enabling the Entente powers to break the German codes systematically.[14]

With both limited mission and the ascendancy of the defensive priority over the offensive in the war as a whole, there could be neither victory nor defeat for the Russians in the Baltic before 1917. Though the army suffered defeats, especially on the Northern Front, the final picture was still inconclusive, and Russia, in any purely military sense, could not have been considered beaten. Loss of territory had been confined largely to the borderlands, and most Russians, both supporters and critics of the government, believed that Russia could still hold out for an Allied victory in the West.

But to carry on a fundamentally defensive posture indefinitely against the combined forces of Germany, Austria-Hungary, and the Ottoman Empire was not enough. Russia had to be victorious in her own right in order to retain political stability, but both the effort to secure military success and the promise of ultimate victory were costing Russia dearly in manpower, resources, and prestige. The Russian bureaucratic machine was also gradually becoming worn down and exhausted by the attempt to prove that the empire still possessed the military capability of a Great Power, a capability commensurate with the gains in territory and strategic position that had been guaranteed by the secret wartime agreements, most especially the long-desired hegemony over the Straits. To analyze fully the effects of this effort upon the fleet, it will be necessary to examine, in turn, conditions within the officer corps and within the ranks of the enlisted men.

CONDITIONS WITHIN THE FLEET DURING THE WAR

It has sometimes been claimed that what Russia lacked during World War I was a professionally trained elite, which later was a product of the Five-Year plans and was so essential to the Soviet military victories in the Second World War. This technically qualified element of the population was indeed small before 1917, but hardly inadequate to Russia's needs. The war had placed extraordinary pressures upon it, however; and the government, for various reasons, was incapable of allocating these talents appropriately. The Baltic fleet certainly possessed sufficient numbers of trained officers and men to operate the complex machinery of a modern navy; the real problem was that they were underutilized. Enforced inactivity became an important source of the mounting frustrations and grievances in the fleet, but another reason for this was the continued influence of older officers, who were more concerned with routine and tradition, who simply lacked an appreciation of technical skills and the potential of a mechanized war machine.

The fleet, under the pressure of war, highlighted the problems of a nation in transition to a modern, industrialized society. The war affected this development in two important ways. The economic transition that was already producing strains in Russia was given a jolt by the needs of a large military effort. While trained workers were siphoned off into the armed forces, especially the navy, urban industries became swollen with new laborers from the countryside. The industrial working force increased at a much sharper rate, with shipyard workers in the Petrograd area, for example, doubling in number between 1913 and 1916 in an effort to rush to completion various shipbuilding and reconstruction projects, while students attending the naval schools rose correspondingly in order to provide the personnel for the anticipated new ships. But delays occasioned by the scarcity of materials, reordering of complex machinery (turbines for a number of large ships under construction had originally been ordered in Germany), and shifts of priorities (submarines, aircraft) meant that a reservoir of technically trained personnel built up by 1917 in the Baltic fleet in depot units and training schools. There was, however, an imbalance in the naval manpower surplus, since it took much longer to train officers than seamen. The sudden large increases in enlisted ranks, in fact, meant that there was a paper shortage of officers, particularly in shore units.

Another important effect of the war was the increase in size and influence of the bureaucracy, which, when applied to the navy, meant the ascendancy of staff over command personnel. The greater number of ships and men, as well as the absorption of a large part of the merchant-marine and naval shipyards, caused a considerable rise in administrative requirements. The relative inactivity of the fleet also fostered the natural tendency for bureaucratization that was already apparent in the prewar navy. The result was an even more badly divided officer corps. Most of the important commands at the beginning of the war were in the hands of the older, basically nontechnical and tradition-minded officers. The smaller and newer ships were more often controlled by the younger officers, who had a high degree of technical proficiency. A third group, also deriving from specialized backgrounds, was composed of those who had gravitated, either by inclination or by accident, into staff positions of the major commands and to the Naval General Staff in Petrograd. But even this rough categorization oversimplifies the situation that faced the command and staff of the fleet.

Though individual testimonies of officers, most of whom supported the anti-Bolshevik cause in the Civil War, may be suspect as biased, collectively they indicate that a serious lack of harmony and trust existed in various levels of the Baltic fleet; this was comparable to a similar situation in the imperial government itself. One officer reflected on the atmosphere in Helsingfors: "Idleness palled me and I was unhappy among the officers, most of whom seemed to enjoy the peace-like routine and comforts of the lovely capital of Finland."[15] Stifled by inactivity, with operations largely reduced to tedious patrolling of minefields, officers had little opportunity to develop an esprit de corps or to win battle laurels and promotions. Many tended to work out their frustrations in petty quarrels and rivalries among themselves and in overdisciplining or overindulging the men of their commands. While some officers earned the reputation of being unduly harsh and cruel toward their men, others appeared to command on the basis of popularity and, even before February 1917, received the epithet "red" from fellow officers. All, however, became more and more vulnerable to abrupt transfers ordered by the Naval General Staff, which were automatically approved through the chain of command.

Admiral Nicholas von Essen emerges from many émigré memoirs as the Stolypin of the fleet, whose own strength and example, had he not died in May 1917, might have prevented factionalization among the officer corps. But it would appear that the forces described above would have eventually been beyond even his control. In fact, von Essen's dislike of administrative work, which was duplicated by Chief of Staff Ludwig Kerber, allowed lower staff officers to gain a great amount of authority and influence in the fleet.[16] The unity of command that von Essen successfully maintained was achieved by constant movement from ship to ship, and his high visibility to both officers and men of the fleet in all kinds of weather, regardless of health considerations, hastened his death. Kerber, who temporarily succeeded him, was the natural replacement, but because of his German name and his opposition to the Petrograd staff, he was passed over in favor of the elderly and mild-mannered Vice-Admiral Vasilii Kanin, who, after scarcely a year, "retired" in the summer of 1916 to a less demanding post in the Naval Ministry.

The next commander in chief, Vice-Admiral Adrian Nepenin, had never commanded a large ship but had attained promotion chiefly by his skillful organization of the communications staff during the war. As such, he represented the partial triumph of staff over command in the fleet. Rear Admiral Sergei Timirev, writing in 1922, believed that the appointment of Nepenin was the critical turning point in the deterioration of command unity in the fleet, especially since it was coupled with Admiral Kolchak's transfer from the Baltic to command the Black Sea fleet. These changes, Timirev claimed, were inspired by Captain Vasilii Altfater of the Naval General Staff, whose purpose was to undermine discipline and loyalty to the tsar on behalf of a clique of liberals in the capital.[17] Dmitrii Fedotov White agreed with the conclusion that the Petrograd staff was getting the upper hand over the fleet, but he pointed the finger at Captain Aleksandr Zhitkov, editor of *Morskoi Sbornik*, as the chief engineer of changes in command.[18] The existence of a real plot to remove dynamic and loyal commanders such as Kolchak and to elevate those who were amenable to political change remains to be proven, but a "progressive bloc" of influential staff officers definitely did exist, led by Altfater and Zhitkov in Petrograd and by Prince Mikhail Cherkasskii, Captain Ivan Rengarten (chief of intelligence), and Fedor Dovkont, who was on Nepenin's staff. Although none ever held important command positions, they controlled vital intrafleet communications and served in high advisory capacities during the crucial winter of 1916–17.

Whether by deliberate plot or by natural tendency, the advance of a number of other "progressives" to important command positions—Aleksandr Maksimov as chief of mine defense, Dmitrii Verderevsky as chief of submarines, Vladimir Pilkin as commander of the First Cruiser Squadron, S. V. Zarubaev as commander of the battleship *Poltava*, Modest Ivanov as commander of the cruiser *Diana*—along with the transfer to other posts of a few of the abler officers, such as Boris Dudorov and Fedotov White, who happened to be friends or protégés of Kolchak, had a significant effect on the fleet's ability to respond to revolutionary threats. The retention of some of the older, senior officers at their posts can be explained by the undermining of their authority or by their unpopularity's serving the purpose of the "progressives." Vice-Admiral Gerasimov, as commander of the Revel base, held virtually no control over the independent commands at that port, and Robert Viren, commander at Kronstadt, held a position that no one else wanted. Viren, who was referred to rather sarcastically as "chief of the rear," was responsible for the thankless tasks of supervising the training reservoirs and of administering the swelling jails and disciplinary units of the fleet.[19]

The "command revolution" in the fleet, if it can in fact be so designated, was not something that could be effected in a few years; it was far from complete by 1917. Nepenin himself represented a compromise, for he was disliked by many of the command officers because of his crude and inexperienced efforts at attaining a high level of discipline. His occasional but unannounced visits to ships, as well as his general lack of diplomacy and tact, caused an increasing deterioration of rapport; and the consequent isolation of the commander in chief caused him to grow more and more dependent upon his staff.[20]

This feeling of isolation and dependence was heightened by one more peculiarity of the wartime operations of the Russian Baltic fleet. Under von Essen, a major ship—the battleship *Sevastopol*—served as the flagship of the fleet, though von Essen actually spent little time on it. But because of the fleet's defensive posture and because of ice in winter, the commander in chief and his staff became increasingly reliant upon telegraphic and cable lines for communication with Petrograd, Stavka, the commander of the Northern Front, and other bases. Even under von Essen the staff of the fleet was located on a requisitioned Finnish passenger ship, the *Polaris*, which was permanently docked in Helsingfors Harbor. Admiral Kanin arranged for the unification of command and staff on a communications vessel, the *Krechet*, which was lavishly refurnished during January and February 1916 and was anchored at Skatudden, an area of Helsingfors Harbor, where Russian base workers were concentrated.[21] From the beginning of 1916, unlike almost all other active fleets, the Baltic fleet had a commander who was not on board a large fighting ship. The pride associated with being the flagship of the fleet might have saved at least one major vessel from revolution in February 1917, as well as affording protection to the commander and his staff. This physical dependence on land facilities also abetted the rising influence of the Petrograd staff.

It had an even greater effect, however, on the growth of political awareness of staff officers on board the *Krechet* during the winter of 1916–17. In the wardrooms and cabins of this vessel the main topics of conversation became internal politics: speeches in the Duma, the murder of Rasputin (in December), Trepov's resignation as minister of the interior (which was greatly welcomed), and increasing unrest in the capital. Rengarten and Cherkasskii constituted an informal "Committee of Action," and as early as 14 January 1917 they discussed the eventuality of a constitution being granted, after which Rengarten noted in his diary: "It is possible to say that the prestige of tsarist authority has never fallen so low."[22] Two weeks later, Nepenin read a copy of Guchkov's letter to General Alekseev, criticizing the deterioration of Russian military capability to an assembly of staff officers, thus opening both a general discussion of a speech by the Menshevik Chkheidze and the position of the fleet in regard to a political revolution in the capital.[23]

Nor was such a state of affairs confined to the commanding staff on the *Krechet*. Captain M. N. Aleambarov, commander of one of the most active destroyer squadrons (the sixth), announced to his officers that he could not order his ships to fire on the people at the behest of "Protopopov [the new minister of the interior] and Co." Fedotov White recalls that this attitude made a vivid impression on him: "At the time of the 1905 revolution such a remark would have been quite impossible. It was obvious that the view-point of the rank and file of the naval officers had undergone a very surprising change since that time, particularly during the last two years," and Fedotov White attributed this in particular to speeches in the Duma by representatives of all political parties.[24] Perhaps just as important in the reformation of officer attitudes was the persistent and growing strength of the revolutionary movement in the fleet.

The same circumstances of inactivity and isolation that affected the officers during the war also resulted in an increase of revolutionary consciousness among the men of the fleet. Normally, combat experience creates a closer relationship between officers and men than that existing in peace-time, but the defensive posture of the navy in the Baltic allowed few opportunities for this to develop, although when such occasions occurred both before and after the February Revolution, it is remarkable to observe a revival of teamwork and cooperation between officers and crews. Such potential was certainly present, though already limited by the prewar distrust that had been developed by mutinies and revolts, arrests and sentences.

An important reason for a widening gap between officers and men during the war—which paralleled a similar rift between tsar and people, government and society—was the rise of national consciousness, along with revolutionary inclination. The complementary character of national and social revolution, so often noted by analysts of revolution, was emphasized in Russia by the war. Not only were officers from different social backgrounds than the sailors, but many were also of different nationality. The problem was most pronounced in the Baltic fleet because of the large number of Baltic Germans and Finno-Swedes who were officers in the fleet. When rumors spread in Petrograd of high-level treason and of German agents in the officer ranks, it was logical for sailors to suspect their commanders who had German names. Officers with names like Körber, Mirbach, Keyserling, Helmersen, Tippolt, Knüpfer, Grünewald, Weiss, Fersen, Stark, Bittenbinder, Graf, and Hildebrand could be easy targets for revolutionary agitators. Even those from loyal Finno-Swedish families who had long served the tsar could easily appear to be "German" to their men. One can imagine the handicap presented by having a name like Fedotov White's friend Baron Nicholas von Hoiningen Huene, who was second in command of a destroyer. While the majority of officers were Russian, there were a few representatives in the officer corps of other sailor ethnic groups, such as Estonians, Latvians, or Ukrainians.[25] Could von Essen or his chief of staff,

The cruiser *Aurora* in 1967 (top); and the battleship *Respublika* (former *Imperator Pavel I*), the most Bolshevized ship of the Baltic fleet (bottom)

Headquarters of Tsentrobalt: the former imperial yacht *Poliarnaia Zvezda* in Helsingfors Harbor (top); and the Baltic fleet preparing to evacuate Helsingfors Harbor in April 1918 (bottom)

Kerber, have been popular commanders to a Russian or Estonian sailor in World War I? Von Essen himself thought not, and shortly before his death he seriously considered changing his name.[26]

The general characteristics of the men of the fleet, which have already been described—high working-class composition, rising national and social consciousness, proximity to port cities and major industrial areas with frustrated and dissatisfied working forces, and inactivity—were aggravated by a host of particular grievances. The war brought increased discipline and a more restrictive leave policy, so that the sailors' vexations had more time to build to a breaking point. A neutral source noted that Russian sailors were treated like "dogs," a common epithet; also that on Ekaterinskii Boulevard in Kronstadt, where many officers lived with their families, a sign was posted: "Entrance with dogs and to lower ranks forbidden."[27] Sailors were stopped on the street by officers' wives, who took their names and numbers for being improperly dressed or for acting insolently. Over one-third of the sailors of the Baltic fleet suffered for infractions of the rules; many were sentenced to terms in disciplinary battalions, which gave them something more to resent.

Several incidents helped to lower morale and to build up suspicion of officers in the fleet. The first was the sinking of the cruiser *Pallada* on 19 October 1914, with the loss of the entire crew. Though the cause turned out to be a well-aimed torpedo from a German submarine, rumors at the time placed the blame on a Russian mine or sabotage aboard ship.[28] That such a loss could occur so suddenly within the Gulf of Finland easily left the impression that it could happen again to any ship. Another incident was the running aground of four battleships at the entrance of Revel Harbor. The presence of the commander in chief, von Essen, on board one of them led to rumors that he intended either to surrender the whole fleet to the Germans or to disable it.[29]

REVOLUTIONARY ACTIVITY IN THE WARTIME FLEET

The cadre of radical revolutionaries in the fleet survived the first few months of "patriotic war" and, augmented by reservists and new recruits, took advantage of each incident to spread propaganda against the officers. The Bolsheviks founded small cells of three to five members, and in order to avoid detection, they limited contact between these units.[30] But this arrangement also had the disadvantage of reducing the prospects for concerted action, at least for the time being. Meanwhile, through the long summer of 1915, dissatisfaction with the course of the war grew in the fleet bases, as it did in Russia as a whole. A sudden increase in the number of industrial strikes in the port cities provided an atmosphere of general unrest. Though there was some access to newspapers, which were filled with official releases anyway, crews and shore units received distorted information about these events through the "mess hall herald."[31]

The first serious trouble appeared on the cruiser *Rossiia* in Helsingfors Harbor in September 1915, when protests focused on the "German" officers, poor food, and strict discipline. After an inspection by Rear Admiral Aleksandr Kurosh, commander of the squadron, sixteen sailors who were considered "an extremely harmful influence on the remainder of the crew" were transferred to Kronstadt, where they were assigned to the First Baltic Fleet Depot Troop. Among these was Timofei Uliantsev, one of the most active Bolsheviks in the fleet.[32]

A month later a much more severe case of insubordination occurred on the battleship *Gangut*, which was also in Helsingfors Harbor. The distribution of antiwar leaflets a few days before may have contributed to the disorder, but the actual occasion, on 19 October, stemmed from the failure of the crew to receive the customary meat supper after the heavy work of loading coal on the ship. The men refused to eat what was offered them, upon which the unpopular executive officer, Captain Fitingof, ordered the meal thrown overboard and attempted to drive the crew below deck with his revolver. After other officers managed to restrain Fitingof, over three hundred sailors (one-third of the complement) raged out of control the whole night.[33] The rioters communicated with the men of the other battleships anchored nearby, and the next day those crews refused to obey orders to level their guns at the *Gangut,* but after considerable agitation, they failed to come out in open revolt.[34]

The appearance of submarines threatening to fire torpedoes into the *Gangut* soon led to the surrender of the rebelling sailors. Most of the ninety-five who were arrested, including Vladimir Polukhin, the Bolshevik leader, were assigned to disciplinary battalions in Arkhangelsk.[35] A similar fate was in store for forty-two sailors of the cruiser *Rossiia* who attempted to prevent the removal of the *Gangut* crew; and a few of the leading agitators on other ships were also detained, including Bolsheviks Vasilii Marusev and Nikolai Khovrin on the *Imperator Pavel I*. According to Dybenko, who was also present, there were relatively few arrests, because officers feared that more arrests might lead to a general revolt. Marusev and Khovrin soon returned to their duties on board ship.[36]

The *Gangut* uprising also illustrated one of the most difficult problems of rebellious sailors and their leaders: the dangers of premature revolt. The ongoing debate ranged from the position that any blow struck was a step toward revolution to the belief that such isolated mutinies were retrogressive, weakening the revolutionary forces for the really decisive general uprising in conjunction with the workers and peasants. Though the latter was, of course, the official Bolshevik position, and has been emphasized by Soviet scholars in retrospect, not all known Bolsheviks adhered to it at the time. Dybenko, for example, advocated coming out in support of the *Gangut* on board the *Imperator Pavel I*. Soviet historians steer a careful line, praising the Bolsheviks for successes in promoting the revolutionary movement in the fleet but also excusing them for the excesses to which it was carried. Their usual method is to blame the SRs and Mensheviks as being in greater prominence, a tactic that also serves to dramatize the tremendous growth in Bolshevik strength during 1917. But little evidence on the activities of non-Bolshevik radical groups in the fleet is available. The general indications are, however, that they were no more numerous or influential than the Bolsheviks in a genuinely organized way, that, in fact, the great majority of the sailors were "unorganized" and acting spontaneously. Perhaps five to ten out of the twelve-hundred-man crew of the *Gangut* were actually affiliated with any political party. But on the other hand, how many leaders are needed to carry out a revolt?

The removals of these and other troublemakers from ships to shore units were beginning to create considerable difficulty at Kronstadt, where Admiral Viren, complaining that the jail was full, proposed to organize a special work battalion.[37] No safe use could be found for such a unit; so, to avoid overcrowding of the already unwieldy disciplinary battalions, many sailors were reassigned to the First Baltic Fleet Depot Troop, where seasoned agitators mixed with new recruits under relatively loose officer control.

Another tactic employed for dealing with unruly sailors was to organize them into separate companies for duty on the Northern Front, but one of the first, from the *Imperator Pavel I*, caused so much trouble for the commander of the Twelfth Army that he requested its recall.[38] It appeared that the radicalization of the fleet in these circumstances could not really be significantly deterred but only contained and concentrated at Kronstadt. What was gained in the way of discipline and control on the ships was lost in the shore units, and they in turn provided centers for further infiltration of ships' crews.

An immediate result of this concentration of radicals in Kronstadt was a step forward in revolutionary organization. At the end of September 1915 several Bolsheviks, at the initiative of Uliantsev, met in the Zaria tearoom and formed the "Main Collective," the first central organization of the Bolsheviks in the Baltic fleet.[39] The purpose of this group, which included long-time sailor-Bolsheviks Ivan Sladkov and Fedor Kuznetsov-Lomakin, was to maintain liaison with the Petersburg Committee of the party, on the one hand, and with the various cells in the ship and shore units of the fleet on the other. The Main Committee, however, was very loosely organized, meeting infrequently in local tearooms or taverns, where its members were watched by police agents. Apparently, its existence quickly became known to the Petrograd Bolsheviks, who had just established their own military organization for the dissemination of party literature in military units and for gathering information about the state of radical activities in the armed forces. The members of this "Voenka" who devoted particular attention to fleet affairs were Vladimir Zalezhskii and Boris Zhemchuzhin, and they in turn designated an old party worker with considerable experience in naval activities, Kiril Orlov (Ivan Egorov), to establish communications with the Kronstadt Bolsheviks at the end of the summer.[40]

This attention from a Russian party center was probably what prodded the Kronstadters to increase propaganda activities and to reach as many as twenty-nine party cells in the fleet, nineteen of which were on active ships, but it also prompted greater attention from the police.[41] Whether this Bolshevik activity in the fleet in the fall of 1915 had any direct effect on a notable rise of dissent among the Kronstadt sailors is still open to question. Certainly of greater significance was the transfer of some of the *Gangut* sailors to the training base for trial, a circumstance that agitators of all political groups exploited. The Kronstadt police chief reported to Viren in early November that the local sailors were in open sympathy with the accused and that there were even rumors of deploying the ships that were based there against Petrograd if the accused sailors were not released.[42]

Port authorities, obviously worried by the situation, prepared to crack down on any organized connection with a revolutionary party. The arrival of the battleships *Tsesarevich* and *Imperator Pavel I* for repairs at the end of November also put the Kronstadt police on special guard.[43] Meanwhile, the scope of activities of the Main Committee increased in December during the *Gangut* trial and in preparation for a 9 January demonstration (on the anniversary of Bloody Sunday of 1905) led by Semen Roshal from Petrograd. One big disadvantage of expanded operations, of course, was increased visibility.[44]

At the end of December, Sladkov, who was then serving as an instructor on the training mineship *Aleksandr II*, went to Petrograd to pick up leaflets pertaining to the call for the January demonstration, but he was under police surveillance the whole time. In fact, his permission to leave the base may have been deliberately arranged by the police. In any event, as soon as he stepped on the *Tsesarevich* to make delivery, he was arrested.[45] Others were soon taken into custody; and a big break for the police came in February 1916 with the seizure in Helsingfors of Nikolai Brendin, a sailor on six-months' sick leave who had chosen to stay and work with the Sveaborg base as chief liaison for the Main Committee. Unfortunately for the Bolsheviks in the fleet, he had a number of papers on him, including an address book listing a number of activists. These documents provided evidence against those who had already been detained and led to new arrests—of Uliantsev, Kuznetsov-Lomakin, and Orlov—and to the decimation of the Helsingfors cells of the party. Altogether, seventeen sailors received the dubious distinction of incarceration in the Peter and Paul and the Kresty political prisons in Petrograd until their trial the following October.[46]

Soviet commentators claim that the Main Committee at Kronstadt was immediately restored, though it was obviously hampered by the police crackdown. A Bolshevik organization did exist, but it operated at a lower profile. Vladimir Zaitsev, who served in a strategically important post in the communications section, replaced Uliantsev as leader, and Petr Kimen took over Orlov's liaison functions.[47] During the summer of 1916 they led an intensive propaganda campaign, distributing a leaflet written by Kimen, "To the Organized Sailors and Soldiers," and printing, on the mimeograph of the Student Mine Detachment, 100,000 copies of an antiwar pamphlet entitled "When Is the End?"[48] A major theme of both of these Bolshevik tracts urged that the sailors act only in concert with the workers and peasants, not alone.

ON THE EVE

Growing disillusionment with the war among the sailors had, in fact, made elimination of such agitation virtually impossible, though attempts were still being made. On one September night in 1916, 107 sailors were searched and questioned.[49] Further evidence of the slackening of control that summer was the appearance of sailors on outings on the shore of the mainland near Oranienbaum and Sestroretsk, where they were met by political orators from the capital.[50] Perhaps the sailors sensed that there was a limit now on the enforcement of law and order at Kronstadt.

More arrests were made, nevertheless, especially in the fortress's artillery and infantry units, where the Bolshevik organization was effectively crushed in October.[51] By this time, the naval units seemed more immune to police supervision, probably because the radicals were so well established in them, often with petty-officer rank, that their removal would have caused further trouble in the command, and for that reason they were even protected by their commanders. Such was the cause with Vladimir Zaitsev, who was briefly detained by the police, but then was released after being vouched for by his commanding officer.

Though most writers on revolution in the fleet assume that a major cause of the growth of revolutionary consciousness in the fleet was the conflict between officers and men, this was not always the case. Officers, especially the younger ones, did have some things in common with their men that were unique to the navy. Technical skills and a common respect for them fostered a relationship toward the machines or apparatus under their care that could bring officers and men together in times of crisis. Another difference between the navy and army was a higher esprit de corps emanating from team association and attachment to a unit or vessel. Each ship of the fleet was distinctive (even sister ships had their individual peculiarities) in design and equipment and in its history. The competitive rivalry that such loyalty and uniqueness engenders was to some degree transferred to radical activity. This situation only added a further dimension to the complexity of relations between officers and crews, which fostered a common resentment to any outside attempts to interfere with their affairs.

By the end of the summer of 1916, multiple fissures were easily discernible in the fleet that directly threatened the functioning of the naval chain of command. The "chief" of the Kronstadt base pointed out the hopelessness of his situation in a private letter that he wrote in mid September to Count Aleksei Kapnist, the naval staff officer at Stavka:

> I will not refrain from extreme, decisive measures and will, if ordered, introduce, instead of lashings with birch rods and sentences of solitary confinement, a week without food, but it must be realized

that my hands are tied. . . . You, count, playing a leading role in the Naval Ministry and in the circle nearest to His Majesty, are obliged to know the whole truth. Under my authority at present is an army of 80,000 men, all kinds of weapons, even trawlers and engineer units for defense against gas attacks. . . . I honestly say that with only one push from Petrograd, and Kronstadt, along with the ships located now in port, would come out against me, the officer corps, the government, and whoever you want. . . . Yesterday I visited the cruiser *Diana*. . . . I felt as if I were on an enemy ship. . . . In the wardroom the officers openly said that the sailors were completely revolutionaries. . . . So it is everywhere in Kronstadt. We can convict them, exile them, shoot them, but this will not achieve the goal: you cannot prosecute 80,000.[52]

Similar depressing reports, it is true, came from other military units, especially from those on the Northern Front, but these were isolated and tended to reflect what might be considered temporary circumstances. What is most remarkable about Viren's statement is that it pertained to such a large body of men located so close to the capital and that it registered a clear sense of irreversibility. Did enough loyal control apparatus still exist in the vicinity of Petrograd to contain this threat through another year of war?

Admiral Grigorovich, who was no doubt receiving regular reports from Viren and other commanders, became especially worried about the deteriorating situation not only in the fleet units but also in the shipyards and armaments factories. While renewing his cooperative efforts with Duma leaders, the minister also went to Mogilev in mid November to see the tsar personally. According to Grigorovich, the resulting private interview was brief and inconsequential: Nicholas II refused to discuss any matters pertaining to internal security.[53] Written reports also met with no response.

One has a sense of important changes occurring in the late summer and early fall of 1916, mainly in northwest Russia, even though there are few specific events and little direct evidence to cite. In January 1917, when some ranking officers of the Baltic fleet considered revolution a likely possibility if not inevitable, Admiral Grigorovich visited the Black Sea fleet, where Kolchak's new disciplinary measures impressed him, but he noted an obvious deterioration in the country as a whole. The minister of the navy returned in time to hold one last official inspection at Kronstadt, on 24 February; he verified Viren's description of the situation: "In the course of inspecting the garrison, I noted with infinite sadness the profound transformation that had occurred in the mentality of the crews. . . . [Viren] said to me, 'The officers and sailors are tired of a war that has submitted them too long to nervous tension. And each day records a widening of the spirit of lack of discipline.' "[54] The sailors were no longer desperate, with a sense of being backed into a corner by authority, where frustrations would mount until they burst in spontaneous riot, protest, or mutiny. The balance had turned in their favor, and authority was now in the corner.

So it was an uneasy state of frustration and dissension that prevailed in the fleet from September to February, into the third winter of the war. If the men on a majority of ships and in the shore units were prepared to revolt, they were also convinced by much experience that they must act in coordination with a broader movement in the rest of the country. The "push" finally did come from Petrograd.

3

THE FLEET REVOLTS

WHILE THE MILITARY CAPABILITY of Russia's armed forces in the winter of 1916–17 may still be subject to varied interpretations, most observers agree that on the home front the situation had deteriorated drastically. Because the transportation system was breaking down, basic supplies were not reaching the cities in sufficient quantities to avoid scarcity, inflation, and falling production. One is reminded of the old adage "For want of a nail. . . ." Locomotives using low-grade coal and wood were falling apart. Even wood, the most common fuel, was scarce, because it was bulky to haul and because, at the places where wood was cut, horses were too few and too weak for the work demanded of them, owing to army recruitment and a poor supply of oats to feed them.[1] As the prices of all fuels rose during the severe winter, bakeries found it too expensive to bake bread from the limited quantity of flour available.

But what made the Petrograd situation intractable was the existense of similar conditions in other parts of the country. The reality of the great Russian economic machine slowing down was accompanied by a sense of general national paralysis. North Winship, the American consul in Petrograd, toured Moscow, Kharkov, and Kiev by train in October and November of 1916 and reported that university students were sleeping in railroad stations to keep warm and that although basic goods were plentiful in the country, acute shortages were occurring in the cities due to inadequate transport. "Russia (the villages and the army) is in no danger of want; the cities are in no real danger, but believe themselves to be, and it is possible that the fear, if persisted in, may yet prove to be the father of reality."[2]

Spiraling inflation, with wages failing to keep up with prices; opposition to the war as the chief cause not only of misery but also of the deaths of relatives and friends; and mounting distrust in the government, which changed ministers so frequently and seemingly from bad to worse—all contributed to an outburst of labor unrest in the fall of 1916 after a relatively calm summer.[3] One specific grievance that the workers found to focus upon in mid October was the trial of the Bolshevik sailors. Over eighty thousand workers in Petrograd and other Baltic ports went on strike in sympathy; in fact, the public protest probably influenced the court in dismissing charges against most of the accused and in sentencing Uliantsev, Sladkov, Brendin, and Orlov to terms of from only four to eight years.[4] Thus the revolutionary movement in the Baltic fleet did play a significant part in launching the tide of labor disturbances in the large Petrograd factories, which eventually culminated in the February Revolution.

As the capital and the symbol of imperial grandeur from Peter the Great to Nicholas II, Petrograd was bound to be critical in deciding the fate of the Romanov dynasty; and as an important reserve center, it was crucial in determining the people's willingness to fight the war. On 24 February 1917, the British ambassador, George Buchanan, cabled to London that for over a year and a half, supplies of coal had been tied up in haggling between railroad officials and mine owners over the price, and finally the large Putilov Works had stopped for lack of material:

> For the past four weeks railways have carried no metal and no fuel for themselves. . . . Russia has got all the raw material but her efforts are constantly (?stifled) by stupidity of her Government. Premier is a nonentity Minister of Interior policeman. There is no co-ordination between Ministers or even between Department(s) of one Ministry. There is no Foresight and push. If we could induce Emperor to commission someone that people Trusted with formation of a Government we might not get efficiency at once but we would have done the only possible step to save situation.[5]

Yet there appeared to be no one whom both tsar and people could trust.

The liberal leaders of the Progressive Bloc of the Duma were already hoping to take advantage of the situation in order to effect political changes that, at the minimum, would sharply reduce the autocrat's powers. A few spoke privately of the necessity of deposing Nicholas II, but they envisaged a regency for the tsar's son, Alexis. A much larger number supported the Left-Center attack on the government's conduct of the war in the November–December session of 1916. Though the Duma was finally prorogued in mid December, criticism of the government continued to grow. Even conservative groups inside and outside the Duma were moving, but in different directions, to bring about an administration that could cope effectively with the deteriorating economic and political conditions. Though the necessity of martial law in the cities and the suppression of radical parties was discussed in these circles, the murder of Rasputin on 17 December was about the only real accomplishment, and that deed failed to check the increasingly hostile public attitude toward the tsar, the empress, and their government. One of the chief problems was that no group—liberal or conservative—or individual leader was able to make much impression on the Nicholas-Alexandra circle, which had become increasingly isolated from public opinion and closed to outside pressures. This failure reflected the weakness and division of the opposition as much as the strength of the government. Everyone seemed to be waiting for decision by crisis, and one likely time was the middle of February, when the Fourth Duma resumed its session.

Even among the officers of the army and navy, where the greatest loyalty to the tsar should be expected, disillusionment developed during the winter. The British military attaché reported that "general lack of confidence in the Government stifles all sense of patriotism."[6] The grand dukes and generals, as well as the Duma, were in a quandary about what to do. There were hostile recriminations and heated arguments, which reverberated down through Russian society. A winter war-bond campaign with a goal of £300 million subscribed only £70 million by February, and most of that was in the form of pledges.[7]

The small radical groups took advantage of the governments' isolation and weakness and of the general malaise in "society" to strengthen their organizations and to expand propaganda activities. Foremost among these were the Bolsheviks, whose Petersburg Committee possessed its own press for the publication of leaflets and circulars that focused on the rising economic complaints and antiwar sentiments. The "Russian Bureau" of the party attempted to coordinate these activities with the leaders of the party abroad and with other local committees throughout Russia. As so many sources show, however, the Bolsheviks were still quite few in number, and though strategically well placed for communications, they were still divided among themselves and plagued by intraparty conflicts with other Social Democrats, particularly the Mensheviks and the Inter-Regional (or unionist) organization. The Socialist Revolutionaries still had the largest popular strength, but they had an even weaker central leadership than the Social Democrats.[8]

The issue that caused the greatest difficulty for radical, liberal, conservative, and imperial government spokesmen during the long winter debates of 1916–17 was the war. In the highest councils of the state, sentiment for a separate peace with the Central Powers was growing, led by Rasputin and his friends, and by A. D. Protopopov, who became minister of the interior in September. A former liberal leader in the Duma from the left wing of the Octobrist party, Protopopov had broken with his former associates and was rumored to be actively working for peace. Though obviously unstable and bordering on insanity, he continued to hold his position. Nicholas II was also considering the possibility of an early peace, and tentative negotiations were begun through Swiss and Bulgarian channels. Nothing definite came of these, however, before the government was overtaken by the February crisis. Some of this peace talk may have been intended only to secure greater Allied support, which in fact was promised at a war council that met in Petrograd in January.

The question of war or peace also divided both conservatives and radicals. The increasingly moralistic tone of the war (democracy versus autocracy) caused some conservatives to have second thoughts about what the ruin of Imperial Germany and Austria-Hungary would do to the viability of the Russian Empire, while others continued to see victory as the best bulwark of the existing system. Both Social Democrats and Socialist Revolutionaries were split by this issue into internationalist-antiwar and patriotic-defensist wings.

Aside from a few defections, such as that of Protopopov, the liberals gained most from Russia's problems, consolidating themselves behind the idea that victory could be won by a more democratic Russian government, a position that would become the basis of the Provisional Government's initial foreign policy. And they gained the support of the Allied representatives in Russia, especially George Buchanan, the British ambassador, who began to interfere in the internal affairs of the country with the goal of improving Russia's military capability and bolstering prospects of future economic dominance. But they, too, moved hesitantly. Even after Buchanan's outspoken interview with the tsar in January accomplished nothing, Allied diplomats were reluctant to commit themselves fully to a policy that might well bring Russia to ruin.[9]

For the bulk of the lower stratum of the population, the broader and more complex political issues were secondary in importance to the economic conditions. While debates and irresolution paralyzed the government, bread lines lengthened, inflation rose, and fuel became increasingly scarce. One round of strikes on 9 January was followed by another in the middle of February, in connection with the reopening of the Duma. While one more series was being planned for the observance of International Women's Day on 23 February, scarcity of materials and labor unrest led the directors of the largest machine factory in Petrograd, the Putilov Works, to close its gates, thus throwing a large number of workers into the streets with additional grievances. By the time that women conductors left their trams in the middle of the streets and threw the starting cranks under the ice in the canals on the morning of 23 February, normal life in the capital city had ceased.[10] The Petrograd garrison and miscellaneous reserve units—composed mostly of new recruits, recuperating veterans, and inexperienced officers—wavered for a few days; then the majority of the soldiers joined the demonstrators on the main streets of the city. The remaining and still loyal military and police units, which had indecisive leadership and were faced with mass opposition, were unwilling or unable to use the force necessary to preserve order. During the ensuing chaos in the capital, a special committee of the Duma, composed mostly of members hostile to the tsar's government, undertook to reestablish law and order and to obtain sufficient independent authority to ensure political reform. Much to everyone's surprise, this led to the abdication of the tsar, on behalf of himself and his son, and the formation of a "provisional government."

The "spontaneous" February Revolution was not as free from violence as it is often pictured to have been. Bloody clashes erupted at a number of places around the city, with the Hotel Astoria, which served as an officers' hostel, becoming a real battleground.[11] Police, officers, a few demonstrators, and bystanders were the chief casualties. For several days, victory belonged to the street and was partially consolidated by those radical leaders who were present in Petrograd under the aegis of the Petrograd Soviet of Workers' and Soldiers' Deputies on 27 and 28 February.

The Preobrazhensky regiment, a famous guards' unit, followed a typical course. A battalion commander was shot while attempting to prevent his unit from joining a demonstration; other officers stayed away from the compound; new commanders were "elected"; and leaders among the soldiers organized unit committees and appointed themselves as delegates to the Petrograd Soviet.

THE REVOLT OF THE PETROGRAD NAVAL UNITS

The first naval unit to become involved was the Second Baltic Fleet Depot Troop, which was stationed in the capital and consisted mostly of new recruits. Late on the evening of the twenty-seventh, Naval Minister Grigorovich himself ordered that the fifteen companies of the troop, numbering 3,500 men, be confined to their barracks. The unit was already restless, and some of the officers opposed this move as being provocative, and then simply went home to sleep. Perhaps because of this opposition the decision was reversed early the next morning, and the whole depot troop—with its commander, Major General Girs, a giant red flag, and a band in front—marched toward the Tauride Palace, where the Duma and Soviet were meeting. But about noon, on the way back to the compound, order rapidly disintegrated. Girs was seized, hanged by his feet in his own office, and later shot. Some of the sailors then swarmed up and down Nevsky Prospect, some occupied the Nikolaevsky and Tsarskoe Selo railroad stations, while others complied with instructions of the Military Commission of the Duma to "guard" the Winter Palace.[12] While the troop was highly visible during the February days and was present at strategically important places, it acted more as part of the Petrograd garrison than as part of the navy.

The first ship of the Baltic fleet to join the revolution was the cruiser *Aurora*, which was docked for repairs at the Franco-Russian Works at the mouth of the Neva. The *Aurora*, as part of the Second (reserve) Cruiser Squadron, had been one of the most active ships in the fleet during the war, serving on minefield patrols in the Gulf of Finland while based at Helsingfors. The performance of these duties had been uneventful, and the men of the *Aurora* had been relatively calm throughout the war, except that they had evinced some unrest after witnessing the sinking of the *Pallada* and had given demonstrations of sympathy for the crew of the *Gangut* in 1915. After a Social Democratic cell was removed from the ship early in 1916, there was apparently not a single Bolshevik among the crew until after the February Revolution.

During the summer of 1916 the *Aurora* was employed as part of a squadron guarding the Gulf of Riga, but in September she left her station for badly needed repairs—the remounting of guns and turbines. Shortly before leaving the Gulf of Riga, the genial and popular commander, Captain Aleksandr Butakov, who was a descendent of famous Russian explorer-admirals, was relieved by Captain Mikhail Nikolskii. Along with Lieutenant Pavel Ogranovich, a new executive officer, Nikolskii attempted to tighten discipline on the ship during the cruise to Petrograd.[13] Though this was a wise move in view of where the ship was headed, it only incurred the hostility of the crew, which was soon working at close quarters with equally disgruntled repairmen from the Franco-Russian Works. And since this factory was a Socialist Revolutionary stronghold, the sailors were soon infected with a more radical spirit.[14]

What would happen when this "typical" ship of the Baltic fleet found itself in the middle of a revolution? The first indication to the crew that something unusual was happening was when the factory workers failed to show up on 22 February. The commander did what was natural under the circumstances and confined his sailors to the ship. A few days later, the Kexholm regiment, which was guarding the factory, arrested a couple of unruly workers and asked Nikolskii to detain them in the ship's brig, which he agreed to do over the objections of several junior officers, who feared that this would agitate the crew. Reports of what was happening in the city were received sporadically by telegraph, and the crew, kept informed by the communications personnel, grew more and more upset at being confined.[15] On the twenty-seventh there was a protest against the detention of workers on the ship, with some sailors shouting, "The Aurora is not a jail!" This resulted in the wounding of two crew members. That night, below decks, the angry sailors made plans to rise, at a signal the next morning, and overpower the machine guns that had been placed on the bridge. Spurred by reports that those who had been wounded the day before were dying in the ship's hospital, and encouraged by a crowd of workers (the Kexholm regiment having abandoned its duties) that had gathered near the ship, the crew broke into the armory, seized rifles and pistols, and overwhelmed Nikolskii and Ogranovich about 9:00 on the morning of the twenty-eighth. In the confusion that followed, the two officers were led off the ship, in order to avoid bloodshed on the decks. Nikolskii was shot immediately, whereas Ogranovich, after summary trial, received a sharp blow from a Japanese sabre. Both were believed to be dead at the time, but Ogranovich was only badly wounded; later he served on Kolchak's staff in the anti-Bolshevik resistance.[16]

The crew, after they had disarmed the other officers and had posted guards, held an assembly to celebrate their victory, crying, "Down with the bloody war" and "To hell with the Tsar." They also listened to words of guidance from the most vocal members of the crew, including Aleksandr Belyshev, a future Bolshevik leader on the ship. After distributing rifles, they liberated two automobiles from the unguarded garage of the Franco-Russian Works, and these were mounted with machine guns from the cruiser. This "armored" task force then cruised the streets of Petrograd and assisted in the seizure of a cadet school; also, at the corner of Lermontovskii Prospect and the Obvodnyi Canal, it removed a troublesome sniper, who turned out to be a retired general. Other *Aurora* sailors led an assault on a tavern, which was barricaded by the police, and participated in other mopping-up operations.[17] By the end of the day, they were joined by the crews of the only other active naval ships in the city, the imperial yachts *Shtandart* and *Ekaterina*.

During the next few days the men of the *Aurora* participated in various meetings and demonstrations both on ship and on shore. The *Aurora* was one of the first units to implement Order Number One of the Petrograd Soviet, which dictated new rules of discipline for military units in the Petrograd area. The order prescribed an elected committee which would represent the enlisted men, control weapons, and see to the carrying out of all directives of the Petrograd Soviet and of the Military Commission of the Duma, so long as those of the latter did not conflict with those of the Soviet. At a general assembly of the crew, apparently on the evening of 1 March, the question of what to do about the command of the ship—a matter that was left open by Order Number One—was debated. They first considered choosing a member of the crew, but the majority of the assembly decided that only officers possessed the necessary experience and capability. The senior officer who was left aboard ship, Lieutenant Nikolai Nikonov, was then designated for the post.[18] At other meetings, representatives of the new government were politely heard, anarchic tendencies (reflected in a desire to stop all repair work on the cruiser) were suppressed, and a ship's committee was elected.

According to the recollections of one *Aurora* veteran, the committee was at first dominated by SR and Menshevik members, because the Bolsheviks were not yet organized on the ship.[19] In fact, there was little organization anywhere during these early days of the revolution, and the committee members simply represented a cross section of the crew. In this situation, the rank and file of the *Aurora*, as those of other military units in Petrograd, tended to follow the leadership of the Soviet, which was Menshevik and SR. But on 2 March, Andrei Zlatogorskii, a senior petty officer and chief machinist on the *Aurora*, who had just joined the Bolsheviks upon the recommendation of party workers of the Franco-Russian factory, organized a cell of the party on the ship, which included Timofei Lipatov, Aleksandr Belyshev, Aleksandr Nevolin, and Petr Kurkov.[20]

Meanwhile the pattern of revolt and retribution spread to the chief bases of the fleet, first to nearby Kronstadt, then to Revel and Helsingfors, where the degree of violence surpassed that at Petrograd. And it is the February–March revolution at the fleet bases that first gave the urban crisis in Petrograd a sense of being at least region-wide, of including more of Russia than the capital city, and of going farther than both the Duma and Soviet leaders in Petrograd had intended.[21] In fact, the deteriorating situation in the tsar's own "pride and glory" may have influenced some critical decisions as much as what happened on the streets of Petrograd. Reports emphasizing the collapse of control in the navy, for example, reached the headquarters of the army of the Northern Front shortly before the tsar's decision to abdicate. Nicholas II must have been especially impressed that a loyal and conservative commander, such as Nepenin, had so quickly decided to recognize the authority of the Provisional Government.

It was impossible to isolate the naval bases from the news of the Petrograd demonstrations because of regular supply channels and links through the telephone exchange and because enlisted men manned the telegraph apparatus. Direct contact also existed. The leading Bolshevik at Kronstadt, Vladimir Zaitsev, who was a petty officer in the naval communications center, visited Petrograd on the twenty-fourth and conferred with members of the party committee of the Vyborg District of the city.[22] Other radical sailors, who were on leave or who had previously deserted, participated in the events in the capital before returning to their units.

KRONSTADT RESPONDS

So, despite the appropriate restrictions of men to compounds and ships, reports about defections of the Petrograd garrison units and about the formation of the Petrograd Soviet of Workers' and Soldiers' Deputies reached Kronstadt by the evening of 27 February. Members of radical parties among workers in the naval factories remained free to move about and to communicate with friends in the military units. The impossibility of maintaining strict discipline, which Admiral Viren had already emphasized, even allowed a conference of Bolsheviks (basically the Main Collective of the Kronstadt Military Organization of the RSDRP) to gather on the evening of the twenty-seventh to plan strategy. According to D. N. Kondakov, this group decided that it would begin a revolt the next night.[23] But other radical groups were no doubt talking along similar lines, following the general wishes of many of the sailors and soldiers.

During the morning of 28 February, new reports from Petrograd spread quickly through the factories and military units at Kronstadt. Soon after lunch the workers of the Kronstadt Steamship Works, one of the largest factories on the island, walked out on strike, demanding the right to leave for Petrograd in mass. Admiral Viren refused to meet with the workers, but he promised to address a general assembly on Anchor Square the next day.[24] As the strike movement spread, however, Viren called a conference of his staff in the afternoon, where he received warnings that a number of military units were completely unreliable. The port commander then insisted on placing machine guns around Anchor Square as a means of controlling the crowds.[25]

Representatives of various radical groups, meeting about 6:00 P.M., reaffirmed plans for a concerted movement into the streets at nine o'clock that night upon a signal of a machine gun at the fortress. General confusion and difficulties in communicating this news to units that were confined in their compounds caused further delays and added to the tensions. Finally, soon after 11:00 P.M., a burst of machine-gun fire was heard;[26] and what one writer later referred to as "the Kronstadt October" had begun.[27]

One of the first naval units to break out of its compound was the Student Mine Detachment. Its sergeant major (boatswain), Spiridon Tikhonov, and a dissident leader, Aleksei Pronin, formed the unit under arms, and they distributed ten rounds of ammunition to each sailor. While this was going on, an infantry regiment, in full dress, marched by with the band, which was playing the *Marseillaise*. The Student Mine Detachment immediately moved to the exit from the street, where it was met by the duty officer, who was brandishing his revolver and ordering the unit back to the barracks. A sailor in the front rank knocked the officer down with the butt of a rifle, and the men streamed out. Their first destination was the nearby compound of the First Baltic Fleet Depot Troop. Breaking down the gate in the darkness, the mine men discovered a company that was being threatened and cajoled by officers. Warning shots were aimed at the invaders, who retreated without returning fire. Opening a second gate, the Student

Mine Detachment succeeded in "liberating" the transfer company of the troop. This success influenced remaining companies to overpower their officers and move out onto the streets.[28]

By the time the First Baltic Fleet Depot Troop was on the streets, the uprising had become general, though some units remained under the nominal command of their officers. The Second Fortress Artillery Regiment, for example, marched out under colors, with its commander at the head. Others broke up into unruly groups whose goal was to overthrow all traditional authority by getting as many others as possible to join them in the streets. First the centrally located base units—student detachments, depot troops, and regiments of artillery and infantry—and workers appeared on the streets. Then the crews of ships, workers in outlying factories, and those sailors and soldiers who were in disciplinary battalions and jails were released, or escaped, from officer or police control. The last group, who were in an especially violent mood, were the perpetrators of much of the bloodshed that followed.

Most of the sailors, soldiers, and workers of Kronstadt met spontaneously in the darkness of early morning at the Naval Arena, where each unit chose representatives for a directorate called the Committee of Movement. In the meantime, however, before any real direction could be established, sailors gathered at the nearby house of Admiral Viren to insist that he come to Anchor Square. The port commander reluctantly agreed, but after assessing the mood of the sailors, he attempted to turn back and was either killed or mortally wounded on the spot by a sailor from a disciplinary battalion. The body of the port commander was then taken to Anchor Square, where it was mutilated in a frenzied posthumous ceremony.[29] This public bloodletting encouraged others to settle private grievances or simply to go on a shooting spree under the cover of darkness. Several high-ranking officers suffered the ignominy of public execution at the statue of Admiral Makarov, but in other respects, considering the chaos that existed, the bloodshed was surprisingly light. Many of the officers simply stayed out of the road, went along with their men, or were quickly taken into custody by the Committee of Movement.

As dawn broke on 1 March, only the headquarters of the Okhrana and the Cadet Corps of the Naval Engineering School remained out of the uprising. After a brief siege, in which six civilians were killed, the Okhrana building fell about noon. The engineering cadets, who were confined to the school during the night, were mostly of noble or middle-class background and therefore were less inclined than ordinary sailors and soldiers to join the revolt. Nevertheless, even here the majority were disillusioned with the war and were openly sympathetic to the sailors. When a delegation sent by the Committee of Movement asked them for their weapons, the cadets and their officers (with the exception of two or three who were arrested) readily agreed and marched out to join the general uprising.[30]

The training center of the fleet had overthrown the traditional chain of command. The Committee of Movement now attempted to restore order, arresting more officers who were suspected of harboring designs for restoration of their own authority, peacefully disarming most of the sailors and soldiers, and delegating regular armed patrols to guard the streets. Virtually no property had been destroyed during the revolt, and on 2 March, according to most reports, life appeared to resume a normal course, with stores and banks open in the town.

For the first few days after the revolt, power at Kronstadt resided in the hands of the Committee of Movement, which has been described by one Soviet authority as "a typical Menshevik-Socialist Revolutionary conciliatory organ"; but the same source also lists three Bolsheviks among the original seven members—Vladimir Zaitsev, Fedor Gromov, and Nikolai Markin—while the one SR, Krasovskii, was also the only officer to be a member of the group.[31] The committee quickly grew in size, it is true, with supposedly one representative from each unit, but the Student Mine Detachment had four members, and a total of twelve Bolsheviks are identified as having been active in the organization.[32] In fact, under the chairmanship of a student who was a Popular Socialist by the name of Khanokh, the committee had little time to establish a party position but was busy handling local problems and reacting in confused panic to rumors of an "invasion" by an infantry regiment from Finland.[33] Despite the committee's efforts at control, mobs settled accounts with two other admirals, Kurosh and Butakov, and a total of more than fifty people lost their lives.

As the chaos continued in both Kronstadt and Petrograd, the Committee of Movement welcomed the arrival of a commissar of the Duma committee, Viktor Pepeliaev, on 3 March, and it organized a garrison assembly, which gave its blessings to the new Provisional Government and elected a Council of Ten to assist the new commissar in restoring order.[34] This local executive, however, proved to be much more temporary than the central government.

THE EXPANSION OF THE REVOLUTION IN THE FLEET

The next important Baltic base to be seriously affected by the revolution was Revel, the main port and provincial capital of Estonia, where cruiser, destroyer, and submarine divisions were stationed. Officers maintained control over their commands until a city-wide general strike occurred on 2 March. Shortly after noon a crowd of workers with red flags approached the docks where the ships were anchored for the winter, and they called for the sailors to join them.[35] Because some sailors wanted to respond, the situation threatened to get out of hand, so most commanders agreed to release their crews. On several ships, however, the sailors refused to join the demonstration and stayed behind with their officers. A large mob of workers, sailors, and soldiers moved through the city to the fortress prison, the Margarita, in the old town wall, where they overpowered the guard and released all of the prisoners, including a few former sailor-revolutionaries of 1905–6. Two prison officials were killed, and the port commander, Vice-Admiral Aleksandr Gerasimov, was struck and wounded on the head while attempting to calm the mob.[36]

At Revel, differences in nationality and language between Estonian workers and Russian sailors prevented as much open fraternization and concerted action as there was at Kronstadt, and the greater degree of isolation and self-containment of the small ships enabled the officers to retain better control. Also, since these ships had been more active during the war, there continued to be better relations between officers and crews. The former, too, tended to be younger and more liberal, more inclined to join and to lead their own men in the demonstrations.[37] Rear Admiral Vladimir Pilkin, the commander of the First Squadron of Cruisers, and Rear Admiral Dmitrii Verderevsky, who was in charge of submarines, made good use of their reputations as liberals and tended to go along with the tide of the revolution. Pilkin kept his superior, Nepenin, informed of the course of events, and in turn, Pilkin received a timely instruction on 2 March to announce support of the Provisional Government.[38] Soviet writers dismiss the Revel insurrection as having been led by Socialist Revolutionaries and Mensheviks. At least, Bolsheviks were less in evidence at the Estonian port than at Kronstadt or Helsingfors.

Clearly, the most important factor in the relative stability maintained at Revel was that the relationship between officers and crews was closer than at the other bases. Fedotov White, who commanded a destroyer at Revel,

71

revealed in his diary of the events that he knew several Social Democrats and Socialist Revolutionaries and had discussed issues with them.[39] Also of significance was the arrival on 3 March of Fedor Evseev, a Petrograd Bolshevik, who presided over a conference of officers and sailor representatives on the training ship *Petr Velikii*. The resolution that was drafted at this meeting was one of the first in the Baltic fleet to indicate firmly that a definite new direction of affairs was at hand. The first article went so far as "to express entire trust in the Temporary Government and assure defense and support in the organization of victory and reestablishment of order, in the hope that the Government prepares as soon as possible the convocation of a National Assembly, which will designate such a form of Government as would be in agreement with the will of the people." The other points, which dealt with long-standing grievances of sailors but more radically than did Order Number One, would have entirely abolished saluting between officers and men (article 2), given crews the right to take part in courts in the same number as officers (article 4), abolished "disciplinary punishments imposed heretofore" (article 12), and established a court "to dismiss persons whose presence is considered undesirable by the crew" (article 9).[40] Even after this apparent agreement between officers and crews, the situation at Revel continued to be precarious as reports of more violence arrived from Kronstadt and Helsingfors.

VIOLENCE IN HELSINGFORS

At the main base of the fleet a rather different course of events unfolded. Although Admiral Nepenin was in constant communication with the Naval General Staff in Petrograd, sailors on the largest ships were less well informed than those in Kronstadt and Revel. Reports tended to be exaggerated, particularly those from officers and sailors returning from leave in Petrograd. The stories related by Admirals Nebolsin and Kedrov, who had returned to Helsingfors by 1 March, were especially alarming, and it is also quite possible, as one émigré officer later charged, that Captain Altfater and Captain Kapnist, of the staff in the capital, and Prince Cherkasskii and Captain Rengarten, on board the *Krechet*, magnified their descriptions of events in an effort to neutralize the fleet for the sake of their own political prejudices against the old regime.[41] Nepenin, who was quite conscious of the importance of communications, may also have overreacted to the news that the revolt at Kronstadt had cut all official channels of direct contact with that base; he was perhaps too ready to believe the rumors about the killing of a large number of officers. On the other hand, Nepenin's alarm at the murder of one port commander and the wounding of another is quite understandable.

Early on 1 March, Nepenin placed the ice-bound fleet on battle alert as a means of tightening discipline and reinforcing control; everyone then knew that something drastic was occurring, and officers and crews both waited expectantly for the next move. Later in the day, in response to reports of the deteriorating situation at Kronstadt and of the revolt on board the *Aurora*, the commander telegraphed directly to the tsar, requesting that he consent to the demands of the Duma leaders in order to preserve Russia's fighting ability.[42] At a conference of staff and command officers the next morning, Nepenin announced his decision to support the new Provisional Government: "We must not interfere in internal affairs, but we must recognize that the acts of the State Duma are patriotic. If circumstances demand, I will openly declare that I recognize the Executive Committee of the State Duma, and I will announce this publicly."[43] The admiral did not seem to realize that public assessments of patriotism and a declaration of support for a new government constituted a type of internal interference. While a majority of officers in command positions opposed Nepenin's statement, the staff officers supported it. Only Rear Admiral Bakhirev, commander of the First Squadron of Battleships, went so far as to tell Nepenin privately that "he would remain loyal to His Highness" no matter what happened, to which the fleet commander replied: "Now there is war, which must be brought to a conclusion. I believe that after it is finished, the tsar, if he so desires, may again take power in his hands; we must not abandon our position, but must remain and fight both the external and internal enemies."[44] Obviously, the admiral was in a difficult position, and he reacted with hesitation and confusion. He placed what he conceived of as his military duty above that of loyalty to the tsar, but the distinction between the two remained blurred.

After reports from Revel came in later on 2 March, Nepenin telegraphed Stavka at 10:40 P.M.:

> With enormous difficulty I continue to control the fleet and retain the trust of the sailors. In Revel the situation is critical, but I have not yet lost hope that it can be saved. Report to His Majesty that I support the intercession of Grand Duke Nikolai Nikolaevich, our

supreme staff, and the commanders in chief of the fronts regarding the demands put forward by the president of the State Duma [Rodzianko]. If the decision is not taken in the course of the next few hours, then will come catastrophe and uncounted misfortunes for our native land.[45]

Thus, the Baltic commander realized the urgency of the situation and added one more important voice to the circles that were applying pressure on the tsar to abdicate.

So far, the Helsingfors base remained under control, though demonstrations were developing in the city, and news about the violence on the *Aurora* and in Kronstadt was creating a mood for imitation in the fleet. Nepenin believed that the quicker the political question could be decided, the better the military situation would be. And on this point the admiral's actions would appear to have been correct. Both Kronstadt and Revel were settling down, and 3 March dawned quietly in Finland.

In fact, only after receipt of news of the tsar's abdication in the late afternoon of 3 March did disturbances again rise, and then, unlike in Kronstadt and Revel, the instigation came directly from the crews of the ships. Exactly why a revolt should begin after the political situation in Petrograd had been decided, at least for the time being, is not entirely clear. Low morale, long-standing grievances, the presence of revolutionaries, and possibly of German agents, and general confusion contributed to the breakdown of authority. The psychology of mob action was perhaps the most important factor in the troublesome Second Squadron of Battleships, which was docked across the frozen harbor at the Sveaborg fortress. There the large complements of the *Imperator Pavel I*, the *Andrei Pervozvannyi*, and the *Slava*, who were unhappy with being confined to ships on battle alert, seized control and raised the red flags. Several officers had been killed, including the squadron commander, Rear Admiral Arkadii Nebolsin, by 7:30 that evening, when Nepenin telegraphed Rodzianko: "The Baltic fleet as a military force no longer exists. What I can do, I will do."[46] Shortly afterwards a red flag was hoisted over the *Krechet* with the admiral's approval.[47]

The revolt quickly spread to other ships. The *Andrei* and the *Pavel* signaled the other crews to "take care of" their most hated officers, and a large delegation from these ships approached the *Petropavlovsk*, the modern flagship of the First Squadron of Battleships, about 9:00 P.M. and called for the sailors to disarm their officers. Admiral Bakhirev, after consulting his staff, agreed that all of his officers would surrender their weapons.[48] By this time, with more bloodshed and less notice, most of the smaller ships of the fleet at Helsingfors were in the hands of their crews.

Only at this time, in desperation, did the fleet commander request that the new authorities in Petrograd send representatives immediately to explain the basis of the new government and to restore calm.[49] Why this had not already been done is something of a mystery, since delegations had been sent to Kronstadt, Revel, and even to the cruiser *Aurora*. Probably the leaders of both the government and the Soviet had been too preoccupied with other events during the day, and perhaps they also thought that the crisis was passing and, with order returning to Petrograd and Kronstadt, that there was little to fear from other quarters. In any event, a near-panic reaction occurred in Petrograd. The newly formed Executive Committee of the Soviet met immediately in emergency session and decided to send one of its best-known members, Matvei Skobelev, the Menshevik vice-chairman, to Helsingfors.[50] The Provisional Government, which was still little more than a committee, chose Fedor Rodichev, a Duma member and a Kadet supporter of Miliukov's, to accompany Skobelev as temporary commissar for Finland; and Alexander Kerensky hurried over to the Naval General Staff to spend part of the night overseeing communications with the Baltic bases.

Nepenin, however, could not wait for the arrival of help. He called a meeting of delegates of sailors from all the ships at 11:00 P.M. At this tumultuous session on board the *Krechet* the commander insisted that officers be released and that those who were guilty of murder be arrested. The sailors demanded assurances that there would be no retribution and that they would be allowed to choose their own commanders. Agreement was impossible, but they quieted somewhat after listening to a long telegram from Kerensky. The meeting on the *Krechet* broke up in the early hours of 4 March with the announcement that a similar one would convene later that morning to hear the deputies from Petrograd.[51]

But meanwhile, rumors spread from ship to ship. An infantry regiment, which Nepenin had requested earlier, made an untimely appearance on the quay about midnight, leading many sailors to believe that Nepenin was forcing them into a trap. A radio message transmitted from either the *Pavel* or the *Andrei* at 5:30 A.M. by the United Fleet Democratic Organization reminded the sailors of an unpopular saluting order that had been issued by Nepenin the previous November. At 10:45 another transmission demanded that no further orders from Nepenin be issued or obeyed.[52] By this time the crews of the battleships had decided to replace Nepenin with the popular "red" Vice-Admiral Maksimov, who had to be rescued from his place of confinement on board the *Chaika*.[53]

About noon, the sailors delivered Maksimov to the *Krechet* in a car decorated with red flags, but Nepenin claimed that he had no authority for such an irregular change of command unless he had instructions from Petrograd.[54] Maksimov then led the way to Railroad Station Square in the middle of the city, where, before the still-unfinished masterpiece of Saarinen's modern architecture, a vast crowd gathered to celebrate the revolution and receive the delegation from Petrograd. The train was delayed, and during the long wait outside the station, restless soldiers and sailors fired shots into the air and provoked brief periods of panic. Violence was averted, thanks to the bravery of a few officers and the stamina of a military band, which frequently struck up the *Marseillaise*; nevertheless, general confusion reigned for several hours.[55] One group decided to bring Nepenin to the station. When the mob reached the *Krechet*, the admiral agreed to accompany them, partly because he was defenseless, the crew of the ship having left, but also in order to safeguard the ship, with its signal equipment and code books. As he made his way on foot to the harbor gates, about 1:45 in the afternoon, a shot rang out from the crowd, and the commander of the fleet fell dead.[56]

When the news of the murder of Nepenin reached the assemblage on the station square, Maksimov was again declared commander, a position that he had held de facto since noon. This was officially confirmed by a cablegram from the new minister of war, Alexander Guchkov, at 3:00 P.M. Maksimov's first order pertained to the lowering of red battle flags and to the releasing of imprisoned officers.[57] Then, with bands playing and banners waving, the train from Petrograd that was carrying Skobelev and Rodichev pulled into Helsingfors about 4:00 P.M. Speeches filled with platitudes about the glories of the revolution were interrupted repeatedly by hurrahs from the mass of sailors, soldiers, and workers, and afterwards the delegation accompanied Maksimov to his command post.[58] But the revolt at the Helsingfors base, unlike that at Kronstadt, was not so much concluded as suspended. The naval chain of command remained intact though weakened, and under Maksimov it drifted along with the tide of the revolution.

ASSESSING THE REVOLT IN THE FLEET

The February Revolution in the Baltic fleet had exacted a high toll and had cut much deeper than was the case in Petrograd. While few high-ranking officials died in Petrograd, the Baltic fleet lost a substantial portion of its top echelon. Though reports at the time were exaggerated, placing the murder of officers at a level between 300 and 500, they still reflect the picture of the real disaster that had occurred. By one count, 76 officers of the Baltic fleet lost their lives in the upheaval—45 in Helsingfors, 24 in Kronstadt, 5 at Revel, and 2 in Petrograd.[59] In addition to the officers who were brutally killed, several more were seriously wounded, and 20 noncommissioned officers also became victims while attempting to maintain order. When civilian and police losses at the bases are added up, the casualties totaled over 150.

But many more officers were removed from their positions either through duress or by arrest. In Kronstadt alone, about 500, including 162 naval officers, were detained, some under severe conditions. Of a total of about 650 arrested at the bases of Helsingfors, Kronstadt, Revel, and Åbo, approximately half were military officers and 90 percent of these were from the navy. The other half were mostly police and noncommissioned officers.[60] Thus, about 10 percent of the officer corps of the Baltic fleet was eliminated by the February Revolution, a percentage that still does not adequately reflect the magnitude of the disaster that overwhelmed the fleet, since most of these held strategically important command positions, several others "escaped," never to return to their duties that year, and many who remained were psychologically affected by what they had witnessed.

The reasons for the excesses can only partly be accounted for by the previous history of conflict, mutiny, and retribution in the navy and by the peculiar circumstances of the Baltic area that have already been described. The violence at Kronstadt was, therefore, predictable and relatively unsurprising, given the nature of the base and the presence of disciplinary units. But to explain the greater bloodshed in Helsingfors, after the abdication of the tsar and the formation of the Provisional Government, is more difficult. The conditions on the large battleships, where there were more distant relationships between officers and crew and where anonymity within the mob made murder easier, contributed to the conflicts. It would be misleading, however, to place too much emphasis on the presence of the largest ships in the fleet as the key to the Helsingfors violence, since actually more officers were killed on the smaller ships, the mine sweeper *Retivyi*, for example, losing all three of its officers to the forty-man crew.[61]

The explosions in the fleet mystified contemporary observers and led them to make a number of charges and countercharges. The American naval attaché wrote, about three weeks after the February–March turmoil:

"The reason for the Naval Revolt is not clear. . . . Officially it is explained that it was a case of misunderstanding, the sailors not believing that the officers were acting in good faith. Their merciless treatment of their officers is not yet understood, except that even after joining the Revolution, some of the officers used severe measures to keep the men under discipline."[62] One can understand that sailors would be suspicious of officers who had adhered to all the old traditions and now were carrying red flags and claiming to be democrats and even socialists. Yet the officers were obviously in a precarious position. Facing an incomprehensible crisis and traditionally apolitical, they were left baffled and paralyzed from fear and frustration. It must be remembered that both officers and crew members in Helsingfors were already aware of what had happened in Petrograd and Kronstadt. So, was the choice to join the mob, and end up hanging by your feet, like Girs, or to go down fighting, like Nikolskii? More at Helsingfors appeared to prefer the latter, perhaps in part because they knew that they were under the direct observation of the commander of the fleet and his staff. But this choice often ended in pitched battle, such as the one of nearly an hour on the *Andrei Pervozvannyi*, which was ended only by the courageous action of the captain, George Gadd, who adroitly won over part of the crew, made them all listen to a stirring speech, and saved a number of officers from nearly certain death.[63]

Soviet sources usually blame the officers for bringing violence upon themselves because of their former brutalities and their present confusion and narrow mindedness. Even the Menshevik Skobelev, addressing the Petrograd Soviet a few days after his dramatic appearance in Helsingfors, substantially agreed with the view that the officers were at fault; but few details were provided for this claim, except to go back to the old issue of past grievances.[64] It is true that violence was almost always directed toward officers in command positions and that staff officers were mostly immune, and one can cite instances of supposedly popular commanders being shot down.

Another common explanation that receives credence in both Soviet and émigré sources is the clash of classes, of officers versus men. Admiral Glennon, the naval representative on the Root Mission, wrote in July 1917, after visiting the Baltic bases and talking with a number of officers: "Some friction resulted, and suddenly mobs of workmen and sailors, intoxicated by the unaccustomed possession of unlimited power, started an indiscriminate killing of officers. Many were killed in their beds, others were shot on the ice attempting to escape, some were tortured and confined to the bare hold

78

of a ship."[65] This was a typical exaggeration which was derived from anti-revolutionary sources and from officers who were giving excuses for subsequent actions, such as failing to reestablish discipline or retiring from active duty. If class warfare had been the chief cause of the disturbances at Helsingfors, many more officers would have been killed. Instead, one can find numerous instances of officers siding with crews and of crews protecting officers. An explanation would also have to be found for the presence of so many officers on ships' committees and Soviet executive committees immediately afterwards. Even at Kronstadt, when the Soviet met in its first session, one-third of the members were officers.

Émigré officers tend to divide sharply on the causes, blaming German agents, Socialist Revolutionaries, and Bolsheviks; and because they differ among themselves, writing years after the events from extremely partisan positions, their analyses can be too easily dismissed. Evidence, of course, is very thin indeed to support any of these contentions. Despite Admiral Timirev's claim that presence of German agents was the main difference between Helsingfors and Revel, no such agents can specifically be named.[66] But Finland's geographic position and the recruitment and training of 2,000 Finns in Germany provided many opportunities for communications. Anti-Russian Finns could easily have acted deliberately or unknowingly as German agents to the extent at least of undermining morale at the naval base. But whether or not actual agents were at work may not be as relevant as the belief that they were. Explosions on board the new dreadnought *Imperatritsa Mariia* in October 1916, which resulted in her sinking in Sevastopol Harbor with the loss of 216 crew members and the injury of 232 more, was widely attributed to German espionage, though, in fact, it is more likely that they were accidental.[67] The ships in Helsingfors were believed to be even more vulnerable because of the closer German presence and the widespread sympathy toward Germany among the nationalistic Finns. This naturally increased feelings of distrust and suspicion of "their barons," on the part of crews, and of any civilian contact with crews, on the part of officers. In this atmosphere, rationalizations could easily be distorted by fear so as to cause the overconfinement of crews, on the one hand, and the "justified" killing of officers, on the other—both conceived as patriotic acts.

A valuable émigré manuscript, written by a midshipman on the *Petropavlovsk*, blames the Socialist Revolutionaries for the violence.[68] Again, firm evidence is lacking, because little light has been shed on the local activities of the SRs in Finland. Helsingfors had been a stronghold of the Battle

Organization. The party had emerged initially as the strongest in the Helsingfors Soviet, and the Finnish capital became a major center of the left wing of the party later in 1917. The picture of underground and long-frustrated SR terrorists finally realizing a golden opportunity cannot be entirely dismissed, despite its implausibility.

The Bolsheviks are naturally an easy culprit for many émigré writers, Graf, for example.[69] This focus is just as naturally denied by Soviet sources, and the weakness of the Bolsheviks in Helsingfors after the arrests of 1915 and 1916 would tend to bear them out. Still there is the strangely coincidental arrival of Nikolai Khovrin on the battleship *Imperator Pavel I* on 1 March. It is known that Khovrin had been influential on the ship at the time of the *Gangut* uprising and that the crew of the *Pavel* was the first to murder officers and spread the word to the other ships. Khovrin's presence and the fact that he was dispatched to the base by the left-wing Vyborg (in Petrograd) District Committee of the party are deliberately ignored by Soviet secondary sources.[70] His name also heads the list of the ship's initial delegation (three out of five of whom were Bolsheviks) to the Helsingfors Soviet. If Khovrin was really the leader that he appeared to be in 1915 and again later in 1917, he must bear some responsibility for the violence of March. His descriptions of participating in the Petrograd street demonstrations may at least have provided one more spark, which landed in the midst of a tense combustible situation, to excite the sailors to rebellion.

The big question that was now posed was whether the Provisional Government, or any central authority, could restore military order in the Baltic bases. But the immediate question was whether it was practical at all to intervene in naval affairs, given the higher priorities assigned to the construction of a new, effective government and the maintaining of fighting ability on the land. Baltic problems were bound to affect even the outcome of these efforts, since both the military and the political pictures were changed by the naval revolt. A memorandum from Stavka on 18 March indicated the beginnings of the dilemma: "The organization of the defense in Finland and that of the approaches to Petrograd call for an increase in strength on the Northern Front, inasmuch as the cooperation of the Baltic fleet cannot be counted upon."[71] If the Provisional Government did not reassert control over the navy and its bases, they could influence the political and military situation of the capital.

4

THE REVOLUTION ORGANIZES

DURING THE FIVE-DAY REVOLUTION in the Baltic fleet, the traditional operating procedure was severely disrupted, undergoing what were probably the most intensive changes for any major military unit other than in battle itself. Yet, the revolution was by no means complete; in many ways it was only beginning. What allowed the course of events of those February and March days to set the tone for the following weeks and to prevent the orderly reestablishment of control?

First of all, there was still the war; therefore, the circumstances and conditions that had been largely responsible for the fall of the imperial government remained. According to Dmitrii Fedotov White, one of the most astute participant-observers in the fleet, "It was not the strength of the Revolutionary organization that brought about the downfall of the Empire, it was the falling to pieces of the armed forces and of the Government machinery under the impact of war." As long as the war was being fought, the revolution would continue, in the sense at least that a stabilization or arrest of the currents of change was impossible: "When a State is in the process of transition from one mode of life to another, when great political changes are impending, a long war, particularly a not successful war, expedites the . . . breakdown of the old regime."[1] But for a revolution to progress, a degree of dynamism and movement must be present, and these are produced by a combination of times and men. As World War I conditioned the times, men made the revolution.

THE ORGANIZATION OF THE BALTIC FLEET
SUMMER OF 1917

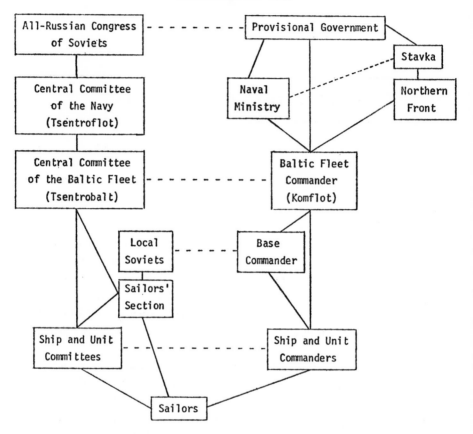

THE RISE OF POLITICAL CONSCIOUSNESS IN THE FLEET

Almost all observers agree that the initial turmoil was devoid of major leaders, that the events of 28 February to 4 March failed to produce heroes. Even Soviet proclivity toward worshiping heroes on anniversaries, which was especially strong in 1957 and 1967, could not find satisfactory evidence that any Bolsheviks had been outstanding leaders in the fleet during those days. This does not mean that the revolution lacked instigation from individuals; rather, it had so much that the question of an overall leadership remains open. The absence of obvious initiators and control groups is what made the revolution in the fleet so spontaneous and elastic. Adherence to a party, as a result, meant very little at this stage. But because of past repression, accumulated incidents, and persistent revolutionary propaganda, the new programs and direct action that were provided by party organization soon attracted many of the men, and this tendency gave previously established radical groups an advantage. Sailors proved to be both leaders and followers.

Unique evidence on the emerging political leadership at the main base is provided by a list of 504 sailor delegates and alternates who were elected to the Helsingfors Soviet in March and who composed the Sailors' Assembly. Only 66 of these names can be identified as belonging to members of other organizations during 1917, and only 30 were definitely affiliated with political parties (18 Bolsheviks, 10 Socialist Revolutionaries, 1 anarchist, and 1 Menshevik), but this number includes some of the most active Bolsheviks of the wartime fleet: Pavel Dybenko, Vasilii Marusev, Nikolai Khovrin, and Grigorii Svetlichnyi. Convincing as the evidence may be that these four men were indeed recognized by their fellow sailors as leaders in March, it should be pointed out that all were from the *Imperator Pavel I*, now renamed the *Respublika*, though Dybenko, after his return to Helsingfors from a few months' detention and sick leave on 3 March, found a new home on the transport *Shcha*. Of the 24 delegates to the Sailors' Assembly from the two other most riotous battleships in the March "days," the *Andrei* and the *Petropavlovsk*, none were apparently active in any political party. Several of those sailors from these and other ships, who are cited by Soviet sources as leaders of Bolshevik cells, are not found among the delegations of those ships in March.[2]

The great majority of rank-and-file sailors obviously belonged to no political party or organization. Many did not even know the difference between the active parties. Unfortunately, there is very little information available about the first party and unit organizations in the fleet. Soviet sources do not agree even on the date of the founding of the Bolshevik committee at Kronstadt, a leading secondary authority placing it sometime between 4 March and 18 March.[3] In fact, the Bolshevik organization came into existence gradually, from the time of an initial meeting on 3 March to listen to a deputation from the Vyborg District Committee, which was led by Fedor Dingelshtedt, until the designation of the Kronstadt Committee by the Russian Bureau of the party on 7 March.[4] After this initiative it still took several more days to get the committee fully operative, with a Petrograd party worker, Semen Roshal, as regular chairman. At Helsingfors, three or four Bolsheviks met rather informally on the transport *Shcha* on 12 March to constitute the first "Bolshevik conference" in the Finnish capital.[5]

Though party membership in the fleet was very small, the political consciousness of the sailors, in its formative stage, was quite definitely socialist. At Kronstadt, perhaps because of a certain revolutionary pride already associated with the radical training base, many sailors wanted to remain independent of a party organization and regarded outside agitators with suspicion. This tendency to retain solidarity and to eschew political factions resulted in a strong "nonparty" (albeit socialist) orientation. Anatolii Lamanov, chairman of the Kronstadt Soviet through most of 1917, adhered to this "neutral" position.

Influenced by the overwhelmingly peasant garrison and the factory workers, the naval units in Petrograd were inclined at first to support the Socialist Revolutionaries. The rapid politicization of the capital, which was promoted by the presence of central party organizations; an intensive circulation of newspapers and pamphlets; and the prestige of the Petrograd Soviet —all caused allegiances to develop more quickly there than in the major fleet bases. Of four delegates to the Petrograd Soviet from the cruiser *Aurora*, none was at first definitely associated with a political party; three of them later became Socialist Revolutionaries, one a Bolshevik.[6] And a similar situation existed at Revel, where sailors, and officers too, were Socialist Revolutionaries when they became politically active. In both Petrograd and Revel, however, the sailors tended to attach themselves to a revolutionary name, rather than to a specific program, and "socialist revolutionary" was best known and sounded most appropriate. The large following gained by that amorphous party during the first few weeks after the revolution in February and March does not reflect a firm adherence either to its goals or to its leaders. Nowhere was it yet really possible to sense which party was most "radical," but among those who knew, the Socialist Revolutionaries seemed more traditional—and more Russian.

At the main base of the fleet the Socialist Revolutionaries initially attracted few sailors; a larger number took the "Social Democratic" label. This is credited mostly to the existence of the well-organized Finnish Social Democratic Party and the timely appearance of Matvei Skobelev, a Petrograd Menshevik leader, on 4 March. Under the leadership of Sergei Garin (Garfeld), a young, intellectual navy petty officer, the Social Democrat sailors tended at first to be "moderate" and more Menshevik than Bolshevik, though Garin considered himself to be a Bolshevik.[7] A more radical center, led by Dybenko, slowly emerged in the course of the first month.

THE RESPONSE OF THE PROVISIONAL GOVERNMENT

While political orientations were developing in the fleet, radical shifts in routine, which might appear minor in retrospect, were quickly effected by the orders of Admiral Maksimov. On 5 March, officers were forbidden to use familiar and degrading terms that the sailors considered abusive, and the officers were to be addressed, in turn, as *gospodin* ("mister") rather than as Your Excellency. "Lower ranks" became "sailors," and they were allowed to smoke in the street.[8] These changes, following the tenor of Order Number One of the Petrograd Soviet, are indicative of a widespread destruction of the regulations and traditions that had maintained and enforced the gap between sailors and officers in the Imperial Navy. They were important psychologically as convincing evidence of the power of mass action, and though largely dictated by the most radical elements in the Baltic fleet, they were applied universally to the whole Baltic naval establishment.

If the revolution in the fleet had accomplished a considerable liberation and unification of the ordinary sailors, it had the opposite effect upon the officers. Besides those who were killed or arrested, many either resigned or were removed from their posts. The American attaché reported: "Officers of the Navy, who can do so are retiring or resigning in numbers. Of those at the Navy Department all except two of the rank of Commander and above have either been retired by the New Government, or have resigned of their own accord. Their spirit is quite gone."[9] In fact, the decrees of the new government, which were issued by traditional means and in routine form, failed to reflect the situation that actually existed in the fleet. Generally, officers were powerless, and sailors performed very few of their regular duties. This was true even on the smaller ships and submarines at Revel, where the British submarine commander reported that his Russian sailors "would not permit any officers to leave or enter the ship until their committee (headed by the man who gets my bath ready every morning) decided what to do with certain officers."[10] And at the outlying bases, such as Moon Sound and Åbo, where smaller patrol squadrons were stationed, the revolution at first was peaceful but then became violent after news arrived from Helsingfors and Kronstadt. Because of frozen seas, no naval unit could escape the consequences of revolution.

The situation in the Baltic fleet that was produced by the uprising was allowed to continue because of the weakness of central authority. In Petrograd, where by 5 March a "Socialist Committee virtually constitutes a Rival Government," General Alfred Knox reported that the minister of war (the army and navy were now combined for the first time), Alexander Guchkov, told him "that he [Guchkov] realized terrible position occupied at present by officers who were never in sympathy with the old regime but he said that it was impossible to arrest agitators as such action would at once cause a second revolution."[11] Guchkov's order of 6 March forbidding soviets to interfere in appointments of officers was generally ignored, and in many cases it was irrelevant since most changes were effected by lower-level unit committees, then approved by the appropriate commanders.

Guchkov, who was primarily interested in the army, preferred to assign naval problems to subordinates and to commissions. The first such commission—which was headed by a popular general, A. A. Polivanov, and the chief of the Naval General Staff, Captain Aleksei Kapnist—on 9 March approved the general principle of self-administration of naval commands, thereby sanctioning the liberal moves of Maksimov. Shortly after this, a fleet delegation from Revel arrived in Petrograd to protest the Provisional Government's lack of positive action. The minister of war listened intently to Fedotov White's description of the rapid collapse of discipline in the navy —"Guchkov was amazed by my words, and exclaimed loudly: 'Well, what should be done?' With those words our audience came to an end."[12]

Another more permanent commission, under the direction of N. V. Savich, a former member of the Duma, was announced on 15 March, but preparatory work for the full membership of thirty-five (seven officers, seven *konduktory*, and twenty-one sailors) began only on 22 March, with the group meeting officially for the first time on 13 April. It was over a month after that before a detailed report on the problem of the relations of sailors to officers was ready.[13]

The policy of the Provisional Government was to ride out the storm, hoping that things would settle down and that the regular routine of naval operations could be resumed when the ice melted. During the kaleidoscope of events in the capital, Revel and Helsingfors seemed very far away; and closer at home, the local commissar at Kronstadt was left to deal with problems as best he could. There was obvious fear among some of the leaders of the Provisional Government that since Kronstadt had escaped from the regular chain of command during the February–March revolution, it would be dangerous to try to restore discipline while their own authority was still weak. A resumption of violence there might easily spread to Petrograd and bring about the fall of the government, or at least it might damage the chances of cooperation from the Petrograd Soviet. Others were confident that the declared democratic intentions of the new government would eventually win over the majority of sailors, or they were simply opposed to shedding more blood.

The instability of the situation was stressed in the reports of the American naval attaché: "Although the temporary government is still in power, the economic, political, and military situation of this district, and especially Petrograd, Helsingfors and Raval [*sic*], is daily becoming more serious."[14] And as reports filtered in from the naval bases, the British ambassador became quite alarmed: "Naval attaché would say that weakness of fleet lies more with shaken nerves of many officers rather than with disposition of crews but hopes that next three weeks which must elapse before active operations can be undertaken by or against fleet will give time to effect much improvement."[15] At about the same time, 17 March, his consul at Kronstadt reported: "On the whole everything is quiet at present. . . . The sailors, however, realize that they have got the power to dictate their own terms, and as there is a vast quantity of explosives at Kronstadt it is generally conceded that the men will have to be handled with tact before they consent to submit to discipline."[16]

While some observers seemed to question whether the Provisional Government had the means to quell a rebellion on an armed naval base, others favored immediate, drastic action. General Knox, the British military attaché, agreed with General Lavr Kornilov, the new commander of the Petrograd region, "that if Government do not act soon it will be too late, [since the] insurgents at Kronstadt have declared they will not fire a shot against enemy."[17] After some prodding, Foreign Minister Paul Miliukov told Buchanan on 22 March "that he was glad to say that Committee of Soldiers and Workers Deputies with whom Government had yesterday discussed naval situation now understood gravity of the question and had recognized necessity for allowing officers to be re-installed and of replacing Admiral Maximoff."[18] Frequently voiced British concern may also have affected the government's decision to issue, on 27 March, the "Declaration to Citizens" which attempted to explain Russia's continuation of the war as a fight for democratic ideals.

On 28 March, Rear Admiral Dmitrii Verderevsky, chief of the submarine division, was named second in command to Maksimov, with the understanding that he would soon become the commander.[19] These preliminary moves were supported by Socialist Revolutionary and Menshevik leaders in the Central Executive Committee of the Petrograd Soviet but were not followed by decisive executive orders. The Provisional Government still chose to try to cajole the sailors into more respectful and orderly behavior. Alexander Kerensky made a personal appeal to the Kronstadt sailors at the Naval Arena on 28 March to release the arrested officers, and the Petrograd Soviet cooperated by sending two of its leaders, Matvei Skobelev and Iraklii Tsereteli, to Kronstadt and Helsingfors, respectively, in March. Even General Kornilov and "the little grandmother," Ekaterina Breshko-Breshkovskaia, addressed a large crowd at Anchor Square on 5 April.[20]

Little objective information on these visits is available. Though apparently catching the sailors by surprise, they were unsuccessful in establishing any greater degree of government control. The American naval attaché, who accompanied the delegation to Helsingfors, reported:

> The great evil of present conditions is a profound sense of distrust between officers and men. Appeals and reason seem to have little effect with the men. The British, French, and American systems have been explained to them, but their point of view is that none of these systems are applicable to the present conditions and they are going to have an entirely new, a Russian system. Now officers have no direct control over their men. They have simply the role of instructors, or technical assistants.[21]

Except for using fruitless "peaceful persuasion," the Provisional Government did little more in the next six weeks to strengthen its control over the fleet.

On 11 April, Buchanan again became alarmed at the situation in the fleet: "Attitude of seamen in the Baltic fleet is (?changing) for the worse; . . . they are becoming more exacting in regard to control over business of the Fleet internal and external and in some cases showing a disinclination to take their ships (?to) (?sea) if called on." A few days later the British consul in Petrograd was sent to Helsingfors to study the situation, and he confirmed Buchanan's fears: "The spirit of the fleet could scarcely be worse. The men have seized the naval chest at Helsingfors and are enjoying themselves with the proceeds. Many are in Petrograd, where they are a real danger, as they openly preach violence and pillage."[22] The consul pointed out two more important features of the situation in the fleet—that the sailors were well financed because they had achieved control over unit and ship mess funds, and that their presence was being felt in urban centers. Probably it was unknown to many observers that the influence of the Baltic sailors was spreading much farther, deep into the countryside. Naum Tochenyi relates that many sailors were directed to the countryside "for agitating for transfer of power to the Soviets and the seizure of land from the landlords." He and two other sailors went to Chernigov Province at the end of April, where, Tochenyi claims, he spoke before the city duma of Nezhin with such effect that he turned the delegates against the Provisional Government.[23]

Many other individuals and groups from the Baltic fleet traveled around Russia on special assignments during April and May; they included a number of the leading radicals among the sailors. Dybenko led a group to the Southwestern Front, while Pavel Khokhriakov and Dmitrii Kondakov, Bolsheviks from Kronstadt, visited the Northern Front. Another detachment left for the Northern Front in April, under the auspices of the Helsingfors Bolshevik Committee and under the direction of Mikhail Gorchaev, who had been a sailor-Bolshevik since before the war. Many of these "tours" were organized by political parties or soviets for the purpose of explaining positions or incidents, but others were more spontaneous or were designed as a means of establishing communications. Most useful in this regard were the "directed leaves" that were sponsored by the many provincial associations (zemliachestva) in Kronstadt and Helsingfors. By the end of May, around six hundred agitators had been dispatched to the countryside by the associations of Kronstadt alone, though how many actually returned is not recorded. At least the success of "sailors' power" was being broadcast far and wide. Perhaps the most effective and significant of the Baltic delegations was the one led by Timofei Uliantsev and Vladimir Zaitsev that left Kronstadt at the end of May and concentrated on urban centers in the Donets Basin of the Ukraine, the ports of the Black and Caspian seas, and all of the major cities along the Volga, returning more than two months after its departure.[24]

The scattering of some of the most radical sailors to towns and the countryside may have made it easier for Maksimov to achieve a degree of combat readiness in May. He boasted to Montgomery Grove, the British consul in Helsingfors, "that the Baltic fleet is working alright, that the men were all perfectly ready to go to sea and to fight, . . . that the big ships were ready for putting out to sea, . . . that the destroyers are doing reconnaisance work regularly, and that the mine layers are getting on excellently." And

Grove admitted: "The state of affairs in the fleet is certainly better than it was quite recently and will probably improve now that they have got most of the big units out of the harbour. What was so absolutely demoralizing for the men was loafing about in town all day and all night with nothing to do: naturally from sheer boredom they got into the hands of women and also went to all the meetings which were daily got up by agitators of every sort and description."[25]

This improvement did not save Maksimov's position. His removal, promised at the end of March, was finally effected on 2 June, after Kerensky assumed the post of minister of war and navy.[26] Maksimov was "promoted" to naval chief of staff at Stavka, and Verderevsky became the fourth commander of the Baltic fleet in a little more than a year. The delay may reflect, in addition to procrastination, genuine concern by leaders in the Provisional Government about the suitability of the popular, easygoing Verderevsky. Kolchak turned down Guchkov's offer of the appointment at the end of April, so there seemed to be few other alternatives. At least Verderevsky was known for his apolitical stance, while Maksimov had not hesitated to become involved in political questions.[27]

The first "revolutionary" commander had courted the sailors' support by addressing crowds on the street and on the ships and by playing the part of the "red admiral" in the sessions of the Helsingfors Soviet.[28] But Maksimov had aided the revolutionary movement in another, more important way. During his three months' tenure, the commanders of almost every unit in the fleet had been changed; most of his 298 orders pertained to promotions and appointments to command positions.[29] Many of these directives were unavoidable, as vacancies had to be filled; but Maksimov also tended to go along with the whims of the sailors, approving their "elections," so that it was not unusual for a capital ship to have three or four different commanders during this period. Thus not only was the chain of command weakened by mutual distrust between the Provisional Government and the commander in chief of the fleet, but it was also undermined by the promotion to strategically important posts of generally weaker, more inexperienced officers, many of whom actually owed their advancement to the sailors under their command. No wonder, then, that there was little immediate improvement in discipline or operational ability when Maksimov was removed. At least a serious possibility that the sailors would oppose the change was eased by Maksimov's ready compliance and Verderevsky's popularity.

THE CREATION OF SAILORS' ORGANIZATIONS

The overall weakening of the command and staff echelon of the fleet would not have been so remarkable except for the simultaneous strengthening of the positions of those who had created the February–March revolution in the fleet. At first the sailors lacked organization, a factor they must have been acutely aware of, for what followed was a mania for committee building. The first ships' committees formed independently and spontaneously, but they were soon regularized by example and were coordinated by higher committees, such as the Committee of Movement at Kronstadt. Their immediate goals were to control and arrest officers, to centralize decision-making within the unit, and to act as communications centers for receipt of information and for coordination with other committees. Still the need for a supreme authority at each base was quickly realized.

The most significant step toward this organization was the creation of soviets, which were made up of elected representatives. This was a natural, spontaneous response to the need for a central communications center; and at the beginning, the organization of the Petrograd Soviet of Workers' and Soldiers' Deputies offered an important example to follow. The exact form, however, did not always follow Petrograd, nor was it uniform at the various bases.

At Kronstadt the Committee of People's Movement called for the selection of an assembly on 3 March. The First Assembly, as it was officially designated, consisted primarily of representatives of military and naval units. Its temporary executive body, the Council of Ten, was presided over by Viktor Pepeliaev, a commissar appointed by the Provisional Government.[30] The workers of the port and factories organized, in the meantime, the Soviet of Workers' Deputies on 5 March. Following this example and the one in Petrograd, the First Assembly and the Committee of Movement simultaneously announced the formation of a Soviet of Military Deputies—to include two representatives and the commander of every military unit, irrespective of size—which would hold its first session at 6:00 P.M. on 7 March. An SR artillery officer, I. A. Krasovskii, was elected first chairman, and an executive committee of eighteen representatives from the navy and eighteen from the army was formed, but the major question of the first session concerned the presence of officers, who, if the order of selection of deputies had been followed exactly, would have constituted one-third of the assembly. After considerable debate, the officers were deprived of automatic membership, and the number of elected delegates was correspondingly increased.[31] Though this action did not preclude the election of officers as regular members, it did prevent any bloc representation for them. It also reflects the degree of radicalism at Kronstadt, since many of the officer-commanders at this time would have been among the most liberal and popular in the navy.

The executive committee of the military soviet met for the first time on 8 March, choosing Artemii Liubovich, a soldier in a telegraph company who had been a Bolshevik since 1907, as its chairman. The first order of business concerned the fate of the officers who were being held in confinement. After a lively debate a special investigative commission was selected, which was headed by another Bolshevik, Ivan Sladkov. This signaled a victory for a leftist hard-line policy in regard to the officers, and it showed that Bolsheviks, with little outside assistance, were both taking the initiative and securing important positions. Meanwhile, Commissar Pepeliaev, who also had little help from Petrograd, was attempting to stem the tide of soviet power by organizing a separate elective body consisting of sixty-five representatives from thirteen occupational groups in the town. Though chosen on 9 March, this embryonic duma seems to have held no real power, having served only as an advisory council to the commissar, who himself could get nothing done without the consent of the soviet.[32]

From the beginning, the military soviet claimed precedence over the more moderate workers' soviet, but in order to avoid possible conflict and to improve centralization, ten delegates of the workers were invited to attend a meeting of the executive committee of the military soviet on 10 March. The two soviets were officially united on that date as the Kronstadt Soviet of Workers' and Military Deputies, with membership in a new executive committee equally divided among three elements—sailors, soldiers, and workers (18 from naval units; 5 from artillery, 5 from infantry, 4 from engineer units, and 4 from port administration; and 18 from the factory workers)—with the chairmanship in the hands of the nonparty leader, Anatolii Lamanov. Of 298 delegates elected to the first session of the combined soviet, 90 were workers. Despite the union, however, the workers' and military deputies continued to meet in separate groups, formally recognized on 17 March as "sections."

On 13 March the new combined soviet ended any ambiguity that still existed by declaring that it, and not the commissar, was the supreme authority on the island. Two days later the Kronstadt Soviet named General Gerasimov to the vacant post of port commander and Lieutenant Petr

Lamanov, brother of the Soviet leader, as commander of the naval units, but it also appointed a special commission to oversee their actions. By this time the Ministry of War and the Ministry of Justice nominally recognized the soviet's power in Kronstadt by sending their directives to the soviet.[33]

Sailors, soldiers, and workers joined in the first meeting of the Helsingfors Soviet on 5 March; but whereas the Kronstadt Soviet was the primary authority for the whole of Kotlin Island, the one in Helsingfors represented only the Russians in a predominantly Finnish city. So, immediately after the revolution, a major problem of the soviet concerned liaison with the Finnish Senate, which, however, was a national representative body that was interested primarily in establishing an independent Finland. With 550 to 600 members, the Soviet of Deputies of the Army and Navy and Workers of the Sveaborg Base, as it was first officially named, was considerably larger than its counterpart at Kronstadt. About 40 percent of the deputies—253—were delegates from naval units, while, in contrast to Kronstadt, worker representatives composed no more than 15 percent.[34] Soldiers, who were inclined to be more moderate than sailors, thus formed the largest bloc in the Helsingfors Soviet.

The sailors resented not having full control, and so by the middle of March they had formed a separate Sailors' Assembly under the chairmanship of Ilia Rastorguev, a sailor from the battleship *Poltava*. Meeting in half-day sessions on an average of four times a week, the assembly handled all matters pertaining to the fleet in the harbor. After a few minor conflicts with the soviet over the publication of protocols and over access to typewriters, the Sailors' Assembly cooperated with a large soviet executive committee of 74 members (24 sailors, 29 soldiers, 6 naval officers, 9 army officers, and 6 workers) but remained largely independent. In both of these organizations, officers, such as Captain Rengarten and Lieutenant Roman Grundman, were instrumental in creating functional subcommissions and committees.[35]

At Revel, the next-largest base of the fleet, the situation was reversed. Only one body, the Revel Soviet of Workers' and Soldiers' Deputies, existed for the city. Since it had a larger representational base, it limited the number of deputies from the fleet to only 10 percent of the total of about 200. The complexion of the Revel Soviet was, therefore, predominantly Estonian and worker in orientation, and it dealt very little with affairs of the fleet. A general assembly of sailors met infrequently, but its executive committee represented the highest revolutionary authority at the naval base. The degree of organizational activity was much lower at Revel than at Kronstadt and Helsingfors, because of the more active operations of the ships, the survival of more qualified officers, and the fact that the sailors were a small element in the local soviet.[36]

The soviets of the outlying bases tended to follow the nearest main base in organization and political orientation. The Åbo-Åland (Turku) Soviet, however, included delegates of Finnish workers as well as those of the Russian workers and military units; and the soviets of the Moon Sound Fortified Position, on the island of Oesel, retained a separation between military and worker sections until later in the year. Given the geographical, social, and other differences between the various Baltic bases, however, the course of soviet development and their methods of operation were remarkably similar.[37]

Meeting on the average of three or four times a week, the soviets debated the most important questions of the day. Their executive committees convened on an even more regular basis, and during crises they met in more or less permanent session. As the center of local political activities, where factional differences and party alignments first became known to the sailors, they were instrumental in provoking a more intense mass involvement in the major issues. Without soviets, sailor radicalism might have burned itself out in isolation. In them the particular complaints of the sailors were integrated with those of the workers and soldiers, and under the prodding of intellectual leadership, these complaints became general grievances. They were the perpetual stokers for the fires of revolution.

For the first few weeks after the February–March Revolution in the fleet, political allegiances were extremely fluid, and party membership in the soviets cannot be accurately counted. One source (Pronin) credits the Bolsheviks with having had only 11 deputies in the first session of the Kronstadt Soviet, while at the Seventh Party Conference (24–29 April) a representative from the training base, probably exaggerating the Bolshevik gains to impress party leaders, boasted of having 60 votes in the soviet.[38] By best accounts, Bolshevik membership was indeed quite small at the beginning but expanded to over 40 within the first two months, as uncommitted deputies joined the party while others switched party membership or were recalled and replaced. Still, this was a relatively small number compared with 108 Socialist Revolutionaries, 72 Mensheviks, and 77 nonparty delegates who were officially recorded.[39] Despite the initial weakness of the Bolsheviks, the Kronstadt Soviet quickly became renowned for its extreme positions. In part, the local Socialist Revolutionaries and Mensheviks never really attained a solid base of support and could conserve their voting strength only by swinging considerably to the left of their central party leaders.[40] As policies became hardened in Petrograd, however, and as the parties consolidated their positions, this option became increasingly difficult to exercise. At the end of April the Kronstadt Soviet was reelected in its entirety for the first time. The Bolsheviks now emerged as the largest single party, with 93 members, but the Socialist Revolutionaries were still close behind with 91. The Mensheviks dropped to 46, and there were 68 nonparty delegates.[41]

The Bolshevik faction was also small at Helsingfors initially. At the Seventh Party Conference a representative of the Finnish base claimed only 29 Bolsheviks in the soviet, while another source credits 80 delegates to the party by the end of April, and by the end of May, Antonov-Ovseenko reported that a total of 130 out of 535 delegates were members of the party. By this time the executive committee was nearly half Bolshevik (32 out of 65).[42] As in other parts of the country, moderates dominated the early weeks of the Helsingfors Soviet, under the leadership of Social Democrats Nikolai Kilianyi and Sergei Garin, but they soon began to lose ground, especially in April and May. From the first, however, Bolsheviks were much more influential in the Sailors' Assembly than in the soviet as a whole.[43]

Surprisingly, Revel, the base with a reputation for the greatest moderation, listed a larger proportion of elected Bolsheviks to its soviet. Out of 66 delegates to the first soviet, 15 or 16 were Bolsheviks and 39 or 40 were Socialist Revolutionaries, according to the memoirs of one of the Bolshevik leaders in Estonia.[44] Party composition at the second session of the Revel Soviet, in May, was as follows: Socialist Revolutionaries, 87; Bolsheviks, 58; Mensheviks, 29; minor parties, 13; and nonparty, 9. In the new Åbo Soviet, in June, Bolsheviks held 40 of the 149 places.[45]

Thus, by June the Bolsheviks had increased their strength in the soviets of the naval bases to between 25 and 30 percent, while the Socialist Revolutionaries, though declining slightly, held from 30 to 45 percent. The Mensheviks had fallen rather sharply, to about 15 percent. But as has already been emphasized, each soviet was different in composition. The sailor constituencies of the Helsingfors and Kronstadt soviets were probably about 50 percent Bolshevik, while at Revel the proportion of sailors who were Bolsheviks fell below that of the soviet. Total membership in the Bolshevik party rose even more dramatically at Kronstadt and Helsingfors—from under 100 at each base in February to 3,000 at the end of April. At Kronstadt, about 40 percent of these members were sailors, whereas the Helsingfors party was well over 50 percent naval, the battleships alone accounting for nearly 40 percent.[46] By contrast, the Revel party membership of about 2,000 was at least 90 percent workers (Russian and Estonian).[47] An important distinction had thus developed by May between the more-radical and better-organized sailors of Kronstadt and Helsingfors and those of Revel. And in comparison with their positions in Petrograd and the rest of Russia, both Bolsheviks and Socialist Revolutionaries at Helsingfors and Kronstadt had moved farther to the left.

THE OFFICERS' ORGANIZATIONS

As might be expected, the officers of the Revel base were much better prepared to control the situation. At all of the bases, however, the delegates to the soviets from the fleet at first included a number of officers. Many sailors reacted simply and naturally in electing their traditional leaders to represent them, or at the same time that they chose a popular officer as commander, they also nominated him to the soviet. Though some of these officers became dedicated to the revolution, most were simply trying to control the revolution by joining it. But the number of officer-delegates decreased sharply by May, partly because of the increasing radicalization of the sailors, and partly because of the withdrawal by the officers to join separate organizations or to abstain from political activity.

The liberal staff officers at the Helsingfors base who had supported changes in the fleet were the first to organize. Led by Rengarten, Cherkasskii, Muravev, and Shchastnyi, this group registered two hundred members by 19 March and affiliated with the Union of Officer-Republicans of the People's Army. The latter switched its allegiance to the left and became the Union of Socialists of the People's Army in mid April, but its influence was limited by the opposition of many members to involvement in political affairs and by the creation of a rival, more conservative organization.[48]

The largest and most effective organization of officers was the Union of Naval Officers of Revel (SMOR). A greater harmony of views among the officers at Revel, who were less affected by killings, arrests, and resignations, made possible the calling of a general assembly of four hundred Revel naval officers in March under the leadership of Captain Boris Dudorov, commander of the Air Squadron. Its "Declaration of 24 March," which received wide circulation, announced full support for the Provisional Government and vowed that its members were prepared "to defend free Russia from its external and internal enemies to the last drop of blood, . . . that any officer who attempts to change the established order is an enemy of the nation and cannot remain in officer position." SMOR also sought full protection of the law for its members.[49]

At the same time that the Revel officers were organizing, a similar assembly of officers—the Union of Officer-Republicans, Doctors, and Officials of the Army and Navy of the Sveaborg Base—met in Helsingfors under the leadership of Lieutenant Vladimir Demchinskii.[50] This organization, like the one in Revel but unlike the People's Army group, not only supported the Provisional Government; it also actively opposed the more radical tendencies of the sailors and led a counter campaign against revolutionary and antiwar propaganda.

Similar organizations existed in the other Baltic ports, though none of them achieved the same degree of local power as the one in Revel. Finally, on 23 May, the officer-republicans joined in forming the All-Baltic Professional Union of Officers, Doctors, and Officials of the Fleet and Bases of the Baltic Sea (PROMOR), which declared that its chief tasks were to strengthen the fighting capability of the fleet and "to defend the professional and service interests of its members." Its central presidium in Petrograd campaigned in the press and through government officials for an improvement in conditions for officers.[51]

Unfortunately, this effort of some officers to organize for the purpose of defending their views and interests only added to the problems of order in the fleet. Committee meetings and assemblies were time-consuming and nerve-racking, and above all, the divisions within the officer staff were only hardened by the existence of formal organizations. At least four distinct groupings can thus be detected among the officers still on duty: a small number who more or less forgot their officer status and devoted themselves completely to party or soviet activity; those inclined to radical-liberal positions who formed organizations that attempted to cooperate with the sailor committees and local soviets; a large group who consolidated for purposes of improving their position by contesting the authority of the sailors and by lobbying in Petrograd; and the majority, who preferred to sit quietly in order to avoid alienating anyone by engaging in organizational activity.

THE CENTRAL COMMITTEE OF THE BALTIC FLEET

While some officers, by nature of their experience, quickly realized the importance of central organization, the sailors were still handicapped in March and April by a large number of diverse committees. Some five hundred ships' committees, two hundred port committees, and one hundred fifty coastal-defense committees were loosely supervised by about eighty committees at the intermediate level of brigade and division.[52] The Sailors' Assembly of the Helsingfors Soviet came close to being a central authority for the men of the fleet, but it was too large and loosely organized for effective leadership; furthermore, it represented only the sailors of the main base.

Acting on the proposals of the ships' committees of the battleship *Grazhdanin* and the cruiser *Admiral Makarov* at Revel, the Sailors' Assembly obtained authority from the Helsingfors Soviet to create a commission to work out plans for a central committee. On 10 April, four fleet representatives from Revel, two from Åbo-Åland, two from Hango-Lapvik, and two from the Second Baltic Fleet Depot Troop in Petrograd joined five members of the Helsingfors executive committee (leaving out "independent" Kronstadt) to draw up a preliminary constitution. Under the chairmanship of Petr Chudakov, a Bolshevik petty officer from Åbo, on 26 April the commission approved the "Provisional Rules for the Central Committee of the Baltic Fleet," which stated that "without the approval of the Central Committee of the Baltic Fleet not one order pertaining to the internal order and administration of the Baltic fleet can have any force."[53] Though opposed by the Provisional Government and the officers' organizations, the commission's work was sanctioned by the Helsingfors Soviet on 27 April, and Tsentrobalt, as it was commonly termed, began its deliberations on the twenty-eighth. (See organizational chart, p. 82.)

At the first meeting of Tsentrobalt, before all of its members could arrive, Lieutenant Roman Grundman of the cruiser *Gromoboi* was elected temporary chairman and Pavel Dybenko vice-chairman. The first order of business concerned clarification of the relationship of Tsentrobalt to the Helsingfors Soviet. Apparently fearing controls or limitations by its parent body, Tsentrobalt resolved that "since its actions pertain only to the 'life of the fleet,' it will be responsible only to the Sailors' Assembly of the Soviet and not to the whole body."[54] Then the committee proceeded to pass and modify its own constitution, so recently debated in the soviet. In one important change, Tsentrobalt declared: "Denying prior control of operations, TsKBF has the right to control operational affairs after their completion, and in their investigation, it has the right to question the commander in chief and to appoint commissions for this purpose."[55] Thus, Tsentrobalt claimed a review authority over all operation orders of the fleet.

At the second meeting, Tsentrobalt refused to admit one representative from Revel who had been chosen by SMOR, the officers' organization there. And at the fourth meeting, on 2 May, with 32 of its 33 authorized members in attendance, a six-man presidium was chosen, Pavel Dybenko was elected permanent chairman, and two officers—Lieutenant Roman Grundman and Midshipman Mechislav Savich-Zablotskii—were named vice-chairman and secretary, respectively. The assistant secretary was Ivan Solovev, a Bolshevik representing the Student Mine Detachment at Kronstadt, who had actually received the most votes in the presidium election.[56] The addition of three more sailors formed a nine-man Executive Bureau; a Soviet source designates three of these as Bolsheviks, five as Bolshevik sympathizers, and one, Aleksandr Sinitsyn, as a Menshevik.[57] The Bolsheviks and their sympathizers easily obtained a working majority in the committee.

Under Dybenko's leadership, Tsentrobalt decided many questions pertaining to the fleet—changes in salaries and uniforms; leave; and removal of officers. Admiral Maksimov chose to cooperate with Tsentrobalt, and a rather remarkable degree of coordination was achieved between the radical sailors' organization and the commander's staff. The first direct challenge to the committee came from the new minister of war, who visited Helsingfors on 9 May. Kerensky asked Tsentrobalt to confer with him on board the command ship *Krechet*, but members of the committee insisted that the minister come to see them instead; Kerensky's short speech on board the *Viola*, to the effect that Tsentrobalt must support the Provisional Government, went over poorly, according to Nikolai Khovrin.[58] Two days later, Fedor Onipko, the commissar for the Baltic fleet who had been left behind by Kerensky, attended a meeting of Tsentrobalt and directly challenged the basis for its organization. Though apparently convinced that Tsentrobalt had the support of most unit committees, he insisted that part of the "Rules" be modified. Onipko and Tsentrobalt finally agreed that any changes should be approved by a general congress of the fleet.[59] The committee then set about working out the procedure for elections of delegates for the First Congress of the Baltic Fleet, which would convene on 25 May.

THE RISE OF BOLSHEVIK STRENGTH IN THE FLEET

How did it happen that the Bolsheviks could rise from such a low status in the fleet to become the largest party at Kronstadt and to hold the commanding position in the Central Committee of the Baltic fleet? A major share of the credit must go to the able and dedicated middle-echelon party workers, who might be called the "first apparatchiks." Left by themselves, the few sailor Bolsheviks of early March might have been swayed by popular, democratic feeling into supporting the Provisional Government.

The Bolsheviks in Petrograd were among the first to understand the significance of what had happened in the military units in and around the capital. On 3 March a Military Organization was created by the Central Committee under the chairmanship of Nikolai Podvoisky.[60] On the same day, three young party workers—Semen Roshal, Petr Smirnov, and Boris Zhemchuzhin (Dmitrii)—were sent to Kronstadt to help organize party activities. Though these young (twenty- to twenty-one-year-old) graduates of gymnasia and polytechnic institutes already had a few years of underground party experience, they were guided and assisted by Bolsheviks with considerable experience—Aleksandr Ilin-Zhenevskii, Fedor Dingelshtedt, Vladimir Zalezhskii, Ivan Smilga, Ivan Egorov (Kiril Orlov), and Ivan Flerovskii—who went back and forth between Kronstadt and Petrograd in March and April. Together they organized the first Bolshevik committee at Kronstadt, with Roshal as chairman, which included a couple of veteran Bolshevik sailors who had just been released from prison, Ivan Sladkov and Timofei Uliantsev.[61]

While Roshal concentrated on party organization, Zhemchuzhin and Smirnov directed their energies toward founding a newspaper. Receiving donations from local units totaling over 4,000 rubles by 20 March, and hiring a private press, they issued *Golos Pravdy,* one of the first legal Bolshevik newspapers outside of Petrograd, on 15 March, beating by two days the appearance of the *Izvestiia* of the Kronstadt Soviet. Besides printing a daily paper at Kronstadt, the young Bolsheviks also acted as distributors of the Petrograd *Pravda* and printed a large number of leaflets and brochures.[62] On 17 March, Fedor Raskolnikov, a midshipman-student at the Marine Academy who had had several years' experience on the editorial staff of *Pravda,* arrived at Kronstadt to assume overall editorship of the Bolshevik publications and to become chairman of the Bolshevik committee.[63] Because of his naval rank, Raskolnikov provided a very useful link between the Bolshevik organizers, who had no prior connection with the fleet, and the sailor-Bolsheviks.

The attention from Petrograd, the energy and dedication of young party stalwarts, and the Kronstadt imprint on a political newspaper gave the Bolsheviks a big boost over their political rivals at the training base of the fleet. Though not as much is known about the activities of other parties, the fact that *Golos Pravdy* was the only party newspaper published at Kronstadt during the first two months provides some measure of respective organizational activities. The Socialist Revolutionaries may still have outnumbered the Bolsheviks in membership at the end of April, thanks chiefly to a flourishing club, Volia i Zemlia, which was established in the former house of Admiral Viren.[64] They and the Mensheviks at Kronstadt, however, had already won a reputation for being to the left of the central party organizations in Petrograd; and the nonparty, maximalist, and anarchist groups were in some respects to the left of the Bolsheviks.

Perhaps even more instructive on how to win support and influence the course of local affairs is the story of the beginning of the Bolshevik organization at Helsingfors. There the Social Democrats remained united and were still cooperating with the Socialist Revolutionaries at the end of March. The Social Democratic leaders, Kilianyi and Garin, refused to recognize the difference between Mensheviks and Bolsheviks, remaining instead under the influence of the Finnish Social Democratic Party. Only a small group of Russian sailors, led by Dybenko, Vasilii Marusev, and Nikolai Khovrin, insisted on "Bolshevik detachment," and after learning of the publication of *Golos Pravdy*, they sent an appeal for help to Kronstadt around 25 March.[65]

A group of "Kronstadters"—Ilin-Zhenevskii (Raskolnikov's brother), Zhemchuzhin, Semen Pelikhov, Fedor Dingelshtedt, and Efim Zinchenko —took the matter up with Podvoisky in Petrograd, who was skeptical about their proposal to go to Helsingfors: "It isn't youngsters like you who should go there, but some members of the Central Committee." Still undaunted, Zhemchuzhin replied, "Won't it make the party generals look small if we establish an organization in Helsingfors and publish a newspaper?"[66]

As Ilin-Zhenevskii relates the story, the young adventurers left for the Finnish capital on 27 March: "We had no contacts, no money and were strangers in Helsingfors. We spent the last money we had on tickets and a little food, and, taking our places in the clean little cars of the Finnish Railway, we set out, as carefree as the birds in heaven, and in the best of spirits." Optimistically, they wrote articles for the first issue of a Helsingfors Bolshevik newspaper while on the train, and upon arrival, they went directly to the soviet, where they were dismissed rather coldly by the Central Executive Committee once their purpose was ascertained.[67]

After renting a large room on Visokogornyi Street, in the former tsarist police headquarters, Zhemchuzhin and Ilin-Zhenevskii went off in search of a printing press, while the others accompanied the Bolshevik sailors Khovrin, Marusev, and Grigorii Svetlichnyi to their ship, *Imperator Pavel I* (the *Respublika*), where after short speeches to the assembled crew, 1,000 rubles were donated out of the ship's mess fund. With this windfall the Gorskhov printing house was immediately contracted for, and the first issue of *Volna* appeared on Thursday, 30 March. Khovrin organized a distribution system by asking ship and unit committees at the base to send a man to the printing press for 100 copies, to be sold at 3 kopecks each.[68]

The first issue of *Volna*, under the slogan "The wave of revolution rises!," contained a lead article by "K. Stalin" and several additional articles by Ilin-Zhenevskii and Dingelshtedt.[69] The next copy, on 31 March, carried an article by Zinoviev and a large block appeal: "Comrade soldiers, sailors, and workers! You know that a workers', sailors', and soldiers' newspaper can exist only through your support. Contribute to the iron fund of *Volna!*"[70] After the first few issues, the editors arranged, through the Finnish Social Democratic Party leaders Tokoi and Vasten, to publish the paper more cheaply on the press of the Finnish Senate.

The Bolshevik newspaper in Helsingfors appeared at an opportune time to publicize the arrival of the party leader. One delegation, including a few sailors, greeted Lenin at Tornio on the Swedish frontier. Boris Zhemchuzhin led another, much larger group to meet Lenin at Riihimäki, a railroad center about forty miles north of Helsingfors. Among the eighteen sailors in the welcoming committee were Grigorii Svetlichnyi and Fedor Dmitriev from the *Respublika* and Evgenii Vishnevskii from the *Diana*.[71]

During April and May, *Volna* appeared regularly, usually headlined with an article copied from *Pravda* or *Soldatskaia Pravda* by Stalin, Zinoviev, Kollontai (6 April), Lenin (8, 11, and 12 April), Gorky (6 and 13 May), or Bukharin (9 May). Most of the material, however, was written by the local staff, headed at first by Ilin-Zheneveskii and then, after 16 April, by Leonid Stark, who made a point of including a number of contributions from sailors in the fleet in the form of articles or letters to the editor.[72]

The sudden appearance of *Volna* and the response that it received, both in the fleet and in the town, caught the united Russian Social Democratic Workers' Party in Helsingfors by surprise. After a general meeting on 4 April, the original Bolshevik Sveaborg Sailors' Collective became the Helsingfors Committee of the RSDLP (b[=Bolshevik]). Following the leadership of Garin, most members of the older Social Democratic party voted to join the new committee (thus becoming Bolsheviks) and to affiliate with *Volna*.[73] During April, Garin, Vasten, and other Social Democrats worked for the new Bolshevik committee. Their intention may have been to capture the new organization by overwhelming it with membership, but cooperation eventually failed, and the real result was the breakup of the older, larger organization, with its membership going in various directions—Bolsheviks, Socialist Revolutionaries, Left Socialist Revolutionaries, and Mensheviks.

The Bolshevik journalistic offensive galvanized the Socialist Revolutionaries to action. Their first general meeting was held on 12 April, under the leadership of Mikhail Kotrokhov and Ter-Mikelov. They decided to publish their own newspaper, to be called *Narodnaia Niva*.[74] With the appearance of the first issue on 25 April, an intensive rivalry between the two party newspapers began in Helsingfors. While *Volna* was characterized by hard-hitting ideological articles and strongly worded appeals for funds and support, *Narodnaia Niva* adopted a softer, more localized tone, publicizing a number of "nonparty" activities such as the Sailors' Club, which was located in the old imperial Marinskii Palace. In fact, the Sailors' Club, which attained a membership of over seven thousand by early June, was started as a Socialist Revolutionary front, as was the Helsingfors Scientific-Educational Circle, which was headed by a leading Socialist Revolutionary, army Lieutenant Brilliantov.[75] *Narodnaia Niva* also devoted considerable space to the "Finnish question," and it heralded the establishment of a satellite group on 7 May, the Peoples' Socialist party, as a kind of welcoming committee for the visit of Kerensky.[76]

The two party newspapers stimulated a variety of activities, publishing the protocols of the soviet and Tsentrobalt and covering lectures, concerts, and assemblies. Financial support for *Narodnaia Niva* came principally from the battleships *Gangut* and *Andrei Pervozvannyi*, the command ship *Krechet* (probably from the "socialist" staff officers), and from various army units. *Volna* received some funds from a variety of fleet units as well as sizable contributions from the Finnish Social Democrats; the latter, being in Finnish marks, were particularly welcome, since Russian rubles had become virtually unnegotiable in Finland.[77] During May, *Volna* was able not only to pay its own way but also to send contributions to *Pravda* and to help finance the Bolshevik publishing house, Priboi, for the printing of leaflets and books. By the end of May, *Volna* had collected over 23,000 Finnish marks, one of the largest single contributions being 2,000 marks from the

Union of Finnish Social Democratic Youth on 24 May.[78] Not surprisingly, *Volna* was taking a strong position in favor of Finnish self-government.

Revel was much slower in obtaining its own Russian-language party newspapers, although the Estonian-language Bolshevik paper *Kiir*, as well as *Volna, Golos Pravdy, Soldatskaia Pravda, Okopnaia Pravda* (Riga), and *Pravda*, were widely distributed. Finally, on 17 May, *Utro Pravdy* commenced publication, but it was mainly directed toward Russian soldiers and workers of this important reserve center. Nevertheless, the sailors' club Union, which in May had 6,250 members, was an important center for distributing all kinds of party literature.[79]

The intensity of publication and dissemination of newsprint in the bases of the fleet was amazing considering the widely held belief in the low literacy level of the Russian populace. The Section for Spreading the Idea of Sovereignty of the People of the Helsingfors Soviet promoted the sale of all kinds of literature, set up libraries, and organized a series of lectures. Talks on the ships in April concerned the land question; relations with Allies; Lenin; and property.[80]

But political ideas and programs can be drowned in a sea of words, or they can be organized out of existence. What caused slogans to crystalize and what renewed the dynamism of revolutionary feelings in the fleet were the incidents and convulsions that shook the bases. Bolshevik fires, ignited by superior leadership and organization, were fueled by mass demonstrations in the street.

THE APRIL–MAY DEMONSTRATIONS

The war was the main concern of mass meetings at the Naval Arena at Kronstadt on 11 and 12 April. A Menshevik from the Petrograd Soviet argued the case for the Provisional Government, but according to *Golos Pravdy*, he was frequently interrupted by hoots and whistles. Following the antiwar mood that prevailed at Kronstadt, the soviet on 14 April asked its Petrograd counterpart to assume a larger role in foreign policy, demanding the publication of secret treaties and suggesting that much more active measures be taken to secure peace.[81]

Sailors responded in mass to the "May Day" celebrations on 18 April. Bolsheviks Ivan Smilga and Vladimir Zaitsev organized a contingent of one thousand Kronstadt sailors for the rally in Petrograd, setting a precedent that was to be an important feature of the year.[82] Miliukov's poor timing of a note to the Allies, promising that Russia would fulfill her treaty obligations and continue the war, helped to extend these rallies into a general crisis. With a showdown expected on 21 April, Podvoisky requested one hundred fifty armed sailors from Kronstadt to protect the Bolshevik headquarters in the capital and to agitate among the garrison units.[83] The number of sailors roaming about the city was probably a factor in the decision of the Central Executive Committee of the Petrograd Soviet to cooperate with the Provisional Government in banning military personnel from participating in the protest demonstration. The Kronstadt Soviet then declared the "criminal acts" of the Provisional Government "completely intolerable" and went on record in support of the Bolshevik call to transfer all power to the soviets.[84]

The meetings of 20 and 21 April demonstrated the rapid politicization of the sailors; more than twenty thousand, according to *Golos Pravdy*, met in front of the Bolshevik headquarters at Kronstadt, where a resolution offered by Semen Roshal was accepted by acclamation: "Considering that the Provisional Government by its note had defied both the proletariat and democracy, and is clearly on the path of counterrevolution, we must use all our forces for the overthrow of the Provisional Government and for the transfer of power to the soviets of workers' and soldiers' deputies."[85] This was going too far even for the executive committee at Kronstadt, which proceeded to expel Roshal, an act that only generated fresh protests and caused a number of units to recall their moderate deputies to the soviet and send more radical ones. It also provided an excuse for the Bolshevik demand that there be a reelection of the soviet. In this context the Bolshevik gains in the general election at the end of April are not surprising.[86]

The Helsingfors Soviet, already reelected, on 21 April passed a strongly worded Bolshevik resolution declaring "that all of its armed forces will support all revolutionary acts of the Petrograd Soviet of Workers' and Soldiers' Deputies, and is ready, upon the first word, to overthrow the Provisional Government."[87] A Bolshevik leaflet published by *Volna* the next day called for renewed demonstrations under the slogans: Off with the Bourgeoisie! and Down with the Provisional Government![88] These slogans and resolutions illustrate that the naval centers were moving more to the left, in many cases beyond the positions taken by parent political parties in the capital. This was true even for the Bolsheviks, as the famous "Kronstadt incident" in May will demonstrate.

But in the meantime, the opposition policies and behavior of Miliukov and Guchkov had resulted in their resignations, precipitating yet another crisis for the Provisional Government. Its resolution in the formation at the end of April of a coalition government that included ten socialist ministers only widened the gap between leaders of the Petrograd Soviet and their nominal adherents at the naval bases; and visits by Mensheviks Voitinskii and Vainberg to Kronstadt on 30 April and 2 May, respectively, to explain the shifts did little more than reinforce the growing opposition there.

THE MAY KRONSTADT INCIDENT

The second session of the Kronstadt Soviet met for the first time on 5 May. It was organized by parties, though the nonparty Anatolii Lamanov was reelected chairman of the executive committee. Raskolnikov, who had not participated in the first session because of his comparatively late arrival, now led the Bolshevik delegation, the largest of the political groups. Early meetings featured debates over the land question, with a Socialist Revolutionary resolution that called for all land to be given to the peasants winning handily, 204 to 94; a long exchange—between SR Aleksandr Baranov and Iogann Neiman, the Menshevik leader at Kronstadt—about the social and political value of holding dances; and on 9 May, an angry outburst by Bolshevik Mikhail Lebedev during a debate over fraternization, which resulted in his being censured by Chairman Lamanov over Roshal's protest.[89] Then a relative calm reigned over the proceedings—until 13 May—when the executive committee resolved: "The single authority in Kronstadt is the Soviet of Workers' and Military Deputies, which in all affairs of state will maintain relations with the Provisional Government."[90] This was partly in response to another government request to release the officers who were still held in jail for trial by Petrograd courts and partly a maneuver aimed at removing Pepeliaev, the Provisional Government's commissar, who was a protégé of Miliukov's. The immediate results were, in fact, the commissar's resignation and his public denunciation of the Kronstadt Soviet.

In the accounts published in Kadet and in pro–Provisional Government newspapers in Petrograd, the resolution was interpreted as an attack on the Provisional Government and a "declaration of independence from Russia," since Kronstadt apparently did not even recognize a higher soviet authority. The whole affair was blamed on the Bolsheviks and their followers, perhaps because of coincidental speeches made by several Bolshevik leaders, including Trotsky, Lunacharsky, Chudnovsky, and Broido, at a meeting of the Kronstadt Soviet on 14 May.[91] On 16 May the resolution was debated by the whole soviet, which, in attempting to mollify some of the sharpest criticism in Petrograd, voted to change the clause "in all affairs of state maintains relations with the Provisional Government" to "in all affairs of state maintains relations with the Petrograd Soviet of Workers' and Soldiers' Deputies."[92] This only made the matter worse by seeming to break off relations with the Provisional Government and by seeming to recognize the "soviet" as the "state."

Soviet historians have argued that the Socialist Revolutionaries maneuvered the Bolsheviks into this position in order to discredit them. If true, this would be a unique case of the Bolsheviks being outmaneuvered by the Socialist Revolutionaries in 1917. In fact, Aleksandr Brushvit, an SR leader, did lead the debate in favor of the resolution, but Mikhail Lebedev gave him strong support, and Petr Malyshev, a Menshevik who was one of the few opponents of the resolution, wondered aloud at the Socialist Revolutionaries' connivance with the Bolsheviks.[93] Raskolnikov later argued that most of the Bolsheviks were away from the soviet, listening to a speech by Lunacharsky,[94] but it seems unlikely that many Bolsheviks would have been absent from a debate on a matter that had attracted so much attention.

For Soviet historians the main significance of the "incident" is Lenin's interfering for the first time in Bolshevik affairs in the fleet by calling Raskolnikov to Petrograd on 18 May to lecture him on the foolishness of alienating Kronstadt from the rest of Russia.[95] What Lenin feared most was that the actions of the Kronstadt Bolsheviks would give more ammunition to the anti-Bolshevik propaganda that was gaining momentum and would tend to isolate the Bolsheviks as a whole at a crucial stage in their expansion. There was also probably some desire on the part of the veteran leaders to put young, heady upstarts like Roshal and Raskolnikov in their places.

With their ardor dampened by Lenin, the Kronstadt Bolsheviks quietly allowed a delegation from the Central Executive Committee of the Petrograd Soviet, headed by Nikolai Chkheidze and Abram Gots, to convince the Socialist Revolutionaries and other supporters of the resolution to retract their position. On 21 May the Kronstadt Executive Committee resolved that its declaration regarding direct relations with the Petrograd Soviet "did not exclude relations with the Provisional Government" and accused the "bourgeois press" of slander in attributing to Kronstadt an attempt to separate from Russia and form an independent republic.[96] Ten representatives from Kronstadt, including Bolsheviks Raskolnikov, Roshal, Flerovskii, and Liubovich, then faced the Petrograd Soviet on the evening of 22 May, but no satisfactory conclusion was reached. At one point in the acrimonious proceedings, Victor Chernov, the new minister of agriculture, suggested that Kronstadt might be starved into submission by cutting off all supplies.

Two of the socialist ministers, Tsereteli and Skobelev, arrived at Kronstadt on 23 May and participated in a stormy all-night session of the executive committee, at which the main issues were the authority of the Provisional Government at the naval base and the release of the arrested officers. Finally a general assembly of the soviet on 24 May agreed to hand over the officers to a special commission; it also reiterated its belief that all power should be in the hands of a single soviet authority, "but while the majority does not yet agree with us and supports the Provisional Government, we will recognize this government and consider its dispositions and orders as applicable to Kronstadt as to the rest of Russia."[97]

The Provisional Government, though claiming a victory, had climbed a mountain in order to gain a molehill in achieving Kronstadt's "recognition." The incident in some ways actually weakened the government's position in the fleet. The bulk of the Socialist Revolutionaries and Mensheviks at Kronstadt, dismayed at their treatment by the Petrograd leaders, moved more decidedly into the camps of the Left Socialist Revolutionaries and Menshevik-Internationalists, both of which were united with the Bolsheviks on the important questions of peace and soviet power. And sizable support from the fleet in turn gave these splinter opposition groups a considerable boost in the capital.

In order to obtain Kronstadt's acceptance of a new commissar, the Provisional Government agreed that the Kronstadt Soviet could nominate its own man as long as he was loyal to the government. The soviet elected one of its own members, Foma Parchevskii, who possessed virtually no authority in the post.[98] But most important of all, the "Kronstadt incident" ended the training base's isolation from the rest of the fleet and promoted support from other bases and units. On 24 May, for example, the crew of the cruiser *Pamiat' Azova*, extended "greetings to revolutionary Kronstadt and to all fighters for freedom, equality and fraternity," continuing: "Comrades, we hope that you will fulfill your duty to the end, as honestly as has been done so far under the red banner. We trust in your strength, your brave soul, and your ability. We share your views and . . . we will support you with all the force that we have at our disposal."[99]

THE FIRST CONGRESS OF THE BALTIC FLEET

Feelings of unity came at a particularly auspicious time, just before the convening of the First Congress of the Baltic Fleet in Helsingfors on 25 May. The 232 delegates, including 12 officers, were divided geographically on the basis of one delegate for every 250 sailors: Helsingfors, 84; Revel and Moon Sound, 76; Kronstadt, 38; Hango-Lapvik, 16; Petrograd, 12; Åbo-Åland, 4; and Nikolaishtadt, 2.[100] Although there was a distinct difference between the radical Kronstadt and the moderate Revel delegations, the keynotes of the congress were unity and harmony. Captain Ilia Lodyzhenskii, the Socialist Revolutionary commander of the battleship *Andrei Pervozvannyi*, became chairman, and Bolshevik Nikolai Markin, leader of the Kronstadt delegates, was chosen vice-chairman.[101]

The most important business of the congress concerned the permanent rules for Tsentrobalt. Bolshevik delegates relented to a modification of the "Provisional Rules" that provided for a clear separation of powers between it (internal affairs) and the commander in chief (operational affairs). Another change doubled the size of the committee without prescribing a date for its reelection, but there was apparently no serious intention of packing the enlarged Tsentrobalt with non-Bolsheviks, and Dybenko remained as chairman. The congress sent Markin and two other delegates to Petrograd to obtain official approval of the new rules.[102] Despite failure to receive the blessing of the Provisional Government, the "Permanent Rules" went into effect; they made Tsentrobalt's position more secure as the congress's permanent "executive committee," though it is important to note that the committee was not elected by the congress but by the lower fleet and unit committees.

The congress, which lasted until 15 June, provided an excellent opportunity for establishing better relations between the various bases and units and between officers and men. The old and new commanders, Maksimov and Verderevsky, addressed the congress, the latter receiving a vote of confidence from the assembled delegates. But the return of Markin with Kerensky's rejection of the rules on 8 June, as well as the simultaneous arrival of a special delegation from Kronstadt, which was headed by Fedor

Raskolnikov, tended to solidify the sailors against the Provisional Government.[103] Speeches by commissar Onipko, Viktor Lebedev, and Captain Boris Dudorov, representing Kerensky, met with a generally hostile reception. What seems to have united the sailors more than anything else was the "fight-on" emphasis in the Provisional Government's messages.

During its final days the First Congress of the Baltic Fleet accepted all but the last of fourteen points submitted by Admiral Verderevsky, which were intended to clarify the working relationships between officers and sailors. But this point, concerning the right of the commander in chief to appoint officers to command posts, was probably the most important. Verderevsky objected especially to the sailors' refusal to allow him to remove Captain S. V. Zarubaev as commander of the First Squadron of Battleships, and so Verderevsky threatened to resign. After the congress closed, the matter continued to be discussed by the Helsingfors Assembly of Sailors and the ship committees. On 16 June over twenty-five members, including Dybenko, spoke for the elective principle; none spoke for the right of appointment by the commander. The assembly then voted unanimously, with one abstention, for a resolution offered by its president, Bolshevik Grigorii Kireev: "Recognizing the principle of election of all responsible posts as the only correct way for realizing the idea of people's sovereignty, the Helsingfors Sailors' Deputies Assembly, combined with ships committees, will insist with all of the means at its disposal upon putting it immediately into practice."[104] The sailors were obviously worried that the new commander would succeed in undermining the power of the ship and unit committees. In fact, the Baltic congress had concluded by giving Tsentrobalt special powers to oversee the work of the commanding staff.[105]

During the deliberations in Helsingfors, the party and soviet presses at the bases paid little notice to the First All-Russian Congress of Soviets, which was meeting in Petrograd. In fact, unlikely as it would appear, no record is available concerning any participation in the Petrograd congress by delegates from the Kronstadt or Helsingfors Soviets, although the Baltic Fleet Congress chose eight representatives on 8 June, to be headed by Markin.[106] Kronstadt, because of the recent May troubles, may have been deliberately omitted, or it may have chosen to abstain. Most of this time the Bolshevik leaders in the fleet, including Markin, can be accounted for as being engaged in other activities, and the Socialist Revolutionaries in Helsingfors were busy reorganizing. On the very day of the beginning of the congress,

3 June, the Helsingfors SR party held an important assembly, which naturally monopolized the attention of the local leadership.[107]

THE JUNE "CALM"

The proceedings of the congress in Petrograd consisted, for the most part, of speeches and resolutions supporting the Provisional Government. It was, in fact, a carefully staged attempt to rally the country behind the new coalition government and its plans for a military offensive. As such, the recent Kronstadt incident loomed in the background as a test of central government vis-à-vis soviet power, and a few pointed references in the opening speeches by Tsereteli and Kerensky promised stern action. But the façade of strength had already been cracked. During the usual Sunday marches in the capital on 28 May, the First Machine Gun Regiment conspicuously supported the Kronstadters. And the next Sunday, on the day after the convening of the congress, five thousand demonstrators from the naval base appeared on the streets of Petrograd along with the machine gunners. An even larger mass protest was being planned for 10 June, but it was hastily declared illegal by the government, which was supported by leaders of the congress. Detachments were preparing to embark on that morning from Kronstadt when the Bolshevik decision to abstain from a test with the government arrived. But then only fierce oratory by Roshal and by a flamboyant anarchist named Khaim Iarchuk could persuade the men to put down their loaded rifles and send a small investigative commission to "inspect" the city.[108]

An unarmed demonstration was then scheduled by the SR-Menshevik leaders of the Petrograd congress for 18 June, but the Kronstadt detachment numbered only a little over one thousand. Lenin, who had been informed of the difficulty in restraining Kronstadt on 10 June, expressed surprise about this weak force to Ivan Flerovskii, one of his Kronstadt lieutenants. The response was that the previous experience had hurt their feelings. Possibly they also realized that they would be greatly outnumbered; but Lenin was impressed: "You have good lads there, especially the sailors." And after Flerovskii had noted that the sailors were fed up with meetings and resolutions, the Bolshevik leader answered: "The impatience of your masses is legitimate, natural. But Kronstadt and Petrograd are not the whole of Russia. For Russia it is still necessary to struggle."[109]

Major demonstrations occurred in many other cities, including Kronstadt and Helsingfors, on 18 June. That day, an assembly of sailors in Helsingfors formally called for all power to be taken by the soviets and asked that Tsentrobalt send a delegation to the Petrograd congress to express this demand.[110] The fleet committee, however, was meeting infrequently during this period, and not until 24 June was a delegation named, to be led by Bolshevik Nikolai Khovrin, which could not have carried out its mission before the First All-Russian Congress disbanded on the twenty-fourth.[111]

June continued to be a month for consolidation of Bolshevik strength in the fleet. While Dybenko and the Bolshevik sailors maintained their control of Tsentrobalt, the regular party apparatus received more expert guidance from Petrograd. Vladimir Zalezhskii not only edited *Volna* but also organized lecture programs through most of the month. Contributions to a special fund enabled the party to buy its own printing press and expand the newspaper.[112] About 11 June, Vladimir Antonov-Ovseenko, one of the best Bolshevik organizers and propagandists, arrived to assume the leadership of the party in Helsingfors. Throughout June the Bolsheviks sponsored a continuous series of lectures, assemblies, and concerts. They also took a lead in staging the massive demonstration of 18 June, when over forty thousand people marched in the Finnish city.[113]

The belated attempts by the Socialist Revolutionaries in Helsingfors to establish an organization comparable to that of the Bolsheviks encountered serious difficulties by the middle of the month, especially over the issues of party participation in the Provisional Government and of a more aggressive campaign against the Bolsheviks, which included charges that Bolsheviks were German agents. The division became clear over the selection of the Finland central committee of the party on 20 June, when one of the SR leaders, Prosh Proshian, was accused of being a Bolshevik. The result was the withdrawal of the left wing and the consolidation of *Narodnaia Niva* under a single editor, Sergei Tsion.[114]

Meanwhile, an apparent calm had settled over Kronstadt—student ships were at sea, delegations were traveling around the Baltic and to the Black Sea, and a number of the most active sailors had taken leave for various parts of the country.[115] Since most foreigners had been evacuated from the "dangerous" base in April, few observations by outsiders are available. M. Philips Price visited the base in June, however; he managed to attend a session of the soviet in the former officers' club and observed that the chairman (Lamanov?) "appeared to be a student. . . . He had long hair and dreamy eyes, with the far-off look of an idealist." He also interviewed either Raskolnikov or Roshal:

> The Bolshevik leader in Kronstadt said that his party were not going to force events. Time, he said, was working for them. The war and profiteering were reducing Russia to misery and famine and pushing the masses steadily to the Kronstadt position. That process was not yet accomplished, but it would be before many months. Then would be the time to act. Meanwhile, he was willing to wait and watch the interesting little experiments which the working-class masses were making on their own initiative, without any prompting from outside. Kronstadt was, he said, but an early development, due to peculiar local conditions of what would happen throughout the rest of Russia.[116]

In keeping with this wait-and-see attitude, at the end of June, Raskolnikov and Roshal both went to Petrograd to spend several days resting.

Even Commander Cromie became optimistic about the naval situation. He wrote privately to Admiral Phillimore:

> Things are improving in spite of what appears to be a well organized propaganda of anarchy. Slowly but surely the men are getting tired of their new toy and officers are gradually being invited to take part in these eternal meetings. I spent a week with my "C" boats in Moon Sound the other day and found things far better in the little ships—no discipline but at least a willingness to work.

This description was particularly true for Revel, as Cromie admitted: "The First Cruiser Squadron [at Revel] had improved greatly but the less said about the battleships the better."[117]

The battleships, however, were able to influence much of the rest of the fleet and to provoke consternation at the highest levels in the fleet. On 21 June the *Petropavlovsk* hosted a meeting of four hundred members of local ships' committees in Helsingfors Harbor; this group decided to send a telegram directly to the government, stating that if the ten nonsocialist ministers did not leave their posts within twenty-four hours, the fleet would bombard Petrograd. Commander in Chief Verderevsky and Commissar Onipko were so upset by this threat, and by the apparent support that it had from the other ships, that they left immediately for Revel.[118] The Sailors' Assembly spent the afternoon of 23 June debating and refining the "*Petropavlovsk* resolution," and it finally voted 126 to 5, with 52 abstentions, for the transfer of all power to the All-Russian Congress of Soviets, the expulsion of the nonsocialist ministers, the move of Nicholas II to Kronstadt, and the publication of secret treaties.[119] These were ominous storm clouds on the Baltic horizon.

5

THE JULY CRISIS IN THE FLEET

DURING THE FIRST WEEK of July a major crisis developed in Petrograd when about four hundred thousand workers, soldiers, and sailors, some of them armed, demonstrated against the Provisional Government. Because of confusion among the leaders of the opposition and because of the hesitant neutrality of most of the garrison of the city, the authorities were able to contain the most radical units by using loyal troops, then to arrest some of the leaders and discipline those who refused to disband. These events, usually termed the July Crisis or July Days, are interpreted by many as a dress rehearsal for the October Revolution, as a premature attempt at revolution.

According to some émigré Russian and Western analysts, Bolsheviks and their anarchist allies provoked the demonstration to a point of open rebellion. Most Soviet accounts depict an instinctive mass action that was being led to an unfortunate show of force by anarchists, Left Socialist Revolutionaries, and, a few admit, by some headstrong Bolsheviks; the Bolshevik leaders then had to take an active part in order to control the rebels for their own good. In fact, unlike the demonstrations of 10 and 18 June, the one of early July occurred in the middle of the week, was more spontaneous or less planned by either the government or its opposition, and was concentrated in Petrograd, where, by all accounts, the Kronstadt sailors were an important element.

Participation by sailors was due to several factors. First of all, the rise of active competition to the Bolsheviks for the support of the sailors must be noted. The Left Socialist Revolutionaries championed much the same program as the Bolsheviks without bothering to fit it into a Marxist timetable.

At Kronstadt, practically the whole Socialist Revolutionary party had moved into the leftist orbit by the end of June. At Helsingfors a dramatic split occurred at that time, particularly over the issue of support for a coalition (socialist and nonsocialist) government. During a general party assembly in the Finnish city on 9 June, an anti-Kerensky resolution, presented by Prosh Proshian, was defeated, 108 to 47.[1] But opposition tendencies continued, and in speeches at an all-Finland congress of the party on 18 June, Proshian and Aleksei Ustinov, who were both on the staff of *Narodnaia Niva*, called for the immediate ouster of the nonsocialist ministers. On 19 June the Congress debated the principle of collective editorship of the newspaper, with Sergei Tsion, the leader of the Sveaborg uprising of 1906, arguing that the central party organization should appoint a responsible editor in chief, while Proshian insisted on retaining leadership by the local collective. By a close vote of 7 to 6 with 2 abstentions, *Narodnaia Niva* was transferred from the Helsingfors committee to the all-Finland committee of the party, and by 23 June, Proshian and Ustinov had lost their positions, leaving full control of the Socialist Revolutionary publications in Finland in the hands of Tsion, who supported the Provisional Government.[2] The "left" faction then organized separately and began publishing its own newspaper, *Sotsialist-Revoliutsioner*, on 9 July. The split within the Socialist Revolutionary party and the development of a separate Left Socialist Revolutionary party in Helsingfors thus began before the July Crisis but was reinforced by it.

Other groups that benefited from the radical mood of the sailors were the "anarchists" and the "maximalists." These were two catch-words of 1917 that were often attached to anyone who was to the left of the Provisional Government. The Bolshevik leaders at Kronstadt, for example, were frequently called anarchist or maximalist in order to denote their radical position. The maximalists proper, however, were ultra-left Socialist Revolutionaries, though some Bolsheviks—former, present, and future—were active in the maximalist group led by Nikolai Rivkin, a Kronstadt port worker and a leading member of the soviet executive committee.

There were also a number of genuine anarchists at Kronstadt, enough to make a cry of alarm valid, though very few of them were represented in the soviets or on committees. Anarchists returning from abroad, particularly Khaim Iarchuk and I. S. Bleikhman-Solntsev, found the Kronstadters receptive to their speeches, and Iarchuk became an active member of the executive committee. The "free" nature of the naval base obviously attracted all kinds of political propagandists, and the frequent and impromptu assemblies were conducive to the spread of anarchist ideas.

Even so, confusion still exists about the role of anarchists in the July Crisis. Some Bolsheviks, especially those writing in the 1920s, emphasized that the anarchists "worked with us," while the later Soviet historical point of view is the opposite—that anarchists opposed the official Bolshevik line of gradual radicalization of the masses through propaganda. Both views are in a sense correct: many of the Bolsheviks at the naval bases had moved to the left of the central party organization and were thus "tinged with anarchism."

Quite clearly the main parties to lose in the growth of these radical offshoots in June were the Mensheviks and the Right Socialist Revolutionaries. There are also signs that the Bolsheviks were beginning to lose strength. At Kronstadt some sailors who had previously been identified as Bolsheviks were definitely flirting with anarchism. One, Anatolii Zhelezniakov, was arrested on 21 June in a government raid on the Durnovo Villa in the Vyborg District, which had become the anarchist headquarters for the Petrograd area.[3] In the protest meetings that followed on 22 and 23 June, it was difficult to separate Bolshevik speeches from anarchist ones; nevertheless, the Provisional Government disregarded petitions from Kronstadt and sentenced Zhelezhniakov to fourteen years at hard labor.[4]

At Helsingfors the fairly harmonious arrangements worked out between Admiral Verderevsky and the Bolshevik-led Tsentrobalt left many of the most radical sailors dissatisfied. In the period 21–23 June a crisis was averted by Tsentrobalt's cooperation with the commander when the crews of the most radical battleships passed utimatums demanding the immediate removal of nonsocialist ministers and then threatened to sink the commander's ship as it attempted to leave for Revel.[5] These same "heavily Bolshevized" battleships were donating considerable sums to the Left Socialist Revolutionaries by early July.[6] A growing problem for the Bolsheviks in the fleet was the "drain off" of the most influential party members to higher, more responsible positions, such as being delegates to Tsentrobalt.[7]

The immediate cause for the rise of tension at the naval bases was the Provisional Government's renewed war effort, the Kerensky-sponsored June offensive. Tensions rose when rumors circulated that units in and around the capital were to be ordered to the front. This seemed to threaten the Kronstadt sailors as well as army units, since voices from some quarters had been insisting all along that the way to deal with radical Kronstadt was to disperse the units to the front, and the sailors knew that there was no logical argument against such an action. Radical propagandists could make much of this situation.

Army units were, of course, more susceptible to immediate reassignment, and the actual transfer at the end of June of a unit of the First Machine Gun Regiment, which was stationed in Petrograd, provoked the beginning of the July Crisis. Rumors persisted that the whole regiment would be sent to the front or disbanded, and conflict within the regiment between the Socialist Revolutionary- and Menshevik-controlled regimental committee and the unit's Bolsheviks and anarchists created a very tense atmosphere.[8] The unhappy machine gunners, who were joined by contingents of Kronstadt sailors, imparted a hostile tone to the regular weekend demonstrations in Petrograd on 1 July.

Meanwhile, the Provisional Government received two significant blows to its position and prestige. The June offensive in Galicia, after some surprising gains, bogged down and began to disintegrate by the first week of July. In the same geographic area, in an effort to bolster that front, the government moved to grant concessions to the Ukrainian nationalist movement, which had organized in the form of the Central Rada in Kiev. A delegation headed by Kerensky, Tereshchenko (the minister of foreign affairs), and Tsereteli agreed to the Ukrainian leaders' insistence on a degree of limited autonomy for the Ukraine. Soon after this concession became known in Petrograd on 1 July, the right-wing Kadet ministers of the government resigned in protest over what they considered an illegal exercise of power by the Kerensky forces, thus precipitating another governmental crisis.[9]

As the mood of rebellion grew rapidly in the First Machine Gun Regiment on Sunday, 2 July, the Bolshevik Military Organization and the Petrograd anarchists held separate conferences to formulate a policy. While the Bolsheviks temporized by seeking guidance from the party leaders, on the one hand, and by sounding an alert among the Bolshevik cadre in the garrison units, on the other, the anarchists decided to force the issue as far as possible and therefore dispatched agitators to various units. At an assembly on 3 July the anarchist leader Bleikhman-Solntsev told the machine gunners to overthrow the Provisional Government immediately, while other speakers, including Trotsky and Lunacharsky, made little attempt to calm the soldiers.[10]

KRONSTADT JOINS THE DEMONSTRATION

Already on 2 July a group of anarchists led by Mikhail Nikiferov and Iosif Gurvich were agitating in Kronstadt for support of a demonstration in Petrograd.[11] The "free" Kronstadt assemblies quickly caught the mood. Dmitrii Kondakov sent an urgent message to Roshal, who was staying in Petrograd with Ilin-Zhenevskii at the time: "Comrade Simeon, come back at once. There was a meeting yesterday [2 July] at which the masses were so revolutionised that they drove us off the platform, saying that we were afraid to attack, and they want to go straightway to Petrograd with arms. Get back here as fast as you can."[12]

Two representatives of the machine-gun regiment arrived at Kronstadt about midday on 3 July. The visitors spoke to a number of units during the afternoon, calling for the ouster of Kerensky and agitating for a general movement to Petrograd. They were supported by the local anarchists and by two Bolshevik sailors, Afanasii Remnev and Fedor Gromov.[13] By evening a large crowd had gathered at Anchor Square. The leaders of the radical political factions spoke to the assembly—Iarchuk and Gurvich for the anarchists; Roshal, Raskolnikov, and Gromov for the Bolsheviks.[14] Despite instructions just received from party headquarters to calm and contain the Kronstadters' desire to protest, Roshal was carried along by the sentiment of the audience and called for them to join the demonstration.[15] Bolshevik policy was obviously confused, and influenced by the moods of the moment, it added to an already dangerous situation.

While these unorganized meetings continued on the streets and squares of the naval base, the executive committee of the Kronstadt Soviet met at 9:30 P.M. under the chairmanship of Bolshevik Lazar Bregman. It allowed the admission of a number of representatives of units and factories to debates on possible courses of action, and after learning by telephone of the decision of the Workers' Section of the Petrograd Soviet to march in the streets the next day, it drew up plans for the movement of a large contingent to Petrograd.[16] As this was being done, the conference received the formal decisions of the two leading parties—Bolsheviks and Left Socialist Revolutionaries—to join the demonstration. A nine-member commission (six Bolsheviks, two Left Socialist Revolutionaries, and one anarchist) was then named to supervise the operation. The major question at the all-night meeting was whether the delegation from Kronstadt should be armed. Since disarming those who already had weapons seemed out of the question, most voted in favor, though a few who were present, notably the Left SR leader Brushvit, refused to sanction the carrying of weapons.[17]

The commission proceeded to issue additional ammunition, but it had some difficulty in obtaining ships, since few naval vessels were then at the base and since the officers of the largest—the training ship *Okean*—not only objected to its use but allegedly plotted to sink the ship in the channel to prevent others from passing.[18] The *Okean* was left immobilized by its crew, and at about 7:00 A.M. the Kronstadt forces embarked on a motley assortment of transports, gunboats, and ferries. The number landing on Vasilevsky Island in Petrograd about 10:30 A.M. on 4 July is often given as 10,000, probably inflated owing to a tendency in 1917 for upward rounding off of figures.[19] An official navy report to Kerensky listed only 7,000.[20] In fact, this was probably closer to the actual count, since more exact figures of the naval participants account for only 2,916 sailors and 17 officers, about half of whom represented two naval units, the Student Mine Detachment (814) and the Machine School (613).[21] Thus the 10,000 Kronstadt sailors mentioned in many accounts of the July Crisis were, in fact, closer to 3,000. The others were workers and soldiers from the naval base. Nearly all of the sailors carried rifles and cartridges, however, and to the British ambassador's daughter they presented an awesome sight:

> 3,000 Kronstadt sailors marched past the Embassy, an endless stream of evil-looking men, armed with every kind of weapon, cheered by the soldiers of the Fortress, though the ordinary public in the streets shrank at the sight of them. . . . Looking at them, one wondered what the fate of Petrograd would be if these ruffians with their unshaved faces, their slouching walk, their utter brutality were to have the town at their mercy.[22]

Though the armed sailors from Kronstadt formed a relatively small contingent, they polarized the July Crisis. While some military units in the city declined to participate as the likelihood of bloodshed increased, others now rushed more quickly to join. The sailors of the cruiser *Aurora*, for example, were waiting for a decision of the Putilov workers, when the Kronstadt "armada" passed by on its way to the Neva. Immediately the sailors left ship to participate in the demonstration, and their action may in turn have influenced the Putilov workers, who decided to join them.[23] In addition, the appearance of "armed anarchists" from Kronstadt may have been decisive in the strong steps taken by the Provisional Government, which had already been shaken by the resignation of the nonsocialist ministers on 2 July, to suppress the revolt.

News of the Kronstadters' arrival spread quickly around Petrograd, and they were met on the quay by Bleikhman-Solntsev and by Ivan Flerovskii and Artemii Liubovich, two Bolshevik members of the Kronstadt executive committee who had been acting as liaisons with the Petrograd Soviet. The Bolsheviks convinced the sailors that they should march to the Kshesinskaia Mansion, the Bolshevik headquarters, instead of directly to the Tauride Palace to confront the Provisional Government.[24] Their aims were apparently twofold: to prevent a premature conflict and to hold a kind of review of forces before the Bolshevik leaders, especially before Lenin, who had just returned to town from a rest in the country.

With their leaders in front—Raskolnikov, Roshal, Flerovskii, Iarchuk— the Kronstadters marched seriously and purposefully along the Neva, across the Stock Exchange Bridge to the island district known as the Petrograd Side. At the Bolshevik headquarters a crowd had already gathered. After short addresses by Sverdlov and Lunacharsky, who were especially popular with the sailors, Lenin stepped out on the balcony to receive an ovation and to respond with a few noncommittal words, calling on the sailors to be both peaceful and vigilant.[25]

After learning that the Tauride Palace was the target of a large number of workers and soldiers converging from various part of the city, most of the crowd in front of the Kshesinskaia Mansion crossed the Troitskii Bridge into the central part of the city. As they approached the palace along Panteleimonovskaia Street, shots rang out at the rear of the column, apparently fired from apartment windows above. Reacting in panic, the sailors fired back indiscriminately. About a hundred workers, sailors, and innocent bystanders were killed or wounded in the confusion.[26] By the time the disorganized column reached the Tauride Palace, many of the sailors were in an even angrier mood. While Raskolnikov checked on the situation inside, a contingent of sailors from the Machine School demanded to see Minister of Justice Paul Pereverzev about the detention of their comrade, Zhelezniakov, but when the minister of agriculture, Victor Chernov, appeared instead, they quickly seized him as a hostage and roughly shoved him into a nearby car. Raskolnikov rushed back outside and, with Trotsky's assistance, managed to secure the release of the Socialist Revolutionary leader.[27]

As the crowd milled about outside the palace, the government and soviet leaders who were inside discussed what to do. Pereverzev managed to circulate an alleged indictment of the Bolsheviks as German agents that, along with reports of troops moving on the city from the front, caused several neutral Petrograd garrison units to support the Provisional Government. Furthermore, the ardor of the armed demonstrators was cooled by evening thundershowers and by prolonged meetings and negotiations. No doubt the Kronstadters were very tired after the all-night preparations, the excitement of the passage to the capital, and a day spent marching around city streets and listening to speeches. The midafternoon panic in the streets may have discouraged many sailors about the chances of positive action, and after midnight, most of them retired to garrison quarters in the city.

When it became clear that the tide had turned against them early on the morning of 5 July, Raskolnikov, Roshal, and Iarchuk arranged terms with the local military authorities for an honorable retreat, an armistice that would allow the release of any sailors who had already been arrested and the retention of arms during the return trip to Kronstadt. It was promised that there would be no reprisals.[28] But immediately after this settlement, the Kronstadt leaders were notified by Mikhail Liber, a Menshevik leader, that a much stronger position had been taken by the Provisional Government after consultation with the Soviet Central Executive Committee. The Kronstadters would have to be disarmed. Quite naturally the Kronstadt leaders could not agree to this and ever hope to face the sailors again. In the absence of any real agreement, most of the Kronstadters made their way back to the base on 5 July, some with arms, some without.

But about two hundred sailors remained behind, along with some machine gunners, to defend the Bolshevik headquarters. Raskolnikov assumed responsibility for holding off a rapidly growing encirclement by forces that were loyal to the Provisional Government. Though hopelessly outnumbered, the Kronstadt sailors and Petrograd machine gunners prevented a surprise raid on the Bolshevik headquarters during 5 July, allowing the Bolshevik leaders to make an orderly escape. Once this main task had been accomplished by the morning of 6 July, the Bolshevik guards retreated from the exposed Kshesinskaia Mansion and made a last stand in the nearby Peter and Paul Fortress, which a detachment of sailors had occupied on the fourth. There they soon surrendered, upon the condition, negotiated by Stalin, that the men could return to their units after turning in their arms. Only the leaders were to be arrested, but in fact, most of them, including Raskolnikov, managed to get back to Kronstadt.[29]

REPERCUSSIONS OF THE JULY CRISIS AT HELSINGFORS

While the immediate threat to the Provisional Government had ended, the repercussions of the events in Petrograd continued to convulse the whole fleet, not just the base at Kronstadt. When troops were being summoned from the front on the afternoon of 4 July, it occurred to the government leaders that some loyal ships would be useful in suppressing the Kronstadt sailors and preventing any reinforcements. From the joint meeting of the Provisional Government and the Central Executive Committee in the Tauride Palace, Viktor Lebedev, the acting naval minister, telephoned his assistant in the Admiralty, Captain Boris Dudorov, to ask his advice about ordering large warships to Petrograd.[30] Dudorov, who was more knowledgeable about naval affairs, advised that smaller, destroyer-type vessels would be more effective around the capital, and after a brief discussion of what particular ships could be trusted, Dudorov drafted a telegram to Verderevsky at Helsingfors, summoning four modern "Novik" destroyers to Petrograd:

> The Provisional Government, in agreement with the Executive Committee, orders the immediate dispatch of *Pobeditel, Zabiiaka, Grom,* and *Orfei* [the First Destroyer Flotilla] to Petrograd, where they should enter the Neva. Go full speed. Keep their dispatch secret. If some of these destroyers cannot leave quickly, do not hold the others. The commander of the division will report upon arrival to me. The Provisional Government charges them with the task of demonstration, and, if necessary, to act against the Kronstadters who have already arrived. If, according to your information, it is completely impossible to send the designated destroyers, substitute another division that is better prepared.[31]

Though this was a legal demand for military reinforcements, similar to the orders going to the army front at the same time, the Lebedev-Dudorov action was foolhardy, since it should have been obvious to them that reports of what was happening in Petrograd would have circulated at the main base. The Petrograd authorities made no effort to ascertain exactly what the situation was in Helsingfors, nor did they send more than fragmentary reports of events in the capital. Still, Dudorov and Lebedev cannot be totally blamed for the havoc created by the telegram.

Unknown to the assistant naval minister, at the same time that he formulated plans for obtaining ships from the main base of the fleet, a joint session of the presidium of Tsentrobalt and representatives of ships' committees met on the former imperial yacht, *Poliarnaia Zvezda* (Polar Star), to decide on a course of action. Rumors of unrest in Petrograd had already reached Helsingfors. In fact, on the afternoon of 4 July the battleships *Respublika* and *Petropavlovsk* had radioed offers of assistance to Kronstadt and Petrograd. The coincidental arrival of a detachment of ships from Revel, headed by the cruiser *Admiral Makarov*, which was loyal to the government, further alarmed the Helsingfors sailors. Suspecting that a counterattack upon them was being planned, the Tsentrobalt and unit committees appointed a "top secret commission" to oversee the communications center of the fleet, which was on board the *Krechet*.[32] This was the first known exercise of the power to supervise the commanding staff that was granted to Tsentrobalt by the First Congress of the Baltic Fleet at the end of its meetings in mid June.

When the three-man commission—Bolsheviks Nikolai Khovrin and Andrei Shtarev, plus Semen Shenbin—boarded the *Krechet* about 7:30 P.M. on 4 July, Dudorov's telegram was in the process of being decoded. Sensing from the attitude of staff officers and telegraphers that it contained something important, the commission demanded that Verderevsky reveal the contents to Tsentrobalt.[33] The commander in chief, perhaps influenced by some of the liberal staff officers and by a rumor, just received, that Kerensky had been killed, agreed to read the telegram to the assembly of Tsentrobalt and committees from the ships. The admiral was also obviously upset over the fact that Dudorov's order placed him in an awkward position.

Other factors may have influenced Verderevsky's decision. During the hurried encoding at the naval ministry (or perhaps during an equally hurried decoding at Helsingfors), the first line had been omitted, so that the high authority of the order (Provisional Government and Central Executive Committee) had not been relayed to Verderevsky.[34] Also, the procedure for indicating an operational order, which could only be sent in code, had not been strictly followed. The fleet commander was probably annoyed because Dudorov had specified that four destroyers be sent, only one of which, the *Orfei*, was actually available in Helsingfors; furthermore, its committee was Bolshevik.[35] The crowning blow was a second message, sent by Dudorov after he apparently had second thoughts about what might happen at the main base upon the sudden departure of four destroyers:

The Provisional Government, in agreement with the Executive Committee, orders that measures be taken that not one ship can go to Kronstadt without your precise order, and do not refrain from sinking any that try; it is suggested that necessary submarines be stationed beforehand in position.[36]

This message was received and decoded in Khovrin's presence and was immediately relayed to the *Poliarnaia Zvezda*. Verderevsky's reading of the first telegram to the sailors certainly went beyond the call of duty, but he was apparently trying to retain the working cooperation of Tsentrobalt. After further consultation with the presidium of Tsentrobalt, Verderevsky finally replied to Dudorov:

> According to the established arrangement, I alone give commands about only purely operational matters. The sending of destroyers to the Neva at the present moment is a political act. All political decisions can be made by me only in agreement with Tsentrobalt, and therefore, considering the secret nature of your telegram, I declare that the dispatch of destroyers to the Neva makes the fleet an instrument of the political struggle and diverts it from direct military tasks; up to this time all the efforts of myself and of Tsentrobalt have been directed towards upholding the military capability of the fleet. Ordering the dispatch of ships introduces disharmony into the fleet and weakens considerably its military power. . . . I agree with them [Tsentrobalt] in opposing this dispatch [of destroyers]. Tsentrobalt and I must retain all forces in order to keep the fleet free of internal strife in which no one has the right to entangle it. Verderevsky.[37]

A remarkable statement—that military units committed to a war role cannot be deployed to preserve internal order—was probably the result of Verderevsky's calculation that the government had fallen or was about to fall.

Still, the commander in chief was not consistent in this position, for he allowed the *Orfei* to leave for Petrograd on a political mission, not as Dudorov wanted, but carrying a protest delegation of sailors. The *Orfei* departed early in the morning of 5 July with sixty-two representatives of unit committees and with four members of Tsentrobalt, led by Bolsheviks Khovrin and Izmailov. Their visits to the Admiralty and the Tauride Palace naturally met with a cold reception on 5 July, and early on the morning of 6 July the leaders were arrested when they appeared at the newly established headquarters of the Central Committee of the All-Russian Navy (Tsentroflot) in the Admiralty building.[38]

Tsentrobalt and the ships' committees, meeting together in continuous session in Helsingfors during 5 and 6 July, learned of the arrest of the first delegation and decided to send a second, headed by Dybenko, on the destroyer *Gromiashchii,* but this delegation was also arrested, soon after its arrival on the morning of 7 July.[39] At the same time, another destroyer, the *Molodetskii,* brought Admiral Verderevsky to explain his course of action to the Naval Ministry. But by this time the Provisional Government was not interested in explanations, and the commander in chief of the Baltic fleet was arrested and jailed too![40] The conclusion to the July Crisis in the fleet thus produced a surprising array of "casualties."

GOVERNMENT REACTION TO THE JULY CRISIS

By 8 July it appeared that the Provisional Government was at last taking decisive, albeit erratic, steps to curb radical activities in the country, especially in the Baltic fleet. The job was simplified by the rash commitment to action of the radical leaders in the fleet, although a relatively small number of sailors, mainly the Helsingfors delegations, were actually under arrest. The last-ditch stand by sailors in the capital in the fortress on 6 July gave the government the excuse it needed to use loyal forces in suppressing mutineers. Even the removal of Verderevsky, which might have made way for the restoration of discipline under a new commander, was easily accomplished by his appearance in Petrograd.

So the government started to take the offensive. Kerensky's general order of 7 July to the fleet demanded the election of new representatives to Tsentrobalt, the arrest of agitators on board ships, and, more specifically, the restoration of complete discipline at Kronstadt and on the battleships *Petropavlovsk, Respublika,* and *Slava.* He gave the crews of the battleships twenty-four hours to turn in the "instigators."[41] Commissar Onipko accepted command responsibility as general commissar of the Helsingfors base until the arrival of a new commander. But this post was promptly filled on 8 July with the appointment of Captain Aleksandr Razvozov, commander of the destroyer division at Revel. That day, Acting Naval Minister Lebedev went to the south shore base, addressed a hostile assembly of ships' committees, won them over with a half-hour speech, and introduced Razvozov, who received an ovation as he was promoted to rear admiral. Following what was, by now, a typical course of action, other emissaries—Bunakov-Fundamenskii and Nikolai Sokolov—went to Helsingfors on 10 July, where they had little trouble obtaining from the soviet a *pro forma* condemnation of the July demonstration.[42]

Yet the government was being pulled in diametrically opposed directions, and it could not move resolutely and quickly to restore complete discipline in the fleet. Some members of the Central Executive Committee who supported the Provisional Government were appalled at the measures of repression that were taken against the Bolsheviks, who so recently had been their fellow revolutionaries. By contrast, officer groups and especially General Aleksei Brusilov, the current commander in chief, counseled that strong action should be taken against Kronstadt.[43] More pressure came from the British ambassador and military advisers. Buchanan complained on 6 July:

> I had always admitted Government was right to temporize till it had necessary force behind it but this excuse no longer obtained and if it now failed to follow up its victory and to stamp out anarchy once and for all we should be confronted with another crisis in a few weeks time. . . . Government's desire to avoid bloodshed was rational but anarchists and agitators who were responsible for the 500 casualties must be punished or far more blood would be shed later on.[44]

The British ambassador blamed the prime minister, Prince Lvov, for the lack of decisive action, which may have influenced Lvov's resignation shortly afterwards.

It was over a week after victory had been attained in the streets of Petrograd before the government took positive steps to restore discipline in the fleet. This allowed time for the sailors to cool their tempers, for the leaders to review what had happened in extended soviet sessions, and for the political parties to develop plans of action. On 13 July, General Gerasimov, the commandant of the fortress complex at Kronstadt, was ordered to close the Bolshevik newspaper, *Golos Pravdy*, and to arrest the Bolshevik leaders Raskolnikov, Roshal, and Remnev. This placed him in an awkward position, but he went before the soviet, whose president, A. N. Lamanov, agreed that something should be done in order to avoid harsher measures. The Bolshevik faction cooperated by closing the newspaper, declaring, however, that it would issue a new one, *Proletarskoe Delo*, the next day.[45] Similarly, P. N. Lamanov, the commander of the naval units at Kronstadt, arranged compliance with his instructions to replace red flags with the old naval banner, the flag of St. Andrew, and to raise two companies of volunteers for the front. These were obviously token gestures, as only one hundred men assembled for dispatch to Petrograd on 14 July (and only fifteen to twenty actually left Petrograd for the front).[46]

Arresting the Bolshevik leaders posed a more serious question. Afanasii Remnev insisted on going into hiding, and Roshal was still in Petrograd. Despite the general opposition of the most revolutionary sailors, Raskolnikov decided, however, to turn himself in to the authorities in Petrograd, especially in view of a threatened blockade of the island.[47] In a dramatic appearance before the Kronstadt Soviet on 13 July, Raskolnikov tied the government action to the world situation:

> This measure [order for arrest] is clearly of a reactionary character and shows that the Provisional Government is attempting to create a united political front with the Allies. It wants to bring to Russia the same order and constraints that exist during the war in France and England. Nowhere up to this time has there existed such freedom as we now know in Russia. But now our government will constrict and oppress the work of internationalists as it is being done in the other leading countries.

And the Bolshevik leader concluded:

> We had many opportunities to escape from Kronstadt, to go abroad through Finland. But we decided not to do this, because we have done nothing wrong. I consider my conscience clear and am fully prepared to go to Petrograd in order to present testimony on the whole affair. I will appear in Petrograd completely voluntarily. Of course, I am sure, comrades, that none of you will doubt my honesty and all of you will consider me as deeply idealistic and sincere as when you invested me with the distinguished title of assistant chairman of the Kronstadt Soviet of Workers' and Soldiers' Deputies (applause).[48]

Commandant Lamanov furnished Raskolnikov with a first-class cutter for his trip to Petrograd, where Captain Dudorov met him and escorted him to a cell on the first floor of the Kresty political prison.

Meanwhile, the Provisional Government was again acting hesitantly and unpredictably. On the morning of 14 July, with no advance warning, Captain Tyrkov arrived at Kronstadt to replace Gerasimov as port commander. He was supported by a two-hundred-man cyclist company under Captain L. K. Artamanov, a Left Socialist Revolutionary. Whether this was intended simply as a follow-up action or whether it resulted from a dissatisfaction with the outcome of the thirteenth is not clear, but the use of force to achieve control was now impossible because of the token compliance that had already been initiated, the weakness of the unit that had actually been dispatched, and the behavior of Tyrkov, who proceeded to belabor and threaten the soviet. In any event, Kronstadt met the small "invasion" passively; the soviet listened politely to the new commandant, even allowing Tyrkov to search the old training battleship *Zaria Svobody* for Lenin (who was believed to be hiding at Kronstadt) and Roshal. The Kronstadt Soviet, in a day-long session, then passed a resolution, offered by its Left Socialist Revolutionary chairman, Fedor Pokrovskii, that refused any further assistance to Tyrkov.[49]

Finally, on the fourteenth, another small detachment of loyal troops arrived at Kronstadt to occupy the fortresses. They took control of Fort Krasnaia Gorka without opposition, but they were unsuccessful in gaining the more strategic Fort Ino, thanks to Bolshevik agitation among the artillerists; and then the detachment was withdrawn completely from the island for fear that it would be "Kronstadtized." On 15 July, Tyrkov and Captain Artamanov managed to search the *Zaria Svobody* for Lenin and Roshal, but the soviet refused to allow them to take the command of the naval units from Lamanov. In an apparent attempt to resolve this impasse, Acting Naval Minister Lebedev arrived on the seventeenth to address a large assemblage of sailors at the Naval Arena. He was met with hoots and whistles and was not able to speak. Fearing the violent mood of the sailors and realizing that the loyal troops were competely outnumbered, Lebedev relieved Tyrkov of his command, then returned to Petrograd, leaving Artamanov as commandant. Tyrkov's "rule" at Kronstadt lasted three days, and his successor was left to pursue Gerasimov's policy of cooperation with the soviet.[50]

The government's attack on Kronstadt was obviously muted, and it concentrated upon the Bolshevik professionals. Practically no arrests were made, and the attempt to silence the press was totally ineffectual. In fact, the Kronstadt Bolshevik newspaper filled an important gap in the capital area after the suppression of *Pravda* by publishing articles by Lenin and also a number of pamphlets and brochures, which were distributed by sailors around the city.[51] The deliberate focus of the government's move against a few Bolshevik leaders was so plain, especially since anarchist leaders such as Iarchuk were left free, that it probably encouraged sympathy for the Marxist party. And since only a few Bolsheviks were arrested from the Kronstadt party organization, it is difficult to note any effect whatsoever on party

129

strength. Lazar Bregman, a popular young doctor, took Raskolnikov's position as the Bolshevik spokesman in the Kronstadt Soviet, while a number of party regulars—Ilin-Zhenevskii, Flerovskii, Smilga, Kolbin, Breslav, and Stal—supervised publications.

In Helsingfors the government's actions likewise encountered effective passive resistance. Rear Admiral Razvozov, who arrived on 9 July, attempted to comply with the letter of Kerensky's directives. An initial advantage due to the absence of about seventy-five sailor-leaders, who had been arrested in Petrograd, was dissipated by the release of most of them, including Bolsheviks Khovrin and Shtarev, who resumed their places in Tsentrobalt. The ships' committees of those unruly battleships that had been singled out for attention by Kerensky agreed to support the new commander's efforts to restore discipline, but there are no records of any arrests on those ships.[52] Tsentrobalt declared itself reelected on 10 July, but this was obviously a sham, and it was once more dissolved, to meet again only on 25 July. For the interim, six members of Tsentroflot joined six delegates chosen by a special assembly, composed of the Helsingfors Soviet and unit committees, which met on the afternoon of 12 July. But of thirty candidates nominated at the assembly, twenty-three withdrew from the balloting, "considering a new election of Tsentrobalt unneeded and illegal."[53]

As at Kronstadt, orders for the arrest of leading Bolsheviks concentrated on the editors of the party newspaper—Antonov-Ovseenko, Stark, and Mikhail Roshal, a brother of the Kronstadt leader—who had little if anything to do with the July Crisis. The arrests were accomplished without resistance on 16 July by the Guard of People's Freedom, a conservative adjunct of the Helsingfors Soviet.[54] Also arrested on 18 July, without any particular reason, were the editors of the Left Socialist Revolutionary newspaper, Ustinov and Proshian. In a farewell "letter to the readers" they denounced the government's action:

> Comrades! They arrested us on the orders of war and naval ministers "Comrades" Kerensky and Lebedev. Goodbye. We trust that our only concern, that of international socialism, will triumph, in spite of socialist traitors working alongside the bourgeoisie. Long live the International. P. Proshian and Al. Ustinov.[55]

Although the last issue of *Volna* appeared on 15 July, *Sotsialist-Revoliutsioner* continued publication, filling an important gap in the radical literature of Helsingfors until another Bolshevik paper, *Priboi*, was launched on 27 July.[56]

The actions against radicalism in the fleet should also be viewed in long-range perspective as part of the Provisional Government's domestic offensive that began in the last half of June in conjunction with the launching of a military advance and the winning of solid support from the First All-Russian Congress of Soviets. These efforts served as one catalyst for the radical "counterattack" of early July, but they were also intensified by it. Thus, not all of the government measures can be traced to the reaction to the July Crisis. Some were inaugurated before those events but were not really effective or noticed until afterwards. The establishment of Tsentroflot as an All-Navy Central Committee that would be dominated by non-Baltic, moderate representatives took place before the July Crisis, but that organization's threat to the autonomy and influence of Tsentrobalt was not apparent until mid July. Likewise, the conversion on 2 July of the old official military newspaper, *Russkii Invalid*, to a much more politically active organ, *Armiia i Flot Svobodnoi Rossii* (Army and Navy of Free Russia), received little notice until after the demonstrations. The strident anti-Bolshevik campaign waged by the editor, Fedor Stepun, in July most likely did not reach the rank and file of the fleet, as the publication was considered an officers' newspaper and was dismissed for what it was, official propaganda.[57] The extensive publicity concerning the restoration of discipline in the fleet in the pages of *Armiia i Flot Svobodnoi Rossii* might have only added to the demoralization of naval officers who realized how little was actually being accomplished.

In all fairness to the Provisional Government, it must be pointed out that a state of crisis continued throughout July and compromised the consistency of the policies that it was pursuing. Measures against radicalism in the fleet, especially the closing of newspapers, coincided with Kerensky's efforts to appease the right wing of the revolution, led by the Kadet party, and culminated in the appointment of Lavr Kornilov as commander in chief of the armed forces on 18 July. The failure to mend the rupture on the Right, however, led to Kerensky's resignation, then to the formation of a second coalition government on 24 July, with Kerensky as prime minister, after which the antiradical campaign eased.

During the period following the July Crisis, when the government's repression of radical activities was most severe, there was hardly a noticeable abatement of antigovernment sentiment in Kronstadt and Helsingfors. Numerous resolutions protesting the repressive acts were issued by organizations of all kinds. On the public squares, assemblies proclaimed, just as vehemently as before, their belief that all power should be in the hands of the soviets. Before their arrests the Bolshevik leaders such as Raskolnikov and Antonov-Ovseenko were perhaps even more active than usual in public. In Helsingfors the Left Socialist Revolutionaries inaugurated a "Propaganda School" with lectures every evening, and the first sailors' theater, sponsored by the Left Socialist Revolutionaries, raised its curtain on 7 July.[58] But the big event of the month at the main base was the grand opening on 14 July of new quarters for the Sailors' Club in the former Apollo Hotel on South Esplanade. Before the July Crisis the Provisional Government had arranged for the purchase of the building, which contained many fine appointments and a luxury restaurant, for 4 million rubles as part of its campaign to win the allegiance of the sailors from the radicals. But all parties welcomed the new facility with its spacious dining and meeting rooms. The Bolsheviks, though they were prevented from speaking at the dedication ceremonies, extended a special welcome in the last issue of *Volna*.[59]

The government's "carrot and stick" policy, if indeed it was a policy, was not applied consistently. Of about three hundred from the naval bases who had been detained as a result of activities during the July Crisis or from the repression that followed, most were released on 9 July. Another group was held for more thorough investigation but was let go about 25 July.[60] Only a few leaders remained in confinement in the old tsarist prison, Kresty. From Kronstadt—Raskolnikov, Remnev, and Semen Roshal; from Helsingfors—Antonov-Ovseenko, Dybenko, Mikhail Roshal, Ustinov, Proshian, and Stark; from Petrograd—Kurkov and Zlatogorskii (from the *Aurora*), who were assigned cells on the same floor as the more illustrious Bolshevik captives Trotsky, Kamenev, and Lunacharskii.[61] After a brief hunger strike, which was led by Antonov-Ovseenko and Raskolnikov, the prison regime was relaxed even more than was normal for Russian political inmates. The cells were locked only at night, and the days were spent in discussion and lectures; friends from outside brought quantities of food and literature of all kinds, and one cell was set aside as a library. As Dybenko romanticized: "Here in Kresty the methods of action for revolution were appraised. The Kresty of Kerensky became for many a school of leadership training for the barricade battles of the Great October."[62]

In addition to providing daily seminars on revolution at government expense, the Petrograd authorities created a tangible grievance for the extremists who remained at the bases. The air was filled with resolutions from the sailors demanding the release of their leaders, who had now become martyrs. The attempt to silence the radical press in the fleet bases turned out to be a farce, and there was apparently no thought of any drastic alteration of the institutions that existed. The convocation of the third session of Tsentrobalt on 25 July provided the first real test of the government's program. One of the first acts of the new committee was to protest the arrest of the delegation that had been sent to Petrograd, though the members cautiously avoided another dissolution by electing Sergei Magnitskii, a Menshevik midshipman, to become Dybenko's permanent replacement as chairman.[63] Starting with only thirty-five members, Tsentrobalt gradually increased in size as delegates arrived from distant bases and others returned from their detention in Petrograd, so that by 9 August about fifty of the authorized sixty members were present. A Soviet source that assumes a total of sixty divides the delegates as follows: fifteen Bolsheviks; eight pro-Bolsheviks; eighteen Socialist Revolutionaries, Mensheviks, and their supporters; and nineteen nonparty.[64] Though a non-Bolshevik was chairman, the other members of the presidium were two moderate Bolsheviks (Aleksei Baranov and Fedor Averichkin) and two pro-Bolsheviks (Roman Grundman and Fedor Likhomanov).[65]

Party divisions should not be overemphasized, however, as the two basic positions within Tsentrobalt—moderate and radical—cut across party lines. Moderates dominated the body until mid August under the leadership of all of those in the presidium, including Bolsheviks. The radicals were led by Bolsheviks Nikolai Khovrin, Nikolai Izmailov, Ivan Sapozhnikov, and Konstantin Sviridov (who might be called the Dybenkoites) and by anarchist Evgenii Blokhin and nonparty members Iakov Mokhov and Pavel Verbitskii. The radicals were not a solid bloc, certainly not in the presidium elections of 7 August, when Izmailov and Mokhov each received one vote. But on 9 August the radicals challenged the moderate temperament of the committee with a strong resolution that called for the release of those who were still being held and that attempted to unite Tsentrobalt with a declaration issued by the Sailors' Assembly on 7 August; but the Tsentrobalt moderates easily defeated the resolution, 28 to 9 with 6 abstentions.[66]

A major issue for Tsentrobalt during most of August was the problem of a change in rules, which Kerensky had demanded. The moderates wished neither to appease nor to confront the government, and so they postponed resolving the matter. The radicals, led by Khovrin and Blokhin, pushed the question to a head in the session of 18 August, demanding either that the old rules approved by the First Congress of the Baltic Fleet be in force or that

Tsentrobalt be dissolved and a new congress be called. The session passed Blokhin's resolution that Tsentrobalt propose to Tsentroflot that the former rules be approved, and then it chose two delegates, Mikhail Shkoliarov and Izmailov, to go to Petrograd to explain the difficult position of Tsentrobalt, which was caught between pressure from the sailors and demands from the Provisional Government.[67]

The Provisional Government did not attempt to limit or modify in any way the powers of the soviets at the naval bases, apparently because of the intimate involvement of some of the members with the institution of soviets and perhaps because they believed that no changes could be implemented. Between 9 and 11 August the Kronstadt Soviet was reelected for the third time, with the following results: Bolsheviks, 96; Socialist Revolutionaries, 73; Mensheviks, 13; anarchists, 7; and nonparty, about 100.[68] The Bolsheviks registered slight gains (from 93), but the Socialist Revolutionaries and Mensheviks lost considerably, and almost all delegates of the latter parties belonged to the leftist factions of their parties. In the executive committee there were now 10 nonparty, 10 Bolsheviks, 8 Socialist Revolutionaries, 1 Menshevik, and 1 anarchist, roughly the same as before, but Lazar Bregman replaced Lamanov as the permanent chairman. Konstantin Shugrin, a Left Socialist Revolutionary, presided over the larger assembly, with the radical Bolshevik Mikhail Lebedev as his assistant.[69]

The Revel Soviet became even more decisively Bolshevik on 26 July: 78 Bolsheviks, 67 Socialist Revolutionaries, 9 Mensheviks, 8 Menshevik-Internationalists, and 20 nonparty. But the soviet still consisted predominately of workers, and the Socialist Revolutionaries remained the strongest party on the ships at Revel, especially on the cruisers *Admiral Makarov* and *Rossiia*.[70] And these Socialist Revolutionaries remained loyal to the government until the end of August.

The party breakdown of the Helsingfors Soviet continued to be more difficult to distinguish. Zalezhskii reported to the Sixth Congress of the Russian Social Democratic Labor Party (Bolshevik) at the end of July that there were 125 internationalists, 70 to 80 of them Bolsheviks, out of 400 members.[71] In general, the soviet remained moderate, and a Socialist Revolutionary, Bishard, presided over most of the meetings in August. But the Sailors' Assembly was more radical, under Left Socialist Revolutionary and Bolshevik dominance. An additional factor in Helsingfors, however, was the swing of the main Socialist Revolutionary party away from the Provisional Government on 23 July in support of Chernov's resignation from the government.[72]

If such analyses of strength, imprecise as they may be, prove the growth of radical control at the main bases, they also reveal the prevailing atmosphere of open meetings and debates, which was quite a contrast from the much greater control on such activities that existed in Petrograd in July and August. This is not to say that radicalism in the fleet was now contained and that it no longer had an influence in the capital, however. In fact, a little-known conference of workers, Kronstadters, and representatives of the military fronts occurred in a factory club on Vasilevsky Island on 21 and 22 July.[73] The resolutions passed at this meeting provide important evidence of the immediate political demands of these groups: (1) not to enter into any kind of negotiations with the "counterrevolutionary Duma," and to take power into their own hands; (2) to remove the death sentence; (3) to cease arrests of revolutionary soldiers and sailors, "especially Kronstadters"; (4) to open all newspapers that had been closed; (5) to take more decisive measures in the struggle with the counterrevolutionary press.[74]

And a sizable Kronstadt contingent—Orlov, Kolbin, Liubovich, Smilga, Flerovskii, Breslav, Uliantsev, and Bikelis—attended the Sixth Congress of the Bolshevik wing of the RSDLP, which was held from 26 July to 3 August. Flerovskii delivered the report on the naval base, which was one of three "city reports," the others being for Moscow and Petrograd. He stressed that "Kronstadt fully realizes 'Soviet power'" and that the Bolsheviks were the leading party.[75] A number of delegates to the congress, including Podvoisky and Dzhaparidze, visited Kronstadt on 6 August, where they received a grand reception. These contacts were especially valuable for communicating to the central leadership echelons of the party the extent of Kronstadt's commitment to the Bolshevik position.

Attempts to restore discipline in the fleet after the July Crisis were half-hearted and ineffectual. The efforts of Rear Admiral Razvozov were nullified by another shakeup of officers—one more new commander in chief, one more staff rotation—and the resulting increase in dissension among the officers. Commander Cromie reported: "In many ways I find it more difficult daily to work satisfactorily with the various Staffs: there is little combination, less organization, communication dreadful, and information nil,—at least I can never get any, even about our own boats."[76] Razvozov drifted into the same policy as his predecessor—seeking a working arrangement with the sailors that would retain a degree of centralized control while maintaining the navy as a fighting unit. As a result, the phenomenal rise of radical forces in the fleet was scarcely slowed by the July reaction.

6

FROM THE KORNILOV AFFAIR
TO THE BATTLE OF MOON SOUND

FAILURE TO RESTORE FIRM CONTROL over the military units in the Petrograd area and to suppress the political groups that were openly calling for the overthrow of the government caused the sentiment against Kerensky to develop into a full-fledged movement, which culminated in the Kornilov Affair. The attempt to introduce a stronger government headed by army officers was probably doomed from the beginning due to lack of secrecy and to divisions among the leaders, who represented a cross section of Right and Center political views. The monarchist Right could not fully trust the generals who had been active in forcing the abdication of the tsar, the generals themselves were not certain of support from below in the army, and some of the Kadets and Center groups hoped for a compromise through negotiations that would avoid a violent clash with the Provisional Government.

Kerensky later argued that the "plot" originated in rightist military and financial circles immediately after the February Revolution, but the real beginning of the August debacle was the minister-president's search for effective discipline after the July Crisis.[1] Boris Savinkov, a colorful veteran of the Socialist Revolutionary terrorist organization who came to Petrograd from his post as commissar on the Southwestern Front, convinced Kerensky of his ability to handle the restoration and was appointed deputy minister of war. He in turn was instrumental in the elevation of General Lavr Kornilov, the commander of the Southwestern Front, to the position of supreme commander in chief on 18 July.[2] Kornilov understood that he would have increased authority to effect the restoration of discipline. But from the perspective of Kornilov and other generals, discipline of front-line units could not be significantly improved unless the contagious sources of rebellion in Petrograd and Moscow were eliminated. The attempt to obtain martial law in the rear areas is what produced the impasse between the generals and the Provisional Government.

As Kornilov tried to remedy a deteriorating situation on the front lines by strengthening the rear areas, Kerensky was trapped between these military pressures and the voices of the street. By shifting to the left to include Mensheviks and Socialist Revolutionaries, the Provisional Government was forced to listen to the Central Executive Committee of the First All-Russian Congress of Soviets, which remained in permanent session; but this body was also caught in a dilemma between the increasingly hard line policies of the Provisional Government and the radicalization of the local soviets in northern Russia. The outcome was likely to be a series of compromises and disagreements, alliances and ruptures.

The Provisional Government was trying to move in the direction of law and order after the July Crisis. Following the formation of a new government on 25 July, which retained Boris Savinkov and Viktor Lebedev as deputy ministers of war and navy, respectively, a series of decrees bolstered executive power: "the right to prohibit and close all meetings and assemblies which may constitute a danger to the war effort or the security of the state" (28 July); the extension of the death penalty (restored to frontline army units on 12 July) to the navy (30 July); "the detention under arrest of persons whose activity constitutes a particular threat to the defense and internal security of the state and to the freedoms achieved by the revolution" (2 August); and the sentencing to hard labor of "a person guilty of an act of violence designed to change the existing structure of Russia or to sever from Russia any of its parts" (4 August).[3] All that remained was a matter of implementing these decrees.

Government leaders were quite aware that revolutionary activity could not be ended by decree and that an effort to enforce the letter of the new laws under present circumstances would result in civil war. The next best alternative was to win over public opinion and to increase confidence in the government. Above all, crises such as the one in July had to be avoided. But even the critical financial situation, which was somewhat obscured by the other problems, had been severely affected by government changes and instability. Minister of Finance Nikolai Nekrasov reported to the Moscow State Conference in mid August:

By examining the subscription list to the "Liberty Loan" which I have at my disposal, you can clearly, consistently, and accurately trace (the relation between) the changes in the subscription (rate) and the changes in the internal situation. It inevitably registers a drop during a governmental crisis or when changes or difficulties occur. And it shows an increase when these difficulties are overcome, and when the country develops confidence in the stability of the contemporary situation.[4]

The task of a government that was facing military necessity and lack of public confidence, on the one side, and the spirit of revolution, on the other, was not easy.

THE GOVERNMENT'S PACIFICATION PROGRAM

Public appeals remained Minister-President Kerensky's most important method. He seems to have had tremendous confidence in the possibilities of mass information (or indoctrination), and it may well be, in retrospect, that Kerensky's government died of overexposure. Press releases, tours, interviews, lectures, and conferences abounded. In an interview published on 28 July, Savinkov said that his first task was the restoration of "iron discipline."[5] His counterpart for the navy, Lebedev, went on another tour of the Baltic bases at the end of July, giving pep talks to anyone who would listen. At Åbo on 31 July he was asked to address a crowd of sailors at the People's House. But at the entrance he was met by a hostile, threatening mob shouting, "Go home!" "Why do we need discipline?" "We want leave!"[6] According to the official government military newspaper, Lebedev then delivered an animated (angry?) speech:

I was not afraid of the tsarist gendarmes and executioners, and I faced death without trembling when the majority of you knew nothing about revolution. And after my struggle for your freedom and happiness, you, here, in front of foreigners [Finns?], so disgustingly misuse that freedom. If you think that I am afraid of your threats, you are sadly mistaken. I was not afraid of Nicholas II and I am not afraid of the people to whom I gave my whole life, all my energies.

I am not afraid of you. And what has happened here just now reaffirms how much discipline is needed. And we will obtain and create revolutionary discipline whatever it costs, whatever severe and merciless measures we have to resort to. Or else not only our liberty but also Russia will be ruined.[7]

The sailors responded, according to the government report, "True! True!"[8]

During an interview in Petrograd a few days later, Lebedev summed up his impressions thus: "My latest tour convinced me that among the mass of sailors a change in mood is occurring. The sailors are beginning to recognize the necessity of continuing the war and, from that, the necessity to get busy and obey their commanders."[9] He praised the units in the Gulf of Riga for their determination to resist the enemy, but he admitted that much work needed to be done, that Tsentrobalt had changed little. He concluded: "In general the situation in the fleet is extremely serious and demands a great amount of effort to set it straight."[10]

Lecture and discussion programs also were aimed at improving the public image of the Provisional Government. In Petrograd the naval ministry opened a series of lectures "on political questions" for sailors at the Physical Sciences Auditorium of the university on Saturday afternoon, 5 August.[11] The "government sponsored" Sailors' Club in Helsinki continued to flourish, and in early August its Cultural-Enlightenment Section opened a "Sailors' University."[12] But a wider discussion of political issues seemed to do more harm than good to the cause of the Provisional Government; graduates of the "university" were assigned to agitational tasks by Tsentrobalt! The government also failed to sustain other efforts. As the situation in Finland continued to deteriorate with strikes and demonstrations in a number of cities in early August, the first Russian-language newspaper to be directly loyal to the Provisional Government, *Obshchee Delo*, appeared; but it closed after two issues.[13]

Meanwhile, Admiral Aleksandr Razvozov, commander in chief of the fleet, had taken steps to improve its operational capability. Several cruisers and battleships were removed from the main base in order to patrol near Åbo and Revel. Unfortunately, scarcity of fuel and the existence of minefields limited their steaming time. The commander and his staff moved on the *Krechet* to Revel, away from Tsentrobalt and the guns of the most radical battleships and under the more friendly protection of the Revel destroyer flotilla. But the transfer to Revel in summer, a pattern that had been established in previous war years, offered little relief to hard-pressed officers, for there the crumbling Northern Front aroused concern. The staff officers, overwhelmed by revolution for five months, were suddenly thrust back into the war. The result was a noticeable lowering of the morale of officers.

Prince Cherkasskii, the chief of staff, confessed to Captain Rengarten that it would take a whole winter of peace and quiet to put the fleet back together again. He divided the officers into four groups: (1) "depressed souls," those who were dissatisfied with the conditions but had no place to go; (2) "incompatibles," those who hoped for a return of the tsarist regime; (3) "true workers," Russian patriots who were devoted to fighting the enemy regardless of the form of government under which they served; and (4) "scoundrels," who took advantage of disturbed conditions in order to promote their own personal gain, often to the extent of actively supporting radical forces. A majority of the officers fitted into the first category, several belonged in the third, and smaller numbers in the other two, according to Cherkasskii.[14] Rengarten's diary also reveals that staff officers shared a common tendency in frustrating situations—to dream of shifting officer personnel up and down the line with the hope that a strategic position filled by the right man would miraculously solve the problems. But few benefits were attained by those changes that were effected. Captain Modest Ivanov, the "red" commander of a battleship, had been released from active duty by Lebedev at the end of July, but loud complaints from his former command produced his reinstatement and the additional demand that he be promoted to admiral.[15]

The radical mood of the sailors at the main bases—Helsingfors and Kronstadt—continued to influence the surrounding area. About fifteen thousand attended the regular Sunday assemblies on 6 August at both bases. The one at Kronstadt, which included "soldiers, sailors, peasants, and workers of Petrograd, Sestroretsk, and Kronstadt," passed a resolution, which was presented by anarchist Iosif Gurvich (Venik), calling for the release of those who had been arrested in the July Crisis and protesting the Moscow State Conference.[16] At Helsingfors, under chairman Eizhen Berg, who was a leader of Bolsheviks on the battleship *Sevastopol*, an assembly voted a series of resolutions warning of the danger of military collapse and of counterrevolution and demanding that the soviets do something about the government and that it free Dybenko, Antonov-Ovseenko, Ustinov, and Proshian. The loyalty of Tsentrobalt to the sailors was also questioned.[17] Perhaps influenced by the mood of the assembly, Tsentrobalt on 7 August strongly attacked Lebedev's report of his tour and chose one of the leading Bolshevik delegates, Aleksei Baranov, as its representative at the Moscow State Conference.[18]

In the four- to five-hour daily meetings of Tsentrobalt during August,

there was relatively little discussion of troubles between officers and men—
that issue was temporarily dead—but there was much concern over Tsentroflot, the Sailors' Assembly of the Helsingfors Soviet, and the Central
Executive Committee in Petrograd. Under the chairmanship of Sergei
Magnitskii, a Menshevik, the fleet committee attempted to steer a middle
course between the progovernment Tsentroflot and the more radical Sailors'
Assembly and Kronstadt Soviet, but the committee tended, when under
pressure, to veer left. When a delegate from the cruiser *Aurora* arrived to
complain about threats of arrests from the government on 9 August, Nikolai
Izmailov, Konstantin Roshkov, and Pavel Sutyrin went to investigate. A
few days later they reported on their visits to the cruiser, the Kronstadt base,
Tsentroflot, the naval ministry, and the Central Executive Committee. They
were dissatisfied with the answers given by Lebedev and Chkheidze to questions regarding the arrests of delegates and of Admiral Verderevsky in July,
the procedure of the investigation commissions, the reelection of Tsentroflot, the transfer of sailors to the front, and the calling of the Moscow State
Conference.[19]

THE BEGINNING OF THE KORNILOV AFFAIR

Meanwhile, during meetings of representatives of various Russian parties
and organizations in Moscow, rumors circulated about the formation of a
counterrevolutionary plot by army generals. The Bolshevik Central Committee discussed this possibility on 14 August, and it assigned two members,
Felix Dzerzhinsky and Jacob Sverdlov, to a special information bureau that
had been set up by the Central Executive Committee.[20] That day, two
veteran Bolshevik agitators, Ludmila Stal and Petr Zalutskii, spoke before
the Kronstadt Soviet, protesting the conference.[21] A large delegation of
Kronstadters visited Sestroretsk, on the nearby mainland, the next day to
declare the conference "a center for consolidating counterrevolutionary
forces," not a bad description, as it turned out.[22] But in the week that followed, protocols and resolutions emanating from the Baltic area seem mun-
dane and inconsequential—the lull before the storm.

Both Kerensky and Kornilov planned to deal with what Kerensky
called "the rotten corner" of Russia by transferring naval units away from
their revolutionized bases.[23] Prior attempts to move sailors had been unsuccessful because of fear of pressing the sailors into open rebellion. At the

end of July, two transfer companies of the First Baltic Fleet Depot Troop were called out, but only seventy men appeared, the balance either deserting or transferring to other units.[24] On 8 August, Kerensky approved a secret report of the Naval General Staff that proposed the complete evacuation of the Kronstadt base, but it was not until 23 August that more detailed plans were offered by Admiral Maksimov, who had formerly been the "red" commander of the Baltic fleet and now was chief of the naval staff at supreme headquarters, the delay apparently having been caused by indecision and by the Moscow State Conference.[25]

The liquidation of Kronstadt thus became an important element in Kornilov-Kerensky relations at the end of August. This base had long been the symbol of the most radical tendencies in the Russian revolution; but given war priorities up to this time, not enough local troops could be spared for purposes of suppressing Kronstadt and, at the same time, of overawing and checking the Petrograd garrison. Why should an attempt now be made in August? Apparently the influence of Boris Savinkov was decisive; he knew that Kornilov had personally loyal units on the Southwestern Front and that Kornilov had directed their transfer into positions for moving on the Petrograd area. By 22 August, Savinkov had edged Lebedev aside and had become deputy minister of both the army and the navy.[26]

Kerensky, Savinkov, and Kornilov agreed on the necessity of suppressing Kronstadt, and the fall of Riga on 21 August added urgency to the military situation. Soviet accounts, which are quite obviously biased in regard to the Kornilov Affair, claim that the move against Kronstadt and the surrender of Riga were the beginnings of a plot to surrender Petrograd to the Germans.[27] Very little evidence for this exists. In fact, the defense of Russia, particularly of Petrograd, is what brought these three dissimilar men so close to agreement on the introduction of martial law. Whatever the reason—differences in ultimate objectives, personality quirks, outside influences, faulty communications—Kerensky, at practically the last possible moment, refused to support what he feared had become a challenge to his own power. Under the influence of anti-Kerensky forces at headquarters, Kornilov may actually have planned a military dictatorship. More likely, he was embarrassingly left at what he thought was a point of no return by the actions of Savinkov and Kerensky and had to proceed with the plan for military occupation of the Petrograd area.

Surprisingly, the plans for dispersing the military units in the Petrograd region and for the establishment of martial law were not publicly known until after the break between Kornilov and Kerensky on 26 August. According to General Aleksandr Lukomskii, Kornilov's chief of staff, arranging the movement of troops upon Petrograd began as early as 3 August and were to culminate at the end of the month, when radical demonstrations were expected in connection with the six month's anniversary of the February Revolution.[28] Groups preparing these celebrations were, in fact, meeting when the news of the advance of General Aleksandr Krymov's cavalry corps became known in Petrograd on 26 August.

Three sailors of the *Aurora*, which was still docked in Petrograd Harbor, brought the news to Kronstadt, where an extraordinary session of the executive committee of the soviet was called on 27 August. Under the chairmanship of Bolshevik Lazar Bregman, the committee dispatched special commissars to all communications, postal, arsenal, and command centers on the island, and it called for the whole soviet to meet at 10:00 A.M. on 28 August.[29] The executive committee continued in permanent session during the crisis but decided that it was not properly equipped for the role of preparing an active defense of the island; therefore, on 28 August it formed a Military-Technical Commission, to which it delegated all "military-technical and operational functions." The commission consisted of eight members of the executive committee (including Bolsheviks Ivan Zherebtsov, Stepan Grediushko, Nikolai Pozharov, and Aleksei Pavlov, and anarchists Khaim Iarchuk and Nikolai Rivkin) and three ranking military authorities at the base—the commandant of the fortress, Captain L. K. Artamanov; the commander of naval forces, Lieutenant Petr Lamanov; and the chief of the militia, Georgii Ivanov.[30] In other actions the executive committee ordered the formation of a "red guard" militia, and delegated its chairman, Bregman, and Georgii Popuridi as the two Kronstadt representatives at the Smolny Institute in Petrograd, where a new soviet body—the Committee for Struggle against Counterrevolution—had been created.[31]

Sailors quickly became the backbone of the defense of Petrograd against the forces of Kornilov. Upon request of the Central Executive Committee in Petrograd, an expeditionary unit of over 3,000 (2,210 sailors, 625 soldiers, and an undisclosed number of workers) from Kronstadt arrived in the capital about 9:00 A.M. on 29 August.[32] Some were sent to the outskirts of the city in order to defend the approaches. By this time a detachment from the cruiser *Aurora* was in defensive position at the Winter Palace, the headquarters of the Provisional Government, which the same men would be attacking two months later.[33] Under the command of Evgenii Vishnevskii, a Bolshevik delegate of Tsentroflot, a larger group of 600 sailors from the Second Baltic Fleet Depot Troop surrounded the Hotel Astoria, allegedly the headquarters of the pro-Kornilov Military League.[34] All of the naval forces were heavily armed and so were able to distribute several hundred new Japanese rifles to the workers' militia.[35]

This support could not be obtained without a price being asked. A small delegation from Kronstadt, led by Bolsheviks Ivan Kolbin and Aleksei Pronin, found time to demand the release of those who had been arrested in July, and it provoked substantial support from the Workers' Section of the Petrograd Soviet.[36] The Kronstadt Soviet, meeting under the chairmanship of Bolshevik Mikhail Lebedev on 29 August, drew up instructions to another delegation headed by Ivan Flerovskii that included demands for (in numerical order) the immediate dismissal of counterrevolutionary generals, with their successors to be chosen by election; restoration of soldiers' organizations under "democratic principles"; abolition of repressive acts, beginning with the death penalty; immediate granting of all land to the peasants; legal establishment of an eight-hour day for all workers; complete democratization of the financial structure; organization of an equitable exchange of goods between town and country; the right of national self-determination; declaration of a free, democratic republic and the immediate calling of the Constituent Assembly; and an exchange of secret treaties with allies and an offer of a general democratic peace:

> The Kronstadt Soviet declares that without the realization of these demands it is impossible to save the revolution. . . . And that the only means to realize these demands are a break with the capitalists, complete liquidation of the bourgeois counterrevolution, and the transfer of power in the country into the hands of the revolutionary workers, peasants, and soldiers. Only such a conclusion can save the country and the revolution from bankruptcy.[37]

The "nakaz" concluded by "charging the representatives to demand . . . the immediate liberation of the comrades jailed in connection with the events of 3–5 July."[38] This document followed the usual pattern of mixing Bolshevik theory with the natural inclinations of the "free" sailors.

THE EFFECTS OF THE KORNILOV AFFAIR AT THE BASES

Contrary to the general impression given by secondary works, the Kornilov Affair did not result in the immediate fulfillment of the sailors' wishes by the Provisional Government in gratitude for their support. In fact, only four men of the Baltic fleet were still in custody: Pavel Dybenko was released on 4 September on condition that he not return to Helsingfors (where he soon reappeared); Anatolii Zhelezniakov gained his freedom on 6 September; Fedor Raskolnikov, however, remained in prison until 10 October; and Semen Roshal had to wait for the October Revolution.[39]

As the July Crisis had done, the Kornilov Affair focused attention on Petrograd but very quickly caused reverberations at the outlying bases. In Helsingfors the reaction of the executive committee of the soviet was very similar to the one of Kronstadt. On 28 August a Revolutionary Committee, which had complete authority over the structure of the military command in Finland, was organized. Unlike the Military-Technical Commission at Kronstadt, the twenty-five members of the Revolutionary Committee included only the representatives of soviets or committees: 14 from the Helsingfors Soviet, 4 from Tsentrobalt, 4 from the Oblast (Province) Peasants' Soviet, and 3 from the Oblast Committee. There were nine sailors: the four from Tsentrobalt (Nikolai Izmailov and Aleksei Baranov, both Bolsheviks, and Pavel Gordeev and Mikhail Tornin-Mitrofanov) and five from the soviet.[40] While the Kronstadt executive committee continued to function, appointing commissars and dispatching delegations, in Helsingfors the Revolutionary Committee displaced the executive committee and was, therefore, much more powerful. The reason for this was apparently the necessity of safeguarding a much wider area—all of Finland—than that encompassed by the executive committee of the Helsingfors Soviet.

The Revolutionary Committee sent commissars to the major units in the area. One sailor, Izmailov, was in virtual command of the Fifth Caucasian Division, which, because of the large number of Cossacks in it, was considered particularly suspect. Another sailor, Mikhail Savoskin, was designated as commissar of the commander of the fleet, who was still in Revel.[41] This appointment raised questions of jurisdiction; for Savoskin, though a member of Tsentrobalt, was a soviet delegate on the Revolutionary Committee. Not only did Tsentrobalt resent its displacement as the supreme sailor's authority, but there was also the question of whether a Helsingfors committee had the right to extend its jurisdiction to Revel. The protocols of Tsentrobalt contain no confirmation of Savoskin's appointment. In fact, the fleet committee assigned its own commissars to *Krechet*.

The Central Committee of the Baltic Fleet met all day and all night on 28 August, convening its sixtieth meeting at 10:20 A.M. and adjourning at

5:35 A.M. the next morning. The members read and discussed reports from Petrograd, and they concluded with a unanimous vote to send four destroyers, requested by Tsentroflot, to Petrograd. A highlight of the meeting came in the early evening during a confrontation between the moderate chairman, Sergei Magnitskii, and Bolshevik Nikolai Khovrin over the powers of commissars who were being sent to separate ships. The Bolshevik sharply denounced Magnitskii for wanting to exclude operational matters from the jurisdiction of commissars. Khovrin's argument that political action could be disguised under operational directives was weakened by his arrogant assault on the chairman.[42]

Soviet scholars have condemned Tsentrobalt for its compromising, pro–Provisional Government position throughout the Kornilov Affair.[43] They fail to note that leading Bolshevik delegates, as well as Bolshevik-leaning ones, were absent much of this time in the Revolutionary Committee and were serving as commissars. Nikolai Izmailov, a leading Bolshevik spokesman, left the meeting of 28 August early and did not appear again until 7 September. Others who were especially active during August are not recorded as having spoken at sessions during the Kornilov Affair—Roman Grundman, Evgenii Blokhin, Pavel Gordeev, and Ivan Sapozhnikov. Also Aleksei Baranov, probably the most influential Bolshevik member, was obviously in and out of Tsentrobalt sessions.[44]

Moreover, the political position of Tsentrobalt is not so easily defined. Baranov himself, in an opening speech on 28 August, proposed "to send a cablegram to Kerensky to express full confidence in him and readiness to support him with all of the force of the fleet."[45] On the other hand, Bolshevik positions were more frequently approved than rejected, Khovrin's fight for comprehensive powers for commissars being an exception of little importance when it is noted that the Revolutionary Committee had already established such powers. In the assignment of commissars, "radicals" clearly predominated. The reelection of Magnitskii as chairman on 4 September was not quite a "moderate" victory, since the other two candidates—Bolsheviks Averichkin and Baranov—together outpolled Magnitskii, 20 to 18. At the same meeting, Khovrin's resolution on the method of electing representatives to the Democratic Conference was overwhelmingly approved, and Baranov and Khovrin, along with another "radical," were elected.[46]

The Kornilov Affair caused another severe shock to the relations between officers and sailors in the fleet, the worst since the March violence. Charges that naval officers were active supporters of Kornilov are for the most part unfounded, though many officers naturally sympathized with the general idea of restoring military discipline. Nevertheless, the atmosphere, which was filled with invectives about counterrevolutionary generals, created strong suspicions. The Revolutionary Committee tried to direct the sailors' efforts into securing pledges of loyalty to the Provisional Government. Most officers signed reluctantly, including the whole commanding staff on board the *Krechet*, which returned to Helsingfors from Revel on 1 September: "We obey the Provisional Government, defending, in cooperation with the central democratic organs, the conquests of the revolution, and we are not on the side of Kornilov."[47] On most of the active-duty ships the whole thing was ignored, but on the battleship *Slava*, which was in the Gulf of Riga, the pledge was made.[48]

Some officers, however, refused to obligate themselves to a political position. The first victim, who was shot on 30 August, was the commander of the Naval Air Station at Åbo; his only crime seems to have been his unpopularity due to disciplinary measures.[49] The most serious incident occurred on the battleship *Petropavlovsk*, a stronghold of Left Socialist Revolutionaries, in Helsingfors Harbor on 31 August. The ship's committee, under pressure from the crew, expanded the pledge to include an agreement to fire upon Petrograd if so ordered. Four young officers balked at this, offering their own version as a substitute:

> We, the undersigned, pledge ourselves to obey unflinchingly all orders that are issued by the commander in chief appointed by the Provisional Government and are directed against our external enemy and sanctioned by the central democratic organ. Not wishing to shed the blood of Russian citizens, we refuse to participate actively in any domestic politics. We protest the charge against us of having antirevolutionary ideas, and ask, in order to prove our fidelity to Russia, to be sent to the Zerel front [Gulf of Riga] so that we may be in direct contact with the external foe of our country.[50]

Despite this affirmation of loyalty, the four officers were arrested and, according to Commissar Blokhin, were sent under guard to the Revolutionary Committee. But apparently in conformance with a decision of a portion of the crew, the four officers were shot on the dock.[51]

The Provisional Government condemned this application of lynch law by the sailors. Kerensky demanded the arrest of the murderers, but the ship's committee of the *Petropavlovsk* replied that all twelve hundred crew members shared the responsibility equally, since they had acted as a legal court.[52] By a vote of 22 to 18, Tsentrobalt, meeting on 3 September, rejected a strongly worded condemnation of the action taken on board the *Petropavlovsk*. During the discussion it was obvious, however, that the majority regretted the action and hoped that another such episode could be avoided.[53] The inability of the Kerensky government to make any arrests added one more stain to its reputation. After details of the affair had been published in a liberal newspaper called *Novoe Vremia*, Admiral Victor Stanley, who had just arrived in Petrograd as British naval liaison officer, advised the British government to make a strong protest on behalf of the hard-pressed naval officers of their ally Russia.[54]

THE GOVERNMENT'S NEW FACE

At this time the government's attention was again absorbed in reforming the ministerial positions. Because of his involvement with Kornilov, Savinkov was among the first to go. Kerensky had stepped down as official minister of war and now headed, still as minister-president, a five-man directorate. The other members were the minister of foreign affairs, Tereshchenko; the new minister of the interior, Aleksei Nikitin; and the ministers of war and navy. Colonel Aleksandr Verkhovskii, the young commander of the Moscow Military District who had been instrumental in suppressing the Kornilov revolt, was now made minister of war, with the rank of general and with the mission to court the support of unit committees by a program of democratization of the armed forces. Much to everyone's surprise, the new naval minister was none other than Admiral Dmitrii Verderevsky, the former commander of the Baltic fleet who had been arrested for his defiance of the Provisional Government during the July Crisis. The reestablishment of a naval minister in the government, for the first time since the February Revolution, did not affect policy formation, as that remained almost entirely in the hands of Kerensky and his closest advisers.

One of the new policies involved the announcement that Russia was now a republic. On 1 September a proclamation signed by Kerensky and his minister of justice, Aleksandr Zarudnyi, was issued:

> General Kornilov's revolt has been suppressed, but the sedition brought by him into the ranks of the army and the country is great. And once again a great danger threatens the fate of our native land and her freedom.

Considering it necessary to put an end to the outward vagueness of the organization of the State and remembering the wholehearted and enthusiastic acceptance of the republican idea at the Moscow State Conference, the Provisional Government announces that the state system by which the State of Russia is governed is republican and proclaims the Russian Republic.[55]

This move by the government immediately aroused controversy because it, perhaps unconstitutionally, removed one of the options that was reserved for the Constituent Assembly and yet did not proclaim a "democratic" republic, as the radical forces wished. This was another example of an attempt by Kerensky to compromise with the forces of the Left that failed to work.

When Aleksei Shchastnyi, the flag captain of the Baltic fleet, announced the formation of a "democratic republic" at the 3 September meeting of Tsentrobalt, the news was received with applause and with the decision to raise red flags in honor of the event.[56] But the published version, which omitted the term "democratic," was greeted by the sailors with protests; and again the *Petropavlovsk* led the way. Upon the initiative of the crew of that battleship, a general assembly of nineteen ships of the First Baltic Squadron carried a resolution on 6 September to raise red "battle flags" at 8:00 A.M. on 8 September as a sign of opposition.[57] On the following day, 7 September, the question was debated in a meeting of Tsentrobalt. A representative of the *Petropavlovsk* spoke for the resolution, arguing against the criticism from one quarter that the act could lead to a vote of confidence in the Provisional Government. Mikhail Savoskin pointed out that the ships would raise flags regardless of the action taken by Tsentrobalt and that unity could best be maintained by Tsentrobalt's support of the resolution. He added that "full trust in the Provisional Government had already broken down."[58] By a vote of 30 to 5, with 5 abstaining, Tsentrobalt passed the following resolution:

The Central Committee of the Baltic Fleet, in its session of 7 September, debated the resolution, which was carried by nineteen large ships, and resolved: considering that the decree of the Provisional Government proclaimed a Russian and not a democratic republic, in sign of protest against . . . the postponement of the introduction of republican institutions for an indefinite time, Tsentrobalt orders that at 8:00 A.M. on 8 September red flags are to be raised on the flag masts of all ships of the Baltic fleet . . . ; and they are not to be lowered until the establishment of a federative democratic republic.

An amendment was then added: "Ships receiving orders to go out to sea must lower their red flags."[59]

Despite objections from staff officers, the red battle flags appeared over the fleet on 8 September, but the next day, Tsentrobalt accepted the advice of the Sailors' Assembly of the Helsingfors Soviet to lower flags on 12 September, the eve of the Democratic Conference. A joint resolution was intended to serve as a political message to that conference:

> The Baltic fleet has raised battle flags. By this means it expresses its firm devotion and loyalty to the revolution. The fleet demonstrates its readiness to fight with all its strength for the transfer of power into the hands of the revolutionary democrats, the proletariat, and the working peasantry, and it insists before the Democratic Conference upon bringing this about. Down with compromises with the bourgeoisie! We demand the immediate transfer of all land to the disposition of land committees before the convocation of the Constituent Assembly. We demand workers' control over production. Flags must be lowered on the day of the convocation of the Democratic Conference, at 8:00 P.M.[60]

The flag incident, moreover, illustrated the ineffectiveness of the government's democratization policy, the growing confidence of the sailors, and the renewed success of Tsentrobalt's attempts to pose as the supreme authority over the fleet.

The generally tense situation and the unsteadiness of the Provisional Government caused other, rather small, disagreements to mushroom into major incidents. In mid September, Tsentroflot expanded its quarters in the Naval Ministry to include an apartment that belonged to the naval chief of staff, Captain Vsevolod Egorev. The government reacted with surprising severity by ordering that Tsentroflot be dissolved and that a new election be held.[61] Cablegrams from Verderevsky to Razvozov were monitored by Tsentrobalt, which asked the commander to make an explanation on 19 September. He attempted to dismiss the whole thing as a minor misunderstanding which should be of little concern to a fleet that was engaged with an outside enemy, but that afternoon an extraordinary session of Tsentrobalt in conjunction with the Sailors' Assembly of the Helsingfors Soviet and the representatives of eighty ships' committees debated the dissolution for five hours under the chairmanship of Pavel Dybenko, who reemerged as the sailors' chief spokesman for the first time since the July Crisis. The meeting culminated in the usual manner by adopting a resolution that strongly condemned the action of the Provisional Government, stating that it did not have the authority to dissolve an elected organization, which was an interesting and probably correct position from the soviet point of view:

> Therefore, the plenary session declares that no more orders of the Provisional Government will be executed, and its authority is not recognized; Tsentroflot is called upon to occupy its legal position as the supreme naval organization, whose orders alone the fleet obeys.[62]

The irony is that Tsentrobalt had seldom been in agreement with Tsentroflot and had demanded its reelection numerous times on the grounds that it was not democratic.

THE SITUATION IN THE FLEET AFTER THE KORNILOV AFFAIR

During September, several problems that had plagued the Baltic fleet throughout 1917 grew more serious: lowering morale of the officers; the supply of food, clothing, and fuel; the national independence movements; and the advance of the German forces. Each problem interacted with the others and thus heightened the psychological atmosphere of conflict, defeat, and political upheaval.

Government authority in a military unit depends both upon the officers who command and upon the chain of command that maintains the line of direction from a central source. The revolution had created disastrous results among the officer corps. Depletion of numbers by murder, expulsion, or escape had reduced the effective control of the officers. By September the chain of command and the morale of the officers was finally breaking down.

The Kornilov Affair destroyed the uncertain harmony that had been restored to the fleet since the February–March Revolution. The majority of officers were in sympathy with Kornilov's attempts to restore discipline in the armed forces, and they were unhappy with the Kerensky government; but despite the claims of Soviet scholars and despite the beliefs of many rank-and-file sailors at the time, very few, if any, officers supported Kornilov openly in his move against the government. Most right-wing officers had already been removed from the fleet, and those who remained were geographically isolated and too psychologically depressed to provide any encouragement to Kornilov. When Major General Pavel Dolgorukov, an emissary from Kornilov, appeared on board the *Krechet* to solicit support, he was promptly placed under arrest by the officers and was escorted back to Petrograd.[63]

From the protests and resolutions it is obvious that the sailors harbored suspicions that most of the officers were likely to support a counterrevolution if given the opportunity. The large cultural and social gulf between officers and seamen was the major reason for this enduring distrust. Understandably, the sailors were not yet sophisticated and experienced in the exercise of their newly won authority. Admiral Stanley, the British naval observer, summed up the situation in the fleet at the time of the Kornilov Affair:

> There is no doubt that the lack of discipline is deplorable. . . . The destroyers appear to be the best, and the battleships the worst, but all are bad. . . . It is a matter of doubt if any order from a higher authority which did not meet with the full approval of the Committee would be carried out. Every sailor is a politician and is swayed by the political events of the moment, and they have little or no respect for their officers.[64]

And after this came the *Petropavlovsk* episode and the furor over the "Russian republic." Prince Cherkasskii, in his most depressed mood yet, told Rengarten on 7 September: "The commanders of large ships are no more —their nerves are finally destroyed, and there is no one to relieve them. The command in the fleet is also nonexistent—no authority, no guarantees, nothing! There is only terror and emptiness."[65] Still, the staff officers were not without some hope of saving the situation. On 8 September, the day that red flags began to fly on all ships of the fleet, they drew up a petition, complaining about the unendurable conditions. According to Rengarten, this was presented to Tsentrobalt, with the result that the sailors offered sarcastically to build the officers a sanatorium.[66]

The officers decided to take their case to Petrograd, where Razvozov, Rengarten, and Cherkasskii arrived on 9 September. Razvozov recognized that he was no longer able to command the fleet, so he planned to retire in favor of Rear Admiral Pilkin or Rear Admiral Zarubaev. The staff officers agreed that Captain Ilia Lodyzhenskii, the left-leaning commander who was president of the ship's committee of the battleship *Andrei Pervozvannyi*, should replace Cherkasskii as chief of staff. The plan, therefore, involved an attempt to transfer the commanding staff into the hands of those officers who had the greatest support from the sailors. Talks with Kerensky and Verderevsky were fruitless, however, which led Rengarten to comment: "What does it matter to Kerensky? Who still considers us?"[67]

The Kornilov Affair had also resulted in new elements in the sailor "command" organizations, as well as in important experience in tactical control. The Military-Technical Commission continued its existence at Kronstadt, although it was largely inactive and was under the jurisdiction of the executive committee; whereas the Revolutionary Committee at Helsingfors was displaced by a new, more active executive committee of the Third Oblast Congress of Soviets of Finland, which met from 9 to 12 September under Bolshevik dominance. More important, however, were the new committees of outlying areas, particularly the Committee of Naval Forces of the Gulf of Riga, which had been inspired by the Bolshevik cell on the *Slava*, and the United Soviet of the Gulf of Bothnia, both of which were formed in September. These intermediate structures provided additional opportunities for communication and coordination, though their importance was far from that claimed by a Soviet assessment: "All these committees were organs through which the Bolshevik Tsentrobalt frustrated the counter-revolutionary impulse of the reactionary commanding staffs and mobilized the forces of the Baltic fleet for participation in the socialist revolution."[68]

It would appear from the above that the officers' authority had virtually ceased to exist. This conclusion should not be hastily made, however. Conditions were certainly bad, but some orders were still being obeyed. The decades of traditional respect for officers and of the performance of routine tasks under supervision were not to be forgotten overnight, or even in six months. Squadrons of small ships, and even a few large ships, continued to patrol the Gulf of Finland. Both officers and sailors at the main bases sat around telling jokes, playing guitars, singing folk songs, and passing scuttlebutt. The talk was mainly of politics—of who would win and why. Officers still had diversions, and they spent many evenings in local coffeehouses, discussing current problems. In the midst of the Kornilov Affair, on 29 August, Admiral Razvozov and several staff officers spent the evening in a Revel coffeehouse.[69] In revolution or war, those who are participating must, to some extent, go on living their daily routine.

THE "FINNISH QUESTION"

During an interview with Buchanan on 26 September, Tereshchenko held out the hope that if Russia could survive the winter, then the dissolution of Austria-Hungary would make victory possible on the Eastern

Front.[70] There were, in fact, good grounds for this ray of optimism, but the question remained as to which of the two empires was dissolving faster. The Finnish independence movement already had a head start on the Russian Revolution. Anti-Russian feelings in Finland led many Finns to volunteer for the German army, and by June 1916, over two thousand of them were training at a special camp, at Lohstadt, near Hamburg.[71] But the Russian Revolution made the course of Finnish independence more complex. As Werner Söderhjelm, a Swedish socialist, explained, "It involves the emergence of a whole class from the rearmost ranks to the foremost—a class that has been taught to distrust middle-class legislation and that is, in the main, unused to the responsibility."[72] Grievances against the stationing of large Russian forces on Finnish territory were mitigated by leftist sentiment that a Social-Democratic revolution could be won with Russian assistance.

Nevertheless, almost all Finns supported autonomy, if not independence; and the Diet, in which the Social Democrats possessed an absolute majority, passed an "Autonomy Act" during the July Crisis by a vote of 136 to 55.[73] The Provisional Government reacted by dissolving the Diet. This was followed by a series of strikes, culminating in a province-wide general strike on 1 August; the Diet defied Petrograd and resumed its sessions.[74] The British consul, Montgomery Grove, reported that the sailors could not make up their minds about what to do, "and therefore decided to keep all men aboard ships and remain perfectly 'neutral.' "[75] The Diet building was then occupied by a Cossack unit on 15 August. On that day the British consul general in Petrograd reported:

> Future events in Finland will turn largely on the attitude of the Russian garrison and fleet, who are alternately courted and reviled by their Finnish comrades. As far as one can judge from their public meetings, this attitude is fairly well defined. It is that the soldiers and sailors will back up, at least passively, any acts of disorder and violence directed against the *bourgeoisie*, but will not tolerate disobedience to the commands of the Russian Government in political matters. But there is no doubt that much of the trouble in Finland has been fomented by Germany, and the possibility of German descent by sea cannot be ignored. In that event the Finns would certainly welcome the invaders, for they are at heart pro-German, whereas the Russian, in spite of his instability and war fatigue, remains at bottom anti-German.[76]

The anti-Russian feelings of the majority of Finns was the main reason that the Russian and Finnish revolutions remained largely separate. The Russian organizations—soviets, committees, clubs, parties—were distinct from Finnish ones. Though there were frequent lectures and articles on the "Finnish question," the Russians, such as those in Tsentrobalt, assumed that Finnish autonomy or independence would be granted, but at the same time, they did not plan on evacuation. While the fleet radicals remained largely silent on the issue of evacuation, for the good reason that this would remove them from their base of power, the Finnish Social Democrats were reluctant to involve themselves in complex and uniquely Russian social and political questions.

The Provisional Government and its representative in Finland, the governor general, were caught in the middle. Lindley summarized the situation on 24 September:

> The Russian Government, as at present constituted, are not at all inclined to accept the demands of the Finns, but they are powerless to act with the troops and fleet in their present mood. Strangely enough it is the behaviour of these same troops and sailors which makes the Finns long more than ever to be entirely free from Russian control. The dirty habits and disorderly conduct of these men are a constant offence to the more civilized and cleanly Finns, and it is probably true to say that race feeling was never so bitter in the days of the old regime as it is now.[77]

THE STRATEGIC AND LOGISTIC SITUATION IN SEPTEMBER

The relations between Finns and Russians were also influenced by the decrease in supplies of basic necessities. This problem consumed more of Tsentrobalt's time in September than anything else. Winter clothing had not been issued, and an early Baltic autumn was already making its appearance. The year 1917 had also been a poor crop year in Finland. Therefore, the population was already looking forward to a hard winter, and the Baltic sailors had gained the impression that the Provisional Government was trying to starve them into submission. Probably the British conclusion that the supply and transport systems were collapsing was more correct. Commander Cromie reported on 11 September that supplies were desperately low, that no flour was left, and that the British submarines, now stationed at Hango, were sailing without adequate provisions of all kinds.[78]

By September the Baltic fleet was being squeezed from different directions. The advance of the Germans northward from Riga, as well as reports that a German naval force was headed toward the Gulf of Finland, caused considerable alarm in the fleet. The Revel base would have to be evacuated before winter, when ice could leave ships at the mercy of German armies, causing an additional concentration of forces on the north shore, in Finnish territory. As late as 8 September, at a conference with Admiral Stanley, Cromie preferred to stay in Revel and take his chances with the Germans:

> I advised Revel as our winter base if possible, largely on the account of provisioning, facilities of dockyard, but mostly because I fear rows between our men and the Russians in Helsingfors during the long winter evenings in a town where they have no friends, few amusements, and [where are located] the most truculent of Russian sailors whom they begin to despise rather openly.[79]

While many officers were still making genuine efforts to keep ships and men together, the Bolsheviks and their supporters moved to consolidate their position through the calling of a Second Congress of the Baltic Fleet, which met from 25 September to 5 October on the yacht *Poliarnaia Zvezda* in Helsingfors. The Bolsheviks, led by Dybenko, insisted, on the grounds of economy, that the number of delegates be restricted by having one representative for every five hundred sailors. Though detailed records of the congress have not been published, the Bolsheviks clearly dominated the proceedings. Of an elected presidium of seven members, four were Bolsheviks, two were Left SRs, and one was an anarchist. Dybenko was chairman, and the Kronstadt anarchist Anatolii Zhelezniakov, under the alias of Viktorskii, was the secretary (which may account for the absence of regular minutes).[80] The veteran Bolshevik organizer Antonov-Ovseenko and a leader of the Left SRs named Maria Spiridonova were the keynote speakers.[81]

The resolutions that were adopted by the congress included a demand for convening the Second All-Russian Congress of Soviets, a refusal to approve the removal of artillery from Kronstadt, insistence on the immediate resignation of Kerensky, and the immediate dissolution of the Pre-parliament.[82] Turning more to the business of the fleet, on 30 September the congress approved in substance the "Rules" of Tsentrobalt, which had been suspended in July. The wording of the preamble was quite similar to that approved by the first congress in May:

> The Central Committee of the Baltic Fleet is the highest elected organ . . . of all fleet committees of the Baltic Sea, which, together

with members of the staff, fulfills all functions of the fleet, excluding those that are purely operative and technical, which are under the authority and the responsibility of the fleet commander.

One can note, however, that there is a greater effort to placate the commander in chief with a tone of respect. In fact, the new "Rules" seem to set up another commanding staff for nonoperational matters:

> All orders, declarations, and dispositions, excluding purely operational and technical ones, do not have force without the approval of Tsentrobalt. All decisions of Tsentrobalt, pertaining to the sphere of its authority, are released in the form of declarations, which will be disseminated throughout the fleet for information and fulfillment. The execution of such declarations is obligatory for all naval units of the Baltic Sea.[83]

The real power in deciding what was operational and nonoperational and in settling disputes between officers and sailors resided in a commissar, to be chosen on each ship, with Tsentrobalt reserving the authority to name the commissar for the commander in chief. The duties of the commissars were spelled out on 2 October: to decipher all radio telegrams along with the duty officer of the ship or staff; to examine all secret packets and to guarantee their safekeeping; to refer all orders of a political nature to Tsentrobalt for decision, or, if they were of an urgent nature, to refer them to the ship's committee for resolution.[84] Further work of the congress was absorbed in a sudden flurry of naval action.

THE BATTLE OF MOON SOUND

An attack on the islands off the west coast of Estonia had been anticipated for some time, and information about the threatening movements of the German Baltic fleet was received in early September from British intelligence.[85] The German goal was clear—to silence the artillery batteries on these islands that covered the entrances to the Gulf of Riga. Then the minefields could be cleared, and sealanes could be opened into the recently captured port of Riga, for the German advance toward Petrograd was hampered by dependence upon a badly damaged and overworked railroad from Memel. With Riga as a major supply base, the front could be strengthened, and the offensive could resume. In order to accomplish this objective a substantial amphibious operation was prepared, which was to include supporting naval forces and was to involve the temporary withdrawal of two infantry divisions from the Northern Front; this, for the time being, would relieve the pressure on the main Russian land defenses. The lateness of the season probably ensured that supplies could not be built up and that the offensive could not be remounted before winter, even if the plan were successful.

The resulting Battle of Moon Sound was the largest single action in which the Russian Baltic fleet engaged during World War I. On 29 September a German force of 24,600 soldiers, under cover of a fleet of over three hundred vessels, which was commanded by Vice-Admiral Ehrhard Schmidt, landed on the north side of the island of Oesel.[86] Several German ships then deployed around the island in order to cut off the Russian shore batteries from support and to gain control not only of the strategic shipping channel, the Irben Strait, which led out of Moon Sound into the Gulf of Riga, but also of a newly dredged channel which connected the Gulf of Finland with Moon Sound. The defending Russian forces consisted of about 12,000 infantry and artillery and a naval squadron of two old battleships (the *Slava* and the *Grazhdanin*), three light cruisers, and several destroyers under Vice-Admiral Mikhail Bakhirev.[87]

The Russian land defenses on Oesel quickly collapsed, but considering the upheavals that it had undergone in 1917, the Russian fleet offered surprisingly effective opposition in Moon Sound. After several days of battle and maneuver, which reached a climax in a furious gun battle on 4 October, the fleet retreated to a second line of defense at the entrance to the Gulf of Finland. How were these revolution-ridden, outnumbered Russian ships able to fight a defensive engagement at all? According to a non-Soviet memoir, when the initial attack began, the Russian sailors refused to obey the orders of officers. But when a German squadron under the command of Vice-Admiral Behncke approached Moon Sound through Irben Strait, a remarkable change occurred in the attitude of the crews, who suddenly began to respond enthusiastically to battle orders.[88]

One factor may have been the sudden effort to cooperate on the part of the fleet's radicals, who perceived the German attack as a direct threat to their bases of influence in the Gulf of Finland. At least the new military activity now absorbed much of the attention of the Second Congress of the Fleet, where Admiral Razvozov appeared in order to appeal for assistance. According to Dybenko, he was assured by the congress that "in battle your order is law." The delegates went on to affirm: "Anyone who dares not obey a battle order will be considered an enemy of the revolution and will be shot."[89] Ironically, this warlike posture was struck by the very elements in the fleet that rose to influence on slogans opposing the war and the death penalty. And it is doubtful that the radical sailors at the congress were acting spontaneously, since a regional Bolshevik party conference, which some of the delegates also attended, was taking place in Helsingfors at the time.[90] The broadcast appeals of the congress may have been one cause of that surprising willingness to fight.

Partly on this basis, the engagement that took place in Moon Sound was later distorted by Soviet writers into a heroic legend. If the concern over the German advance provided the impetus for the cooperation of the Bolshevik-controlled sailor's organizations and the commander of the fleet, the men on the spot in Moon Sound responded more to a natural defensive esprit. Even the officers were able to rally to a central task and were able to carry out their duties, inspired by instances of truly heroic leadership; the commander of the destroyer *Grom* had to be carried off by force in order to prevent him from going down with a sinking ship.[91] And whether Bolshevik or not, the sailors were obviously affected by such examples of bravery under fire. Moreover, the squadron in Moon Sound had been on patrol for over a month, and the officers and men were both more experienced and better prepared for action than those on most of the other Russian ships.[92]

But the quality of the Russian defense should not be overrated. The Russians held a superior position behind extensive minefields. In the opinion of a high-ranking German officer, they failed to exploit fully their strategic advantage and to conduct an active defense.[93] The main German objective was, after all, accomplished. Furthermore, the Russians lost the battleship *Slava* and the destroyer *Grom*, although before the latter sank, a senior machinist, Fedor Samonchuk, managed to maneuver the vessel into a position that would block the channel. The artillery batteries on the islands surrendered without much opposition, but the Germans also suffered heavy losses—serious damage to two dreadnoughts and two large transports by mines and the loss of several smaller ships.[94] Moreover, the back door to the Gulf of Finland through Moon Sound was still covered by Russian guns on the Estonian coast. According to Admiral Scheer, this discouraged any further German naval advances that year.[95] The Germans remained especially wary of the Russian mines, and they exercised caution because of their own recent trouble with discipline—a few abortive mutinies had occurred in

August at the Baltic base of Wilhelmshaven. And it would still take weeks of tedious minesweeping to open the Gulf of Riga to shipping.

The fighting off the Estonian coast added one more dimension to the tension and strain between the government and the Baltic fleet. As the German attack developed, on 29 September, Kerensky issued an order to the commander of the Northern Front which failed to conceal his feelings toward the fleet: "Tell the Baltic fleet that the terrible hour of trials has come to it. . . . It is time to collect one's senses, and one must stop playing, wittingly or unwittingly, into the hands of the enemy." And after commenting that the men of Kronstadt were shirking their duty, Kerensky concluded: "Let the atrocious crime of the *Petropavlovsk* be expiated, and let the navy, under the command of its officers whose supreme love for their native land is known to all of Russia, repel the enemy with speed."[96] Such a tone could not help but arouse bitterness among the sailors, and the final proclamation of the Second Congress of the Baltic Fleet contained the reply: "We will fulfill our duty. We will fulfill it not by order of some kind of pitiful Russian Bonaparte, reigning by grace of a long-impatient revolution. . . . We will execute the supreme command of our revolutionary consciousness." The strongly worded declaration concluded: "Raise the banner of revolt! Long live the world revolution! Long live a just, general peace! Long live socialism!"[97]

The German success in capturing the islands provoked more alarm in Petrograd, where ministers of the Provisional Government openly discussed moving to Moscow on 4 October.[98] Rumors of surrender and betrayal were soon circulating in the fleet, but there is no evidence to support the Soviet claim that officers were conspiring with Kerensky to surrender Petrograd to the Germans. One could more easily charge the Bolsheviks with having used the German approach for their own propaganda purposes against the government.

Nevertheless, it is true that the Russian commanders did not react as effectively as they might have. Captain Cromie of the British submarine squadron was especially upset that he could not get orders to move his ships into the action. In diary form he recorded his frustration:

[1 October]—No news of any plan of action on the part of the C-in-C, nor can I find any signs of concerted movement on the part of other admirals.

[3 October]—No telegrams or information received today, and I

161

find we are working on the same information as the newspapers get, usually 24 hrs. old.

[4 October]—No plan of action for the submarines has yet been received from the C-in-C, . . . The position calls for the gravest alarm, and I fear that the major part of the Russian forces in the Moon Sound will be lost.

[5 October]—Admiral Valdislavleff commander of submarines cannot be found, consequently the leader of the first division, Captain Doutkin, and myself have taken charge jointly. It is believed that the Admiral has committed suicide as there are no traces of him.

[7 October]—There is still no definite plan of defense, but the C-in-C expects to give battle with his big ships as the enemy try and force the outer minefields.[99]

Cromie's straining at the leash certainly proves that the British navy was not part of a conspiracy to surrender Petrograd, as some Soviet commentators absurdly claim.

The Battle of Moon Sound was a clear indication of the German intention to continue the offensive on the Northern Front, but also, to those who scrutinized the situation more closely, it was evidence of enemy supply problems which would give the Russians a respite, probably until spring. But as the war pressure in reality relaxed, the revolutionary tensions continued to mount. Three weeks after the sinking of the battleship *Slava* by German guns, the cruiser *Aurora* would fire on the Winter Palace.

7

THE BALTIC FLEET
IN THE OCTOBER REVOLUTION

THE BATTLE OF MOON SOUND occurred in the middle of a period of intense political activity in the Baltic region, which culminated in the calling of the Second All-Russian Congress of Soviets and the coup d'état staged by Bolshevik-led forces against the Provisional Government. Of major importance to the outcome of these dramatic events were the strategy and tactics of the radical opposition leadership, in particular Lenin, of the government, and, to a lesser extent, of the Allies.

The radical mood of the majority of the sailors of the fleet was made clear by the selection of delegates for committees, conferences, and congresses; in the membership of local soviets; and in the resolutions passed by these organizations and by the many ad hoc meetings and assemblies on ship and on shore. But did these views register with party leaders? Why didn't the government act more decisively against this open display of opposition? How did the Allies, particularly the British, react to the political and military situation in the eastern Baltic? What influence did sailors actually exert in the crucial decisions that preceded the "Great October"? Finally, just how significant was sailor support to the Bolshevik victory in Petrograd?

The most important political development in the Baltic area in 1917 was not so much the steady and overwhelming rise of the Bolsheviks' strength as the decline of that of their socialist opponents. The regular Socialist Revolutionary and Menshevik parties, especially because of the identification of leaders such as Chernov and Tsereteli with antifleet positions and with the Provisional Government, were caught in a vortex of rising leftist and rightist political currents, worsening military and economic situations, and declining credibility. From the beginning, it is true, the Bolsheviks devoted more attention to the fleet than did their rivals, sending enthusiastic and experienced organizers—Raskolnikov, Roshal, Zhemchuzhin, Stark, Antonov-Ovseenko—to the major fleet bases at Kronstadt and Helsingfors. The round of arrests in July brought replacements—Flerovskii and Breslav to Kronstadt and Ivan Smilga to Helsingfors. None of the central organizations of other parties devoted such attention to the fleet. The achievement of all these Bolshevik efforts remains open to question, however. The rank-and-file sailors were still free to choose from among the various radical positions—Bolshevik, Left Socialist Revolutionary, anarchist, nonparty. Bolshevik membership in the fleet does not appear to have increased much, perhaps none at all, between July and October. In fact, in comparison with some other areas of the country, Bolshevik support was stagnating in northwest Russia in September. Among a selected list of soviets that showed considerable Bolshevik membership in September and October, the Kronstadt Soviet had a surprisingly low percentage of Bolsheviks: Saratov, 60 percent; Minsk, 54 percent; Samara, 40 percent; Revel, 40 percent; Kronstadt, 30 percent.[1]

This does not mean that the radicalism of the Baltic fleet was declining just before the October Revolution. On the contrary, hostility towards the Provisional Government was stronger than ever. Simultaneously, the non-Bolshevik radicals—anarchists, Menshevik-Internationalists, and especially the Left Socialist Revolutionaries—were growing in strength, but none of these were exactly opponents of the Bolsheviks. All were handicapped by intellectual ideologies that few sailors understood and by the inability to achieve broader objectives after being in power positions (in the fleet) for several months. The Left Socialist Revolutionaries, in particular, could appeal directly to the land-and-peace psychology of the sailors; but they were also victims of an ideology, one which caused them to concentrate on agrarian issues to the neglect of the more immediate problems of power and authority, and they lacked a strong central organization and enough experienced agitators.

The Bolsheviks, on the other hand, had been able to build up a solid nucleus of leaders, a working organization that gave them considerable electoral advantage and, at the same time, an ability to pose as the elder brothers of the revolutionary movement in the fleet, those who could best lead a successful coalition against the Provisional Government. They were careful to avoid clashes with their allies, allowing, for example, a Left Socialist Revolutionary to be president of the Kronstadt Soviet during the month of October. The other parties simply could not match the radical reputations of seasoned leaders such as Lenin, Trotsky, and Sverdlov, nor the organizational experience of Antonov-Ovseenko and Dybenko. When the latter was chosen chairman of the fourth session of Tsentrobalt on 16 October, it was not because of an increase in Bolshevik membership on the committee, but because he was the "traditional" leader, the obvious choice.

ASSEMBLIES FOR REVOLUTION

The Bolsheviks in the Baltic area exercised their organizational supremacy particularly in dominating a series of congresses and conferences held in September and October. These meetings served not only to maintain revolutionary fervor among the participants but also to establish communications within a geographical area and to provide contacts and experiences for local leaders. They were, in fact, indispensable for promoting participation of the fleet in the October Revolution.

The first such congress during this intense period of organization was the Third Oblast Congress of Soviets of the Army, Navy, and Workers of Finland, meeting from 9 to 12 September in Helsingfors. Notwithstanding the name and location of the conclave, this was an entirely Russian affair with no Finns included. Almost half (63) of the 128 voting delegates were registered as Bolsheviks, but following a common pattern, Bolsheviks predominated in the new Oblast Committee, which was selected at the congress: 37 Bolsheviks, 26 Left SRs, and 2 Menshevik-Internationalists.[2] Aleksandr Sheinman, who would soon become the Bolshevik chairman of the Helsingfors Soviet, presided over the congress. The new head of the committee was Ivan Smilga, one of the few Bolsheviks who had regular contact with Lenin during his "exile" in Finland. Dybenko and Antonov-Ovseenko played a leading part in enlarging the power and scope of the Oblast Committee. By a vote of 97 to 4, with 7 abstaining, the congress declared that "the political line of the Oblast Committee had been distinguished by a lack of control," causing it to lose ground in the revolutionary movement in Finland. A Bolshevik resolution that was designed to correct this fault passed by a narrower margin of 74 to 44; it stated that "power must be transferred into the hands of the proletariat and the poor peasantry."[3] On 20 September the Oblast Committee decided to establish "the most vigilant control" over the central-government institutions in Finland, in order that "not one disposition of the Provisional Government could be fulfilled without its consent."[4]

The Second Congress of the Baltic Fleet, which was meeting at the end of September and early October, was overshadowed to some extent by the Battle of Moon Sound; but at this congress also the Bolsheviks, led by Dybenko and Antonov-Ovseenko, controlled the proceedings. The influence of the new Oblast Committee of Finland was also notable, as it was in the smaller Second Congress of the Forty-second Separate Army Corps, which met in Vyborg on 2 October.[5] During the congress of the fleet, from 28 to 30 September, the First Oblast Conference of the RSDRP (b) in Finland convened, with sixty-five delegates representing a membership of nine thousand.[6] So frequent and overlapping were these meetings that local Bolshevik leaders must have had a difficult time keeping up with the demands of congresses and conferences.

On 5 October the First Conference of Soviets of the Petrograd Guberniia met at Kronstadt, which was hardly neutral ground. Only three out of forty voting members from such outlying towns as Sestroretsk, Peterhof, Gatchina, Narva, Luga, and Schlüsselburg opposed a resolution that called for the withholding of support from the Provisional Government and the transfer of power to the soviets. Little is known of the proceedings, but the predominance of Kronstadt Bolsheviks is evident from the election of Ivan Flerovskii as chairman and Ludmila Stal, secretary of the Kronstadt Bolshevik Committee, as vice-chairman.[7] Organizers hand-picked the most likely delegates, who, if one can believe Trotsky, "took the very highest note set by the tuning-fork of the Baltic sailors."[8]

The procedure for selecting delegates to these meetings was far from democratic. This is particularly true of the most important "convention" to be held immediately before the October Revolution, the Congress of Soviets of Northern Provinces, which met in the Smolny Institute in Petrograd from 11 to 13 October, after being postponed and moved from Helsingfors. Though most of the delegates came from the Baltic littoral—Petrograd, Revel, Helsingfors, Kronstadt, Vyborg, Narva—some represented Moscow, Arkhangelsk, and the Southwestern and Rumanian fronts. Almost one-third (thirty) were from Petrograd, and the Bolsheviks, of course, claimed a majority: there were fifty-one Bolsheviks, twenty-four Left Socialist Revolutionaries, ten Right Socialist Revolutionaries, four Mensheviks, and one Menshevik-Internationalist, by one count.[9] The few Mensheviks, led by

Boris Bogdanov, walked out during the first day. Nikolai Krylenko, a Petrograd Bolshevik and army officer, became chairman, with L. L. Kallis (a Left Socialist Revolutionary from Kronstadt) and Dybenko as his assistants. Boris Breslav, the Bolshevik leader at Kronstadt, was one of the secretaries and a chief source of information on the congress. He claimed that over 90 percent of the delegates were in favor of giving immediate power to the soviets.[10] Under the obvious influence of the northern military centers, the congress passed one Bolshevik resolution after another and set up an executive committee—of eleven Bolsheviks and six Left SRs—that included Krylenko, Dybenko, Antonov-Ovseenko, and Raskolnikov.[11] The last-named came directly to the congress from the Kresty prison and became the head of the Organizational Bureau of the committee. The congress attracted considerable attention in Petrograd, but the statement of a Soviet scholar that "this was an extremely representative forum, expressing the will of many millions of workers, soldiers, and peasants," is obviously an exaggeration.[12]

Few top-echelon Bolshevik leaders attended these regional meetings, because they either were in hiding (Lenin) or were too busy with other duties, although Trotsky appeared as the keynote speaker at the Congress of the Northern Soviets.[13] While these radical congresses served as excellent vehicles to dramatize Bolshevik strength, to prepare for the Second All-Russian Congress of Soviets, to propagandize by resolution, and, most importantly of all, to improve lines of communication between the various local soviets and committees, they could also influence the policy of behind-the-scenes radicals as well as that of the government. In the final analysis, they could not create a revolution, but could only reflect a growing demand for it.

THE GOVERNMENT ON THE EVE OF REVOLUTION

The interaction of policy formulation and events is one of the most fascinating aspects of 1917. Rebounding from the Kornilov Affair, Kerensky steered the Provisional Government in a policy of closer cooperation with the moderate Left—the Mensheviks and Socialist Revolutionaries, who composed the forces of "revolutionary democracy." Supported by the Central Executive Committee of the First All-Russian Congress of Soviets, he sponsored the Democratic Conference, which met in Petrograd from 14 to 22 September, and its successor, the Democratic Council of the Republic (Preparliament), which continued in session until the Bolshevik occupation of its headquarters in the Marinsky Palace on 25 October. The two most critical problems, besides their own credibility, that the government and its allies faced were the military situation and the rising radicalism of local soviets. Together they presented an enigma, for the solution of one seemed to be blocked by the other. How to get out of this impasse was the big question faced by the leaders of the Provisional Government during the last six weeks of its existence.

Consistency in policy, moreover, was not one of the strong points of the Provisional Government. While Verkhovsky and Verderevsky pursued a plan of cooperation with unit committees in order to bolster combat efficiency in the army and navy, other high-ranking officers favored more direct methods of reestablishing discipline along the lines that Kornilov had followed. And Kerensky kept the door ajar for such a course by treating Kornilov and his supporters leniently and by approving a more specific project that was drawn up at the end of September by Rear Admiral Kapnist of the Naval General Staff for the evacuation and disbanding of the most radical units at Kronstadt.[14] Implementation of the project, however, would have required a sizable military force, thus reviving the question of the loyalty of army units to the Provisional Government, interfering with the effort to bolster the Northern Front, and risking both the provocation of a civil war in the region of the capital and another Kornilov Affair. Success was still conceivable in the confused and complex Russian situation, but the government's overreaction to the German activity in the Estonian islands at the beginning of October led to consideration of the opposite course—removing the government to Moscow and abandoning the whole area to the Germans. The Battle of Moon Sound was thus influential at a critical time when a show of force might have stemmed the tide of opposition in local soviets. By highlighting Russia's military vulnerability, the German action reduced the government's options, or rather, it postponed the coming wintertime relaxation by several weeks.

The continued drift of government policy toward building a democratic front, basically a policy of appeasement, did not inevitably lead to the Bolshevik seizure of power. There were the possibilities that the Bolsheviks, too, would lose steam on their own accord (and signs of that were appearing) or that one round of congresses and conferences would simply be followed by another indefinitely, that radicalism would eventually weaken by being overexposed, much as had the Provisional Government itself. The growing moderation of some of the most visible Bolshevik leaders in the capital—in particular, Kamenev and Zinoviev—lent support to the premise that the mechanics of organization and the formality of speeches and debates in open forum were reducing revolutionary action to words. The exposed tip of this radical iceberg deluded many in the government who believed that it indicated the shape of things below. The configuration of radical policy was eventually determined, however, by Kerensky's chief opponent, who had not been "visible" since July; but that individual was also under the influence of events and conditions of the Baltic area.

LENIN AND THE BALTIC FLEET

Vladimir Lenin spent several quiet weeks in Finland in August and September, out of range of the police and army units that were still loyal to Kerensky. For about a month (about 17 August to 17 September) he was in Helsingfors, some of that time in the apartment of the chief of the city militia, Gustav Rovio. Most of his contacts were with Finnish Social Democrats, and apparently no more than three Russians besides Krupskaya—Ivan Smilga, Boris Zhemchuzhin, and Vladimir Antonov-Ovseenko—knew of his presence.[15] Lenin, however, received a steady supply of information through reading the Russian-language newspapers, especially *Priboi* and *Sotsialist-Revoliutsioner*, and from conversations with Finnish leaders and with Smilga and Zhemchuzhin. Though the Bolshevik leader did not appreciate the Kronstadters' enthusiasm for revolution in May, June, and July, he could now see that the "Kronstadt line" was not as isolated as he had once thought, that ultra-radical sentiment was strong among Russians based in Finland too. But he was also concerned that the situation could change through German conquest of the Gulf of Finland or, even worse, that the same thing would happen to the Bolsheviks as had already happened to the Mensheviks and Socialist Revolutionaries: namely, that their followers would go elsewhere.[16]

After the Kornilov Affair the Petrograd and Moscow soviets passed antigovernment resolutions and came under the effective control of the Bolsheviks. The radical attitude of the Third Oblast Congress of Finland and the raising of red flags on the ships of the fleet (which Lenin could probably see from Rovio's apartment) from 8 to 12 September dramatized the fact that Bolshevik influence was not confined to Petrograd and Moscow. The question now became how to maintain and expand this momentum. A decided note of urgency for seizing power appeared suddenly in Lenin's writings. It appeared in a sharply worded pamphlet, "The Threatening Catastrophe and How to Fight It," which was penned between 10 and 14 September in Helsingfors. And one of Lenin's briefest yet most consequential messages, not published until 1921, was in the form of a letter to the Central Committee of the party in Petrograd. A few excerpts will illustrate the Bolshevik leader's new mood in mid September.

> Having received a majority in the Soviets of Workers and Soldiers Deputies of both capitals [Petrograd and Moscow], the Bolsheviks can and *must* take state power into their hands. . . .
> The majority of the people are *behind* us. . . .
> Why must the Bolsheviks take power *now*?
> Because the forthcoming surrender of Piter makes our chances a hundred times worse.
> But we do not have the forces to prevent the surrender of Piter by the armies headed by Kerensky & Co.
> And it is impossible "to wait" for the Constituent Assembly, since by the surrender of Piter, Kerensky & Co. *can ruin* it. Only our party, by seizing power, can assure the meeting of the Constituent Assembly. . . .
> Only our victory in the capitals can bring the peasantry behind us. . . .
> To wait for a "formal" majority for the Bolsheviks is naïve; not a single revolution waits for that. And Kerensky & Co. do not wait but prepare to surrender Piter.[17]

Two recurring themes in Lenin's letter are the spread of Bolshevik influence beyond Petrograd and the threat of the surrender of the capital.

This message and another one, which attempted to connect the call for an uprising to Marxist theory and to prescribe, as an example, the specific steps required for gaining control of Petrograd, were carried by Smilga to Petrograd on 15 September, where they caused something of a sensation in the Central Committee of the party, which generally opposed a risky attempt to seize power on the streets.[18] But if the radical sailors of the fleet had known of Lenin's views, their reaction would have been: "It's about time!" And Lenin, from his reading and conversations with Smilga and others, must have known this. On 17 September, Lenin hurriedly left Helsingfors for Vyborg to prepare for an appearance in Petrograd. There Lenin turned to the practical problems of seizing power. On 27 September he wrote to Smilga from Vyborg:

> It seems, uniquely, that we have in our *complete* control that which will play a *serious* military role—the Finnish troops and the Baltic fleet. I think that you must take advantage of this, shift all of the minor and routine work from yourself to your aides and secretaries in order not to waste time on "resolutions," and devote *all your attention* to the preparation of the Finnish troops and fleet for the approaching overthrow of Kerensky. Create a *secret* committee from *reliable* troops, discuss with them *in detail*, gather (and examine *yourself*) exact information about the composition and disposition of troops around Piter and in Piter, and the transport of Finnish troops to Piter, and about the movement of the fleet, etc.[19]

The Battle of Moon Sound reinforced Lenin's conviction that the Germans definitely meant business in the North, and it increased his suspicions that Kerensky would make a deal with the Germans that would include a "policing action" by German units in the Petrograd area. In Moscow, Michael Rodzianko, former president of the Duma, stated publicly on 8 October that the surrender of Petrograd would not be a serious loss since most of its military production went to the Baltic fleet, which would be surrendered anyway. This caused a furious reaction in the left-wing press.[20]

Lenin's plans for an insurrection now depended heavily upon the Baltic fleet. In his instructions to the Bolshevik delegates to the Congress of the Northern Soviets—which were written on 8 October, probably the day after his return to Petrograd—Lenin reiterated Marx's dictum that "insurrection, like war, is an art," adding: "In the application of this to Russia and to October 1917 this means: a simultaneous, sudden and swift attack on Piter is possible both from outside and from inside, from the workers' quarters and from Finland, from Revel, from Kronstadt, an attack of *the whole* fleet, an accumulation of *giant preponderant* forces. . . ."[21] Among the "three chief forces" to occupy the telephone, telegraph, and railroad stations and the bridges, Lenin listed the fleet first: "To encircle and cut off Piter, to take it by the combined attack of the fleet, workers, and soldiers—such is the task that demands *art and threefold daring*."[22]

On the same day, Lenin issued a longer statement which denied that "the Baltic fleet, in going to Piter, would open this front to the Germans." The fleet was already enveloped, he argued, by Kerensky's decision to surrender Petrograd to the Germans:

Only the immediate movement of the Baltic fleet, Finnish troops, Revel, and Kronstadt against the Kornilov troops around Piter can save the Russian and world revolutions. . . .

The fleet, Kronstadt, Vyborg, Revel can and must go to Piter, defeat the Kornilovite regiments, arouse both capitals and stir up mass agitation for power, the immediate transfer of land to the peasants, and the immediate negotiation of peace, in order to over-throw the government of Kerensky and to bring about this power.[23]

Ironically, Lenin's thinking bears some similarity to that of some of the leaders of the February Revolution—action was necessary in order to save Russia from defeat by German armies which were aided and abetted by a corrupt, treasonous government. Timing was crucial, and on this point Lenin was not clear. Lenin was convinced, according to Trotsky, that the uprising had to take place before (the implication being just before) the meeting of the Second All-Russian Congress of Soviets, which was originally scheduled for 20 October. But a number of ranking Bolsheviks opposed this on the grounds that meager military support made such a move risky and that the soviets must literally take power themselves, not have it handed to them. It is possible, therefore, that Lenin exaggerated his perception of the military situation in order to convince them of the necessity of an earlier strike. He probably also calculated that the uprising must begin before the winter freeze would immobilize the Baltic fleet. It is also quite possible that Lenin actually believed in the German threat and in Kerensky's pur-ported plan to surrender Petrograd while, at the same time, he was using them for his own revolutionary ends. He was, nonetheless, as much a victim of rumor and propaganda as anyone else in Russia, perhaps more so because of his relative isolation during August, September, and part of October.

Another important addition to Lenin's strategy may have been influ-enced by his Finnish environment in September and early October—his realization of the value of support from sympathetic radical groups. In the above-mentioned letter to Smilga, Lenin emphasized the necessity of making use of allies in order to win the allegiance of the peasantry. Stressing the importance of agitation in the countryside, Lenin advised Smilga to send out teams consisting of one Bolshevik and one Left Socialist Revolutionary.[24] He also asked for copies of Helsingfors' Left Socialist Revolutionary news-paper. According to Podvoisky, Lenin also insisted on including the left-wing SRs in the Military Revolutionary Committee that was set up by the Petrograd Soviet; and its first chairman, Petr Lazimir, was, in fact, a Left

Socialist Revolutionary.[25] The unique strength of the Left Socialist Revolutionaries in the Baltic ports may have given Lenin the impression that a tidal wave of peasant radicalism was sweeping the countryside.

Baltic sailors were indeed active in the Russian countryside in the late summer and early fall of 1917, but their influence is not easy to assess. One can only note that they were present in nearly every province and that "news from the villages" was a daily feature in the radical press of the Baltic area. In some places, notably in the bases of the Black Sea fleet, the *baltiitsy* caused major disruptions; these failed, however, to bring about a significant, lasting political shift. Others were apparently more successful. In early October, Pavel Khokhriakov, a Bolshevik sailor from the battleship *Zaria Svobody*, led a small group of Baltic sailors to Ekaterinburg. A Soviet scholar praises his role in organizing a local Red Guard and in advancing the Bolshevik cause in that important Ural industrial center.[26] In Kronstadt and Helsingfors, sailors' organizations actively discussed the "land question," promoted contacts with villages by sailors on leave, and set up special agrarian sections. Naturally, the Left Socialist Revolutionaries were most active in this sphere, so much so that by October they were neglecting urban affairs, leaving those to the Bolsheviks.

As Lenin apparently overestimated the growth of organized peasant radicalism in Russia, he also badly misread the military situation. After the Battle of Moon Sound had proved that the sailors of the Russian Baltic fleet could still fight and that minefields remained a formidable obstacle to an advancing fleet, the German high command called off additional offensive operations on the Northern Front. A British naval staff report of 13 October stated: "It is possible that the German main operations in this direction have ceased for the winter, and it is understood that they are relieving part of their land forces, leaving only garrisons in the Islands, and the more powerful ships of their fleet are being replaced by battleships and cruisers of older type."[27] In fact, things were rather quiet on the Northern Front.

The monthly report of the American military attaché indicated a considerable shift of forces away from the Russian Front in October. Of a total of 156 divisions of the Central Powers in this sector on 18 September, 143 remained a month later. Most of the ones that moved were German (six and one-half) and Austro-Hungarian (four and one-half) infantry divisions, with the remainder apparently being Turkish units. German divisions on the Northern Front had been reduced from fifteen and one-half on 28 September to eleven, including two divisions on the Baltic islands, on 18

October.[28] Germany was taking advantage of Russian military weakness and disorganization in order to strengthen other fronts, particularly the Western Front, in anticipation of an American build-up. Petrograd was definitely out of danger of German capture until spring, and this realization was bolstering the spirit of the Provisional Government. Some now thought that there would be an opportunity to gather reliable forces and to rally the republic behind the Constituent Assembly. Lenin and Kerensky continued on two different tracks, the one now sounding the alarm from inside and outside, the other gaining confidence and considering the possibility of peace overture to Germany (see below), on the one hand, and of a show of strength against the Bolshevik-led radical forces, on the other.

THE BRITISH PERSPECTIVE

Much still depended upon the Allies, who really did not know what to do. Kerensky and his leading emissary, Tereshchenko, begged for an increase in military and supply assistance. They could not understand why the British navy did not crash through into the Baltic while the Germans were tied up in the Battle of Moon Sound.[29] Where were the promised supplies—shoes, boots, food, and so forth? At a conference of ambassadors on 28 September, which was reminiscent of Buchanan's famous interview with the tsar in January, Kerensky berated his allies for lack of support. As Buchanan reported the scene, Kerensky read a speech denouncing the assembled company for retarding the shipment of war material, then he jumped up, waved his arms, and rushed out of the room.[30] Perhaps this time his theatrics were justified, for the Allies, especially the French, opposed sending much-needed guns to Russia, where they might easily fall, unfired, into the hands of the Germans.

And the British Foreign Office, having clumsily backed Kornilov, still lacked confidence in Kerensky. Lord Hardinge of Penshurst wrote (on 10 October) to Buchanan that there were rumors that Kerensky was in the Germans' pay, and Harold Nicolson reported (on 17 October) that a friend who had just returned from Russia had assured him that Kerensky was just waiting for the opportune time to throw his lot in with the Bolsheviks.[31] Buchanan replied that there was not a word of truth in these reports: "He has shown great weakness and vacillation in past owing to his socialist leanings but I believe that he is as Minister of Foreign Affairs [Tereshchenko] once assured me, 'an honest man.' "[32]

The Russian government was making strong hints about a separate peace. Tereshchenko and Verkhovsky, the minister of war, both warned the British that Russia could not stay in the war for another year under present conditions.[33] Somerset Maugham reported (too late to make any difference) that Kerensky had told him on 18 October that Germany would not accept his first peace offer, but after that he (Kerensky) believed that a trimmed-down army would be more willing to fight—if properly equipped by the Allies.[34] Though the British, who were hard-pressed financially and militarily, remained skeptical of investing any more in Russia, the United States was becoming more involved, thanks mainly to British pressure. Large shipments of supplies were arriving in Vladivostok, Murmansk, and Arkhangelsk. On 22 October, Secretary of State Lansing notified the British ambassador in Washington that the president would consider sending a contingent of American troops to Russia.[35] A large force, everyone recognized, could not be adequately transported and supplied in Russia. Moreover, Buchanan, for one, was quite dubious about the growing American presence in Russia and about what this indicated for the future.[36] His general pessimism even led to a suggestion that the British government buy off the Bolsheviks as he thought the Germans were trying to do.[37] A variety of different-minded people were all groping toward the same conclusion—that Russia could not fight any longer. The question was becoming more and more how to make, or to prevent, a separate peace. But a de facto end of the war in Russia was bringing about the situation that Kerensky had predicted in September—namely, chaos.

Captain Cromie left his submarines for a quick tour of the Northern Front in mid October. He found everything in nearly a complete state of collapse:

> General Vicheroff (45th div.) informed me that the Skazelski Regt. and one other stationed at Hapsal had totally destroyed 47 estates and farms in the last 10 days, driving off or killing the live stock and destroying such corn as was not ground. Several murders have occurred, and the troops are completely out of control. . . . The number of divisions or regiments is no indication whatever of the troops available. The estates are being abandoned in fear of the soldiers, who pillage and burn everywhere: the country is full of wandering soldiers for the most part without arms.[38]

Neither the Provisional Government nor the Bolsheviks could count on much support from units on the Northern Front.

A high-level conference was held at Revel on 21 and 22 October; it was attended by the governor general of Finland, the minister of the navy, the commander of the Northern Front (General Cheremisov), and the commander of the Baltic fleet. Pessimism reigned. Even Cromie, who must have been beyond shock by now, might have been surprised to learn of the message that Verderevsky proposed to send him: "We thank our allies for the help and service they have given us. Our power of resistance has collapsed; we can no longer accept your services. The Baltic fleet has ceased to exist. Do what you think best with your submarines; we shall give you what assistance we can."[39] The minister was right with respect to what the government could expect from the fleet.

THE FLEET PREPARES FOR REVOLUTION

The remaining officers who were on duty with the fleet waited in complete frustration, with the distinct impression that a crisis was approaching. Many thought that a Bolshevik attempt to seize power would coincide with the convening of the Second All-Russian Congress of Soviets, which was originally scheduled for 20 October.[40] In contrast to the apparent inactivity on the government side, the revolutionaries were very busy organizing and reorganizing committees, commissions, and delegations during the last two weeks before the congress. Communications, transportation, and disposition of troops and weapons—all created problems for the leaders of the insurrection. Besides, they also had to devote time and energy to two complex elections—for delegates to the congress and to the Constituent Assembly.

In early October the Second Congress of the Baltic Fleet chose fourteen delegates to the Second All-Russian Congress of Soviets: ten Bolsheviks, two Left Socialist Revolutionaries, one anarchist, and one Right Socialist Revolutionary.[41] The official fleet delegation was thus initially weighted 13 to 1 against the government, including a number of well-known representatives of the Baltic fleet—Dybenko, Khovrin, Zhelezniakov (the lone anarchist), and Baranov. But after the fleet delegates arrived in Petrograd on 19 October, they decided, in agreement with some of the Black Sea delegates, to prohibit the seating of members of Tsentroflot, which was still too "sympathetic." Tsentrobalt was asked to make up the difference, so it added three more delegates—Bolsheviks Pavel Malkov and Pavel Raimo, and Left SR Pavel Sutyrin—all of whom were members of Tsentrobalt.[42] In addition, the Oblast Committee of Finland selected three Bolsheviks and two Left SRs on 17 October; therefore, with the Kronstadt Soviet sending three of its leaders—Flerovskii, Iarchuk, and Rivkin—the Baltic "vote" in favor of revolution rose to 24 to 1, without counting either the three Baltic sailors whose names were "mysteriously" found on the delegate lists or the heavily Bolshevik delegation of seven men from Revel.[43] Obviously the representatives of the Baltic fleet were neither systematically nor democratically elected, but they did reflect the general attitude of the fleet.

Unlike the choosing of delegates to the congress, the election campaign for the Constituent Assembly received wide publicity in all fleet newspapers in October. Although the Bolsheviks lacked a central organization that corresponded to the electoral district, which comprised all naval and army units under the commander of the Baltic fleet, they had little difficulty in selecting their candidates. In the number one spot on the electoral list was "Ulianov, Vladimir Ilich (N. Lenin)," and in second place was Pavel Dybenko. The petition, which contained two hundred signatures, apparently solicited by the Bolsheviks of Tsentrobalt, was submitted to the electoral commission by 12 October.[44] The Left SRs chose Prosh Proshian and Pavel Shishko; the Right SR's, Tsion and Maslov; and the officers, Demchinskii and Rengarten.[45]

For Russia in 1917 it was not ironic that an intense election campaign would coincide with preparations for a military coup d'état. Until the actual event, the election was more certain than the revolution. Although at the historic meeting of 10 October, Lenin was able to convince the inner core of the Bolshevik Central Committee of the necessity for the uprising, many leading members remained reluctant and cautious. Nikolai Podvoisky and Vladimir Nevsky, of the important Military Organization of the party, remained opposed and were somewhat aghast at facing the problems of a tactical seizure of power.[46] As far as the fleet was concerned, the prime movers, besides Lenin, were Sverdlov and Trotsky. Sverdlov conferred with Dybenko at the time of the Congress of Northern Provinces, and they made tentative plans for bringing sailors from Helsingfors to support an uprising in Petrograd.[47]

Upon returning to Helsingfors, Dybenko attended an assembly of representatives from ship and unit committees at which Alexandra Kollontai spoke on "the structure of Soviet power" and concluded by jokingly inviting the assembly as "guests" to Petrograd.[48] Tsentrobalt reorganized on 16

October with a clear Bolshevik majority. The next day the following declaration was issued:

> Ship's committees of battleships and cruisers, and also of shore units composed of more than 200 men, are instructed to form permanent battle platoons which can be at the disposition of Tsentrobalt upon notice. Inform Tsentrobalt exactly about the formation of platoons, naming the platoon commanders. The Military Section of Tsentrobalt will be instructed on technical affairs. Note: On those ships and units where there are no arms, inform Tsentrobalt precisely.[49]

An alternate organization of the fleet was being created, because the leaders realized that the sailors who participated in the revolution would have to be ready for land combat.

This problem was also being faced simultaneously at the highest level in Petrograd. A secret conference of the party's military "experts"—Podvoisky, Nevsky, and Antonov-Ovseenko—and Lenin was held on the night of 17 October. At this meeting, Antonov-Ovseenko assured the group of the Baltic fleet's readiness for action, but Nevsky pointed out the impossibility of moving the larger ships through the minefields from Helsingfors, noting that most of the sailors would have to come by train to Petrograd. Lenin insisted that a way be found to bring warships to the capital. The next day, Nevsky departed for Helsingfors to check on this problem, and Antonov-Ovseenko made a brief tour of the Petrograd coastal area.[50]

The Bolshevik leaders in Petrograd assumed that Kronstadt was ready to take part in a move against the Provisional Government. They may, in fact, have been overconfident; when Raskolnikov came to Sverdlov for an assignment, expecting to be sent back to Kronstadt, Sverdlov told him that he was not needed there, and dispatched him instead to Luga.[51] The Military-Technical Commission, which had first been organized during the Kornilov Affair, had been revamped by 10 October to include representatives of the political parties; but as a result, it became large and unwieldly and included a larger proportion of non-Bolsheviks than was the case in Helsingfors. Petr Smirnov, a Bolshevik party organizer, soon emerged as its head; but since a smaller number of sailors at Kronstadt were assigned to ships, control was harder to maintain. Many Kronstadters were wandering about the Petrograd area, some recruited by Red Guard units to instruct them on how to fire the weapons that they were now receiving in large numbers,

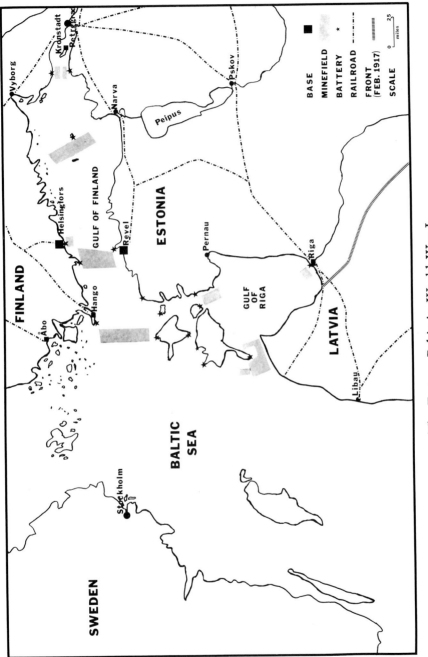

The Eastern Baltic in World War I

SWEDEN

FINLAND

Vyborg

Kronstadt
Petrograd

Abo

Helsingfors

Hango

GULF OF FINLAND

Narva

Peipus

Pskov

ESTONIA

BALTIC
SEA

Stockholm

Revel

Pernau

GULF OF
RIGA

Riga

LATVIA

Libau

BASE ■

MINEFIELD

BATTERY ★

RAILROAD –·–·–·

FRONT
(FEB. 1917)

SCALE

0   25
miles

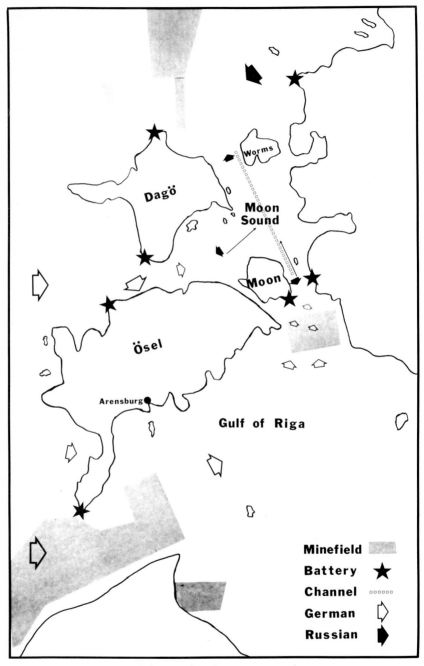

Minefield

Battery ★

Channel ⬚⬚⬚⬚⬚

German ⬦

Russian ◗

The Battle of Moon Sound

thanks to the collapse of government control over the Sestroretsk arms warehouses.[52]

Weapons for the naval centers became a belated concern in mid October. For various reasons—government precautions, carelessness, losses during the July Crisis, "donations" to Red Guards—the sailors were not well armed in October. On 18 October the Military-Technical Commission discovered that the weapons inventory of the Kronstadt naval base included only 920 Russian rifles, 1,811 Japanese rifles, 16 machine guns, 10 Berdan rifles, and 9 revolvers.[53] The artillery fortresses had many more, so they were immediately approached, as were the depots in Petrograd.

A similar situation prevailed at Helsingfors earlier, but Tsentrobalt's success in obtaining arms from the Sveaborg arsenal during the Battle of Moon Sound had relieved the situation. Then Nikolai Izmailov was also able to bring back from Petrograd 3,000 rifles, 500 machine guns, 1,000 revolvers, and a large quantity of ammunition. These were not used at the time but were stored in case of future need. Izmailov returned for more weapons on 19 October.[54]

By 20 October, preparations were advancing in both Kronstadt and Helsingfors, though relatively little "art" and "daring" were being demonstrated. Petrograd was another matter. Fortunately for the Bolsheviks, who were trying to adhere to Lenin's timetable, on 17 October the Central Executive Committee announced the postponement of the opening of the All-Russian Congress until 25 October, giving them five more days in which to get ready. Convinced that the revolution should not be accomplished purely by party organizations, Lenin placed responsibility for it on a Soviet military leadership that included Left Socialist Revolutionaries and other allies but was closely linked to the military-revolutionary center of the party. Details had been worked out and approved by the Soldiers' Section of the Petrograd Soviet on 13 October, helped along by a rousing speech of a guest Baltic sailor, Dybenko. But the Military Revolutionary Committee officially met for the first time only on 20 October, under the chairmanship of Lazimir, who soon proved to be a figurehead for the Bolshevik directors, Trotsky, Podvoisky, and Antonov-Ovseenko. There was still little overall coordination and planning, the Military Revolutionary Committee serving less as an organizing body than as a cover for extraordinary powers for individuals.[55] That is, it provided a stamp or letterhead that would impress garrison and Red Guard units in the capital. Like other special committees or commissions of this period, it increased rapidly in size, quickly losing the ability to perform its original functions.

Events were now building to a climax, overtaking everybody. The Bolsheviks and their allies were committed to an armed uprising on the streets of Petrograd. The Provisional Government expected it; some ministers even hoped for it. At a ministerial conference on 17 October there were suggestions, especially from Tereshchenko and Kishkin, that the government take the offensive, but they were firmly opposed by other ministers, particularly the military ones—Verkhovsky and Verderevsky. The fighting capability of troops in the vicinity of Petrograd was obviously a consideration, but the Provisional Government was continually plagued by dissension and confusion. On the nineteenth, Tereshchenko, a veteran supporter of Kerensky, told Knox that the minister-president should be replaced. The next day, Verkhovsky advised the Defense Commission of the Council of the Republic that only a military dictatorship could save the situation but that, in any event, Russia would have to sue for peace. After an uproar in the press over these statements, the minister of war resigned on the twenty-second. Though the "Verkhovsky affair" may have affected the Provisional Government's response to the mounting threat, Kerensky was also waiting for a scheduled military conference, which was held on the twenty-third and was attended by the commander of the Northern Front, Cheremisov, who came directly from the depressing meeting in Revel that was witnessed by Rengarten.[56] Finally, the government struck, early in the morning of 24 October, seizing the presses that published the two Bolshevik newspapers of the capital, *Rabochii Put* and *Soldat*, and ordering the confinement of garrison units to their compounds and the arrest of members of the Military Revolutionary Committee. As usual, execution of the scheme left much to be desired.

Meanwhile, the side of revolt stumbled through delays and confusion. It took time to organize a staff, appoint commissars, collect vehicles, and issue weapons; and one day, Sunday the twenty-second, had already been preempted as the "Day of the Petrograd Soviet," which was to be celebrated with parades, assemblies, and speeches all over the city. Interrupting these festivities would be awkward, and it was also logical to wait until this additional opportunity for agitation among the workers and soldiers had passed. Nearly everyone now expected a showdown on the twenty-fifth.

ON THE EVE

Communications continued to be a big problem, even with all of the central revolutionary organizations gathered at the Smolny Institute. Even before the lines were cut to Smolny on 24 October, the telephone and telegraph seemed to be regarded with suspicion, perhaps with good reason, considering the confusion that had been created by telephone conversations during the July Crisis. Sverdlov went out to Kronstadt himself on 21 October to see how matters stood, and on the twenty-second, Antonov-Ovseenko sent sailor Vasilii Marusev of Tsentroflot to Helsingfors to see what was going on. From the twentieth to the twenty-fourth the main line of communication between Petrograd and Kronstadt seems to have been a little cutter, the *Ermak*, on which Aleksei Pronin, who had also been quite active in the February Revolution, and Stepan Grediushko went back and forth. It was small enough to go under the bridges and to dock right at Smolny; also, it attracted little attention, except for one poorly aimed fusillade from Nikolaevsky Bridge. The message for Kronstadt was: "We don't need you yet but be ready."[57] A golden opportunity to issue more explicit instructions to Kronstadt was apparently missed on the afternoon of the twenty-fourth, when Flerovskii and Iarchuk ambled into Smolny to register as delegates to the congress. Trotsky came across them, however, and he ordered them to return to Kronstadt immediately, but without elaborating any details.[58]

Actually, Kronstadt had already been alerted, along with all other units in the Petrograd vicinity, by the radio of the cruiser *Aurora*. Various naval, Red Guard, and garrison units in the Petrograd area sent representatives to a meeting called about midday on the twenty-fourth by the Military Revolutionary Committee. During the afternoon, commissars were appointed to these units, most of whom were trusted Bolshevik or Left SR agitators from among the delegates who appeared at Smolny. The Kronstadt base, as usual, took care of its own local appointments. But the delegation of special powers tended to displace the existing committee structure. From the Military Revolutionary Committee there emerged a "troika" of Podvoisky, Antonov-Ovseenko, and Chudnovsky which was to lead the tactical operations of the seizure of power. At Kronstadt the executive committee appointed a "military staff" to displace the unwieldly Military-Technical Commission; this staff consisted of Bolsheviks Flerovskii and Smirnov, Left Socialist Revolutionary Kallis, and anarchists Iarchuk and Grimm. Apparently by coincidence, another "troika" sprang up in Tsentrobalt in Helsingfors—Dybenko, Izmailov, and Averichkin—all of whom were Bolsheviks.[59]

As the climax approached, centralization of authority became more and more the order of the day, but spontaneously rather than following a preconceived plan. Individuals, by virtue of their positions and personalities—especially Sverdlov, Trotsky, and Podvoisky—often acted independently in completing the crucial arrangements to call in armed forces—from Kronstadt, Helsingfors, the cruiser *Aurora*, and so forth—on the evening of the twenty-fourth (at the last possible moment to be effective for the twenty-fifth), before Lenin's surreptitious and unexpected appearance at Smolny about midnight.[60]

What one did during these hectic hours depended much on circumstances. For example, Aleksei Mokrousov, who could "unofficially" be counted as a Baltic sailor, became the first official Soviet censor somewhat by accident. A miner from the Donets Basin who had been recruited for the Baltic fleet before the war, he was arrested for revolutionary agitation in 1912. But he escaped, went abroad, and after adventurous travels through Scandinavia, Argentina, and Australia, returned to Russia in the summer of 1917 by way of Manchuria. The Russian consul there assigned him to the Sevastopol naval base. Partly because the political mood in the Black Sea fleet did not suit him, Mokrousov journeyed northward to visit his old shipmates in Helsingfors. He happened to be passing through Petrograd on his way back to Sevastopol on 23 October, so he decided to delay his trip in order to watch the revolutionary excitement. On the evening of the twenty-fourth he ran into Leonid Stark, a leading member of the Helsingfors Bolshevik committee, and Mokrousov helped Stark to organize a detachment of two hundred sailors to take over the Petrograd Telegraph Agency, Russia's main link with the outside world. After driving off the small guard about 9:00 P.M. and negotiating with the director, they allowed the telegraphers to resume operations. Since Mokrousov knew English, Stark handed him a large red pencil and designated him as censor: "The Bolsheviks must control not only rifles but also the pen and pencil, especially here and now. Take this pencil and strike out all lies, anything that is against the revolution, that would harm it. Don't pay any attention to the complaints of correspondents. If necessary communicate with Smolny. Here is your telephone." Mokrousov worked without relief all night and throughout the twenty-fifth, rejecting a Reuters dispatch that reported a repulse of the Bolsheviks in front of the Winter Palace, but approving an American story that the Bolsheviks had won (before the Winter Palace had fallen). He was relieved in time to attend the first session of the Second All-Russian Congress, and then he returned to the Black Sea.[61]

Meanwhile, one important thing was accomplished by the little *Ermak*. After the closing of the Bolshevik press, a call to arms was sent by the Bolshevik publishing house Priboi to Kronstadt for printing, and two thousand copies were delivered to Petrograd on the evening of the twenty-fourth. As if the arrival of these proclamations were a signal, Smolny finally issued the awaited directives. Podvoisky told Pronin:

> The Kronstadters must be in Petrograd tomorrow afternoon to march against the Winter Palace. The Kexholm regiment and other units will assist them. The *Aurora* will be in place on the Neva at Nikolaevsky Bridge in case we need her guns. However, all this is spelled out in the order of the Military Revolutionary Committee, which is in this packet; you must be sure to get this to Kronstadt safely.[62]

The Kronstadt Executive Committee, although only one-third of its members were Bolshevik, had voted unanimously on the afternoon of 24 October to support a call to arms. At a special session that night the committee authorized "the creation of seven detachments, apart from ships, numbering not less than 1,000 men each," but detailed arrangements had to wait for the arrival of Podvoisky's packet on the slow cutter from Petrograd, which arrived about 3:00 A.M. on the twenty-fifth.[63]

ENTRY OF THE CRUISER AURORA

By this time a larger ship—the cruiser *Aurora*—was getting into action. Perhaps it is indicative of Russia in 1917 that government officials did not fully awaken to the fact that there was a sizable warship, manned by a radical crew, lurking at the entrance to the Neva in Petrograd—until 22 October. The *Aurora*, which had finished mounting new guns and engines, was then ordered "to go on trials" to Helsingfors. The ship's committee refused to carry out the directive unless it was approved by Tsentrobalt, which, of course, countermanded the order. Another effort, by a couple of armored cars, to drive the cruiser away on the morning of the twenty-fourth was notably unsuccessful.[64]

At about 11:00 A.M. on the twenty-fourth, Aleksandr Belyshev, chairman of the ship's committee, received a message from the Military Revolutionary Committee, requesting that two representatives be sent to Smolny. He and another sailor crossed the city on foot to the revolutionary headquarters, where they met Sverdlov. Belyshev was officially designated commissar of the ship just after noon. His "document" read, "Comrade Belyshev is delegated as commissar of the Military Revolutionary Committee of the Petrograd Soviet of Workers' and Soldiers' Deputies for the cruiser *Aurora*." Belyshev replied to Sverdlov, "The decision of the party is for me an order,"[65] with some apparent confusion of party and soviet. The new commissar then returned to the *Aurora* to await further instructions.

The revolutionary leaders were puzzled about what to do with a cruiser at first. In the early evening of the twenty-fourth, with the crucial Palace and Nikolaevsky bridges still controlled by junkers (cadets), someone, perhaps Vasilii Zakharov, thought of bringing the cruiser up the river to Nikolaevsky Bridge in order to overawe the defenders and to inspire the attackers. Orders were issued at Smolny at about 7:00 P.M.,[66] but when they reached the *Aurora* sometime between 8 and 9 P.M., the commander of the vessel, Lieutenant Nikolai Erikson, refused to carry them out, claiming that the shipping channel of the Neva had not been dredged since the beginning of the war and was too shallow to allow the cruiser to pass. Belyshev then took command, locked Erikson in his cabin, and sent a member of the committee ahead in a small boat to take soundings. Other sailors set off to find tugboats to pull the ship away from its moorings.[67] Apparently, no one had thought of making these arrangements in advance.

After the tugboats had tied on, the engines had been started, and soundings had been taken to assure that the channel was deep enough, Lieutenant Erikson informed the sailors that he would guide the ship up the river after all, in order to prevent the inexperienced crewmen from running the ship aground. With a light snow falling, the cruiser *Aurora*, a survivor of the Battle of Tsushima, inched its way up the river in the early hours of the morning under the helm of Erikson, a man who had been regarded as one of the best navigators in the navy; and she dropped anchor in the middle of the Neva, directly downstream from Nikolaevsky Bridge, at 3:30 A.M. Shortly afterwards, the "junkers" abandoned the bridge to sailors of the Second Baltic Fleet Depot Troop, while the whole scene was illuminated by the searchlights of the cruiser.[68] As dawn broke on the twenty-fifth and the sun shone briefly through the clouds, the still quiet warship signified to those who saw her that the denouement was at hand.

THE ARRIVAL OF OTHER NAVAL DETACHMENTS

Although the cruiser *Aurora* was of real psychological impact and although it was immediately designated, along with Peter and Paul Fortress, as a field command center for the revolt, it had not furnished many men to the leaders of the uprising, and that was what they needed at the moment. Sailors of the guard and depot troops in Petrograd; soldiers of the garrison, especially the Kexholm and Pavlovsky regiments; and assorted Red Guards were controlling the bridges, guarding Smolny and the Bolshevik printing plant, and patrolling the streets. During the morning the Pavlovsky regiment occupied Kresty and liberated the Bolshevik leader Semen Roshal, while a detachment of the Second Baltic Fleet Depot Troop, under the command of Kronstadter Ivan Sladkov, occupied the port area, including the chief Petrograd radio transmitter, "New Holland." Shortly after noon, sailors from the Naval Guard Depot Troop helped to seize the Marinsky Palace and to depose the Council of the Republic. Especially valuable in strategic police actions were the Second Baltic Fleet Depot Troop, which was augmented to three thousand by the survivors of the Battle of Moon Sound, and the Kexholm regiment, which was directed by Commissar Artemii Liubovich from Kronstadt. Men from both of these were engaged in one of the few serious, or potentially serious, confrontations of the daylight hours in defending the telephone center against an attack by a few cadets who were led by the government's chief army commissar, V. B. Stankevich.[69]

The first contingent of three thousand Kronstadters sailed up the Neva at approximately 2:00 P.M. on transports, training ships, and the heavy (3,000-ton) minelayer *Amur*; they received a loud welcome from the crew of the *Aurora*. These men were at the moment a more useful addition to the revolutionary forces than the cruiser, especially since they were familiar with the Petrograd streets and had been placed under direct command of the Military Revolutionary Committee. Supervising the landings on both sides of the Neva was Ivan Flerovskii, one of the "unsung heroes" of the Bolshevik Revolution. The *Amur* also symbolized something more, since she was a recently battle-tried veteran of the Battle of Moon Sound and since she mounted seven 120 mm. guns and eight heavy-caliber machine guns. Several smaller vessels accompanied the *Amur*, so that there was quite a flotilla gathered around the *Aurora* by the evening of the twenty-fifth. They included another, older minelayer, the *Khoper*; the training ships *Afrika* and *Vernyi*; the *Zarnitsa*, an old imperial yacht which had been converted to a hospital ship and was still flying a Red Cross flag; two small minesweepers; and several transports and barges. Because Flerovskii was on it, because of its heavy armament, and because its shallow draft permitted mooring near the right (north) bank of the river, the *Amur* became the Bolsheviks' naval headquarters (instead of the *Aurora*) during the seizure of power. All of these vessels were manned by full crews, including officers who, in the case of the *Amur*, passed the time telling stories about the Russo-Japanese War, as if what was currently happening reminded them of that disaster.[70]

Soon after the arrival of the Kronstadt "armada," Antonov-Ovseenko came aboard the *Amur* to relay the plans for the capture of the Winter Palace that he, Pavel Malkov, and Lazimir had drawn up on behalf of the Military Revolutionary Committee. Upon a signal from Peter and Paul Fortress (a flag at half-mast would be raised to full-mast), the *Aurora* would fire three blank shots as a signal for a general attack upon the palace.[71] The theory behind this relay of signals was that the forces that were being massed around the Winter Palace had no adequate means of communication. A six-inch gun of the cruiser would produce an unmistakable sound that everyone could hear for coordinating a mass surprise attack. Psychologically, the attackers' courage might also be strengthened by the belief that they had heavy artillery behind them, whereas that of the defenders would weaken. If the attack failed, live ammunition would be fired from Peter and Paul Fortress and then by the cruiser if necessary.

The plan was not very well worked out in regard to details, and when Antonov-Ovseenko saw the battle-ready *Amur*, he was anxious to move it under the bridges into position opposite the Winter Palace. But unfortunately, the current was too swift for a safe passage, and Nikolaevsky Bridge was in the line of sight from where the *Amur* was anchored.[72] The planners were then surprised to discover that Peter and Paul Fortress contained only ceremonial cannon and a few rusting museum pieces. Like many Russian generals on campaign, the revolutionaries found themselves woefully short of artillery. This caused frustrating delays, and the troops around the Winter Palace grew more impatient. In the meantime it was learned that the armaments of the *Aurora* would not be much good except to make noise.

The six-inch guns would cause much more damage than the leaders desired and, more importantly, could not be fired with accuracy, especially at night, since the guns were new and the sights had not been aligned. The *Aurora* might destroy much of the city before it hit the Winter Palace from its awkward position down river, and a bad overaim could even hit the Smolny Institute. A gun crew from the *Aurora* was sent to Peter and Paul Fortress to see what they could do with the old guns at point-blank range.[73]

This allowed time for more naval forces to go into action. The old training battleship *Zaria Svobody* dropped anchor in the shipping channel between Petrograd and Kronstadt in order to control sea traffic and to train its guns on the Baltic Railway along the coast, which led to the Northern Front. The Seventh Kronstadt Detachment (of about seven hundred men), under commissar Breslav, landed near Oranienbaum on the afternoon of the twenty-fifth. After some confusion, owing to a lack of maps, the sailors captured an officers' school, a quantity of weapons, and a train; and they also accomplished their main objective—securing the railway and telegraph stations along the Baltic line. Posting guards along the way, the Seventh Detachment provided one of the major successes for the revolutionaries that day, and it arrived at the Baltic station in Petrograd at 8:00 p.m., in time to take part in seizing the Winter Palace.[74]

The Helsingfors sailors met with more difficulty on the road to the Winter Palace. After the prearranged signal—a telegram reading "Send Regulations"—reached Helsingfors at about 8:00 p.m. on the twenty-fourth, men prepared to board trains and ships for Petrograd. Collecting cars and assembling arms and supplies consumed time; and the main railroad station in the center of the city saw a turmoil of activity throughout the night. In three echelons on separate trains, four thousand Baltic sailors departed at 3:00, 5:00, and 8:00 a.m.[75] Extra precautions were taken with the ships, since many sailors feared that they would be torpedoed by loyal submarines. After some awkward negotiations with Admiral Razvozov, which were conducted by Dybenko, it became clear that the admiral would do nothing to stand in the way. Soon after 9:00 a.m. a small squadron consisting of two modern "Novik" destroyers, the *Zabiiaka* and *Samson*; two smaller torpedo-boat destroyers, the *Deiatelnyi* and *Metkii*; and the guardship *Iastreb* set off across the Gulf of Finland.[76] Besides their regular complement of officers and men, the ships carried additional contingents from other ships as well as an extra supply of arms. Only the two destroyers would reach the capital that day, however, while the trains, which were normally faster, encountered obstacles (sabotage?) and did not arrive until the next day.[77]

THE SIEGE OF THE WINTER PALACE

While the sailors from the main fleet base were in transit, those in Petrograd were preparing for the final showdown with the Provisional Government. During the afternoon, various revolutionary forces in the capital re-formed, some of them being Kronstadt detachments at the Kexholm barracks. They then began to take up positions around the Winter Palace in the evening about 6:00 P.M. Three field command posts directed the activity, one at Peter and Paul Fortress, under Podvoisky; one at the Pavlovsky barracks to the east of the Winter Palace, directed by Konstantin Eremeev; and the third, in charge of Grigorii Chudnovsky, in the barracks of the Second Baltic Fleet Depot Troop. The Kronstadters served as a unifying thread in the siege, being deployed in detachments at the key points in the extended semicircles that reached to the Neva on both sides of the palace. The Fourth Kronstadt Detachment, consisting mostly of sailors from the First Baltic Fleet Depot Troop, moved from Vasilevsky Island through the Petrograd Side to join Red Guard units from the Vyborg District at the Troitsky Bridge, from where they moved along the Neva toward the Winter Palace. Two more Kronstadt detachments, including twelve hundred men of the Student Mine Detachment, formed one of the important salients behind the General Staff Arch, directly across the Palace Square. Another detachment, along with a large contingent of sailors from the Second Baltic Fleet Depot Troop, held positions at the end of Nevsky Prospect, while the remaining units from Kronstadt completed the encirclement to the Neva, one even being deployed across Palace Bridge to the area around the Academy of Sciences on Vasilevsky Island.[78]

The total number of sailors involved in the siege was at first about six thousand but increased to over ten thousand as the night wore on. About an equal number were in Red Guard units that were important especially for morale purposes—to show that the workers of Petrograd supported the action—but were relatively useless for actual combat. And another third of the total were soldiers, chiefly from the Pavlovsky (on the east side) and Kexholm (on the west side) regiments and from the Kronstadt garrison.[79] Strategically placed in command positions in these units were several veterans of revolution in the fleet: Anatolii Zhelezhniakov, Vladimir Zaitsev, and Ivan Sladkov. The Baltic sailors represented the largest bloc of relatively disciplined and trained combat forces that was at the disposal of the leaders of the uprising, and almost all sources, both Soviet and non-Soviet, attest to their crucial importance.

Even though the Winter Palace was defended by only twenty-five hundred men and women, most of whom were cadets from various military schools in the Petrograd area, the attack was still delayed. Besides general confusion in communications, the reason was that the leaders hoped to achieve a bloodless victory; and indeed these tactics were rewarded with a trickle of defections in the early hours of the confrontation, though an initial ultimatum to surrender was rejected. Another cause of hesitation and delay was the absence of the Helsingfors sailors, whom Lenin and Antonov-Ovseenko had counted on as valuable reinforcements. Whether they now still believed in the need for these additional forces or simply were influenced by preconceived notions of a battle plan is not clear. Perhaps they only wanted them not to miss a commitment to revolutionary action. Anyway, at about 7:00 P.M., Antonov-Ovseenko dispatched an urgent telegram to the Baltic base: "Awaiting regulations. No information whatever."[80] Almost immediately afterwards the first Helsingfors contingent, a hundred sailors from the battleship *Respublika*, arrived on the destroyer *Samson*, along with the information that larger forces were somewhere between Helsingfors and Petrograd.

Shortly after this, while Aleksandr Nevolin was leading a detachment of the crew of the *Aurora* along the Admiralty Gardens about eight o'clock, he heard gunfire from the square, and then he met some retreating and wounded sailors from the Kronstadt Machine School who had been prodded into an initial sortie by their commissar, Zhelezhniakov, but had been repulsed by hand grenades.[81] The battle had begun, probably simply from impatience, but it was quickly halted for another round of parleys. Under the murky Baltic sky, with a cold, gusty wind at their backs, the sailors resumed their tedious vigil.

Darkness had necessitated a change in signal plans, and further delay resulted when awkward difficulties were encountered in trying to run a lighted lantern up the flagpole in Peter and Paul Fortress.[82] Finally, at 9:40 P.M., there was a loud explosion, and a flash of light lit up the sky over the Neva. "The cruiser *Aurora* by the thunder of its guns [*sic*], directed at the Winter Palace, announced the beginning of a new era—the era of the Great

Socialist Revolution," as an official Soviet version describes the event.[83] On the square, loud hurrahs were followed by a period of sustained gunfire. The cruiser's shot had proven to be as loud as everyone expected; it had caused considerable consternation among the defenders in the palace and was one factor in encouraging the defection of a thousand cadets about 10:00 P.M.[84] But a cautious attack was repulsed again. Then the field guns of the fortress opened fire on the beleaguered palace. Though several witnesses attest to hearing a sizable barrage, not more than three shells actually hit the Winter Palace, most of the others apparently being blanks.[85]

Soon after midnight the combination of infiltration, especially on the weakly defended Neva side, and general assault across the square brought what was left of a desultory defense of the Provisional Government to an end. After a confusing period of milling around in corridors and up and down stairways, the remaining ministers were captured; they officially surrendered to Antonov-Ovseenko at 2:10 A.M. A guard of sailors escorted them to Peter and Paul Fortress for safekeeping, but not without difficulty in the confusing melee of drunks and undisciplined, reveling groups.[86] Despite some reports at the time, apparently few acts of violence were committed against the last defenders of the palace, and in the early hours of the morning the first train load of Helsingfors sailors, under the command of Tikhon Grishin, arrived at Finland Station. Having missed most of the excitement, they now performed valuable guard duties around the palace.

The Second All-Russian Congress of Soviets, which opened in the middle of the attack on the Winter Palace, at 10:45 P.M., could now officially "receive" the power that had been won for it by the coup d'état. But to describe the events in Petrograd in October either as a carefully arranged military operation,[87] or as a series of fortuitous accidents, ignores both the role played by the Baltic sailors and the history of the revolutionary movement in the fleet. The sailor-revolutionaries of 1917 possessed the political wisdom that is acquired by survival through crises; the patience and endurance that is gained by the many hours logged in committees, conferences, assemblies, soviets, and congresses; and the esprit that comes from years of association with men and machines. For them the October Revolution was only the climax of a long period of intense radical agitation and organizational activity. Some had worked toward this goal most of their adult lives. Few dreamed that this was only the beginning skirmish of a disastrous civil war.

8

THE BALTIC FLEET
AND SOVIET POWER

FROM A BROAD PERSPECTIVE the clumsy and confused maneuvering in Petrograd from 24 to 26 October scarcely punctuated a tumultuous year of unrest and disorder that witnessed the supplanting of one weak provisional government by another. The new executive that was approved by the Bolshevik-controlled Second All-Russian Congress of Soviets—the Council of People's Commissars—possessed only the authority that could be sustained by propaganda devices and the limited and fragmented armed forces at its disposal. It was, however, given a decided boost by early positive measures, especially the decrees concerning land and peace that were presented by Lenin and then acclaimed by the congress. But was this "Great October Socialist Revolution" what Marxists had envisaged as the initial stage of the world proletarian revolution?

To many of the Baltic sailors, the events of October were not so much a new revolution as an extension of the revolution of February, which had been strengthened and consolidated in the fleet, and a recapture of the birthplace of that event. They believed, so far as their primitive political consciousness would allow, that they were acting in the best interests of the masses of the people of Russia and of the common man throughout the world. To be sure, their limited knowledge of political realities and their isolation, which had been enforced by the war, narrowed their perspectives and made them naïve accomplices to the Bolshevik "crime" of changing the course of Russian and world history. This is not to say that the sailors were unwitting dupes of power-hungry Bolsheviks, but that they were allies in a common cause, and they still possessed the freedom of action and the capability—for at least a few more months—of withholding their support to the new government, as they had to the old one. That they would not, in fact, do so was because both Bolsheviks and sailors were trapped by the myth that they were the vanguard of a truly democratic socialist revolution.

The question of whether the Baltic sailors represented a genuine proletarian "voice" is obviously complicated by their possession of a revolutionary discipline that was far in advance of that possessed by Russian workers. As Trotsky so succinctly wrote: "In working out the plans of the insurrection, Smolny rested great hopes on the Baltic sailors as a fighting detachment combining proletarian revolution with strict military training."[1] In other words, the battle capability of the sailors made it possible for Smolny to plan and carry out a "proletarian" seizure of power. Or as S. P. Melgunov, another shrewd analyst of the October Revolution, put it: "The soldiers were peasants; it was the sailors who, in the class concept of Bolshevik Marxism, represented the proletariat, déclassé to be true."[2] In any event the Baltic seamen had been a major factor in the Bolshevik success in October, not so much for their numbers as for their superior experience, discipline, and enthusiasm and for the impressive war equipment—from rifles to destroyers and cruisers—that they delivered to the cause of revolution.

Granted the sailors' important contribution to the seizure of power in Petrograd, their role was perhaps even more important in protecting the new government. "Truly devoted to the revolution,"[3] the Baltic sailors formed the backbone of the Soviet offensive and defensive operations during the first few months of power, when the weapons of the Baltic fleet, literally, became the critical fire power for the new regime.

During the first few days after the fall of the Provisional Government, the sailors were widely dispersed in and around the capital in small groups, some providing essential guard services, but most being disorganized and leaderless. The leaders of the revolution were naturally concerned about effective management of these forces, especially after the results of the previous day. Between sessions of the congress, Sverdlov summoned one of the Bolshevik sailor delegates, Ivan Vakhrameev, to the third floor of Smolny, where Lenin conferred with them about creating a new Naval Revolutionary Committee to act as a central directorate in the Admiralty. The ninety-one sailor-delegates to the congress then hastily met in an assembly to formally initiate the institution; to elect eleven of their members to it, with Vakhrameev as chairman; and to declare the dissolution of Tsentroflot, several of whose members had sided with the anti-Bolshevik opposition.[4]

But when reports arrived on the twenty-seventh that Kerensky was preparing forces for a counterattack on the capital, Lenin could not wait for the new committee to proceed with the awkward process of taking over the machinery of the old naval ministry; instead he conferred directly with leaders of the fleet—with Izmailov at Tsentrobalt in Helsingfors by direct telegraph and personally with Aleksei Pronin and Raskolnikov of Kronstadt at Smolny. To Izmailov, Lenin revealed his ignorance of naval capabilities by insisting on the passage of battleships up the Neva.[5] Lenin's direct methods, however, were instrumental in the dispatch of fresh detachments from the Baltic bases. At Kronstadt, Pronin quickly put together a force of over three thousand who were armed with machine guns and field guns, while the destroyer *Pobeditel* set off from Helsingfors to Revel, whence it accompanied the cruiser *Oleg* to Petrograd.[6] On the afternoon of the twenty-ninth the *Oleg* anchored beside its sister ship, the *Aurora*, in the Neva. By that time, several smaller ships—destroyers and minelayers—had taken up positions in the river, a few going on up beyond Petrograd to assist in the occupation and defense of the region to the east of the city.

THE BATTLE OF PULKOVO HEIGHTS

Another vital reinforcement to the revolutionary forces of Petrograd was the arrival, on the morning of the twenty-eighth, of the dynamic and experienced leader of Tsentrobalt, Pavel Dybenko, who was quickly appointed an associate people's commissar of defense for naval affairs in the new government; he was to be responsible for assuming overall command of the sailors and for spearheading the defense of the city against the small force that Kerensky had assembled under the command of General Petr Krasnov. After reports of the occupation of Gatchina, which was 25 miles to the south of Petrograd, various navy, army, and Red Guard detachments were being hurriedly dispatched to take up positions astride the main road from Gatchina at Pulkovo Heights.

As Dybenko and Antonov-Ovseenko were preparing to depart from Smolny for the front on the twenty-eighth, two American journalists, John Reed and Albert Rhys Williams, happened along and talked themselves into going in the same car. As Williams tells the story, Dybenko had not eaten since departing from Helsingfors the day before by train, so they stopped at a small food store to pick up some sausage and bread, but it turned out that

193

neither "commissar" had any money. The Americans bought the food, and they were on their way again; but soon the car broke down. Dybenko commandeered a passing automobile that was bearing an Italian flag, and in this they motored on to the front, passing many leaderless groups of workers and soldiers, to whom Dybenko repeatedly shouted: "The sailors are coming!" Near Pulkovo they encountered a better-organized Red Guard unit which was digging trenches but had no weapons. Antonov-Ovseenko started to write out an order, but he discovered that neither he nor Dybenko had paper and pencil. Again the Americans came to the rescue.[7]

After returning again to Smolny to report and to quicken the paces of the Kronstadt detachments, Dybenko returned to Pulkovo the next morning to supervise, with the assistance of Semen Roshal, the final emplacements of forces on the strategically important Pulkovo Heights. These forces included at least twenty-four hundred Kronstadt sailors, fifteen hundred sailors from Helsingfors, and several hundred more from other naval units in the Petrograd area.[8]

Fortunately for the makeshift Soviet army under the general command of Antonov-Ovseenko and Konstantin Eremeev, the attackers on the morning of the thirtieth were few in number and also were lacking in coordination and courageous leadership. A Cossack charge was nonetheless quite spirited, and only the steadiness of the defensive right flank, where the sailors were concentrated, prevented a breakthrough that might have forced the new government out of Petrograd. The sailors, who were heavily armed and well supplied with reserves of food and medicine, proved to be extremely valuable in this first serious combat test of the new regime. Quite fittingly, it was Dybenko who led the rout of what remained of Krasnov's army and who negotiated a surrender in the palace at Gatchina.[9]

The outcome of the "battle" of Pulkovo Heights was especially crucial to the existence of Lenin's new government, since a counterattack by opposition groups that remained in the capital, which were taking advantage of the absence of so many of the pro-Soviet units, had resulted in the seizure of a number of strategically important points around the city on the twenty-ninth, including the telephone and telegraph centers. Though Smolny and the Winter Palace may also have been vulnerable, despite the hasty defense organized by Pavel Malkov, control of the Neva, which was maintained by cruisers and destroyers, provided a definite bastion that could only be taken by substantial forces, which were not available in or around Petrograd. The failure of Krasnov's Cossacks to reach the city also dealt a psychological

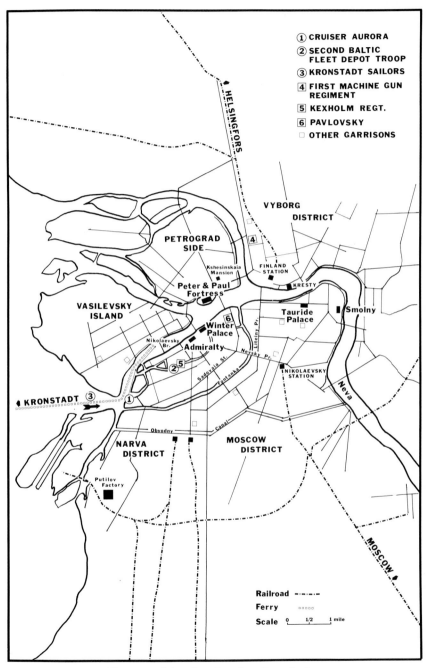

① CRUISER AURORA
② SECOND BALTIC
 FLEET DEPOT TROOP
③ KRONSTADT SAILORS
④ FIRST MACHINE GUN
 REGIMENT
⑤ KEXHOLM REGT.
⑥ PAVLOVSKY
☐ OTHER GARRISONS

HELSINGFORS

VYBORG
DISTRICT

PETROGRAD
SIDE

Kshesinskaia
Mansion

FINLAND
STATION

④

KRESTY

Peter & Paul
Fortress

VASILEVSKY
ISLAND

⑥
Winter
Palace

Tauride
Palace

Smolny

Nikolaevsky
Br.

Admiralty

Liteiny Pr.

Nevsky Pr.

② ⑤

Sadovaia St.

Fontanka

KRONSTADT ③

①

NIKOLAEVSKY
STATION

Neva

Obvodny

Canal

NARVA
DISTRICT

MOSCOW
DISTRICT

Putilov
Factory

MOSCOW

Railroad —·—·—
Ferry   □□□□□
Scale   0   1/2   1 mile

Petrograd in the October Revolution

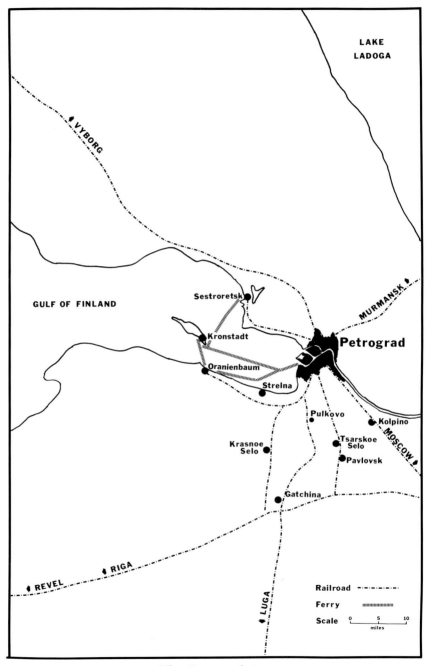

LAKE
LADOGA

VYBORG

GULF OF FINLAND

Sestroretsk

Kronstadt

Oranienbaum

Strelna

MURMANSK

Petrograd

Pulkovo

Kolpino

MOSCOW

Krasnoe
Selo

Tsarskoe
Selo

Pavlovsk

Gatchina

REVEL

RIGA

LUGA

Railroad
Ferry
Scale   0   5   10
              miles

The Petrograd Area

blow to the anti-Bolshevik cause in the city, and sailor reinforcements again led the way in reestablishing Soviet authority over the inner city. Some accounts, Melgunov's in particular, stress Bolshevik vulnerability; they blame mismanagement and lack of coordination of the opposition for failure to reverse the "decision" of 24–26 October, but they also ignore the practical difficulty of countering heavily armed warships in the Neva. The echo of the *Aurora*'s blank shot was still fresh in the memory of the anti-Bolshevik leaders; it was aggravating their frustration and indecision.

THE EXPANSION OF SOVIET POWER

The leaders of the insurrection were quick to capitalize on the situation by taking the offensive and extending the beachhead at Petrograd far into the interior. A firm foundation of Bolshevik strength in the local soviet and the presence of large numbers of sympathetic or neutralized garrison units provided the opportunity in Moscow, where a desperate struggle nonetheless ensued from 27 October to 2 November, the outcome of which was no doubt affected by the events in and around Petrograd. Ability to reinforce the rebels in Moscow was hampered by tedious negotiations with the "neutral" Vikzhel (All-Russian Executive Committee of Railroad Workers) as well as by the needs of the capital. Still, on 29 October a detachment of five hundred Kronstadters was organized to relieve Moscow, and a second detachment of two thousand sailors and soldiers entrained for the second city of the empire on the thirty-first, arriving in time to participate in the final battles for the city, and according to a Soviet source, they "hastened the victory of the October armed uprising in Moscow."[10] A third, even larger detachment of Pulkovo veterans left on 2 November under Raskolnikov, Konstantin Eremeev, Anatolii Zhelezhniakov, Ivan Kolbin, and "Captain" Ilin-Zhenevskii. They secured the vital Petrograd-Moscow Railroad, seizing in the process an enemy armored train and stationing guards at strategic points along the route.[11] Sixty sailors from the *Aurora* were included in the latter group, some of whom voiced reluctance to join an operation so far from the sea.[12]

While Petrograd and Moscow were being secured, important negotiations were taking place to determine the nature of the government. Influential voices on the new Central Executive Committee, which was chosen by the Second All-Russian Congress of Soviets, advocated a coalition government that would include SRs and Mensheviks along with the Bolsheviks. The Left SRs and several Bolsheviks, including Kamenev, Zinoviev, and Riazanov, were joined by remnants of the other socialist parties and Vikzhel in an attempt to prevent further bloodshed and the political dominance of one party. The Bolshevik Central Committee, meeting on 1 November, refused to sanction Lenin's demand for a majority in the government, voting instead to continue negotiations with Vikzhel on the subject. Lenin then turned to the Petrograd Committee of the party, declaring to the advocates of coalition: "If you want a split, go ahead. If you have a majority, take power in the Central Executive Committee and carry on. But we will go to the sailors."[13] The threat seemed to work; for on the next day, 2 November, the Central Committee voted a narrow majority for Lenin's position, and despite resignations in protest, one-party government was assured.

As with the consolidation of the Petrograd-Moscow corridor, when special demands needed to be met during the first few weeks, sailors were usually called upon, performing guard duties in both cities, as well as bolstering morale. Smaller groups spread out south of Petrograd as far as Luga and Pskov, but beyond these points the rapid disintegration of large army units produced chaos that could not be controlled by the small number of reliable forces that were available. Outbreaks of violence and disorder were thus frequent, such as the murder of General Dukhonin, the commander-in-chief of the Russian army, which was witnessed by a few sailors from the *Aurora* at Mogilev. And from Moscow, Nikolai Khovrin, Dybenko's old comrade from the *Respublika*, commanded the first Soviet expedition into the Ukraine. Composed mostly of sailors, including Zhelezhniakov and Ilin-Zhenevskii, the four-hundred-man detachment arrived in the Kharkov area in mid November, in time to prevent army units there that were loyal to General Kornilov from joining others in the Don basin under General Kaledin.[14]

What posed a more direct threat to the new government than did remnants of the old army was the disruption of the normal supply of food for the urban areas, a problem that became the concern of a special commission of the Military Revolutionary Committee as early as 5 November. To Timofei Uliantsev, a twenty-nine-year-old former peasant from Orlov Province, was delegated the responsibility of organizing ten detachments of fifty Kronstadt sailors each for the purpose of supervising the distribution of basic supplies for the capital. He had already achieved surprising success by 8 November, a factor that was of considerable importance in pacifying the population of Petrograd.[15] But this was obviously only a temporary effect, for the stores in the capital would soon be exhausted. To avert this, several more detachments, totaling 355 Kronstadt sailors, set off for more-distant provinces, each group armed with 2,000–6,000 rubles for the purchasing of grain. While one unit of 44 sailors, led by commissar Ilia Blinkov, seized the Murmansk Railroad in order to bring imported goods from the northern port, the others went to the main grain-producing provinces—as far as Kherson, Tambov, Kursk, Samara, and Kharkov, even to Orenburg. Just how much the food supply was augmented is not clear, since the collapsing transportation system continued to be a major obstacle, but these roving sailors may have provided important support to local pro-Bolshevik forces at a critical time.[16]

THE EFFECTS OF THE OCTOBER REVOLUTION ON THE FLEET

The involvement of Baltic seamen in the October Revolution and their performance of so many duties in behalf of that revolution would naturally have had an effect on the fleet itself, although it must be emphasized that in contrast with the February–March events, no violence occurred on ships or at the bases. Admiral Aleksandr Razvozov and his staff remained in charge of "operations," though, as before, they were under constant review of a commissar of Tsentrobalt.[17] What happened in Petrograd was no surprise to the officers, and at a commander's conference on board the *Krechet* on 27 October their leading representatives voted to remain at their posts as long as the war situation demanded. But the events that followed caused some to change their minds. After Tsentrobalt overruled his objection to sending the *Oleg* from Revel to Petrograd on the twenty-eighth, Razvozov tendered his resignation to the naval ministry. It was intercepted, however, and returned by Tsentrobalt with a special plea that he reconsider.[18] Rear Admiral Timirev, who had just replaced Pilkin as commander of the First Squadron of Cruisers in October, wrote that the order of Tsentrobalt, reducing the crews of each large ship by 100 to 150 men in order to provide reinforcements to Petrograd, made the fleet incapable of further naval action and furnished justification to those who wished to leave.[19] Still, by this time, most of the officer corps was largely either neutral or sympathetic to the revolution and remained with their ships and units through November.

A new policy in regard to naval organization formed slowly and haphazardly. Despite the study by Lenin and Trotsky of military strategy and despite their natural skills for outmaneuvering enemies, none of the Bolshevik leaders was really an expert on the details of command structure, weapons capability, and combat operations. Since the Military Revolutionary Committee proved clumsy and inefficient in operation, it was quite natural for the leadership to turn to those second-echelon Bolsheviks who had military experience, particularly the "triumvirate" of Krylenko, Antonov-Ovseenko, and Dybenko, who headed the new People's Commissariat of Defense, and they were soon busy on special assignments. The central chain of command of the Russian army, moreover, was virtually destroyed by the revolution. Having only physical control of the old war ministry, the Soviet government was forced to improvise a shaky command structure through the use of special commissars who had extraordinary but indistinct authority.

But the navy, in particular the Baltic fleet, was different, surviving the October days with its chain of command intact. Admiral Verderevsky, it is true, was arrested—for the second time that year—in the Winter Palace, but he was released and, unlike the other ministers, resumed control of his old ministry.[20] The new Naval Revolutionary Committee formally replaced Tsentroflot on 27 October, but in fact, it actually merged with the older body, as sixteen Tsentroflot members joined the new committee.[21] Tsentrobalt, which was in Helsingfors, was firmly in control of that base well before October, and Kronstadt had worked out its own organizational structures. Since links existed between these organs and the new government leaders through the Bolshevik party organization, Lenin, Trotsky, and Sverdlov knew whom to go to for advice, and they knew who commanded authority. Their consultations with Raskolnikov, Pronin, Vakhrameev, Izmailov, and Khovrin during the first week is evidence of that ability. These men, and probably even the party leaders, were fully cognizant of the fact that moving ships through minefields or up the Neva involved a much more complicated operation than that of stationing men on Pulkovo Heights.

For this reason and because the naval chain of command was practically the only military one in existence, the new government took pains to ease the transition of the fleet to the new regime. Officers were encouraged to remain at their posts on board ship; they were also assured of jurisdiction over "operational" matters and the cooperation of fleet committees. In some instances there was even an improvement in sailor-officer relations. The British submarine officers now found themselves courted by the sailors' committees, though one obvious reason for this was the capability that these few ships had to immobilize the whole fleet. The British ambassador reported: "Strict injunctions have been given not to molest foreigners and British Naval Forces are having no trouble with Russian Fleet Committees."[22]

Indeed this paradoxical picture of peace and harmony in the fleet, where so much violence had occurred, presented the outside world with a confused picture of the nature of the changes in Russia. This was not helped by the interruption in telegraphic communications for a week—from 27 October to 3 November—which allowed rumors to circulate in the Allied capitals. A report from Sweden, originating with the Italian ambassador, claimed that "all Political Parties without exception have deserted Bolsheviks who [are] now supported by sailors only," which was not far from the truth.[23] The British naval attaché, Captain Grenfell, managed to leave Petrograd on 30 October, to relay dispatches from Stockholm and to report personally that everything was quiet in Russia.[24] But another report from Tokyo recommended immediate and drastic intervention, causing Sir Robert Cecil of the Foreign Office to note, "Everyone in and connected with Russia appears to be insane."[25]

This was not a bad description of the atmosphere in Russia as the Bolshevik leaders tried to collect the remnants of central authority. During the first week, Lenin summoned Captain Modest Ivanov, who was well known for his Bolshevik sympathies, to become a member of a naval collegium, giving him the official title of "minister of the navy," although Verderevsky still remained in charge of the Admiralty.[26] Ivanov appeared in Helsingfors to inform Tsentrobalt of his "promotion" on 8 November, was introduced as the minister "elected by us," and received a promise of cooperation from Izmailov.[27] The old ministry continued to function, although Verderevsky explained to Cromie on 9 November that "the entire Ministry of Marine is quite united, and have sent a note to the Smolney that they do not recognize Smolney as the Government and will not carry out their orders." The ministry, Verderevsky added, was prepared to turn its affairs over to "properly authorized and responsible officers," but if any member were removed by force, the entire ministry would leave at once. Cromie concluded his report, "Admiral Verderevsky said the time for keeping up appearances had passed, and, much as it hurt his pride, it was necessary to lay the bare facts of the case before the Allies, and discuss matters openly."[28] In fact, two days later, on the eleventh, Verderevsky officially retired, and a new "naval collegium," composed of Dybenko, Ivanov, and Vikentii Kovalskii, a Bolshevik sailor from the Black Sea fleet, assumed direction of the Admiralty.[29]

THE "NEW" COMMAND OF THE FLEET

While the reorganization of the central naval administration was going on in Petrograd, practical responsibility for the fleet rested with Tsentrobalt in Helsingfors. But the sailor's committee, which was bombarded by special requests from both sailors and officers and from Petrograd, was hard-pressed to perform its duties. The bellicose Izmailov, hampered by the absence of several of Tsentrobalt's leaders, had definite problems in asserting control, and the votes on important questions became noticeably smaller and closer.[30] A short period of revolutionary harmony was restored by Dybenko, who returned to Helsingfors on 10 November to secure one thousand men for an expeditionary force to the Don River area, where Cossack units under General Kaledin had seized control. Tsentrobalt agreed, by a vote of 36 to 1, but objections were raised that the drain of sailors from the ships was crippling the fighting capability of the fleet. Dybenko then told the committee that they could pick specialists from the 129th Infantry Division to replace the departing sailors.[31] This authorization of the local transfer of soldiers to naval units illustrates not only the rapidity of the breakdown of the old military apparatus but also the degree of personal power that Dybenko had assumed for himself.

The "peaceful" transition of officers to the service of a Soviet government could not survive long, though the naval officers did enjoy the advantage of having had time, since March, to get used to the idea of committee structures. Cromie, who had been a keen observer of the course of events in 1917, foresaw the collapse of the officers' control, but he could still hope that the Baltic fleet would yet rally around the flag:

> I still maintain that the Navy might be reformed with the aid of 200 officers and 1,000 men (selected), but the strategic value of such a reformed force is another question. The majority of Russian sailors are easily led, if handled properly, and the crews of small ships, where they have closer contact with their officers, do listen to those who continue to have some real interest in the service, and remain sober. But, on the whole no one can be expected to respect, much less follow, officers who behave as the Russians do at present. The following incidents, both personal observations, will indicate what I

mean. Two officers in the wardroom of the *Pamiat Azova* quarreled, and laid their differences before the sailors committee to settle. Another officer of the same ship reported his captain to the committee for some fault. Drunken officers are a common sight in public restaurants.[32]

What probably upset the officers most was not the existence of a new, radical government in Petrograd, but the chaos of command and the disintegration of the fleet under their very eyes.

The situation in Finland was aggravated by a lack of funds to pay and supply the fleet and by the Finnish independence movement. Montgomery Grove reported from Helsingfors on 28 October that the Russian governor general had departed for Petrograd and that his assistant had resigned, leaving no Russian civil authority in Finland. He urgently asked London to instruct him on what to do if the Finnish Diet declared independence.[33] A general strike began, and all of Finland seemed to be degenerating into chaos within a week after the overthrow in Petrograd. Cromie believed that the British submarine squadron prevented the fleet from disintegrating: "For some reason not very clear, we are the moral police of the fleet, and there are some extraordinary rumours as to what this flotilla has done and prevented from being done, and we are certainly treated with a suspicious respect by the crews of the larger ships."[34] By 3 November, firing in the streets was a common occurrence, and the absence of reliable news and the shortage of money plagued the leaders of the fleet. On 5 November, Cromie wrote: "At the present moment, the majority of the fleet is without Finnish marks of credit, the Government credit notes are not honoured, and there are no marks in the Government pay office. There are many officers and men who have not been paid, and there is now no service money for food. In the *Pamiat Azova*, we have enough food for one week, and no money or credit."[35] Some of the first grumbling came from the Left Socialist Revolutionaries; on 4 November, before the central committee of his party, Prosh Proshian denounced the Military Revolutionary Committee and the Council of People's Commissars for being too independent of soviet control.[36] But gradually the Finnish Red Guards, with the help of weapons from the fleet, restored order in Helsingfors, and the arrival of 20 million marks from Petrograd on 7 November eased the financial distress of the fleet.[37] The return of a degree of stability in the town only spurred the move for Finnish independence, which was formally declared by the Diet on 21 November.

THE POST-OCTOBER PARTY ALIGNMENT IN THE FLEET

The Russian sailors who remained in Finland, however, became more divided and less confident in the absence of clear and constant central direction. Three weeks after the October Revolution and only four days after Dybenko won support for the dispatch of Baltic sailors to South Russia, Tsentrobalt deposed its pro-Bolshevik chairman and elected a new presidium that was entirely non-Bolshevik and was headed by Ivan Balakin, Leopold Zubov, and Petr Surkov, all of whom had participated actively in the affairs of Tsentrobalt during the summer and fall of 1917 but then had not occupied any important positions.[38] The departure of leading Bolshevik sailors—such as Dybenko, Khovrin, and Averichkin—and many radical "volunteers" for revolutionary service in Petrograd and elsewhere had obviously weakened the Bolsheviks' control capability in the fleet. Resentment was rising in Helsingfors over the "orders" that were being received from the Petrograd "outsiders." A clear Bolshevik supremacy in the new government also agitated the Left SR and nonparty membership, as Balakin indicated in his opening remarks as chairman.[39] Though no one in the new leadership can be accurately identified with a political party, Pavel Sutyrin, the most active Left SR in Tsentrobalt, was clearly ascendant during the following two weeks.

These signs that the Kronstadt Revolt of 1921 was already on the horizon does not mean that the Baltic fleet as a whole was swinging away from the Bolsheviks so soon after the seizure of power, but they serve as reminders that Bolshevik dominance in the fleet was far from complete and that strong rivals among the Left SR, anarchist, and nonparty elements still existed. Izmailov, moreover, had been (and perhaps still was) an SR in 1917, and he retained an important position as head of the Military Section of Tsentrobalt, which was gaining in importance at the top level of the command structure. The organization remained united on most of the questions that it faced: drunkenness in the streets; resolutions against Kaledin, Kornilov, and others; the disciplining of a couple of officers who voiced opposition to the new government; and the working out a modus vivendi with Admiral Razvozov.[40]

The results of the "free" election to the Constituent Assembly, which was held on 12 November, provide a better indication of the true sentiments of the Baltic sailors, especially since they had their own special district. Although the Bolsheviks had a clear advantage because of big names—Lenin and Dybenko—on their list and because of the timing of the election in the wake of a successful seizure of power in which so many sailors had taken part, the fleet as a whole voted only 58 percent for the Bolsheviks (contrasting with about 24 percent in the country as a whole), and that majority was won only by an overwhelming Kronstadt victory of 84 percent. In Helsingfors the vote was 50 percent Bolshevik, 31 percent Left Socialist Revolutionary, 16 percent Right Socialist Revolutionary, 2 percent for the officers list, and 1 percent nonparty, according to official Soviet figures.[41] The Left SRs gained a majority in the Åbo-Åland region of Finland, where mostly small ships were stationed, while the Bolsheviks swept the battleships with over 70 percent. The balloting on the command ship *Krechet* was reported as follows: Left SRs, 113; Bolsheviks, 105; officers, 30; and Right SRs, 10.[42] One result is undebatable—that the election to the Constituent Assembly confirmed an overwhelming dissatisfaction with the Provisional Government by a combined Bolshevik and Left SR vote of 85 percent, probably higher than in any other district in the country. Lenin, incidentally, was elected in other districts, including Moscow and Petrograd, but he decided to accept the mandate of the sailors and be their delegate to the Constituent Assembly rather than to represent the more "proletarian" constituencies.[43]

QUESTIONS CONCERNING THE FUTURE OF THE BALTIC FLEET

Before all of the votes could be counted, however, another major crisis loomed at the command center of the fleet. Captain Ivanov arrived in Helsingfors unannounced on 19 November, went aboard one of the cruisers, raised his flag as minister of the navy, and ordered the commanding staff of the fleet to attend him. Razvozov and the other flag officers, who already disliked Ivanov for courting the Bolsheviks, refused to comply, claiming that the minister had no right to board a ship without following proper procedure.[44] At a special session of Tsentrobalt, Ivanov and Razvozov confronted each other. After Razvozov explained his position, Izmailov sharply denounced his action, and Ivanov asked him if he recognized the existing authority in the country. The fleet commander answered: "I cannot recognize any authority since there is not a single one and not all people have acknowledged that the Bolsheviks have an absolute majority. I will recognize that authority which will be established by the Constituent Assembly."[45]

The meeting ended with the problem unsolved. But the next day, Ivanov addressed a council of flag officers and obtained a compromise solution by apologizing for his action, on the one hand, and appealing to the officers' sense of patriotic duty, on the other.[46]

Conflicting but generally pessimistic reports on the military situation in northern Russia caused considerable concern in the Allied capitals. To the British, who were more mindful of naval matters than the other Allies, it suddenly seemed quite possible that the Baltic fleet, with its relatively new and "unworn" equipment—dreadnoughts, cruisers, and modern destroyers and submarines—complete with an arsenal of torpedoes, mines, and so forth, could fall into the hands of Germany, either by connivance within the fleet or through an early spring offensive. When asked to appraise these possibilities, Admiral Stanley responded, on 8 November:

> I do not consider there is more than barest possibility of Russian Fleet or part of it being delivered to Germans treacherously. Practically all power over Fleet now vested in Baltic Fleet Committee and I think there are sufficient right minded men to prevent such an act. What appears to me more likely (will be?) handing over of four dreadnoughts might be made one of preliminary conditions of peace and this would be difficult to prevent.[47]

That Germany might receive all or part of the Russian Baltic fleet just for the asking created even more consternation in London, especially since Stanley's report was followed by news of the beginning of peace negotiations at Brest-Litovsk. The First Sea Lord, Admiral J. R. Jellicoe, responded immediately to Stanley's report. He ruled out using the British submarine squadron to sink the large Russian warships because of the shallowness of Helsingfors Harbor and "the consequences as regards the safety of the British colonies in Russia and our diplomatic representatives."[48] An alternative was to approach "some loyal Russian officers" with the idea of damaging "the ships so seriously as to prevent their use by the Germans at any rate for a considerable period." Regarding the destroyers, "which are more valuable certainly to ourselves and possibly to the Germans than the battleships," Jellicoe proposed to get them out of the Baltic with British assistance.[49] A more detailed Admiralty study, however, found that very likely this plan would fail, because of the German defenses and the limited steaming capability of the smaller ships. The same reasoning applied to the British submarines, whose crews, moreover, were considered to be more valuable than the ships.

The War Cabinet contemplated opening negotiations with the Soviet government, with the goal of preventing the Baltic fleet from passing into German hands, even, if necessary, through a British purchase of the whole fleet followed by its immediate destruction.[50] Though some antiwar idealists among the Bolsheviks might have deemed such a proposal quite acceptable, the Soviet government could never have allowed a course of action that would have led to charges of collusion with the British, especially when it would have involved the destruction of the seedbed of much of its most active support in the October Revolution. For various reasons, the British also decided that "in the present confused situation it was not possible to enter into negotiations on the subject, but that the matter should be reopened when a suitable occasion arose."[51] The Baltic fleet was thus saved for the temporary immobility that the winter ice would bring.

Meanwhile, in Petrograd, in the midst of the consolidating of a new central authority, the beginning of peace negotiations, and increasing signs of civil war, another congress was held—the First All-Russian Congress of the Navy—from 18 to 25 November. Though somewhat anticlimactic, the congress of 190 delegates (82 from the Baltic fleet) served as a useful forum for rebuilding revolutionary enthusiasm through a series of proclamations calling upon the sailors to keep up the fight against the enemies of the revolution.[52] Aleksei Baranov, former leader of Tsentrobalt, chaired the sessions in Petrograd, at which the major speeches were delivered by Dybenko and Lenin. The chairman of the Council of Peoples' Commissars extended greetings from the Soviet government on the afternoon of 22 November; and although he was interrupted several times by "stormy applause,"[53] he then proceeded to outline the policies for peace and for national self-determination of peoples of the old Russian Empire. He also emphasized the importance of discipline in order to preserve the battle strength of the fleet. In terms of length and the material covered, this message to the sailors was one of Lenin's most important public speeches of 1917, and a British reporter made special note of the Bolshevik leader's hint that the war against Germany might continue.[54] In conclusion, the congress elected twenty of its members to form the Sailors' Section of the All-Russian Central Executive Committee.[55]

Other meetings occupied the time and consumed the energies of the revolutionary leadership. In Helsingfors, Ivan Smilga opened the Fourth Oblast Congress of Finland on 25 November.[56] Other Russian activities centered around the Left Socialist Revolutionary–controlled Oblast Peasant

Soviet, though some may have considered an assembly that represented Russian peasants in Finland rather absurd (the "peasants" were all sailors, soldiers, and workers). Many passed the time at the People's University, which was sponsored by the Helsingfors Soviet and the Sailors' Club. The local press was absorbed with the publicity for the courses, which concentrated on economics, government, and history.[57]

Until the beginning of December an uneasy truce existed in what remained of the Baltic fleet. Many important questions seemed to be in suspension, and one has the impression that the fate of the fleet, perhaps of Russia, had not yet been decided, that several options remained open. At least from the vantage point of Helsingfors and Kronstadt, if not from Petrograd itself, the problems of peace or war or civil war, of what the Constitutent Assembly would be allowed to do, of the nature of the new government, and of the future organization of the fleet appeared unsolvable. While some of the most optimistic sailors busied themselves with the People's University, with hopes of building some sort of better future, others viewed the storm clouds gathering over the Russian steppe and began to construct a different destiny for the Baltic sailors.

While the fleet drifted through November with practically nobody at the helm, it was impossible to grapple with a very practical problem—the marooning of most of the ships in what were rapidly becoming foreign ports (Finnish independence was recognized by the Soviet government in December). Confusion, lack of forethought, and preoccupation with other matters, perhaps, account for the inability to see the susceptibility of the fleet to German attack in the winter and early spring, as well as the failure to move at least some of the better ships to Kronstadt. While Tsentrobalt was going off on its own course in November, the man who was most responsible for naval matters in Petrograd, Dybenko, was steering erratically, infatuated by another commissar, Alexandra Kollontai, to the amusement and consternation of the new Petrograd elite.

Perhaps the hardening of attitudes, which was noticeable in the fleet by the beginning of December, was inevitable—as inevitable, at least, as the results of the election to the Constituent Assembly, which gave the anti-Bolshevik parties a clear majority, and the failure of the Allies to accept a working relationship with the Soviet government. An air of arrogance and bravura crept into Bolshevik policy statements. Dybenko told the British military attaché at the end of November that a "strong army was unnecessary as Russian Fleet would defend revolution against Imperialists and counter-revolutionaries."[58] The commissar apparently had the sailors, not the ships, in mind.

THE REORGANIZATION OF THE FLEET

The approach of winter and the state of neither war nor peace did not give the Baltic fleet a new lease on life, it only prolonged the agony. On 2 December another big step was taken in dissolving the old order in the fleet. Dybenko again appeared suddenly and dramatically in Helsingfors, while Razvozov was visiting the Bothnian coastal bases and at the time that Tsentrobalt was coming to grips with a ticklish problem—the transfer of all Ukrainian sailors to the Black Sea fleet. He called an extraordinary meeting of all officers and ships' committees, by-passing both the commander and Tsentrobalt. Though faced with a much bigger turnout of officers than he expected, Dybenko proceeded to outline a stepped-up "democratization" of the fleet. Besides extending the elective principle to all units, the new system provided for the merging of the commanding staff of the fleet with Tsentrobalt, which would now be divided into sections, as specified in the rules adopted at the Second Congress of the fleet in September but never fully put in force. Most of the old fleet staff, including the commander in chief himself, would now be members of the Military Section, which was headed by Izmailov. Admiral Razvozov would become the director of the Operations Subsection under him.[59] To give added weight to Dybenko's words, and apparently for no other reason, the cruiser *Aurora* also made a surprise and triumphal visit to Helsingfors on 2 December, a hazardous voyage that late in the year.[60]

The reorganization of the administration of the fleet, which had emanated officially from the Supreme Naval Collegium in Petrograd, raised a fundamental issue of the revolution. As might be expected, many officers were opposed to the new "collegial" direction of the fleet. At two conferences of flag officers, on 4 and 5 December, the question was debated at some length. Captain Klavdii Shevelev, the commander of a destroyer flotilla, presented the most eloquent argument for the opposition, saying that no navy in history had operated successfully under such an arrangement; but other voices noted that no navy had ever been in such a situation before.[61] At the second assembly the majority appeared to agree with Captain Georgii Stark's opinion that "if the fleet passes into the hands of a collegium, that will be the ruin of the fleet." But others disputed this view, and staff commissar Stepan Zhuravlev, a Bolshevik sailor from the *Gangut*, interjected: "It cannot be that you or we are guilty; the guilty are those we overthrew on 25 October. . . . I do not want to be in power, I do not want you to be in power, I want us to work together, that is the plain fact. The people must be sovereign . . . , a decree, which they declare, must take precedence . . . , but to blame each other is completely useless."[62]

To this, Rear Admiral Nikolai Patton replied: "Comrade Zhuravlev! We are agreed with the principle of sovereignty of the people, but we are against collegial direction, because such irregular administration will produce devastation and ruin." Another rear admiral, Aleksandr Ruzhek, supported the commissar with the simple argument that at present the masses did not want authority vested in one man and that the officers had to obey that desire.[63]

A few high-ranking officers refused to participate in the collegial administration and so resigned. Commander Cromie received the following letter from Admiral Razvozov on 5 December, the date that the new system went into effect:

Dear Sir,

Resigning my position as commander-in-chief of the Baltic Fleet, I consider it my duty to express to you, as Captain of the English Flotilla, my sincere admiration of the valiant war service and brilliant accomplishment of all war operations, and of the officers and crews under your command.

Accept my deepest thanks for the great help given to us during the present war.

Yours very sincerely,

(signed) Razvosoff. Rear-Admiral.[64]

A few days later, Cromie received orders recalling him to London. The revolution and the de facto end of the war for Russia were indeed causing repercussions in the fleet.

But departure of senior officers did not by itself cripple the fleet, as those leaving at this time were those who were most dissatisfied with the state of affairs. Many of the younger and more liberal and popular officers —Ivanov (director of the naval ministry), Berens, Altfater (the Russian naval representative at the Brest-Litovsk peace negotiations), Shchastnyi, Kapnist, Ruzhek (who temporarily replaced Razvozov), Zarubaev, Dmitriev, and Weis—stayed at their posts for a variety of motives: for enduring patriotism, to advance in rank and responsibility, to avoid an irrevocable decision, to maintain a salary and stay with their families, to participate in a revolutionary experiment, or to undermine the Bolshevik regime from within.

Simultaneously with Dybenko's last visit to Helsingfors, Tsentrobalt also adapted to the new course. Balakin, who had supported autonomous authority for the organization against the developing centralism, disappeared from the scene.[65] Whether Dybenko personally forced this change or whether his visit tipped the balance in favor of returning Dybenkoites—Averichkin, Shtarev, Sapozhnikov—is not clear. But the drain of the most active and experienced sailors for land operations, which was reducing the crews of many ships to skeleton levels, remained an important issue. When Raskolnikov arrived in Helsingfors to form another one-thousand-man special detachment for South Russia, he did not have the same success as Dybenko had had. Tsentrobalt, taking its new role seriously, refused his request, explaining that the men had to be retained on the ships, that there should be no more diversion of naval forces for dealing with domestic conflicts.[66] This opposition demonstrated a continuing resentment within the fleet of the Soviet government's policies; and it was probably the beginning of the end of Tsentrobalt.

Meanwhile, other matters—Brest-Litovsk, Ukrainian separatism, the Constituent Assembly—occupied the attention of Petrograd. Heightened tensions and fear of disorder in connection with the meeting of the Constituent Assembly during the first week of January was one reason for suspending further reform in the navy. Insecurity and near panic were revealed in the urgent orders to Kronstadt and Helsingfors to send sailors to guard and contain the body that represented the voice of the people, as registered by democratic election. This time, Tsentrobalt, prodded by a dramatic appeal from Nikolai Khovrin, agreed to send one thousand men, provided that they be allowed to return to their units after a short stay.[67] As it turned out, they were not needed, since the Kronstadt sailors under the command of Dybenko and Zhelezniakov were quite capable of controlling the opening session, and when the sailors grew tired and cold in the early hours of the morning of 6 January, they curtly told the delegates to go home. Thenceforth, the doors to open and free political debate in Petrograd remained closed.

In early January 1918, just as the Constituent Assembly was meeting, Dmitrii Fedotov White, who was serving as assistant Russian naval attaché in London, returned to Russia to gather information for the other attachés abroad about the new Soviet government and about the extent of the opposition to it. Upon arriving in Petrograd, he looked up his old friend, Captain Evgenii Berens, whom he found "inclined to take things for granted, to accept the fact of the Bolshevik rule and merely look for ways and means to preserve the personnel, particularly the officers, from the rigors of the new regime, and the ships from capture and destruction by the enemy." Berens also told Fedotov White about Lenin's response to suggestions for improving discipline in the navy: "Why, all this is much too loose-jointed. We want real discipline and you will revise all your propositions accordingly. We are building now. The destructive period is over!" The attaché also conferred with Raskolnikov ("I liked Raskolnikov personally; he impressed me as a frank, intellectually honest man"), who tried to recruit him for Soviet service.[68] After declining an invitation to command a naval unit that was headed for South Russia, Fedotov White returned to London, convinced by Berens and Raskolnikov that the Bolsheviks were firmly in power.

In fact, both Raskolnikov and Berens, as well as Dybenko and his cohorts in the naval administration, were deeply involved during January in a new constructive effort. A commission composed of the Supreme Naval Collegium, the Naval Section of the All-Russian Central Executive Committee, and, as a special concession to the Baltic fleet, representatives of Tsentrobalt, worked throughout January on a draft decree that Dybenko presented to the Council of People's Commissars, chaired by Lenin, on 29 January. On the next day the old navy was declared "dissolved," and the new Worker-Peasant Red Navy came into being. In theory the navy was to be completely voluntary, with reenlistment by contract, in which each sailor would indicate, along with other service details, his party affiliation and would provide "a recommendation of a democratic organization that stands for Soviet power."[69]

To institute the new regime, the Council of People's Commissars designated a chain of command of commissars. Dybenko now headed the collegium of a separate People's Commissariat of Naval Affairs, with Raskolnikov, Vakhrameev, and Sergei Saks as assistants. And to no one's surprise, Nikolai Izmailov became the chief commissar of the Baltic fleet, with Andrei Shtarev (Bolshevik), Evgenii Blokhin (anarchist), and Pavel Shishko (Left SR) as assistants.[70] The majority of Tsentrobalt opposed these measures, and in angry debates on 31 January and 15 February (new style—the calendar having changed on 1 February to the Western dating, a jump of 13 days), it attempted to forestall implementation. Hostility only increased its isolation from the new power structure, though the Bolshevik Central Committee still sent its most glamorous member (and Dybenko's lover), Alexandra Kollontai, to Helsingfors, where her efforts to cajole Tsentrobalt were notably unsuccessful.[71]

The elected central committee of the fleet, which had been used so effectively by the radical leadership in 1917, was at a definite disadvantage in fighting the tide of central authority. The Bolshevik organization, with at least some support from Left SRs and anarchists and more definitely from officers, moved quickly to dismantle the committee structure throughout the fleet. A perceived new emergency, which was caused by the rupture of the peace talks at Brest-Litovsk and by a new German advance, also added to the weight against Tsentrobalt, as Admiral Ruzhek and Nikolai Izmailov combined forces to rally the fleet behind the "socialist fatherland is in danger" decree, which was issued by the Council of People's Commissars on 21 February.[72]

The pro-Bolshevik members of Tsentrobalt scurried to find posts as commissars. On 3 March, the day of the signing of the Treaty of Brest-Litovsk, the Council of Commissars of the Baltic Fleet (Sovkombalt) was formed; this action was followed the next day by the official dissolution of Tsentrobalt.[73] In one sense, the Baltic fleet had traversed a complete circle in exactly one year with the return of a clearly demarcated and centrally based channel of command. But the fleet was now almost as battle-scarred as after the Battle of Tsushima—it was weakened by losses and defections among officers and by the drain of manpower for revolution and civil war, with as much physical and psychological exhaustion as there would have been during a full year of actual combat.

The last campaign of the old Russian Baltic fleet now began with the effort to bring the ships from Helsingfors to the relative safety of Kronstadt and Petrograd. Already by the end of February a squadron of cruisers and several smaller ships had escaped, with the help of icebreakers, from Revel to Helsingfors, just before Revel fell to the Germans. But the move to Kronstadt had to wait until the thicker ice of the eastern section of the Gulf of Finland had broken up. The German ships, however, were able to sail into the other end of the gulf, and troops landed at Hango, to the southwest of Helsingfors, on 3 April. That day the old heavy cruiser *Riurik* set off from Kronstadt to open a passage, but it ran into difficulty.[74]

An attempt to negotiate an arrangement with Admiral Meyer, commander of the German task force at Hango, also turned out rather badly for the Russians. Meyer interpreted the clause in the Treaty of Brest-Litovsk that gave the Soviet government the right to keep all ice-bound ships as giving him the power to disarm them first.[75] So, with men and fuel in short supply, the grueling and hazardous voyage through the ice began on 7 April. Some of the larger vessels were already partially disabled and had to be towed; others suffered damage en route.[76] But most of the ships reached Kronstadt safely—an achievement of heroic proportions. The success should be credited to the new commissar command structure, but especially to the officers who conducted the operation: Shchastnyi, Zarubaev, and Dmitriev. A few older and smaller vessels were scuttled at their docks or were left behind intact; at least one of the latter was released by Finnish and German authorities in May, in accordance with the treaty.[77] To avoid having to serve either the Germans or the Bolsheviks, the British submarine squadron was blown up in deep water near Helsingfors on 10 April.[78]

Despite the institution of an essentially military command and despite a display of ability to get a job done under unfavorable circumstances, the Russian Baltic fleet soon came to an end as a distinct fighting unit. A large number of the small destroyers, minelayers, and trawlers went inland over the canal system to the Volga, where they fought in the civil war as river flotillas. Few large ships would escape the general pillaging for weapons in the summer of 1918, when the civil war reached major proportions. From the vessels of the fleet came many of the guns for the armored trains and field artillery of the new Red Army, and much of the manpower was transferred to that army in the form of expeditionary detachments. An American naval intelligence report made the following assessment of the Baltic fleet at the end of 1918:

> The Baltic Fleet cannot be considered as a fighting force; it is practically at the mercy of any enemy force that may occupy Cronstad or Petrograd. . . . On the dreadnoughts and battleships only one turret on the average is in working order, owing to serious disorder of the electrical installations and want of experienced men. There is no hope of any improvement in the future. . . . It is expected to get one dreadnought into proper order by taking the missing parts out of the others.[79]

More specifically, the report listed the effects of the civil war: "The guns from the *Bajan* have been removed and sent to the front. The *Rossiia* and *Gromoboi* have been dismantled. The *Makarov* and *Bajan* are in every respect very much neglected." Another source noted that the 120 mm. guns had been removed from the *Respublika* and that 60 four-inch guns had been taken from the destroyers and sent to the front. "All destroyers disarmed. 75 mm. guns and ammo sent to the front. *Aurora*: all guns dismantled and sent to the front."[80] Most of the large ships were, in fact, eventually sold to Germany for scrap.[81]

Almost all of the radical leadership of the fleet during 1917 also was decimated in order to support the war effort on land. For example, on the battleship *Petropavlovsk*, the Bolshevik collective—which had numbered 150, with 300 sympathizers in May 1917—had nearly disappeared by the fall of 1918.[82] Some of the sailors who had managed to avoid volunteering for the front continued the "independent" spirit of 1917—protesting the Treaty of Brest-Litovsk, passing resolutions condemning the arbitrariness of Soviet decisions, joining the SR revolt during the summer of 1918, and in general rebuffing central authority. But those who remained were, from the beginning, the least bolshevized and the most likely to be influenced by anti-Bolshevik radicals; they also opposed the government's piracy of the fleet. The Swedish naval attaché described the situation at Kronstadt in December 1918:

> The sailors are against the Bolsheviks and only a month ago were fully prepared to overthrow the government and only by the leaders giving an extra eight hundred roubles to each man was this movement stopped. . . . The commissars have no control whatever over their men. The Navy is also approaching starvation, for the sailors have sold and pocketed the returns from a two years supply of food which [was] formerly kept at Cronstadt. They have also sold everything movable for which they could find a buyer until now there is practically nothing left.[83]

By the fall of 1920, with the civil war reaching a conclusion, a rebuilding campaign was begun under the leadership of Commissar-Commander Raskolnikov. The attempt to restore discipline upon "free" Kronstadt, where new recruits mixed with veterans who remembered the hopes and ideals of 1917, helped to provoke the Kronstadt uprising of 1921, which was the last effort of the Baltic fleet to influence the course of a Russian government.[84] Only a few of the Baltic leaders of 1917—for example, Anatolii Lamanov and Khaim Iarchuk—were active in the Kronstadt Revolt. The great civil war had already taken a greater toll of the fleet. Among the leaders, Semen Roshal, the ardent revolutionary of the July Crisis, was one of the first to fall; he was captured and executed on the Romanian front in December

1917. Others who sacrificed themselves so that the Bolsheviks could remain in power were Uliantsev, Markin, Zhemchuzhin, Zhelezhniakov, Khokhria-kov, and Berg.

Many of those who distinguished themselves as leaders of the sailors in the revolution and the civil war found themselves enmeshed in the apparatus of the new power, occupying important government and party posts but eventually falling victim to the purges—Dybenko, Antonov-Ovseenko, Ilin-Zhenevskii, Smilga, and less directly, Raskolnikov, who was minister to Bulgaria at the beginning of the purges but defected and died under mysterious circumstances in France in 1939. A surprising number of the sailor-leaders of the fleet survived into the 1950s to herald anniversary celebrations with their reminiscences: Izmailov, Khovrin, Vakhrameev, Flerovskii, Kondakov, Pronin, Belyshev, Malkov, and Baranov.

Over the past six decades, much of the reality of the activities of the sailors of the Baltic fleet in the Russian Revolution has been simplified and distorted into myth. The cruiser *Aurora*, which has been preserved in Leningrad, is now both a museum piece symbolizing the revolutionary spirit of 1917 and an active ship in the Soviet navy representing the triumph of a powerful Soviet system. On the eve of every November 7, when fireworks light up the Neva and vividly outline the warships that are anchored in the river, at least a few thoughts must go back to the aspirations and hopes—and disillusionments—of the sailors of '17.

9

THE SAILORS AND THE REVOLUTION

A study of the revolution in the Baltic fleet and its influence on the surrounding area provides new insights into the nature and course of the twentieth-century revolution that has had immense impact on the world as a whole. After an extensive history of agitation, repression, revolt, and retribution, the Baltic fleet exploded with violence during the February–March Revolution, which marked the real turning point for the sailors. The growth of organizational sophistication within the fleet in 1917—from spontaneous ship and unit committees to party-activated soviets and congresses —was a major feature of the year. This development provided the potential for the offensive deployment of the sailors in the October Revolution. Though the sailors were thoroughly radicalized, "truly devoted to the revolution," and organized for positive action, they were far from being united in support of Leninism. Bolshevik success in using them was partly the result of a superior program and leadership, but it was due more to the particular circumstances of the fleet.

The fleet, first of all, presents physical proof of Russia's valiant effort to keep up with the rapid changes in military technology of the early part of the century, and the ambitious naval construction also highlighted the problems of a country that was caught between escalating progress and deep-seated backwardness, between the demands of technical efficiency and the constraints of political and social tradition. The strain that was produced by the effort to modernize caused further imbalance in the political and social spheres, which are the breeding grounds of dissension and disaffection.

What is notable in regard to revolution in the fleet is the clash of the old and the new—of the traditions of a hierarchical structure of power with a new sense of individual destiny and achievement. The old military chain of command was being weakened and eroded, then overthrown and replaced by a new order of authority. This upheaval was produced not so much by the "will of the masses" (the ordinary sailors) as by a relatively small number of individuals, both officers and seamen, who had the support of outside proponents of new ideas about the future of society.

The impetus for change had been building for at least a generation, since the 1870s; it was represented in the fleet in the form of an active revolutionary movement that instigated a series of local conflicts and incidents. The germs of revolt, once planted in the fleet, could not be removed under the conditions that prevailed in Russia; they only grew and multiplied as part of the general revolutionary development in Russia from which isolation of the fleet was impossible due to its location and its dependence on bases that were centers of radical activities. Political and economic unrest in urban Russia thus closely interacted with revolt and mutiny in the fleet, especially in 1905–6, and again in 1917.

The course of the Great War, especially the sense of impending defeat, aggravated the conditions of daily life in Russia, thus increasing the potential for revolution while limiting the ability of traditional authority to maintain order. The peculiar defensive position of the Baltic fleet during the war obviously exacerbated psychological and physical strains to the point that serious disturbances and revolts would probably have taken place in 1917 regardless of what happened in Petrograd, just as unrest occurred independently in the German navy and the French army that year. The war was thus the single large issue of 1917 for the officers and men of the fleet, far outweighing concern for long-term grievances of workers and peasants. The revolution in the fleet was preconditioned by a rapidly diminishing will to fight to "victory," unless victory meant the triumph of a new government dedicated to making peace and correcting social abuses. The great upheaval of February–March in the Baltic bases was not so much directed against war itself as against the type of war that was being fought and against the nearest symbols of authority, the officers in command positions. The violence in the fleet, it is worth noting, was not aimed at the fighting capability of the navy, since cases of sabotage of the ships, which would have been easy to accomplish, were extremely rare.

There seemed, instead, to be a natural instinct for self-preservation and reconstruction of the fleet on the part of the sailors, which would support the view that natural revolutionaries are intent on securing the military forces of the government that they intend to overthrow. The Provisional Government tried to maintain Russia's armed forces, both as a measure of its own authority and in order to crystallize national support behind military victory; but this meant continuing the same style of war and postponing basic reforms. That the fleet was practically outside of its control did not seem at first to be crucial, since victory was to be gained, if at all, on land. The Provisional Government was unsuccessful for a number of reasons, not the least of which was the revolutionary momentum that continued to build in the major urban areas and interacted with the growth of conscious radicalism in the fleet.

The Provisional Government hoped to weather the storm, and it hesitated to introduce the necessary force in the form of martial law for fear of provoking a revolution or civil war that would endanger the success of its policies and even its own existence. Obviously, Kerensky and his supporters faced complex questions with little political sophistication and experience. But one important miscalculation in the equation of their decision-making was their inattention to the hostile revolutionary power base that was developing in the fleet. Petrograd finally might be pacified, as it essentially was after the July Crisis, but what about Kronstadt? The failure of the Provisional Government to do anything substantive about gaining firm control over the fleet's bases left it vulnerable to attack in a strategically awkward position (as long as the capital was in Petrograd).

That the Baltic fleet posed such a threat to the internal security of Russia in 1917 was due to the strength attained by the new institutions that quickly filled the vacuum of social and political opportunity that traditionally exists in a wartime military force. The assemblies, committees, and soviets of the naval bases, in which the sailors and radical officers played such an important role, represented as much of a fortress opposing outside authority as the guns of the battleships themselves. This alternate bureaucracy, which is often included in the phrase "dual power," really constituted the single major power in the fleet after the February Revolution, inasmuch as it controlled the possibility of change. "Dual power" was, therefore, as much a geographical as a political phenomenon, at least in northwest Russia. The general situation was not unlike that of the Maoist revolution, in which the surrounding countryside is gradually won over and then, finally, the urban citadels.

The soviets and assemblies in the fleet's bases—with their constant barrage of protocols, lectures, clubs, and newspapers—served to educate and politicize the sailors to their new role as the vanguard of a new force for reforging Russian society. Their growth was nurtured by the competition offered by the government, and it was abetted and supported by the revolutionary parties that hoped to realize their ideals and ambitions with the support of the sailors. But the soviets and local committees were too large, clumsy, and inefficient to provide an effective apparatus of control; so, quite naturally, the real voice of authority in the fleet became the smaller, more immediately responsive bodies such as the executive committees of the soviets and the Central Committee of the Baltic Fleet. These organizations served as the strategically important lynch pins in a working chain of command, which was enhanced and reinforced by extraordinary structures that appeared in time of crisis.

By October the soviets in the fleet had become little more than symbols of power, lecture halls for the ratification of the slogans of the left-wing activists. And the lower-level unit and ship committees were also in the process of becoming mere links in a new system of centralized control. This emerging substitute chain of command was still weak and incomplete in respect to what is normally operative in large military units, but it was comparatively strong in relation to what actually existed in the way of an "official" military chain of command or to what one normally thinks of in connection with an "anarchic" revolutionary situation. Even the real anarchists in the fleet—men like Zhelezhniakov and Iarchuk—found themselves enmeshed and dependent upon the new organizational apparatus of the fleet.

But revolutionary institutions are made strong and viable by the men who compose and lead them. The Baltic fleet possessed a cadre of men who were both experienced sailors and active revolutionaries before 1917, and this fact was soon known to the most radical parties, whose leaders were not far away. The great majority of the names that frequent the protocols of committees and that appear in the lists of presidiums of congresses were those of experienced sailors who were trained to operate complex machinery. They were not those of undisciplined or new recruits, but mostly of mature young men ranging in age from twenty-four to thirty (both Dybenko and Averichkin were twenty-eight in 1917), who occupied middle-echelon positions in the ranks of petty or noncommissioned officers. Several, in fact, were designated as instructors in the training detachments. These active leaders were not numerous; perhaps less than a hundred men formed the revolutionary core of the fleet. Of course, several hundred more participated in the committees and soviets, affiliating with voting blocs, making up their minds on crucial issues, and vocally approving and even encouraging their leaders.

The revolution in the fleet would have been only a spontaneous revolt, however, without the vision and spirit of the active radical parties, which already recognized the revolutionary potential of the Baltic fleet. The success and achievement that were produced in the violence in the fleet during the February and March days naturally attracted even more attention from the regular party organizations. This was particularly true of the Bolsheviks, who were conscious of the value of organization and leadership and who were intent on increasing their strength wherever opportunities existed. It is practically a cliché to note that the Bolshevik regulars who became involved in fleet affairs were educated, dedicated, and ambitious. They represented, moreover, a combination of the young and eager radicals, who were anxious to prove to themselves and to the party leaders what they could do, and of the older, more-experienced revolutionaries, who were more cautious and certainly more knowledgeable in Marxist-Leninist theory. The formula for Bolshevik success was thus to supply to the fleet a party cadre composed of optimistic men and women in their early 20s—such as Roshal, Raskolnikov, and Zhemchuzhin—and ones in their 30s—such as Flerovskii, Kiril Orlov, Smilga, and Antonov-Ovseenko—who had a more far-sighted view of the revolutionary potential of the fleet and could transmit their perspectives to the highest leaders of the party.

The crowning Bolshevik achievements in the fleet in 1917 were to gain working control of the key committees and to win over enough revolutionary and rank-and-file sailors to carry resolutions in the various soviets, assemblies, and committees, thus lending strength to the growing alternate command structure. And one notable foundation of their success was the early and continuous publication in the fleet's bases of newspapers that were aimed specifically at the sailors.

The lines of direct Bolshevik control in the fleet were thin and shallow. Neither the party nor any single leader possessed as all-encompassing an organization of control as many writers, both Soviet and Western, assert. Effective party machinery existed only at the highest level in the main bases of the fleet, and the "bolshevized" crews of the ships were largely beyond its direct control. Instead, and quite wisely, the Bolshevik hierarchy depended upon the existing organizations that had been created out of the confusion of the February Revolution. The limits of Bolshevik power are indicated by the continuing strength of the Left Socialist Revolutionary, anarchist, and nonparty affiliations of so many sailors well beyond October 1917. Gaining firm control over the organizational structure of the fleet, however, was the key to the maintenance of power both in the fleet and in the country.

As far as the fleet was concerned, the seizure of power in Petrograd was a phase of a democratic revolution for the creation of a government that would focus its attention on peace, social justice, and economic equality. But the sailors lacked the political sophistication that was necessary in order to control the revolution which they helped to make and which would become more and more dependent for guidance upon the party that was able to gain leadership both before and after October. One of the ironies of the Russian Revolution is that the natural and sensitive expressions of discontent that had provided so much fuel for radical change now had to be suppressed in the interests of preserving the "revolution."

The events of 1917 were especially shaped by the immediate environment, by the peculiar circumstances that existed in northwest Russia. As a result of the war, large numbers of professionally trained sailors were trapped on ships and at bases that were in or near urban centers; thus, they had time to ponder their current conditions and their future fate. Kronstadt could not be isolated from Petrograd, and Kronstadt was only the "vanguard" of the Baltic fleet. The triumph or tragedy, depending upon one's point of view, of the revolution in the fleet, was a triumph or tragedy for Russia—and for the world.

NOTES

The following abbreviations are used in the notes:

ADM   Admiralty Papers
AREEH   Archive of Russian and East European History, Columbia
           University
CAB   Cabinet Papers
DMI   Director of Military Intelligence
FO   Foreign Office, London
HI   Hoover Institution
MA   Military Attaché
NA   National Archives, Naval Attaché
ONI   Office of Naval Intelligence
PRO   Public Record Office
RG   Record Group
SA, VK   Sota Arkisto, Russian Collection, Helsinki

CHAPTER 1

1. Russian naval histories in English are of limited use. The following
   may be consulted for background information: Sir Cyprian Bridge,
   The Navy under Peter the Great (London, 1898); Fred T. Jane, *Russian Imperial Navy* (London, 1904); Mairin Mitchell, *Maritime History of Russia* (London, 1948); David Woodward, *Russians at Sea: A History of the Russian Navy* (New York, 1966); and Donald W. Mitchell, *A History of Russian and Soviet Sea Power* (New York, 1974).
   Prerevolutionary Russian historians produced numerous mono-

graphs, documentary collections, and articles (mostly in the official naval journal *Morskoi Sbornik*), but there is not one definitive history of the whole period. The most reliable authors are Feodosii Veselago, Aleksandr Sorokin, Sergei Elagin, and Viktor Golovachev. Soviet historians who have made notable contributions to imperial naval history include L. S. Berg, Evgenyi Tarle, Aleksandr Shapiro, R. N. Mordvinov, and L. S. Beskrovnyi. One émigré work that should be mentioned is N. Monasterev and Serge Terestchenko's *Histoire de la Marine Russe,* trans. Jean Pereau (Paris, 1932).

2. K. F. Shatsillo, *Russkii imperializm i razvitie flota nakanune pervoi mirovoi voiny (1906–1914 gg.)* (Moscow, 1968), pp. 52–57.

3. Ibid., p. 58.

4. For example, see Robert Massie, *Nicholas and Alexandra.* Much of the information regarding Russian shipbuilding was found in the records of the United States Office of Naval Intelligence: "Russian Shipbuilding Program," NA, RG 38, index 98 (naval attaché reports), P-2-a, f. 851; and "Renovation of the Russian Navy," NA, RG 38, index 98, E-8-c, f. 2214.

5. See Ben-Cion Pinchuk, *The Octobrists in the Third Duma, 1907–1912* (Seattle and London, 1974), pp. 70–80; and Shatsillo, *Russkii imperializm,* pp. 163–68.

6. Shatsillo, *Russkii imperializm,* p. 170.

7. As quoted in ibid., p. 183. See also A. Ia. Avrekh, *Stolypin i tret'ia duma* (Moscow, 1968).

8. Shatsillo, *Russkii imperializm,* pp. 128–32.

9. Ibid., pp. 79–89.

10. Though Klado wrote several books and articles during this period, the best presentation of his views is in the items on naval questions that he wrote for the military encyclopedia *Voennaia Entsiklopediia* (St. Petersburg, 1915). See also M. A. Petrov, *Podgotovka Rossii k pervoi mirovoi voine na more* (Moscow, 1926); and L. G. Beskrovnyi, *Ocherki voennoi istoriografii Rossii* (Moscow, 1962), pp. 306–8.

11. Shatsillo, *Russkii imperializm,* pp. 48–50, 176–77. In his unpublished memoirs, Grigorovich describes how the new public-relations effort included tours by Duma members of bases and ships, where they inspected guns and machines and behaved "as children in the presence of a new toy." Admiral Ivan C. Grigorovich, "Memoires, 1853–1930," AREEH, f. 4723, p. 188.

12. For an exaggerated description of Sukhomlinov see Barbara Tuchman, *The Guns of August* (New York, 1962), pp. 61–64.

13. As quoted in Shatsillo, *Russkii Imperializm,* p. 77.

14. Ibid., and "Russian Naval Estimates, 1914," NA, RG 38, index 98, D-11-c, f. 7621.
15. Shatsillo, *Russkii imperializm*, p. 223.
16. "Putiloff Works," NA, RG 38, index 98, E-12-c, f. 1644.
17. Shatsillo, *Russkii imperializm*, pp. 256-62.
18. NA, RG 38, index 98, E-12-c, f. 1644.
19. "Oboukoff Works," NA, RG 38, index 98, E-12-a, f. 08-532; "Wages in Russian Works and Yards," attaché report no. 66, 15 May 1911, NA, RG 38, index 98, C-3-a, f. 1073.
20. Shatsillo, *Russkii imperializm*, p. 224 and passim, especially chart, p. 355, and Shatsillo, "Inostrannyi kapital i voenno-morskie programmy Rossii nakanune pervoi mirovoi voiny," *Istoricheskie Zapiski* 69 (1961): 73–100; "Russian Shipbuilding Contracts for Baltic Fleet," US naval attaché report no. 160, 2 November 1912, NA, RG 38, index 98, E-8-b, f. 870.
21. "Russian Naval Academy," NA, RG 38, index 98, E-8-b, f. 870.
22. A number of officers wrote autobiographical accounts of their experiences, but few ventured into objective analysis of general conditions among officers. By far the best reminiscences are those by Dmitri Fedotoff White (naval cadet school, class of 1910), who refers to himself as "by inclination a Westerner, in the Russian sense of the word," who sought "the solution of the various Russian problems in terms of European civilization rather than those of Russian tradition." In *Survival through War and Revolution in Russia* (Philadelphia, 1939), p. 10. In a lecture delivered a number of years later, Fedotoff White noted: "Even the Navy, for a long time a stronghold of the Nobility, began to admit commoners into its Officers' ranks. The new class of Officers came from various ranks of society." In "Outline for lecture at Gettysburg, 15 May 1935," Fedotoff papers, AREEH, f. 23. 7. 3. 1.
23. S. N. Timirev, *Vospominaniia morskogo ofitsera: Baltiiskii flot vo vremia voiny i revoliutsii (1914–1918 gg)* (New York, 1961), p. 3; Donald W. Mitchell, *A History of Russian and Soviet Sea Power* (New York, 1974), pp. 280–81.
24. Timirev, *Vospominaniia morskogo ofitsera*, p. 11; Grigorovich, AREEH, f. 4723, p. 177.
25. "Discipline, efficiency of Russian Navy," NA, RG 38, index 98, E-12-a, f. 3065.
26. For a contrasting view of a unified German naval officer corps, see Daniel Horn, *The German Naval Mutinies of World War I* (New Brunswick, N.J., 1969).
27. S. S. Khesin, "Lichnyi sostav russkogo flota 1917 godu," *Voenno-*

Istoricheskii Zhurnal 11 (November 1965) : 102. Another Soviet study of social background includes four recruiting years (1913–16) and apportions 48,853 draftees for the Baltic fleet as follows: workers, 36.2 %; fishermen and commercial seamen, 15.3 %; peasants, 23.2 %; and others (telegraphers, clerks, artisans, etc.), 25.3 %. V. V. Petrash, *Moriaki Baltiiskogo flota v bor'be za pobedu oktiabria* (Moscow-Leningrad, 1966), p. 21. Khesin places less emphasis on the importance of social background for the revolutionizing of the fleet than Petrash does. In purest Marxist terms a sailor cannot be a worker, because he has no direct relationship to the means of production. Therefore, Khesin argues that the chief cause of the growth of radical feeling in the fleet was its proximity to the industrial centers, its absorption of worker unrest, rather than its "proletarian" character.

28. L. T. Senchakova, *Revoliutsionnoe dvizhenie v russkoi armii i flote v kontse XIX–nachale XX v.* (Moscow, 1972), pp. 20–21.

29. "Organization and Administration of the Russian Navy, compiled for the use of midshipmen at the naval school by Major General Eickar, translated in the office of U.S. naval attaché, Petrograd, 1915-1916," p. 29, NA, RG 45 (Naval Records Collection of the Office of Naval Records and Library, subject file, 1911–27), WA 6, box 612, f. 8248.

30. L. G. Beskrovnyi, *Russkaia armiia i flot v XIX veke: Voenno-ekonomicheskii potentsial Rossii* (Moscow, 1973), pp. 550–51. Literacy is only one indicator and an inconstant one at that, for sources vary considerably. These percentages probably include those who could write their own name.

31. Ibid.; Senchakova, *Revoliutsionnoe dvizhenie*, pp. 20–21. Even considering the much larger size of the army—over one million men, contrasted with around fifty thousand for the navy in 1900—more workers ended up as sailors than as soldiers.

32. For the navy as a whole, 95.42% of the sailors were either Russian, Ukrainian, or Belorussian. S. S. Khesin, *Oktiabr'skaia revoliutsiia i flot* (Moscow, 1971), p. 26.

33. After a visit to Kronstadt in 1915, the U.S. naval attaché gave Russian naval training a high rating: "The distinguishing peculiarity of the Russian system of instruction is its intimate association with practice throughout an entire course. In every specialty the actual apparatus with which the men is [*sic*] later supposed to deal is [utilized], and they are constantly required to demonstrate their proficiency in work with it." In "Russian Naval Schools at Kronstadt," NA, RG 38, index 98, E-8-c, f. 5460.

34. "Organization and Administration of the Russian Navy," pp. 57–58, NA, RG 45, WA 6, box 612, f. 8248.
35. Captain Karpov, "Mysli o vozstanii na flote," *Chasovoi* 78 (15 April 1932): 11.
36. Petrash, *Moriaki Baltiiskogo flota*, p. 17.
37. Leon Trotsky, *1905*, Vintage ed., trans. Anya Bostock (New York, 1971), p. 207.
38. Senchakova, *Revoliutsionnoe dvizhenie*, pp. 42–43.
39. Ibid., pp. 48–59.
40. Ibid., p. 61.
41. Ibid., pp. 61–66.
42. Ibid., p. 143. The reference is to Lenin's "Letter to a Comrade on Our Organizational Tasks," written in September 1902; but other pointed remarks on the importance of securing bases in the military forces are found in several pamphlets and articles of this period, particularly in "What Is to Be Done" and "On Demonstrations," the latter published in *Iskra* in October 1902.
43. Senchakova, *Revoliutsionnoe dvizhenie*, pp. 147–48; S. F. Naida *Revoliutsionnoe dvizhenie v tsarskom flote, 1825–1917 gg.* (Moscow-Leningrad, 1948), pp. 71–77.
44. Senchakova, *Revoliutsionnoe dvizhenie*, pp. 191–92.
45. Ibid., pp. 161–66.
46. *Revoliutsionnyi bronenosets—vozstanie v Chernomorskom flote* (Geneva, 1905), pp. 9–11, 29–33. For a popular account, see Richard Hough, *The Potemkin Mutiny* (Englewood Cliffs, N.J., 1963).
47. Platonov, "Moriaki v revoliutsii 1905 goda," *Krasnyi flot* 10 (October 1925): 15.
48. Ibid.
49. Trotsky, *1905*, p. 123 and passim; W. S. Woytinsky, *Stormy Passage: A Personal History through Two Russian Revolutions to Democracy and Freedom, 1905–1960* (New York, 1961), pp. 44–53.
50. R. [Fedor] Raskol'nikov, *Revoliutsionnyi flot* (Kronstadt, 1918), p. 4.
51. Trotsky, *1905*, pp. 166–67; Woytinsky, *Stormy Passage*, pp. 53–54.
52. As quoted in Woytinsky, *Stormy Passage*, p. 55.
53. Trotsky, *1905*, pp. 167–69.
54. Platonov, "Moriaki v revoliutsii 1905 goda," p. 16.
55. *Istoriia goroda-geroia Sevastopolia, 1783–1917*, ed. S. F. Naida (Kiev, 1960), pp. 310–21.
56. As quoted in P. Z. Sivkov, *Kronshtadt: stranitsy revoliutsionnoi istorii* (Leningrad, 1972), p. 34.
57. Ibid., pp. 33–47.

58. N. Kryzhanovskii, "Vozstanie na kreisere 'Pamiat' Azova' v 1906 godu," *Morskie Zapiski* 6 (December 1948): 5–10.
59. Ibid. 7 (March 1949): 3:12.
60. S. A. Tsion, *Tri dnia: vozstaniia v Sveaborge* (Helsingfors, 1907).
61. Kryzhanovskii, "Vozstanie," pp. 17–21; Sivkov, *Kronshtadt*, pp. 47–51.
62. Sivkov, *Kronshtadt*, p. 46.
63. M. A. Stoliarenko, *Syny partii—baltiitsy (rabota partii bol'sheviki v Baltiiskom flote, 1907–fevral' 1917 g.)* (Leningrad, 1969), pp. 21–27.
64. Ibid., pp. 30–34; A. Taimi, *Stranitsy perezhitogo*, 2d ed. (Petrozavodsk, 1955), p. 102.
65. A. Drezen, "Baltiiskii flot v gody pod"ema (1910–1913 gg.)," *Krasnaia Letopis'* 3 (1930): 132–33.
66. Stoliarenko, *Syny partii—baltiitsy*, pp. 43–46.
67. Ibid.; Sivkov, *Kronshtadt*, p. 56.
68. Aleksandr Egorov, *Baltflot v gody reaktsii, 1909–1913* (Moscow, 1928), pp. 40–44.
69. Stoliarenko, *Syny partii—baltiitsy*, pp. 49, 76–77.
70. Sivkov, *Kronshtadt*, pp. 59–60; Stoliarenko, *Syny partii-Baltiitsy*, pp. 68–74. The fact that two leaders, Avdeev (*Riurik*) and Iung (*Tsesarevich*), are not mentioned in these Soviet sources indicates a non-Bolshevik, probably SR, leadership. See Grigorovich, "Memoires," AREEH, f. 4723, p. 186; and [Tipol't], "Dnevnik russkogo morskogo ofitsera, 1917–1918," Golder Collection, HI, box 17, pp. 17–18.
71. Sivkov, *Kronshtadt*, pp. 60–61; Lenin, *Polnoe sobranie sochineniia*, 5th ed. (Moscow, 1958–65), pp. 48, 84, 22, 3–4.
72. Sivkov, *Kronshtadt*, p. 57; "Disciplinary Action in the Russian Navy," 5 February 1913, NA, RG 38, index 98, f. 2568.
73. Egorov, *Baltflot*, p. 73. It is significant that, though Soviet sources emphasize the importance of these disciplinary actions, few Bolsheviks are listed among the accused. Several later became Bolsheviks, however. See Stoliarenko, *Syny partii—baltiitsy*, p. 82.
74. Stoliarenko, *Syny partii—baltiitsy*, p. 88; Dybenko, *Iz nedr tsarskogo flota k velikomu oktiabriu* (Moscow, 1958), pp. 20–23.
75. Sivkov, *Kronshtadt*, pp. 63–65.
76. Grigorovich, "Memoires," AREEH, f. 4723, pp. 197, 222–23.

CHAPTER 2

1. Appendix by Sergei Tereshchenko, in G. Graf, *Na "Novike"* (Munich, 1922), pp. 458–68.

2. Adm. A. I. Rusin, "Imperatorskii russkii flot v velikuiu voinu," *Chaso-voi* 148–49 (May 1935): 11. Grand Duke Nicholas at first objected to the request to start laying mines, but he was convinced by Ianushkevich, the chief of staff. See also Dmitrii Fedotoff White, *Survival through War and Revolution in Russia* (Philadelphia, 1939), p. 34. Fedotov, who added the name White after the revolution, served on the mine-laying cruiser *Rossiia* at the beginning of the war, then was appointed assistant naval attaché in Washington; he rejoined the Baltic fleet in 1916 as second in command of the destroyer *Strashnyi*.
3. Capt. V. Merkushov, "Otvergnutyi plan," *Zarubezhnyi Morskoi Sbornik* 13 (Pilzen, 1931): 31.
4. As quoted in "The Russian Navy: 1914–1918," in *The Times History of the War*, vol. 16 (London, 1918), p. 306.
5. V. V. Petrash, *Moriaki Baltiiskogo flota v bor'be za pobedu oktiabria* (Moscow-Leningrad, 1966), p. 52; S. S. Khesin, *Oktiabraia revoliutsiia i flot* (Moscow, 1971), pp. 30–32.
6. M. A. Stoliarenko, *Syny partii—baltiitsy* (Leningrad, 1969), p. 117.
7. "Russian Volunteer Fleet," NA, RG 45, box 613, WA 6.
8. *"Ariadne,"* brochure of Finnish Steamship Line (Helsinki, 1969).
9. See Michael Futrell, *Northern Underground* (London, 1963).
10. Capt. V. Merkushov, "Kratkii ocherk razvitiia russkago podvodnago flota," *Chasovoi* 99 (1 March 1933): 14.
11. R. H. Bruce Lockhart, *Memoirs of a British Agent* . . . (London and New York, 1932), p. 146. Commander Cromie, who died tragically on the steps of the British Embassy in Petrograd on 23 August 1918, was born at Duncannon Fort, Ireland, in 1882, was commissioned in 1898, and entered submarine service in 1903.
12. Coal imports for St. Petersburg and Kronstadt amounted to 2,899,152 tons in 1913. At the beginning of the war, reserves at Kronstadt consisted of 40,000 tons of New Castle, and 30,000 tons of Welsh, coal. "Russia: Coast Report, Part II: Baltic and Arctic: Sect. 1: Russo-Swedish Frontier to Petrograd (March 1915)," pp. 39–42, NA, RG 45, box 605, f. 9304. These coast reports, which were prepared by British intelligence, contain excellent detailed maps of Baltic port facilities.
13. Fedotoff White, *Survival*, pp. 33–34. A good summary of the battle actions of the Baltic fleet is found in Donald Mitchell, *A History of Russian and Soviet Sea Power* (New York, 1974), pp. 283–310. For a more complete description, but one containing a number of unfortunate errors, see H. Graf, *La Marine russe dans la guerre et dans la révolution* (Paris, 1928); and for the fullest details, see *Flot v pervoi mirovoi voine*, 2 vols., ed. N. B. Pavlovich (Moscow, 1964).

14. Fedotoff White, *Survival*, pp. 28–32.
15. George N. Vesselago, "Episodes Recalled," Vesselago Collection, HI, box 8. Other valuable officer memoirs, both published and in manuscript, are those of Fedotoff White, Graf, Tipolt, Rengarten, and Timirev.
16. S. N. Timirev, *Vospominaniia morskogo ofitsera: Baltiiskii flot vo vremia voiny i revoliutsii (1914–1918 gg.)* (New York, 1961), pp. 26–27.
17. Ibid., pp. 73–75.
18. Dmitri Fedotoff White, "Untitled Autobiography," AREEH, p. 14.
19. Timirev, *Vospominaniia morskogo ofitsera*, pp. 78–82 and passim. For the most complete list of squadrons and ships with their commanders, as of 1 March 1917, see the appendix by Tereshchenko, in Graf, *Na "Novike,"* pp. 458–73.
20. For an example, see Timirev, *Vospominaniia morskogo ofitsera*, p. 77.
21. Ibid., pp. 17, 58.
22. I. I. Rengarten, "Fevral'skaia revoliutsiia v Baltiiskom flote," *Krasnyi Arkhiv* 32 (1929): 92–93.
23. Ibid., pp. 94–95.
24. Fedotoff White, *Survival*, p. 77.
25. Limited information is available on the national composition of the Baltic fleet. Army attached units were definitely more diverse, however. The First Grenadier Infantry Battalion, which was stationed at the Hango-Lapvik base in late 1917, consisted of 694 Great Russians, 76 Ukrainians, 8 Belorussians, 9 Tatars, 7 Bashkirs, 6 Chuvash, 6 Poles, 4 Jews, 2 Lithuanians, 1 Armenian, 1 Latvian, and 1 Finn. The crew of the submarine tender *Oland* was divided as follows: 35 Great Russians, 3 Ukrainians, and 1 Estonian; on four submarines there were 155 Great Russians, 16 Ukrainians, 3 Poles, 2 Estonians, 2 Latvians, 1 Lithuanian, and 1 Finn. "Delo 1917 g. po opisi no. 7v, rasnyia perepiski," SA, VK, 3213. The composition of the submarine units (86.8 % Great Russian, 8.7 % Ukrainian, 3.2 % Baltic, and 1.4 % Polish) may accurately reflect that of the fleet as a whole.
26. Timirev, *Vospominaniia morskogo ofitsera*, p. 26.
27. "Kronshtadtsy," *Moriak* 11 (2/15 September 1917): 242. *Moriak* was the weekly journal of the nonparty Sailors' Club in Helsingfors in 1917.
28. P. E. Dybenko, *Iz nedr tsarskogo flota k velikomu oktiabriu* (Moscow, 1958), p. 37. Unless otherwise indicated, citations will be to this edited version of Dybenko's original memoirs, which were originally published in 1928.

    For the great impression on the officers and crews of the cruisers who witnessed the sinking, see Fedotoff White, *Survival*, pp. 28–29, and

A. S. Nevolin, *Avrorovtsy* (Moscow, 1967), p. 17. The crew of the *Aurora* was especially shocked that a small piece of the deck was all that could be found of their sister cruiser.

29. Dybenko, *Iz nedr tsarskogo flota*, pp. 37–39.
30. Stoliarenko, *Syny partii—baltiitsy*, pp. 92–97.
31. Dybenko, *Iz nedr tsarkogo flota*, pp. 22, 38. The Russian term was *bakovyi vestnik*, i.e., "scuttlebutt."
32. Stoliarenko, *Syny partii—baltiitsy*, p. 131.
33. Ibid., pp. 132–33; and Dybenko, *Iz nedr tsarkogo flota*, pp. 41–42, where the date of the *Gangut* uprising is erroneously recalled as November.
34. Dybenko, *Iz nedr tsarkogo flota*, p. 42.
35. The attention of Soviet scholars to the *Gangut* affair provides some measure of Bolshevik strength at this time. Among the ninety-five arrested, only one other sailor besides Polukhin—Konstantin Pronskii·— is credited with being a Bolshevik, but at least four other Bolsheviks —A. M. Afanasev, Vasilii Lemikhov, S. V. Pinchuk, and Dmitrii Ivanov—escaped detention. Stoliarenko, *Syny partii—baltiitsy*, pp. 134–35. Both Polukhin and Pronskii played prominent parts in the Bolshevik revolution and the Civil War, with the former being executed as one of the 26 Baku commissars in 1918.
36. Dybenko, *Iz nedr tsarkogo flota*, p. 43.
37. Viren to Chief of Naval General Staff K. V. Stetsenko, 13 December 1915, in *Revoliutsionnoe dvizhenie v armii i vo flote v. gody pervoi mirovoi voiny 1914–fevral' 1917: Sb. dokumentov*, ed. A. L. Sidorov (Moscow, 1966), p. 323.
38. Dybenko, *Iz nedr tsarkogo flota*, p. 43.
39. P. Z. Sivkov, *Kronshtadt: stranitsy revoliutsionnoi istorii* (Leningrad, 1972), p. 67. The existence of this committee was not widely known either then or later. Stoliarenko, writing a few years earlier than Sivkov, calls this organization the Central Communications Group, which more graphically describes its operations. Stoliarenko, *Syny partii-baltiitsy*, p. 144.
40. V. N. Zalezhskii, *Iz vospominanii podpolshchika* (Kharkov, 1931), pp. 143–44; Stoliarenko, *Syny partii—baltiitsy*, p. 141.
41. Stoliarenko, *Syny partii—baltiitsy*, p. 146.
42. *Revoliutsionnoe dvizhenie*, p. 321.
43. Stoliarenko, *Syny partii—baltiitsy*, p. 143.
44. *Revoliutsionnoe dvizhenie*, p. 353.
45. Sivkov, *Kronshtadt*, pp. 69–70; Stoliarenko, *Syny partii—baltiitsy*, pp.

148–50; V. Nelaev, "Matros-Bol'shevik Timofei Ul'iantsev," *Voenno-Istoricheskii Zhurnal* 10 (1968): 107.

46. These sailors were most likely almost entirely Bolsheviks, but the number does not include Orlov, his wife, Zalezhskii, and several other party workers who were arrested in connection with the incident. Sivkov, *Kronshtadt*, p. 71; Zalezhskii, *Iz vospominanii podpolshchika*, p. 146; *Revoliutsionnoe dvizhenie*, pp. 346–53.

47. Sivkov, *Kronshtadt*, pp. 72–74; Stoliarenko, *Syny partii—baltiitsy*, pp. 153–54.

48. Sivkov, *Kronshtadt*, pp. 78–80.

49. Ibid., p. 79.

50. Stoliarenko, *Syny partii—baltiitsy*, p. 154.

51. Sivkov, *Kronshtadt*, p. 99. The question of exactly how many Bolsheviks were actually at Kronstadt at the beginning of 1917 may never be answered. Only twenty-six (twenty sailors, three soldiers, and three workers) have been identified by name, and given the Soviet penchant for detail in such matters, this may be the total figure! The list with "and others" added is found in ibid., p. 85. But it should also be noted that some who were not Bolsheviks were connected with their organizations and even attended meetings of the Main Collective.
    A Western scholar, David Longley, has questioned the existence of a strong Bolshevik organization at Kronstadt in 1916; he points out that only five of the seventeen tried can be identified as Bolsheviks, apparently Sladkov, Uliantsev, Brendin, Kuznetsov-Lomakin, and Khovrin (Longley does not provide names). Available sources are indeed ambiguous on the particulars, but police reports at the time list a number of other "Social Democrats"—F. E. Resanov, S. D. Polishchuk, U. V. Zhuk, Gabril Bozhanov, Ivan Bozikov, Ivan Rudakov, Andrei Sergeev, and Liudvig Tomson. Sivkov also mentions Pisarev, Zakupnev, Veshchev, and Marusev. The problem is whether these men were correctly identified by the police and also whether they were actually among those arrested and tried as the "Kronstadt Seventeen," as seems probable. That all names have not been cited in Soviet secondary sources may be because they did not remain Bolsheviks. The evidence would also tend to show that some of the fleet's Bolsheviks, Uliantsev and Khovrin in particular, had a number of friends and supporters who were probably not officially Bolsheviks at this time. For Longley's discussion, see "Some Historiographical Problems of Bolshevik Party History (The Kronstadt Bolsheviks in March 1917)," *Jahrbücher für Geschichte Osteuropas*, n.s. 22 (1974, no. 4): 502.
    Of the five definite Bolsheviks before the court, Sladkov, Uliantsev,

and Brendin received prison terms, while Khovrin and Kuznetsov-Lomakin were sent to front-line units. Khovrin, in his recollections of these events, describes how "we" escaped after a few weeks and found refuge back in Petrograd among friends in the Vyborg District of the city. N. Khovrin, "V dni fevral'skoi revoliutsii," *Sovetskaia Ukraina* 3 (1957) : 128; Sivkov, *Kronshtadt*, p. 72.

52. As quoted in *Izvestiia Kronshtadtskago Soveta*, 20 July 1917.
53. Grigorovich, "Memoires," AREEH, f. 4723, pp. 261–63.
54. Ibid., p. 270.

CHAPTER 3

1. "It does not occur to government that oats should be requisitioned." Buchanan to Foreign Office, 9 March 1917, PRO, FO 371/2995.
2. Winship to State Department, 10 November 1916, NA, RG 45, WA 6, box 608.
3. On the background to the February Revolution, see E. N. Burdzhalov, *Vtoraia russkaia revoliutsiia: vosstanie v Petrograde* (Moscow, 1967); Marc Ferro, *The Russian Revolution of February 1917* (London, 1972); and George Katkov, *Russia 1917: The February Revolution* (New York, 1967).
4. *Istoriia rabochikh Leningrada*, vol. 1, ed. S. N. Valk et al. (Leningrad, 1972), pp. 501–2; M. A. Stoliarenko, *Syny partii-baltiitsy* (Leningrad, 1969), pp. 151–52. Other Bolsheviks, including Khovrin, Marusev, and Kuznetsov-Lomakin, were sent to front-line units, from which they soon deserted.
5. Buchanan to Foreign Office, 9 March 1917, PRO, FO 371/2995. One of the best appraisals of Russia on the eve of the revolution is that of Captain Newton A. McCully, the American naval attaché, who was an experienced witness of Russian affairs, having been an observer on the Russian side in the Russo-Japanese War and a resident in Petrograd since the beginning of World War I: "In the principal towns, particularly Moscow and Petrograd, reside the revolutionary and other elements of disorder, and it is here that any organized movement is likely to commence. In political matters recently British influence has become very strong, and occupies itself almost as much with the internal politics of Russia, as with the financial and commercial conditions, where it is in supreme control. In Petrograd, the British ambassador acting in cooperation with the Progressive 'block' of the Duma, is hardly less powerful than the Emperor himself. . . . Great as are the

difficulties in administration, labor, and supply, those of transportation are now by far the greatest. . . . Moral restraint and self control have diminished. One of the most striking evidences of this is the increasing vogue of spiritualism. . . . Combined with the general disturbance of moral ideas, uncertain means of existence, and loss of the sense of responsibility due to war conditions, the problem of preserving internal order becomes more and more difficult. An organized movement of any kind against the Government would find support from many elements in Russia. Flesh and blood is the cheapest thing in Russia." McCully to ONI, 6 March 1917, NA, RG 165, f. 6497–12.

6. MA for DMI, in Buchanan to FO, 12 March 1917, PRO, FO 371/2995.
7. Lindley to Buchanan, 9 February 1917, PRO, FO 371/3005. The sense of impending doom that prevailed in British dispatches from Russia in the winter of 1916–17 influenced the views of British statesmen, who were already pessimistic about Russia's chances to continue the war. The ambassador in Paris wrote, in reference to the news received from Petrograd: "What is depressing is the disorganization, the increased cost of living and the incapacity of the Government." Bertie to Hardinge, 16 October 1916, PRO, FO 800/178 (the Private Papers of Sir Francis Lord Bertie of Thame). And as hope for Russian fighting declined in London, efforts to get the United States into the war increased.
8. Burdzhalov, *Vtoraia russkaia revoliutsiia*, pp. 87–91.
9. Ibid., pp. 72–76; A. V. Ignat'ev, *Vneshniaia politika vremennogo pravitel'stva* (Moscow, 1974), pp. 42–66.
10. On the starting cranks, see Commander Cromie's letter to Admiral Phillimore (diary form), in Admiralty War Staff, "Report on the Situation in the Baltic," 1 April 1917, PRO, ADM 137/500. Another, undated version is published in "Documents on British Relations with Russia, 1917–1918," vol. 2, comp. and ed. David R. Jones, *Canadian-American Slavic Studies* 7 (no. 3, Fall 1973) : 356–61.
11. Cromie to Phillimore, 1 April 1917, PRO, ADM 137/500; and "Report of British Naval Armoured Car Division (Commander Locker Sampson)," 19 March 1917, PRO, ADM 137/1388.
12. *Baltiiskie moriaki v podgotovke i provedenii velikoi oktiabr'skoi sotsialisticheskoi revoliutsii*, ed. R. N. Mordvinov (Moscow-Leningrad, 1957), p. 330 n.2; "Iz vospominanii B. V. B'erkelunda," MS, AREEH, pp. 12–22. B'erkelund was a midshipman on leave from the battleship *Petropavlovsk* who was assigned to the depot troop. In attempting to restore order after the murder of Girs, he was hit over the head, but managed to walk out of the compound, never to return to naval duty.
13. A. S. Nevolin, *Avrorovtsy* (Moscow, 1967), p. 23.

14. Workers in this shipbuilding factory, which had been owned by the Admiralty since 1913, were among the most militant in Petrograd. The strike of three hundred masters of the foundry for a 100 % increase in salary on 22 February was a major boost to the unrest in the capital. A. G. Shliapnikov, *Semnadtsatyi god*, vol. 1 (Moscow-Petrograd, 1923), p. 80.

15. E. Iunga, *Bessmertnyi korabl'* (Moscow, 1957), pp. 19–26.

16. P. Kurkov, "1917 god na 'Avrora,'" *Morskoi Sbornik* 80 (October 1927): 16–19. Nevolin credits a machinist by the name of Bragin with the shooting of Nikolskii. Nevolin, *Avrorovtsy*, p. 41.

17. Nevolin, *Avrorovtsy*, pp. 43–45.

18. Ibid., p. 46.

19. Ibid., pp. 48–50; but Kurkov writes that the original ship's committee consisted of only four men—one anarchist and the others "leaning toward" the SRs. P. Kurkov, "Kreiser Avrora," *Bor'ba Klassov* 6–7 (1931): 11.

20. Nevolin, *Avrorovtsy*, pp. 49–50.

21. George Bury, a British businessman who was present in Petrograd, reported to the War Cabinet in April: "The Revolution was confined mainly to Petrograd and the Navy. There was little, if any, disturbance elsewhere throughout Russia." "The Russian Revolution," memorandum by George Bury, 5 April 1917, PRO, CAB 24/9, f. 409.

22. P. Z. Sivkov, *Kronshtadt* (Leningrad, 1972), p. 84.

23. "V revoliutsionnom Kronshtadte," in *Voennye moriaki v bor'be za pobedu oktiabr'skoi revoliutsii*, ed. S. F. Naida (Moscow, 1958), pp. 289–90. The exact chronology of the events in Kronstadt continues to be confused in Soviet sources. Sivkov, whose account should be the latest and most reliable, places the planning of signals for the uprising at a Bolshevik conference on the twenty-fourth, which is highly unlikely, since no one could then foresee the course of events in Petrograd. See Sivkov, *Kronshtadt*, pp. 84–85.

24. "Iz vospominanii matrosa uchebno-minnogo otriada A. G. Pronina," in *Baltiiskie moriaki v podgotovke*, pp. 19–20.

25. Ibid., p. 20.

26. Ibid.

27. Evgenyi Bakhmetev, "Oktiabr' v fevrale (Kronshtadtskie vospominaniia)," *Krasnyi Baltiets*, no. 10 (October, 1920), pp. 35–42.

28. *Baltiiskie moriaki v podgotovke*, p. 21.

29. Sivkov, *Kronshtadt*, p. 88. Sources vary about the moment of Viren's death. Quite possibly he was only unconscious when taken to Anchor Square. Bakhmetev, writing soon after the event and in a source read

by many of the participants, relates that Viren was shot by a released prisoner not far from his house, after which a deranged woman (Viren's wife or daughter?) appeared and succeeded in shooting two sailors before being overpowered. Bakhmetev, "Oktiabr' v fevrale," p. 38.

30. Bakhmetev, "Oktiabr' v fevrale," p. 39; A. F. Nazarov, *Nikolai Markin* (Moscow, 1964), p. 19.

31. Sivkov, *Kronshtadt*, pp. 89–90.

32. *Baltiiskie moriaki v podgotovke*, p. 21.

33. Sivkov, *Kronshtadt*, p. 90; Bakhmetev, "Oktiabr' v fevrale," pp. 41–42.

34. Sivkov, *Kronshtadt*, pp. 92–93.

35. Diary of destroyer commander N. A. Tipol't, in *Baltiiskie moriaki v podgotovke*, p. 26.

36. Rear Adm. V. A. Belli, "Dni fevral'skoi revoliutsii v minnoi divizii Baltiiskogo flota v Revele," in *Sbornik dokladov voennoistoricheskoi sektsii, Leningradskii dom uchenykh im. M. Gor'kogo*, vol. 2 (Moscow-Leningrad, 1959), pp. 40–41; V. A. Liubinskii to A. I. Nepenin, 6:00 P.M., 2 March 1917, in *Baltiiskie moriaki v podgotovke*, p. 25; Dmitri Fedotoff White, *Survival through War and Revolution in Russia* (Philadelphia, 1939), p. 87.

37. Fedotoff White, *Survival*, pp. 79–89.

38. S. S. Khesin, *Oktiabr'skaia revoliutsiia i flot* (Moscow, 1971), pp. 40–42.

39. Fedotoff White, *Survival*, p. 91.

40. The text of the resolution, which cannot be found in Soviet sources, is an enclosure in the U.S. naval attaché's report of 20 May, NA, RG 38, 6220B (U-1-i).

41. S. N. Timirev, *Vospominaniia morskogo ofitsera* (New York, 1961), p. 93.

42. Capt. I. I. Rengarten, "Fevral'skaia revoliutsiia v Baltiiskom flote," *Krasnyi Arkhiv* 32 (1929): 102.

43. Ibid., pp. 90–91, 103.

44. H. Graf, *Na "Novike"* (Munich, 1922), p. 356.

45. In *Baltiiskie moriaki v podgotovke*, p. 27.

46. Ibid., p. 29. On the initiative of the crew of the *Imperator Pavel I*, see E. P. Perovskii, *Vernyi dolgu revoliutsii* (Leningrad, 1964), pp. 42–45.

47. Rengarten, "Fevral'skaia revoliutsiia," p. 107.

48. Flag officer's journal, Second Squadron of Battleships, in *Baltiiskie moriaki v podgotovke*, pp. 30–31; Rengarten, "Fevral'skaia revoliutsiia," pp. 103–6.

49. Perovskii, *Vernyi dolgu revoliutsii*, p. 45.

50. N. N. Sukhanov, *The Russian Revolution of 1917*, ed. and trans. Joel Carmichael, 2 vols. (New York, 1962) 1:178–79.

51. Rengarten, "Fevral'skaia revoliutsiia," p. 107.
52. *Baltiiskii moriaki v podgotovke*, pp. 33–34. Adding to Nepenin's problems was his basic unpopularity among both officers and sailors. Timirev, *Vospominaniia morskogo ofitsera*, pp. 73–81; "Russkaia revoliutsiia i Imperatorskaia Rossiia," MS, AREEH, 22. 7. 7. 2, 1:1–20. The latter, the memoirs of an anonymous former sailor stationed at Åbo in 1917, was written outside of the Soviet Union, in Riga, in 1932.
53. Nepenin to Stavka, 4 March, in *Baltiiskie moriaki v podgotovke*, p. 34. The initiative for Maksimov's election apparently came from a group of liberal staff officers led by Capt. Lev Murav'ev. Rengarten, "Fevral'skaia revoliutsiia," p. 109.
54. Flag officer's journal, in *Baltiiskie moriaki v podgotovke*, pp. 36–37; Rengarten, "Fevral'skaia revoliutsiia," p. 110.
55. H. Graf, *La Marine russe* (Paris, 1928), pp. 218–19; Timirev, *Vospominaniia morskogo ofitsera*, p. 95.
56. Graf, *Marine russe*, pp. 220–21; Rengarten, "Fevral'skaia revoliutsiia," p. 110. Whether the first bullet killed the admiral is not known for certain. Several other shots were fired into the body, which also suffered mutilation.
57. Order no. 1 of A. S. Maksimov, SA, VK, 3184.
58. Graf, *Marine russe*, p. 221.
59. V. V. Petrash, *Moriaki Baltiiskogo flota v bor'be za pobedu oktiabria* (Moscow-Leningrad, 1966), p. 52. These figures are based upon documentary study, but the confusion of the times defies absolute accuracy.
60. Petrash, *Moriaki Baltiiskogo flota*, pp. 59–60.
61. Graf, *Marine russe*, p. 237; B'erkelund, "Iz vospominanii," MS, AREEH, p. 46.
62. McCully's report to ONI, in "Revolution in Russia," 3 April 1917, NA, RG 45, WA 6, box 608 (6220A).
63. Graf, *Marine russe*, pp. 224–28.
64. Sukhanov, *Russian Revolution*, 1:179.
65. "Report of Rear Adm. Glennon's Movements in Russia, and Naval Information," app. 4, p. 5, in "Report of the Special Mission to Russia, June–July (Root Mission)," NA, microcopy 367, roll 48.
66. Timirev, *Vospominaniia morskogo ofitsera*, pp. 93–96. See also N. Monasterev and S. Terestchenko, *Histoire de la marine russe* (Paris, 1932), pp. 320–21.
67. V. Gaidamak, "Na Chernom more," *Sovetskaia Ukraina* 3 (1957): 131. Gaidamak, a Baltic Bolshevik sailor and an expert diver, was sent to assist in an attempt to raise the battleship.
68. B'erkelund, "Iz vospominaniia," MS, AREEH, p. 56. The author, it is

true, was not present in Helsingfors at the time, but he had ample opportunity to converse with fellow officers later and to consider the views of other émigrés.

69. Graf, *Marine russe*, p. 242.
70. N. Khovrin, "V dni fevral'skoi revoliutsii," *Sovetskaia Ukraina* 3 (1957): 129–30. After describing his activities among the workers of the Vyborg District of Petrograd in February, Khovrin states, "I was directed to Helsingfors." This evidence might support David Longley's interesting analysis of the divisions within the Bolsheviks in February and March and the ultra-left position of the Vyborg committee. See "Some Historiographical Problems of Bolshevik Party History (The Kronstadt Bolsheviks in March 1917)," *Jahrbücher für Geschichte Osteuropas* 22 (1974): 494–514.
71. Cited in N. N. Golovin, *The Russian Army in the World War* (New Haven, Conn., 1931), p. 261.

CHAPTER 4

1. "Outline for lecture at Gettysburg," 15 May 1935, Fedotoff White Papers, AREEH.
2. "Spisok deputatov . . . ," SA, VK, 3901; V. V. Petrash, *Moriaki Baltiiskogo flota v bor'be za pobedu oktiabria* (Moscow-Leningrad, 1966), pp. 59–60.
3. Petrash, *Moriaki Baltiiskogo flota*, p. 57.
4. P. Z. Sivkov, *Kronshtadt: stranitsy revoliutsionnoi istorii* (Leningrad, 1972), pp. 100–104; F. N. Dingel'shtedt, "Vesna proletarskoi revoliutsii," *Krasnaia Letopis'* 12 (no. 1, 1925): 195–97. See also David Longley, "Some Historiographical Problems of Bolshevik Party History (The Kronstadt Bolsheviks in March 1917)," *Jahrbücher für Geschichte Osteuropas* 27 (1974): 497–98.
5. E. P. Perovskii, *Vernyi dolgu revoliutsii* (Leningrad, 1964), p. 53.
6. P. Kurkov, "1917 god na 'Avrora,'" *Morskoi Sbornik* 53 (October 1927): 19.
7. V. N. Zalezhskii, *Iz vospominanii podpol'shchika* (Kharkov, 1931), p. 183. Though at first a "moderate" who supported the Provisional Government, Garin considered himself a Bolshevik and attended the Seventh (April) Conference of the party.
8. A complete file of the orders of the commander in chief is in SA, VK, 3184.
9. McCully to ONI, "Revolution in Russia," 21 March–3 April 1917, NA, RG 45, WA 6, box 608.

10. Cromie to Phillimore, in "Situation in the Baltic," 18 March–1 April 1917, PRO, ADM 137/500. Cromie concluded pessimistically: "The Baltic Fleet as a force does not exist as officers are quite powerless and are not even saluted (nor are we). . . . If we can only get sweepers and miners going the submarines who are a good lot will do well but how can you trust a big ship?"

11. MA for DMI, in Buchanan to FO, 18 March 1917, PRO, FO 371/2998. All British reports were channeled through Buchanan for purposes of telegraphic control. Communications from various British military agents kept the ambassador so busy that at one point he complained that he felt like a postal clerk.

12. Dmitri Fedotoff White, *Survival through War and Revolution in Russia* (Philadelphia, 1939), pp. 120–21.

13. S. S. Khesin, *Oktiabr'skaia revoliutsiia i flot* (Moscow, 1971), pp. 101–3.

14. McCully to ONI, 27 March 1917, NA, RG 165, 6497-12.

15. Buchanan to FO, 31 March 1917, PRO, FO 371/2995. The cumulative effect of these reports caused the Admiralty War Staff to circulate a secret memorandum, "The effect of the revolution on the Situation in the Baltic," dated 1 April 1917, which concluded: "It is of urgent importance that law and order should again be established in the Baltic Fleet without delay, or the results, once the Baltic is clear of ice, may very well be disastrous not only to Russia, but to our cause in general." PRO, ADM 137/1249.

16. Report of A. Fishwick, in A. W. Woodhouse to Buchanan, enclosure in Buchanan to FO, 30 March 1917, PRO, FO 371/2996.

17. MA for DMI, in Buchanan to FO, 6 April 1917, PRO, FO 371/2995.

18. Buchanan to FO, 4 April 1917, PRO, FO 371/2995. The day before, the minister of finance, Tereshchenko, admitted, "Maximoff had no authority over his men and that he would have to be removed." Buchanan to FO, 3 April 1917, PRO, FO 371/2995.

19. NA for DNI, in Buchanan to FO, 9 April 1917, PRO, ADM 137/1249. The views of Commander Grenfell, the naval attaché, were considerably more moderate than those of other reporters. London considered him too friendly with socialists, and after Miliukov complained, he was recalled.

20. N. Tochenyi, "Kronshtadttsy i vremennoe pravitel'stvo," in *Voennye moriaki v bor'be za pobedu oktiabr'skoi revoliutsii*, ed. S. F. Naida (Moscow, 1958), pp. 318–19; Sivkov, *Kronshtadt*, pp. 133–35.

21. McCully to ONI, 24 April 1917, NA, RG 45, WA 6, box 606 (P-2-b). Suspicion and distrust between officers and men obviously increased after the revolution. As McCully observed, "The men ever fear that the

officers will run the ships on mines and destroy them in order to get even." To ONI, 17 April 1917, NA, RG 45, WA 6, box 608: "A number of Russian Military and Naval Officers have been to the Embassy asking if they could get a commission in our services." "Conditions in Russia," Office of Naval Intelligence report, 31 July 1917, based upon McCully's report of 10 April 1917, NA, RG 45, WA 6, box 608.

22. Buchanan to FO, 24 April 1917, PRO, ADM 137/1249; Lindley's report, 13 May 1917, PRO, FO 371/2996.

23. Sivkov, *Kronshtadt*, pp. 170–72, 212; Khesin, *Oktiabr'skaia revoliutsiia i flot*, pp. 260–78.

24. Tochenyi, "Kronshtadttsy," pp. 321–22.

25. Grove's report, 24 May 1917, PRO, FO 371/3007. Grove also warned, "Admiral Maximoff is, as you know, a thorough faced revolutionary and republican and also a confirmed socialist, hence he looks on everything through very rosy glasses."

26. Maksimov's last order, no. 298, 2 June 1917, SA, VK, 3184, transferring authority to Verderevsky.

27. Louis Guichard and Dmitri Novik [Tereshchenko], *Sous la croix de Saint-André* (Paris, 1929), pp. 188–97; S. N. Timirev, *Vospominaniia morskogo ofitsera* (New York, 1961), pp. 95–98.

28. Zalezhskii, *Iz vospominanii podpol'shchika*, p. 183.

29. List of orders, SA, VK, 3184.

30. A. Blinov, "Pervye revoliutsionnye organy vlasti v Kronshtadte v 1917 godu," in *Voennye Moriaki*, pp. 136–37.

31. Ibid., pp. 138–40.

32. Sivkov, *Kronshtadt*, pp. 97–98.

33. Ibid., pp. 99, 131; Petrash, *Moriaki Baltiiskogo flota*, p. 71 n.88.

34. SA, VK, 3901. The "Sveaborg Soviet," which from the beginning met in the city, was officially renamed the Helsingfors Soviet.

35. Khesin, *Oktiabr'skaia revoliutsiia i flot*, pp. 76–79; I. I. Rengarten, "Fevral'skaia revoliutsiia v Baltiiskom flota," *Krasnyi Arkhiv* 32 (1929): 114–15. The sailors' section began its formal sessions on 22 March. The unpublished protocols of meetings are in "Dela za 1917 god: Gel'singforskago Matroskaia Deputatskago Sobranii," SA, VK, 3896.

36. Petrash, *Moriaki Baltiiskogo flota*, p. 72. Among the most active officers of the fleet in the Revel Soviet was Fedotoff White: "To remain passive and to observe the activities was not sensible, as there were comparatively very few educated people politically active at Reval. To leave the whole thing in the hands of a small group of workers and professional socialist politicians would be sheer stupidity. *Therefore the only proper line of action was to work in cooperation with the Soviet*" (underlin-

ing in original). "Diary," Fedotoff papers, MS, AREEH. Another officer, Captain Koptelov, was the head of the Revel fleet committee. A. Vorob'ev, "Revel'tsy," in *Voennye moriaki*, p. 403.

37. Petrash, *Moriaki Baltiiskogo flota*, p. 76. For an analysis that sharply differentiates the developments at the three main bases—Kronstadt, Helsingfors, and Revel—see David Longley, "Officers and Men: A Study of the Development of Political Attitudes among the Sailors of the Baltic Fleet in 1917," *Soviet Studies* 25 (1974): 29–50.

38. Petrash, *Moriaki Baltiiskogo flota*, pp. 72–73; A. Pronin, "Burnye gody," *Oktiabr'* 8 (August 1957): 148.

39. Blinov, "Pervye revoliutsionnye," p. 142. The number was probably not constant. Tsereteli lists 93 Socialist Revolutionaries, 91 Bolsheviks, 70 nonparty, and 46 Mensheviks in the Kronstadt Soviet in May. Irakli Tsereteli, *Vospominaniia o fevral'skoi revoliutsii*, 2 vols. (Paris, 1963), 1:414.

40. There is little evidence to support the contentions of Soviet scholars, as well as many Western ones, that the Socialist Revolutionaries ever held an "overwhelming majority in the Kronstadt Soviet." For an example of such a claim, see Longley, "Some Historiographical Problems," p. 512.

41. Petrash, *Moriaki Baltiiskogo flota*, p. 73.

42. Ibid.; M. Kh. Kiuru, *Boevoi rezerv revoliutsionnogo Petrograda v 1917 g.: iz istorii russkikh bol'shevistskikh organizatsii v Finliandii* (Petrozavodsk, 1965), p. 53.

43. Evgenyi Vishnevskii, "Matrosskaia fraktsiia Gel'singforskogo Soveta," in *Oktiabr'skii Shkval* (Moscow, 1937), pp. 53–56.

44. G. Pegel'man, "Revoliutsiia 1917 goda v Estonii," *Krasnaia Letopis'* 56–57 (1933): 118–21.

45. Petrash, *Moriaki Baltiiskogo flota*, p. 74.

46. In an incomplete listing in April, 1,512 Bolshevik sailors are accounted for. On the battleships: *Respublika*, 520; *Petropavlovsk*, 160; *Gangut*, 150; *Andrei Pervozvannyi*, 155; *Poltava*, 100; *Slava*, 73. *Baltiiskie moriaki v podgotovke i provedenii velikoi oktiabr'skoi sotsialisticheskoi revoliutsii*, ed. R. N. Mordvinov (Moscow-Leningrad, 1957), pp. 64–65.

47. Based upon figures for August, which list 2,926 workers of a total of 3,182 Bolsheviks. Pegel'man, "Revoliutsiia 1917," p. 124.

48. Petrash, *Moriaki Baltiiskogo flota*, p. 91.

49. Ibid., p. 94. The full text of the Revel officers' resolutions is also found in Robert P. Browder and Alexander F. Kerensky, eds., *The Russian Provisional Government, 1917*, 3 vols. (Stanford, Calif., 1961), 2:872–73.

50. Petrash, *Moriaki Baltiiskogo flota*, pp. 88–89.

51. Ibid., pp. 98–99.

52. A. Blinov, "Matrosskie komitety Baltiiskogo flota v 1917 godu," *Voenno-Istoricheskii Zhurnal* 9 (no. 11, November 1967) : 112.
53. N. F. Izmailov and A. S. Pukhov, *Tsentrobalt* (Kaliningrad, 1967), pp. 30–33; S. S. Khesin, "Tsentrobalt, (k 50 letiiu sozdaniia)," *Voenno-Istoricheskii Zhurnal* 9 (no. 4, April 1967) : 120. One of the two officers on the commission was a member of the Union of Naval Officers of Revel. After approving a list of delegates to the new body on 23 April, the Sailors' Assembly rejected a proposal that it disband. Protocol no. 14, SA, VK, 3896.
54. "Protokol Tsentral'nago Komiteta Balt. flota," 28 April, SA, VK, 3178. The mimeographed protocols of Tsentrobalt have been published without serious omissions in *Protokoly i postanovleniia tsentral'nogo komiteta Baltiiskogo flota, 1917–1918*, ed. D. A. Chugaev, comp. I. Z. Livshits and A. A. Muravev (Moscow and Leningrad, 1963), which includes valuable notes and an annotated biographical index.
55. SA, VK, 3178.
56. "Protokol zasedaniia Tsentral'nogo komiteta Baltiiskogo flota," 5 May 1917, in *Protokoly i postanovleniia*, p. 39. The presidium was apparently chosen by each member voting for six names, with these results: Ivan Solovev (Bolshevik), 24; Pavel Dybenko (Bolshevik), 23; Mechislav Savich-Zablotskii (pro-Bolshevik), 22; Lt. Roman Grundman (pro-Bolshevik), 20; F. Efimov (Bolshevik), 19; Lopatin (pro-Bolshevik), 11; Aleksandr Sinitsyn (Menshevik), 11; and Georgii Galkin (Bolshevik), 8, with several others receiving a total of 104 votes.
57. Izmailov and Pukhov, *Tsentrobalt*, pp. 34–35.
58. N. Khovrin, "1917-i god," in *Voennye moriaki*, p. 249; Pavel Dybenko, *Iz nedr tsarskogo flota k velikomu oktiabriu* (Moscow, 1958), p. 67.
59. "Protokol zasedaniia Tsentral'nogo komiteta Baltiiskogo flota," 11 May, in *Protokoly i postanovleniia*, p. 47.
60. N. Podvoiskii, "Voennaia organizatsiia RSDRP (b) i Voenno-revoliutsionnyi komitet v 1917 g.," *Krasnaia Letopis'* 6 (1932) : 65–66.
61. Zalezhskii, *Iz vospominanii podpol'shchika*, pp. 180–83; Petrash, *Moriaki Baltiiskogo flota*, pp. 56–58.
62. A. Il'in-Zhenevskii, "Bol'shevistskie gazety Kronshtadta i Gel'singforsa v 1917 g.," *Krasnaia Letopis'* 3 (1927) : 83–84; I. N. Kolbin, "Kronshtadt organizuetsia, gotovitsia k boiu," in *Oktiabr'skoi shkval*, p. 30.
63. Il'in-Zhenevskii, "Bol'shevistskie gazety," pp. 83–84. Raskolnikov, whose real name was Ilin, was the younger brother of Ilin-Zhenevskii. Although he was the illegitimate son of a priest, Raskolnikov received a first-rate education in church boarding schools and began the study of economics at St. Petersburg Polytechnic Institute in 1909; there he dis-

covered the works of Marx and Lenin and became a Bolshevik in 1910. He held a number of important posts in the Soviet government and was serving as minister to Bulgaria in the 1930s, when, because of his record, he defected and died under suspicious circumstances on the French Riviera in 1939. Partially rehabilitated in the 1960s with the republication of his memoirs of the revolution, his role in 1917 has again been minimized in Soviet accounts published after 1964. For a brief biography see A. P. Konstantinov, *F. F. Il'in-Raskol'nikov* (Leningrad, 1964), and Norman E. Saul, "Fedor Raskolnikov, a 'Secondary Bolshevik,'" *Russian Review* 32 (April 1973): 131–42.

64. P. Smirnov, D. Kondakov, and A. Liubovich, "Retseniia F. Raskol'nikova, *Kronshtadttsy: iz vospominaniia bol'shevika,*" *Krasnaia Letopis'* 56–57 (nos. 5–6, 1933): 213. Under Bolshevik pressure, the club became a general socialist center after April.

65. Dybenko, *Iz nedr tsarskogo flota*, pp. 55–56; "Dybenko Pavel Efimovich," in *Vospominaniia uchastnikov velikogo oktiabria*, ed. V. T. Loginov et al., *Istoricheskii Arkhiv* 5 (1957): 199. The latter consists of Dybenko's answers to a questionnaire circulated to 350 participants in the revolution by the Historical Commission of the party in 1927.

66. A. F. Il'in-Zhenevskii, *Ot fevralia k zakhvatu vlasti* (Leningrad, n.d.), p. 24.

67. A. F. Ilyin-Genevsky, *From the February Revolution to the October Revolution, 1917* (New York, 1931), p. 27 (trans. and rev. ed. of above).

68. Ibid., pp. 28–31; Dingel'shtedt, "Vesna proletarskoi revoliutsii," pp. 213–14.

69. *Volna*, no. 1 (30 March 1917).

70. *Volna*, no. 2 (31 March 1917).

71. M. A. Stoliarenko, *V. I. Lenin i revoliutsionnye moriaki* (Moscow, 1970), p. 76.

72. A nearly complete file of *Volna* is available in Helsinki, in the University of Helsinki Library and in the Työvän Arkisto (Labor Archive).

73. Ilyin-Genevsky, *From the February Revolution*, pp. 40–42; V. I. Miller, *Soldatskie komitety Russkoi armii v 1917 g.* (Moscow, 1974), pp. 174–75.

74. "Ocherk o zarozhenii i razvitii otdela partii sotsialistov-revoliutsionerov v g. Gel'singforse," *Narodnaia Niva*, no. 1 (25 April 1917), p. 2.

75. *Narodnaia Niva*, nos. 5 and 9 (29 April and 4 May 1917). At the beginning the Sailors' Club received considerable publicity in *Narodnaia Niva* and was not mentioned in *Volna*, but by June the Bolsheviks were participating actively in the club's affairs.

76. *Narodnaia Niva*, no. 12 (7 May 1917).

77. One ruble (approximately 50 cents) was worth 2.67 marks by the offi-

cial exchange rate, but because of the heavy purchases from Finland during the war the actual rate fell to 2.14 at the beginning of 1917. In April the ruble was worth 2.06 marks, but the decline in the ruble became quite rapid in the summer of 1917, with the Finnish bank at times refusing to take Russian rubles. By November the mark equaled the ruble. The Provisional Government managed to secure a large loan from the Finnish bank to help stabilize the exchange in May. But after that the Provisional Government had to purchase marks with hard currency, using precious British and American loans—over $100 million. The Baltic fleet was thus constituting a much heavier financial burden than usual, for all sailors and soldiers based on Finnish territory had to be paid in marks after May 1917. Leo Harmaja, *Effects of the War on Economic and Social Life in Finland*, Economic and Social History of the World War (New Haven, Conn., 1933), pp. 45–49.

78. *Volna*, nos. 44 and 49 (24 and 30 May 1917).

79. M. Petrov, "Moriaki Revel'skoi bazy v bor'be za sverzhenie samoderzhaviia i pobedu oktiabr'skoi revoliutsii," in *Voennye moriaki*, pp. 152–53.

80. Protocols 4 and 5, 14 and 19 April 1917, "Sobraniia chenov sektsii rasprostraneniia idei narodovlastiia," SA, VK, 3232.

81. *Izvestiia Kronshtadtskago Soveta*, no. 24 (16 April 1917).

82. Ibid., no. 25 (18 April 1917).

83. Petrash, *Moriaki Baltiiskogo flota*, p. 107.

84. Ibid., p. 110.

85. Ibid.

86. Fedor Kuznetsov, a Socialist Revolutionary member of the Kronstadt Soviet, emphasized the importance of the Roshal incident for the Bolsheviks' ability to secure a new election, in his testimony before an investigatory commission in July. *Baltiiskie moriaki v podgotovke*, pp. 90–91.

87. *Izvestiia Gel'singforsskago Soveta*, no. 34 (26 April 1917). A few days later the Helsingfors Soviet voted against the Provisional Government's Loan for Freedom, 217 to 125, but accepted a Narodnik and Menshevik resolution that the loan would be acceptable if it were controlled by the Petrograd Soviet and if it included a direct tax on capital and military profits and the confiscation of church and monastery capital reserves. *Volna*, no. 27 (2 May 1917).

88. Petrash, *Moriaki Baltiiskogo flota*, p. 112.

89. *Izvestiia Kronshtadtskago Soveta*, nos. 44, 53, and 58 (11, 24, and 30 May 1917). The newspaper was about two weeks late in publishing the protocols of the soviet sessions.

90. Quoted in V. F. Shishkin, "Kronshtadskii intsident v mae 1917 goda," *Uchenye zapiski, Leningradskii gosudarstvennyi pedagogicheskii institut imeni A. N. Gertsena,* no. 152 (Leningrad, 1958), p. 4.
91. *Izvestiia Kronshtadtskago Soveta,* nos. 46 and 54 (14 and 25 May 1917).
92. Ibid., no. 71 (14 June 1917).
93. Petrash, *Moriaki Baltiiskogo flota,* p. 121; I. P. Flerovskii, "Kronshtadskaia respublika," *Proletarskaia Revoliutsiia* 58 (November 1926): 31–40. The vote was 211 to 41, with 1 abstaining; so, not more than 45 were absent, and the majority of the Bolshevik delegates did vote.
94. F. F. Raskol'nikov, *Na boevykh postakh* (Moscow, 1964), pp. 78–79.
95. Petrash, *Moriaki Baltiiskogo flota,* p. 122; Raskol'nikov, "Tov. Lenin i Kronshtadtskaia 'Respublika,'" *Krasnaia Letopis'* 10 (1924): 45–59.
96. *Baltiiskie moriaki v podgotovke,* pp. 71–72. One of the investigators, V. A. Anisimov, assured the Petrograd Soviet on 22 May 1917 that the Kronstadt Soviet had not declared a republic and had recognized the Provisional Government, "but they do not trust the coalition government and consider the Soviet the single actual authority. We told them that the Soviet is not the power. Then they answered that they wanted to set an example for us because of our indecision." Shishkin, "Kronshtadskii intsident," p. 16; *Izvestiia Petrogradskaia Soveta,* 24 May 1917.
97. *Baltiiskie moriaki v podgotovke,* pp. 72–73; P. Z. Sivkov, *Kronshtadt: stranitsy revoliutsionnoi istorii* (Leningrad, 1972), pp. 191–97.
98. In an article entitled "A Question of Principle," which was published in *Pravda* on 28 May 1917, Lenin wrote: "The Kronstadt incident has two related principles of significance for us. First, it has revealed the fact, already noted by us in the official resolutions of our party, that *in the districts* the revolution has gone farther than in Piter. . . . Secondly, the Kronstadt incident has raised a very important question of principle and program, which not one honest democrat, let alone socialist, can pass by with indifference. This is the question of the right of central authority *to approve* responsible people elected by the local population." *Polnoe sobranie sochineniia,* 3rd ed., 32:218–19. But Lenin admitted to the party committee on 30 May that the incident had brought serious damage to the party. Khesin, *Oktiabr'skaia revoliutsiia i flot,* p. 249.
99. *Volna,* no. 44 (24 May 1917).
100. Petrash, *Moriaki Baltiiskogo flota,* p. 77. The number of delegates rose to 256 by the end of the congress. "Vozzvanie ot s "ezda predstavitelei Baltiiskago flota," *Moriak,* no. 4 (16/29 June 1917), back of front cover.
101. Information on the party composition of the congress is scanty. Dybenko reported that only 25 Bolsheviks and 21 sympathizers were pres-

ent but claimed that 50 percent of the presidium was Bolshevik. P. E. Dybenko, *Oktiabr' na Baltike* (Tashkent, 1934), p. 32. Another source estimates that one-third of the delegates were either Bolsheviks or their sympathizers; one-fourth were Socialist Revolutionaries, Mensheviks, and anarchists; and the remainder belonged to no party. Izmailov and Pukhov, *Tsentrobalt*, p. 51.

102. Izmailov and Pukhov, *Tsentrobalt*, pp. 52–54. Markin is one of the Bolshevik leaders in the fleet who has been neglected. Becoming a party member soon after his father's death in a riot in Saratov in 1906, he was recruited for the navy in 1914. Markin was killed in action in October 1918. A. F. Nazarov, *Nikolai Markin* (Moscow, 1965), pp. 5–23.

103. The Kronstadt delegation, nominated by the soviet on 6 June, stopped over in Vyborg on 7 June, spent three days in Helsingfors before going on to Åbo, and arrived in Revel on 14 June. It consisted of three Bolsheviks (Raskolnikov, Ivan Kolbin, and Sergei Semenov), four Socialist Revolutionaries (Aleksandr Baranov, Genadii Pyshkin, Nikolai Izmailov, and Leshchev), and two Mensheviks (Ivan Alnichenkov and Nikolai Shchukin). Raskolnikov's report to the Kronstadt Soviet is in *Baltiiskie moriaki v podgotovke*, pp. 108–10.

104. Protocol no. 38, 16 June 1917, *Narodnaia Niva*, no. 46 (18 June 1917).

105. N. Khovrin, "1917-i god," in *Voennye moriaki*, pp. 251–52.

106. Khesin, *Oktiabr'skaia revoliutsiia i flot*, p. 239.

107. *Narodnaia Niva*, no. 35 (6 June 1917).

108. Sivkov, *Kronshtadt*, pp. 215–16. Iarchuk blamed the Bolsheviks for the debacle, but he admitted: "It is impossible to go without the Bolsheviks; without organization, without leadership we cannot win." Ibid. Another colorful anarchist, Asnin, proved to be more difficult. He was killed in the government's seizure of Durnovo Villa, the anarchist center, in the Vyborg District. Sivkov, *Kronshtadt*, p. 216; Paul Avrich, *The Russian Anarchists* (Princeton, N.J., 1967), p. 132.

109. I. P. Flerovskii, *Bol'shevistskii Kronshtadt v 1917 g.* (Leningrad, 1957), p. 48.

110. *Baltiiskie moriaki v podgotovke*, pp. 99–100.

111. *Protokoly i postanovleniia*, p. 75.

112. *Volna*, various issues in June; Zalezhskii, *Iz vospominanii*, pp. 197–204; Vladimir Antonov-Ovseenko, *V semnadtsatom godu* (Moscow, 1933), pp. 158–64

113. Petrash, *Moriaki Baltiiskogo flota*, pp. 146–47.

114. *Narodnaia Niva*, nos. 48–51 (21–24 June 1917); *Volna*, no. 73 (28 June 1917).

115. The Baltic delegation was able to stir up the first serious trouble in the

Black Sea base of Sevastopol in early July in the presence of an American naval mission. Admiral James S. Glennon, who was a member of the Root Mission, is credited by his aide with calming several of the ships. Captain Alva Bernhard to secretary of the navy, 26 November 1940, NA, RG 45, VM, box 587.

116. M. Philips Price, *My Reminiscences of the Russian Revolution* (London, 1921), pp. 35, 41.

117. Cromie to Phillimore, 11 July 1917, PRO, ADM 137/500. Admiral Glennon, who toured the Baltic on the destroyer *Samson* in mid June, was less impressed with the progress and found conditions at Helsingfors especially bad: "The mining division, submarines, and about half of the destroyers are loyal but German money is in evidence and the officers never know when their crews will rebel and their lives may be forfeit." Root Mission Report, app. 4, Admiral Glennon's Report, NA, microcopy 367, roll 48.

118. Notes of a meeting between Verderevsky and members of Tsentrobalt, 21 June 1917, in *Baltiiskie moriaki v podgotovke*, pp. 101–3.

119. Protocol no. 42, 23 June 1917, SA, VK, 3896. A delegation headed by Vishnevskii carried the resolution to Petrograd.

CHAPTER 5

1. "Protokol zasedaniia predstavitelei iacheek i chenov partii s.-r. . . . 9 iiunia 1917 goda," *Narodnaia Niva*, no. 42 (14 June 1917).

2. "S"ezd Finliandskikh organizatsii P. S.-R.," *Narodnaia Niva*, no. 50 (23 June 1917). According to Evgenii Vishnevskii's statement at a meeting of the Helsingfors Assembly of Sailors' Deputies a few days before, the attack on Proshian and Ustinov originated in Petrograd. Protocol no. 38, 15 June 1917, *Narodnaia Niva*, no. 46 (18 June 1917). A new policy of central direction was, ironically, driving a section of the Socialist Revolutionaries towards the Bolsheviks and was weakening the local party. On 22 June a letter to the editor, published in *Narodnaia Niva*, complained that a Bolshevik who was posing as a Socialist Revolutionary was giving lectures to military units. He turned out to be Proshian.

3. I. Flerovskii, "Iiul'skii politicheskii urok," *Proletarskaia Revoliutsiia*, no. 7 (1926), pp. 71–72.

4. Alexander Rabinowitch, *Prelude to Revolution: The Petrograd Bolsheviks and the July 1917 Uprising* (Bloomington, Ind., 1968), p. 187. For an excellent summary of anarchist activities in 1917, see Paul Avrich, *The Russian Anarchists* (Princeton, N.J., 1967).

5. *Baltiiskie moriaki v podgotovke i provedenii velikoi oktiabr'skoi sotsialisticheskoi revoliutsii,* ed. R. N. Mordinov (Moscow-Leningrad, 1957), pp. 101–4.

6. The Left Socialist Revolutionaries needed 1,000 Finnish marks in order to launch their newspaper; 615 marks came from the *Petropavlovsk,* which was generally considered to be a "Bolshevik" ship. *Sotsialist-Revoliutsioner,* no. 1 (9 July 1917).

7. A number of the leading Bolsheviks in Tsentrobalt were from the battleships: Pavel Dybenko (*Respublika*), Nikolai Khovrin (*Respublika*), Andrei Shtarev (*Sevastopol*), Grigorii Svetlichnyi (*Respublika*), Vasilii Kisliakov (*Petropavlovsk*).

8. Rabinowitch, *Prelude to Revolution,* pp. 136–38.

9. Irakli Tsereteli, *Vospominaniia o fevral'skoi revoliutsii,* 2 vols. (Paris, 1963), 2:133–36; William G. Rosenberg, *Liberals in the Russian Revolution* (Princeton, N.J., 1974), pp. 170–76.

10. Rabinowitch, *Prelude to Revolution,* pp. 138–46; O. N. Znamenskii, *Iiul'skii krizis 1917 goda* (Moscow-Leningrad, 1964), pp. 45–48. Podvoisky, among other Bolsheviks in Petrograd, placed special stress on the role of the anarchists. "Iiul'skie dni," *Pravda,* 18 July 1925.

11. V. V. Petrash, *Moriaki Baltiiskogo flota v bor'be za pobedu oktiabria* (Moscow-Leningrad, 1966), p. 150.

12. As quoted in A. F. Ilin-Genevsky, *From February to October* (New York, 1932), p. 60.

13. Petrash, *Moriaki Baltiiskogo flota,* p. 151.

14. "Postanovlenie sledstvennoi podkomissii po delu ob uchastii Kronshtadtskikh matrosov v voorushennoi demonstratsii 3–4 iiulia v Petrograd," 5 September 1917, in *Baltiiskie moriaki v podgotovke,* pp. 164–65. Brushvit attempted to argue against an armed demonstration but was driven from the platform.

15. Raskolnikov, who had been advised by Kamenev over the telephone not long before the meeting that the Bolsheviks would not support the demonstration, could not restrain Roshal and Gromov. The latter concluded: "Comrades! We have fed ourselves enough with hopes; let's go to the barracks, take our weapons, and set off for Petrograd." Ibid., p. 165.

16. Ibid., pp. 165–66; P. Zaitsev, "V Kronshtadte," *Novyi Mir* 7 (1957): 167–68; P. Z. Sivkov, *Kronshtadt: stranitsy revoliutsionnoi istorii* (Leningrad, 1972), pp. 223–24. Since a majority of the members of the executive committee were absent from the meeting on the night of 3–4 July, those who favored moderation wanted to postpone a decision until there was a session of the whole soviet, but they were overruled. This

assemblage, which planned Kronstadt's participation, was thus actually outside of any existing organization—a fact that Soviet historians, concerned with the "legality" of the demonstration, prefer to ignore. Znamenskii (*Iiulskii krizis 1917*, pp. 60–61), moreover, erroneously lists Raskolnikov as a member of the executive committee. Petrash (*Moriaki Baltiiskogo flota*, pp. 149–50) cites 300 members in attendance (only 70 in the executive committee); and although he admits that two-thirds of the executive committee were absent, he still insists on calling the meeting "a session of the executive committee." Both of these scholars ignore the lengthy debate between Raskolnikov and Lamanov on this subject at the soviet sessions of 7 and 8 July, which is published in *Izvestiia Kronshtadtskago Soveta*, no. 95 (14 July 1917).

17. Petrash, *Moriaki Baltiiskogo flota*, p. 152; *Baltiiskie moriaki v podgotovke*, pp. 115–16.

18. Petrash, *Moriaki Baltiiskogo flota*, pp. 153–54.

19. Ibid., pp. 154–55; Rabinowitch, *Prelude to Revolution*, p. 182. Both Raskolnikov and Roshal reported that there were about 10,000, half with arms, but everything happened too fast for a very accurate count of workers boarding the ships, and some apparently made their way independently to Petrograd on various small craft. "Exact" figures for the naval units are in *Baltiiskie moriaki v podgotovke*, p. 345. Ivan Novikov (pseudonym?), chairman of the ship's committee of the *Okean*, who claimed to be in charge of the embarkation, gives an even higher figure—12,000. "Vospominaniia uchastnika iiul'skogo i oktiabr'skogo perevorotov v 1917 godu," *Krasnyi Baltiets*, no. 6 (November 1920), p. 24.

The chronology of events during 3 and 4 July is not always clear. Developments overlapped and interrelated. For example, according to Trotsky, it was Raskolnikov's report on what was happening at Kronstadt that brought about the Bolshevik decision to participate in the demonstrations. Leon Trotsky, *The History of the Russian Revolution*, 3 vols. (New York, 1932–34), 2:30.

20. *Baltiiskie moriaki v podgotovke*, p. 126. And Captain Dudorov scaled the figure down to 5,000 in his brief report to Admiral Verderevsky. Ibid., p. 118.

21. Ibid., pp. 154–55.

22. Meriel Buchanan, *Petrograd: The City of Trouble, 1914–1918* (London, 1919), pp. 136–37.

23. P. Kurkov, "1917 god na 'Avrora,'" *Morskoi Sbornik* 80 (no. 10, October 1927): 21. *Morskoi Sbornik*, the official naval journal, is one of the

few publications that continued consecutive and uninterrupted printing through the revolution and up to this day.

24. A. Pronin, "Burnye gody," *Oktiabr'*, no 8 (1957), pp. 150–52; *Baltiiskie moriaki v podgotovke*, pp. 168–69; Rabinowitch, *Prelude to Revolution*, pp. 182–83. The change was protested by Petr Beliaevskii, a Socialist Revolutionary, but to no avail.

25. According to Podvoisky, Lenin at first refused to appear because he was not feeling well and also because he wanted to show his disapproval of the demonstration, but then he relented at Raskolnikov's insistence. This short public appearance was the Bolshevik leader's last until the seizure of power in October. Rabinowitch, *Prelude to Revolution*, p. 184.

26. *Baltiiskie moriaki v podgotovke*, p. 169.

27. Fedor Raskol'nikov, *Kronshtadt i Piter v 1917 godu* (Moscow, 1925), pp. 123–29; Rabinowitch, *Prelude to Revolution*, p. 186. The sailors were particularly incensed by the memory of Chernov's threat to cut off supplies from Kronstadt a month earlier. Sivkov, *Kronshtadt*, p. 227. Trotsky cites Raskolnikov's initiative in this affair. *My Life* (New York, 1960), p. 312.

28. *Baltiiskie moriaki v podgotovke*, pp. 170–72; A. P. Konstantinov, *F. F. Il'in-Raskol'nikov* (Leningrad, 1964), pp. 66–68.

29. *Baltiiskie moriaki v podgotovke*, pp. 172–73; Novikov, "Vospominaniia," pp. 24–25; A. Gribakov, "Iiul'skie dni v vospominaniiakh rabochikh: Kronshtadtsy v Petrograde v iiul'skie dni," *Petrogradskaia Pravda*, no. 158 (13 July 1922); Sivkov, *Kronshtadt*, pp. 228–29. For Stalin's role as a mediator, see the protocols of the Kronstadt Soviet in *Izvestiia Kronshtadtskago Soveta*, no. 95 (14 July 1917).

30. Petrash, *Moriaki Baltiiskogo flota*, p. 158; "Baltflot v iiul'skie dni," *Krasnyi Arkhiv* 46 (1931): 94–95.

31. *Baltiiskie moriaki v podgotovke*, p. 121; V. P. Avtukhov, "Iiul'skie dni," *Morskoi Sbornik* 77 (no. 6, June 1924): 15.

32. P. Dybenko, *Iz nedr tsarskogo flota k velikomu oktiabriu*, rev. ed. (Moscow, 1958), pp. 88–89; N. Khovrin, "1917-i god," in *Voennye moriaki v bor'be za pobedu oktiabr'skoi revoliutsii* (Moscow, 1958), pp. 254–56.

33. N. F. Izmailov and A. S. Pukhov, *Tsentrobalt* (Kaliningrad, 1967), pp. 71–73; Khovrin, "1917-i god," pp. 256–57; Petrash, *Moriaki Baltiiskogo flota*, p. 162.

34. *Baltiiskie moriaki v podgotovke*, p. 121.

35. Krovrin, "1917-i god," p. 257; Cromie to Phillimore, 18/31 July 1917, PRO, ADM 137/500 (extract from private letter).

36. *Baltiiskie moriaki v podgotovke*, p. 122.
37. Avtukhov, "Iiul'skie dni," p. 16.
38. Izmailov and Pukhov, *Tsentrobalt*, pp. 73–75; Khovrin, "1917-i god," pp. 257–58.
39. Dybenko, *Iz nedr tsarskogo flota*, p. 92; Izmailov and Pukhov, *Tsentrobalt*, p. 75.
40. Avtukhov, "Iiul'skie dni," pp. 22–23. The formal charges against Verderevsky were: (1) revealing secret orders; (2) refusing to obey orders; (3) failing to explain the circumstances relating to the orders at the meeting of ships' committees and Tsentrobalt. Verderevsky had taken the extraordinary step on 4 July of ordering the appointment of commissions in all naval units for the purpose of inventorying all secret documents, plans, maps, etc., and "on the commission, by the agreement of the ships' committees, must be included representatives of the sailors." Order no. 107, 4 July 1917, SA, VK, 2586.
41. The text of Kerensky's order is in *Baltiiskie moriaki v podgotovke*, pp. 131–32, and in several newspapers, for example, *Volna*, no. 82 (9 July 1917).
42. Vl. S., "Iiul'skie dni i flot," *Krasnyi Flot*, no. 7 (July 1925), pp. 7–8; S. S. Khesin, *Oktiabr'skaia revoliutsiia i flot* (Moscow, 1971), p. 291.
43. Petrash, *Moriaki Baltiiskogo flota*, p. 175.
44. Buchanan to FO, 19 July 1917, PRO, FO 371/2997.
45. P. N. Lamanov, "V Kronshtadte posle iiul'skikh dnei," *Krasnaia Letopis'* 24 (no. 3, 1927): 28; Sivkov, *Kronshtadt*, pp. 257–58.
46. D. Kondakov, "V revoliutsionnom Kronshtadte," in *Voennye moriaki*, p. 307.
47. Raskol'nikov, *Kronshtadt i Piter*, pp. 153–56.
48. *Izvestiia Kronshtadtskago Soveta*, no. 100 (20 July 1917).
49. *Izvestiia Kronshtadtskago Soveta*, no. 95 (14 July 1917). On the fourteenth the soviet issued a long proclamation "to all soldiers, sailors, and workers of the fortress of Kronstadt," accusing the bourgeois newspapers of the capital of "never lying so much as now." The statement continued: "The Kronstadt Soviet declares that any kind of obvious persecution of any political party or of any political figure is alien to the revolution. Consciously, or unconsciously, it harms the general revolutionary affairs, it causes ruin, unavoidable schism, and turmoil in the ranks of democracy, and . . . it plays into the hands of the dreamers of counterrevolution." *Izvestiia Kronshtadskago Soveta*, no. 95 (14 July 1917).
50. Lamanov, "V Kronshtadte," p. 33; Sivkov, *Kronshtadt*, pp. 262–64.
51. Sivkov, *Kronshtadt*, pp. 272–73. Dmitrii Kondakov describes the special

efforts made to improve and safeguard distribution of newspapers and leaflets. Sailors carried packages of literature by different routes in order to increase the chances of getting through. Kondakov and others operated a regular pickup service to underground party centers for collecting material to be published. In *Voennye moriaki*, pp. 303–6.

52. *Baltiiskie moriaki v podgotovke*, pp. 140–41.
53. Protocol no. 35, *Izvestiia Gel'singforskago Soveta*, no. 104 (20 July 1917). Tsentroflot (the Central Committee of the All-Russian Navy) was established by the Central Executive Committee of the First All-Russian Congress of Soviets, in cooperation with the Provisional Government, on 1 July. The organization included representatives of all naval units in the country, though apparently only the Baltic fleet formally elected its delegates. Socialist Revolutionaries and Mensheviks, therefore, controlled the committee until its dissolution after the October Revolution. Unfortunately, few records of this institution have been published. *Krasnaia Letopis'* 30 (no. 3, 1928): 78–84.
54. M. Roshal', "Bol'sheviki Gel'singforsa," in *Voennye moriaki*, p. 376.
55. *Sotsialist-Revoliutsioner*, no. 9 (19 July 1917).
56. The new Bolshevik paper retained an experienced core of editors— Vladimir Zalezhskii, Boris Zhemchuzhin, and Fedor Dmitriev. Petrash, *Moriaki Baltiiskogo flota*, p. 180.
57. See, for example, the issues of 6, 15, 19, and 23 July 1917.
58. *Sotsialist-Revoliutsioner*, no. 2 (11 July 1917).
59. Cromie to Phillimore, 18/31 July 1917, extract in PRO, ADM 137/500; *Moriak*, no. 5 (15/28 July 1917), pp. 97–99; *Volna*, no. 82 (15 July 1917).
60. "Baltiiskii flot ot iiulia k oktiabriu 1917 g.," *Krasnaia Letopis'* 32 (no. 5, 1929): 175; Izmailov and Pukhov, *Tsentrobalt*, pp. 86–87; Nikolai Khovrin, "V 1917 godu vo flote—vospominaniia matrosa," *Krasnaia Letopis'* 20 (no. 5, 1926): 66.
61. Raskol'nikov, *Kronshtadt i Piter*, p. 190.
62. Pavel Dybenko, *Iz nedr tsarskogo flota k velikomu oktiabriu* (Moscow, 1928), p. 120. In the "rehabilitation edition" of 1958 the text was edited to remove several references to Trotsky, as well as this quotation.
63. Izmailov and Pukhov, *Tsentrobalt*, p. 87.
64. Ibid., p. 88. Unfortunately, not all of the protocols of Tsentrobalt for this period are available. The one for 26 July shows 43 members attending. Petrash, *Moriaki Baltiiskogo flota*, pp. 188–89, counts 19 Bolsheviks in the membership by 6 August. *Protokoly i postanovleniia tsentral'nogo komiteta Baltiiskogo flota, 1917–1918* (Moscow-Leningrad, 1963), pp. 85–126. Actually, according to the protocols, average attendance at the meetings of Tsentrobalt was about 42, with the highest

number 48, on 8 August. SA, VK, 3178. Therefore, if 15 to 19 Bolsheviks are definitely accounted for, the Bolshevik weight in Tsentrobalt may have been even greater than is claimed by Soviet writers.

65. Petrash, *Moriaki Baltiiskogo flota*, p. 189. Though Magnitskii was chosen chairman by a close vote during the session of 8 August, the actual presiding officer rotated. Between 26 July and 26 August, for the 20 out of 24 meetings for which records are available, Grundman, Baranov, Magnitskii, and Averichkin each presided five times. *Protokoly i postanovleniia*, pp. 85–147.

66. Protocol no. 47, *Protokoly i postanovleniia*, pp. 110–12.

67. Protocol no. 53, *Protokoly i postanovleniia*, pp. 121–23.

68. Petrash, *Moriaki Baltiiskogo flota*, p. 186. The figures vary slightly in other sources. Kolbin lists 98 Bolsheviks, 93 nonparty, 72 Left Socialist Revolutionaries, 12 Menshevik-Internationalists, and 7 anarchists. I. N. Kolbin, "Kronshtadt ot fevralia k Kornilovskikh dnei," *Krasnaia Letopis'* 23 (no. 2, 1927): 159. Sivkov (*Kronshtadt*, p. 278) counts 98 Bolsheviks, 96 nonparty, and 73 SRs.

69. Petrash, *Moriaki Baltiiskogo flota*, p. 186.

70. Ibid., p. 187; A. Vorob'ev, "Revel'tsy," in *Voennye moriaki*, pp. 403–6.

71. *Baltiiskie moriaki v podgotovke*, p. 158.

72. *Narodnaia Niva*, no. 77 (26 July 1917). Tsion was ousted as editor, and protests were sent to Kerensky, but the rift was healed by the Kornilov Affair.

73. Of around 200 delegates present, 103 were from Petrograd factories, 35 from Kronstadt, 15 from trade unions, and the remainder from 29 front regiments. *Izvestiia Kronshtadtskago Soveta*, no. 105 (22 July 1917).

74. Sivkov, *Kronshtadt*, p. 269.

75. Ibid., pp. 274–77.

76. Cromie to Phillimore, 18/31 July 1917, PRO, ADM 137/500.

CHAPTER 6

1. For Kerensky's interpretation of the background, see his *Russia and History's Turning Point* (New York, 1965), pp. 359–72.

2. N. Ia. Ivanov, *Kornilovshchina i ee razgrom: iz istorii bor'by s kontrrevoliutsiei v 1917 g.* (Leningrad, 1965), pp. 36–41.

3. Robert Paul Browder and Alexander F. Kerensky, eds., *The Russian Provisional Government, 1917: Documents*, 3 vols. (Stanford, Calif., 1961), 3:1440–41; S. S. Khesin, *Oktiabr'skaia revoliutsiia i flot* (Moscow, 1971), p. 287.

4. Browder and Kerensky, *Russian Provisional Government*, 3:1474.
5. *Armiia i Flot Svobodnoi Rossii*, no. 174 (28 July 1917).
6. "Sluchai s V. I. Lebedevym v Abo," *Armiia i Flot Svobodnoi Rossii*, no. 183 (8 August 1917).
7. Ibid.
8. Ibid.
9. "Beseda s Upravliaiushchim Morskim Ministerstvom V. I. Lebedevym," *Armiia i Flot Svobodnoi Rossii*, no. 181 (5 August 1917).
10. Ibid.
11. Ibid.
12. "O Matrosskom Universitete," *Moriak*, no. 8 (12 August 1917).
13. *Obshchee Delo: organ sotsialisticheskoi mysli*, nos. 1 and 2 (17 and 18 August 1917).
14. I. I. Rengarten, "Baltiiskii flot nakanune Oktiabria," ed. A. K. Drezen, *Krasnyi Arkhiv* 35(1929): 9.
15. Ibid., p. 10. He never actually left his post.
16. Khesin, *Oktiabr'skaia revoliutsiia i flot*, pp. 317, 320, 333; *Baltiiskie moriaki v podgotovke i provedenii velikoi oktiabr'skoi sotsialisticheskoi revoliutsii*, ed. R. N. Mordinov (Moscow-Leningrad, 1957), pp. 176–77.
17. Khesin, *Oktiabr'skaia revoliutsiia i flot*, p. 320.
18. *Protokoly i postanovleniia tsentral'nogo komiteta Baltiiskogo flota* (Moscow-Leningrad, 1963), pp. 102–4.
19. Ibid., pp. 110–12.
20. "Protokol zasedaniia uzkogo sostava Tsentral'nogo Komiteta RSDRP (b)," *Revoliutsionnoe dvizhenie v Rossii v avguste: razgrom Kornilovskogo miatezha* (Moscow, 1959), pp. 33–34.
21. *Izvestiia Kronshtadtskago Soveta*, 18 August 1917.
22. *Revoliutsionnoe dvizhenie v Rossii v avguste*, pp. 408–9.
23. "Among ourselves in the government we used to call the triangle formed by these places 'the rotten corner' of Russia." Kerensky, *Russia and History's Turning Point*, p. 230 n.6.
24. Khesin, *Oktiabr'skaia revoliutsiia i flot*, p. 336; *Armiia i Flot Svobodnoi Rossii*, no. 174 (28 July 1917).
25. *Revoliutsionnoe dvizhenie v Rossii v avguste*, pp. 424, 627 n.218.
26. "Prikazy po armii i flotu," no. 42, SA, VK, 1230.
27. For examples, see Khesin, *Oktiabr'skaia revoliutsiia i flot*, pp. 341–44; Ivanov, *Kornilovshchina*, pp. 86–89; and V. V. Petrash, *Moriaki Baltiiskogo flota v bor'be za pobedu oktiabria* (Moscow-Leningrad, 1966), pp. 197–99.
28. General A. S. Lukomskii, *Vospominaniia*, 2 vols. (Berlin, 1922), 1:227.
29. *Baltiiskie moriaki v podgotovke*, pp. 185–86.

30. Ibid., p. 187; Khesin, *Oktiabr'skaia revoliutsiia i flot*, p. 345 n.290.
31. *Baltiiskie moriaki v podgotovke*, p. 186.
32. Petrash, *Moriaki Baltiiskogo flota*, p. 201.
33. Ibid., p. 203.
34. E. P. Perovskii, *Vernyi dolgu revoliutsii* (Leningrad, 1964), p. 120. Vishnevskii was probably a relative of Vsevolod Vishnevskii, who wrote "An Optimistic Tragedy" and other plays and film scripts dealing with the Baltic sailors. Interview with Slava Yashemsky, a student of the Soviet theater, in Lawrence, Kansas, December 1975.
35. Petrash, *Moriaki Baltiiskogo flota*, pp. 203–4; Khesin, *Oktiabr'skaia revoliutsiia i flota*, pp. 346–47.
36. I. N. Kolbin, "Kronshtadt ot fevralia k Kornilovskikh dnei," *Krasnaia Letopis'* 23 (1927): 160; Khesin, *Oktiabr'skaia revoliutsiia i flot*, pp. 346–47.
37. *Baltiiskie moriaki v podgotovke*, pp. 200–201.
38. Ibid., p. 201.
39. Khesin, *Oktiabr'skaia revoliutsiia i flot*, p. 366.
40. Petrash, *Moriaki Baltiiskogo flota*, pp. 204–5; N. F. Izmailov and A. S. Pukhov, *Tsentrobalt* (Kaliningrad, 1967), p. 97.
41. *Baltiiskie moriaki v podgotovke*, p. 189.
42. "Protokol ekstrennogo zasedaniia Tsentral'nogo komiteta Baltiiskogo flota," 28 August 1917, in *Protokoly i postanovleniia*, pp. 150–57.
43. See, for example, Khesin, *Oktiabr'skaia revoliutsiia i flot*, p. 349.
44. *Protokoly i postanovleniia*, pp. 150–98.
45. Ibid., p. 151.
46. Ibid., pp. 175–79.
47. Rengarten, "Baltiiskii flot," p. 19.
48. K. I. Mazurenko, *Na "Slave" v Rizhkom zalive* (Jordanville, N.Y., 1949), p. 57. One officer refused and was moved to a staff position.
49. Rengarten, "Baltiiskii flot," p. 20.
50. Harold C. Graf, *The Russian Navy in War and Revolution, from 1914 up to 1918* (Munich, 1923), p. 165; Khesin, *Oktiabr'skaia revoliutsiia i flot*, p. 359.
51. *Protokoly i postanovleniia*, pp. 170–74.
52. Ibid.
53. Ibid.
54. Stanley's report to the Admiralty, 4/17 October 1917, PRO, ADM 137/1249. *Novoe Vremia* noted that the officers were shot on the Elizabeth Pier at 9:00 P.M. on 31 August. *Novoe Vremia*, 26 and 30 September 1917. British interference in Russian internal affairs was a continuous but largely ineffectual feature of 1917. For an example, see Norman E.

Saul, "British Involvement in the Kornilov Affair," *Rocky Mountain Social Science Journal* 10 (January 1973) : 43–50.

55. Kerensky and Browder, *Russian Provisional Government*, 3:1657.
56. *Protokoly i postanovleniia*, p. 175.
57. *Baltiiskie moriaki v podgotovke*, p. 210.
58. *Protokoly i postanovleniia*, p. 192.
59. Ibid., p. 193.
60. *Baltiiskie moriaki v podgotovke*, p. 211.
61. *Protokoly i postanovleniia*, p. 220; Rengarten, "Baltiiskii flot," p. 31.
62. *Baltiiskie moriaki v podgotovke*, p. 217.
63. Rengarten, "Baltiiskii flot," p. 18.
64. Stanley's report to the Admiralty, 1/14 September 1917, PRO, ADM 137/1249. The Foreign Office copy has a notation scribbled across it: "Should be communicated to the French." PRO, FO 371/3016.
65. Rengarten, "Baltiiskii flot," p. 23.
66. Ibid., p. 24.
67. Ibid., pp. 25–26.
68. Khesin, *Oktiabr'skaia revoliutsiia i flot*, pp. 407–8.
69. Rengarten, "Baltiiskii flot," p. 16.
70. Buchanan to Foreign Office, 8 October 1917, PRO, FO 371/3011.
71. "Memorandum on Situation in Finland," Intelligence Bureau, 12 November 1917, PRO, FO 371/3007.
72. Howard (Stockholm) to Foreign Office, 26 June 1917, PRO, FO 371/3007.
73. Tuomo Polvinen, *Venäjän vallankumous ja Suomi, 1917–1920*, vol. 1: *Helmikuu 1917–toukokuu 1918* (Porvoo and Helsinki, 1967), pp. 82–83.
74. Grove (Helsingfors) to Foreign Office, 20 August 1917, PRO, FO 371/2997; Buchanan to Foreign Office, 17 August 1917, PRO, FO 371/3007.
75. Grove to Foreign Office, 1 September 1917, PRO, FO 371/3007. For a more detailed and excellent analysis of the Finnish question, see David Kirby, "The Finnish Social Democratic Party and the Bolsheviks," *Journal of Contemporary History* 7 (January–April 1972) : 181–98.
76. Lindley to Foreign Office, 28 August 1917, PRO, FO 371/2997.
77. Lindley to Foreign Office, 7 October 1917, PRO, FO 371/2997.
78. Cromie to Admiralty, 24 September 1917, PRO, ADM 137/1570.
79. Cromie to Admiralty, 21 September 1917, PRO, ADM 137/1570.
80. *Protokoly i postanovleniia*, pp. 218, 447–49; *Baltiiskie moriaki v podgotovke*, pp. 219, 352–53 n.124.
81. Pavel Dybenko, *Iz nedr tsarskogo flota k velikomu oktiabriu* (Moscow, 1928), p. 147. Spiridonova was "purged" from the 1958 edition of Dybenko's memoirs.

82. *Baltiiskie moriaki v podgotovke*, pp. 319–25.
83. "Ustav Tsentral'nogo komiteta Baltiiskogo flota, priniatyi 2-m s"ezdom predstavitelei Baltiiskogo flota," *Protokoly i postanovleniia*, p. 430.
84. *Baltiiskie moriaki v podgotovke*, p. 229.
85. Rengarten, "Baltiiskii flot," p. 27.
86. Lieutenant General von Tschischwitz, *The Army and Navy during the Conquest of the Baltic Islands in October, 1917: An Analytical Study Based on Actual Experiences*, trans. Col. Henry Hossfeld (Fort Leavenworth, Kans., 1933), p. 33.
87. Mazurenko, *Na "Slave" v Rizhkom zalive*, p. 57. It is difficult to obtain a balanced picture of this neglected battle. Tschischwitz, who saw it from the German side, takes a dim view of Russian fighting ability; nevertheless, he notes the heavy damage sustained by the German fleet. Mazurenko was an officer on the *Slava*. A. S. Pulkhov, in *Moonzundskoe srazhenie* (Leningrad, 1957), glorifies the "Bolshevik-led" Russian sailors. Khesin, writing in 1971, takes issue with previous Soviet versions and marks the battle as a clear Russian defeat caused by conspiring officers, which added urgency to the Bolshevik seizure of power in order to save Petrograd from the Germans. Khesin, *Oktiabr'skaia revoliutsiia i flot*, pp. 414–18. For complete details of the action, see N. B. Pavlovich, ed., *Flot v pervoi mirovoi voine*, 2 vols. (Moscow, 1964), 1:262–304.
88. Mazurenko, *Na "Slave" v Rizhkom zalive*, pp. 58–61.
89. Dybenko, *Iz nedr tsarskogo flota* (1928 ed.), p. 139; Dybenko, "Moriaki Baltflota," in *V dni velikoi proletarskoi revoliutsii*, ed. E. Gorodetskii and E. Burdzhalov (Moscow, 1937), p. 126.
90. Khesin, *Oktiabr'skaia revoliutsiia i flot*, p. 404.
91. Mazurenko, *Na "Slave" v Rizhkom zalive*, p. 59.
92. Ibid., p. 55; Jürgen Rohwer, "The Russians as Naval Opponents in Two World Wars," in *The Soviet Navy*, ed. M. G. Saunders (London, 1958), p. 52.
93. Tschischwitz, *Army and Navy*, pp. 146–47.
94. Ibid., p. 248.
95. Adm. Reinhard Scheer, *Germany's High Sea Fleet in the World War* (London, 1920), p. 301.
96. Browder and Kerensky, *Russian Provisional Government*, 3:1629. The order was published in *Izvestiia* on 1 October.
97. *Baltiiskie moriaki v podgotovke*, p. 239.
98. S. P. Melgunov, *The Bolshevik Seizure of Power*, ed. S. G. Pushkarev, trans. James S. Beaver (Santa Barbara, Calif., and Oxford, England, 1972), p. 18.

99. Cromie to the Admiralty, PRO, ADM 137/1570. According to one source (Petrash, *Moriaki Baltiiskogo flota*, p. 231), Adm. Petr Vladislavlev was later shot as a deserter at Hango.

CHAPTER 7

1. A. M. Andreev, *Sovety rabochikh i soldatskikh deputatov nakanune oktiabria: mart–oktiabr' 1917 g.* (Moscow, 1967), p. 322.
2. S. S. Khesin, *Oktiabr'skaia revoliutsiia i flot* (Moscow, 1971), p. 396.
3. Ibid., pp. 396–97.
4. Ibid. This usurpation of power was not accomplished without protest. The small Menshevik organization, headed by Nikolai Kilianyi, a leader of the Helsingfors Soviet in March, called a special conference on 23 September; and its newsletter, *Golos Sotsial-Demokrata*, editorialized: "'Russian' Finland, from 20 September, lives under a Bolshevik dictatorship: the Revolutionary Committee, originating in the Kornilov days, transferred, on 20 September, its authority to the Oblast Committee consisting, as is well known, exclusively of 'internationalists.' Because of the political situation that arises when one government has almost passed away, and another is 'almost' created, it is difficult to raise a question about the legality of a dictatorship in Finland." The first sentence shows the usual Menshevik perception of what the Bolsheviks were doing; the second, their own inability to stop it. *Golos Sotsial-Demokrata*, no. 9 (24 September 1917).
5. *Bor'ba bol'shevikov za armiiu v trekh revoliutsiiakh*, ed. L. G. Beskrovnyi et al. (Moscow, 1969), p. 185.
6. Khesin, *Oktiabr'skaia revoliutsiia i flot*, p. 369.
7. *Rabochii Put'*, no. 34 (6 October 1917); P. Z. Sivkov, *Kronshtadt: stranitsy revoliutsionnoi istorii* (Leningrad, 1972), pp. 303–4; Andreev, *Sovety rabochikh*, p. 363.
8. Leon Trotsky, *The History of the Russian Revolution*, 3 vols. (New York, 1932), 3:195.
9. V. A. Breslav, *Kanun oktiabria 1917 goda: s"ezd sovetov severnoi oblasti, 11–13 oktiabria 1917 g.* (Moscow, 1934), pp. 16–17.
10. Ibid.; Andreev, *Sovety rabochikh*, pp. 365–67.
11. Pavel Shishko and L. L. Kallis led the Left Socialist Revolutionaries. The other members of the committee were: SRs—Rybin, Iosanov, Kudinskii, and Gelmingorian; Bolsheviks—Zof, Dashkevich, Sergeev, Stuchka, Ignatev, Korolev, and Rabchinskii. *Sotsialist-Revoliutsioner*, no. 74 (17 October 1917).

12. Andreev, *Sovety rabochikh*, p. 364.
13. *Sotsialist-Revoliutsioner*, no. 72 (14 October 1917). Breslav, writing in 1934, does not mention Trotsky's presence.
14. L. S. Gaponenko, *Rabochii klass Rossii v 1917 godu* (Moscow, 1970), p. 458.
15. Soviet scholars have consolidated extensive materials on Lenin in 1917, but much of it is still in inconvenient form. For Lenin's exile in Finland, see G. S. Rovio, "Kak Lenin skryvalsia u Gel'singforsskogo 'politsmeistera,'" and Iu. K. Latukka, "Lenin v 1917 godu v podpol'e v Finliandii," in *Lenin v 1917 godu: vospominaniia* (Moscow, 1967), pp. 144–62. Rovio (p. 152), however, claims that only Smilga knew of his presence. Smilga, incidentally, had been one of the "radical" Bolsheviks since July. For a more complete analysis of Lenin's underground environment, see M. A. Stoliarenko, *V. I. Lenin i revoliutsionnye moriaki* (Moscow, 1970), pp. 101–10, and Norman E. Saul, "Lenin's Decision to Seize Power: The Influence of Events in Finland," *Soviet Studies* 24 (April, 1973): 491–505.
16. This interpretation is drawn from an examination of Lenin's writings and takes into consideration his Finnish environment.
17. *Polnoe sobranie sochinenii*, 5th ed., vol. 34 (Moscow, 1962), pp. 239–41. Italics in original.
18. Robert V. Daniels, *Red October: The Bolshevik Revolution of 1917* (London, 1968), pp. 53–54.
19. Lenin, *Polnoe sobranie sochinenii*, 34:265. Italics in original.
20. N. Ia. Ivanov, *Kornilovshchina i ee razgrom: iz istorii bor'by s kontr-revoliutsiei v 1917 g.* (Leningrad, 1965), p. 226.
21. Lenin, *Polnoe sobranie sochinenii*, 34:383. Italics in original.
22. Ibid., p. 384. Lenin's "navy consciousness" may also have contributed to an unwarranted optimism about a German revolution. At least there are references in his writings at this time to the German naval revolts. See, for example, ibid., pp. 275, 340.
23. Ibid., p. 390.
24. Ibid., p. 266.
25. N. I. Podvoiskii, *Krasnaia gvardiia v oktiabr'skie dni* (Moscow-Leningrad, 1927), pp. 16–19.
26. Khesin, *Oktiabr'skaia revoliutsiia i flot*, pp. 434–35.
27. "German Operations in the Gulf of Riga: Admiralty Memorandum for the War Cabinet," 26 October 1917, PRO, ADM 137/500.
28. "Monthly Report," 8 November 1917, NA, RG 165, 9707–8.
29. Buchanan to FO, 23 October 1917, PRO, FO 371/3012. Lindley reported a week later: "The failure of the British fleet to enter the Baltic and

annihilate the German squadrons before Oesel has been seriously exploited by our enemies and by the pacifist press, who share with practically the whole Russian public an abnormal ignorance of naval matters." Lindley to FO, 1 November 1917, PRO, FO 371/2997.

30. Buchanan to FO, 10 October 1917, PRO, FO 371/3011.

31. Hardinge to Buchanan, 23 October 1917, PRO, FO 371/2999; "Foreign Office Minute," 26 October 1917, PRO, FO 371/3016.

32. Buchanan to FO, 25 October 1917, PRO, FO 371/2999.

33. Buchanan to FO, 30 October 1917, PRO, FO 371/3012.

34. The untitled, undated report has a note appended by hand: "Communicated by Sir W. Wiseman who had received document from Mr. Maugham who has just returned from Petrograd, 18.11.17." PRO, FO 800/205. Over two weeks earlier, on 2 October, Verkhovsky suggested a similar plan to General Knox, the British army attaché, that would have involved all of the Allies. Knox cited this as evidence of Verkhovsky's inexperience and confused thinking. See Sir Alfred Knox, *With the Russian Army, 1914–1917*, vol. 2 (London, 1921), p. 696.

35. C. Spring Rice to FO, 4 November 1917, PRO, FO 371/3017. This followed by three days Rice's report from Washington that Russia would make peace in two months.

36. An anti-American theme appears in Buchanan's correspondence. The ambassador was particularly suspicious of the mission of the American Red Cross and "their railway commissioners, among whose members are several prominent financiers who, under the Red Cross flag, intend to spy out the land and spoil the Egyptians." Buchanan to Hardinge, 14 August 1917, PRO, FO 371/2998.

37. "It is therefore worth while considering whether it would be possible for us to win over some of their leaders by out-bidding Germany." Buchanan to FO, 25 October 1917, PRO, FO 371/2999.

38. Cromie to Admiralty, 2 November 1917, PRO, ADM 137/1570. Colonel Judson, the American military attaché, wrote what turned out to be a sad epitaph for pre-Bolshevik Russia: "All the time in the background is the great inert 99 per cent, the active elements being but the froth on the surface, which when it settles down for a moment is disturbed by the slightest heave of the great mass beneath. . . . It may be that a tragedy is approaching which will dwarf that of the Great War. . . . It is time for the whole world to give consideration to the plight of Russia, some day destined perhaps to be the greatest of the nations. Perhaps the collapse of Russia may be even a greater blow at democracy than would the continued political existence of the Kaiser. In fact the one might

necessarily involve the other." "Monthly Report," 8 November 1917, NA, RG 165, 9707–8.

39. Rengarten's diary, "Oktiabr'skaia revoliutsiia v Baltiiskom flote," ed. A. K. Drezen, *Krasnyi Arkhiv* 25 (1927): 47.

40. "13 October, 1500. The 20th is approaching: the double expectation of revolution and mutiny. Everything is inextricably linked together." Ibid., p. 36. "In Petrograd itself the Bolsheviks are officially reported to be planning a *coup d'état*, and in the factories agitators are busy preaching to the men the doctrine of class hatred. November 2nd [20 October] is the day openly proclaimed for the outbreak but it is doubtful whether anything will take place then." Lindley's report, 1 November 1917, PRO, FO 371/2997.

41. Khesin, *Oktiabr'skaia revoliutsiia i flot*, p. 460.

42. Ibid., p. 461.

43. Ibid. Khesin counts 91 delegates who "expressed the will of the sailors and soldiers of the navy": 47 Bolsheviks, 19 Left SRs, 5 internationalists, 4 Right SRs, 2 Mensheviks, 2 anarchists, 6 nonparty, and 6 of unclear political position. This represents a substantial portion of approximately 650 delegates.

The official Bolshevik claim of a majority of 390 delegates is the one usually found in the basic texts on the Russian revolution. This was probably determined sometime after the congress met, as the picture on 25–26 October was not nearly so certain. A Left Socialist Revolutionary source listed the delegates registered by the night of 25 October as follows: 250 Bolsheviks, 69 Left SRs, 150 Right SRs, 60 Mensheviks, 14 Menshevik Internationalists, 3 anarchists, 6 national socialists, 3 nonparty socialists, and 22 nonparty. These figures may be as reliable as any, since they list fewer Left SRs than the official Bolshevik accounting. *Sotsialist-Revoliutsioner*, no. 83 (27 October 1917). The vote would still be about 361 to 225 against the government.

44. *Baltiiskie moriaki v podgotovke i provedenii velikoi oktiabr'skoi sotsialisticheskoi revoliutsii*, ed. R. N. Mordinov (Moscow-Leningrad, 1957), p. 241.

45. *Sotsialist-Revoliutsioner*, no. 76 (19 October 1917).

46. Daniels, *Red October*, pp. 89–92. For the general outline of events in October, I have relied heavily upon Daniels's excellent study, S. P. Melgunov, *The Bolshevik Seizure of Power* (Santa Barbara, Calif., and Oxford, England, 1972), and E. F. Erykalov, *Oktiabr'skoe vooruzhennoe vosstanie v Petrograde* (Leningrad, 1966).

47. P. E. Dybenko, "Baltflot v oktiabr'skie dni," in *Shagi revoliutsii: velikii oktiabr' glazami sovremennikov* (Moscow, 1967), p. 124.

48. Pavel Dybenko, *Iz nedr tsarskogo flota k velikomu oktiabriu* (Moscow, 1958), pp. 126–27.

49. *Baltiiskie moriaki v podgotovke*, p. 247.

50. N. I. Podvoiskii, *Krasnaia gvardiia v oktiabr'skie dni* (Moscow-Leningrad, 1927), pp. 16–17; V. I. Nevskii, "V oktiabr'," *Katorga i Ssylka* 96–97 (nos. 11–12, 1932): 35; Stoliarenko, *V. I. Lenin*, pp. 111–12. Podvoisky claimed that this conference with Lenin was decisive in uniting the party's military "experts" for support of the uprising. If true, their leaders' fantasy about warships in the Neva may have been influential. At least the most cautious member of the military "troika," Nevsky, was now out of town. See Podvoiskii, *God 1917* (Moscow, 1958), p. 105.

51. A. P. Konstantinov, *F. F. Il'in-Raskol'nikov* (Leningrad, 1964), pp. 83–85. Kolbin's claim that Raskolnikov helped to reorganize the Military-Technical Commission at Kronstadt in October is probably in error. See I. N. Kolbin, *Kronshtadt v 1917 g.* (Leningrad, 1932), p. 64.

52. Daniels, *Red October*, p. 111; Khesin, *Oktiabr'skaia revoliutsiia i flot*, p. 442.

53. V. V. Petrash, *Moriaki Baltiiskogo flota v bor'be za pobedu oktiabria* (Moscow-Leningrad, 1966), pp. 245–46.

54. Ibid., pp. 230, 241; N. F. Izmailov, *Baltiiskii flot v oktiabr'skie dni* (Moscow, 1957), pp. 36–37.

55. Soviet scholars naturally credit Lenin with the crucial though indirect role in the formation of the Military Revolutionary Committee. For a fairly sophisticated discussion of this issue, see Erykalov, *Oktiabr'skoe vooruzhennoe vosstanie*, pp. 202–6. Documents pertaining to and emanating from the Military Revolutionary Committee have been published in *Petrogradskii voenno-revoliutsionnyi komitet: dokumenty i materialy*, 3 vols. (Moscow, 1966–67). A wide variety of signatures is found on the documents, and the list of 82 members (3:661–62) includes Lenin, Trotsky, and Stalin, along with the Kronstadt leaders Flerovskii and Iarchuk.

56. Erykalov, *Oktiabr'skoe vooruzhennoe vosstanie*, pp. 277–82, 299–300; Knox, *With the Russian Army*, 2:701–5.

57. V. Marusev, "Ot tsentroflota k VMRK," in *Voennye moriaki v bor'be za pobedu oktiabr'skoi revoliutsii* (Moscow, 1958), p. 445; A. Pronin, "Kronshtadttsy v oktiabr'skie dni 1917 goda," in ibid., pp. 270–77; Pronin, "Matrosy v oktiabre," in *Oktiabr'skii shkval* (Leningrad, 1927), pp. 107–16.

58. Trotsky, *History of the Russian Revolution*, 3:222–23. Trotsky, however, is inaccurate on several details.

59. I. Flerovskii, "Kronshtadt v oktiabr'skoi revoliutsii," *Proletarskaia Revoliutsiia,* no. 10 (1922), p. 136. This "naval" triumvirate in Helsingfors was anticipated by a soviet-oblast "troika"—Smilga, Dybenko, and Shishko—established on 23 October. Dybenko, *Iz nedr tsarskogo flota,* pp. 135–36; N. F. Izmailov and A. S. Pukhov, *Tsentrobalt* (Kaliningrad, 1967), p. 187.

60. Soviet scholars vary on the question of when the revolution actually began. While some place it as early as the twenty-second, others divide between the morning and the afternoon and evening of the twenty-fourth. For a discussion, see Erykalov, *Oktiabr'skoe vooruzhennoe vosstanie,* pp. 336–37. Obviously, maneuvering for position intensified over several days, but the actual orders that brought the key forces into play were issued between 7:00 and 9:00 P.M. on 24 October. Daniels, a good Western authority, claims that the appearance of Lenin at midnight was the vital event that galvanized Smolny to action; he cites the sudden early morning attacks on the telephone and postal centers as evidence. See *Red October,* pp. 162–65. But it seems unlikely, given the general clumsiness of operations, that Lenin, who was still disguised and unobtrusive at Smolny, could have caused the movement onto the streets by 1:00 A.M. of sizable detachments of Red Guards and of the Kexholm regiment, the forces that captured the main post office; and the telephone exchange was not occupied until 7:00 A.M. Besides, the more important telegraph centers had been seized by 9:00 P.M. on the twenty-fourth. Erykalov, *Oktiabr'skoe vooruzhennoe vosstanie,* pp. 381–83. See also Rabinowitch, *The Bolsheviks,* pp. 266–70.

61. Erykalov, *Oktiabr'skoe vooruzhennoe vosstanie,* p. 382; A. Mokrousov, "V noch' na 25 oktiabria," in *Voennye moriaki,* pp. 464–74.

62. A. G. Pronin, "Kronshtadttsy v oktiabr'skie dni 1917 goda," in *Voennye moriaki,* p. 274.

63. D. N. Kondakov, "Krepost' revoliutsii (Kronshtadt ot fevralia k oktiabriu)," in *V ogne revoliutsionnykh boev (raiony Petrograda v dvukh revoliutsiiakh 1917 g.),* p. 351.

64. M. Mitel'man, *Oktiabr'skoe vooruzhennoe vosstanie v Petrograde v 1917 g.* (Moscow, 1938), p. 23; Dybenko, *Iz nedr tsarskogo flota,* p. 131; D. Cherevin, "Nezabyvaemoe," *Vodnyi Transport,* no. 79 (2 July 1957).

65. A. V. Belyshev, "'Avrora' v dni Oktiabria," in *Petrograd v dni velikogo oktiabria* (Leningrad, 1967), p. 370. Some sources, Dybenko, for example, cite Petr Kurkov as the *Aurora*'s commissar; he was actually only a member of the ship's committee who later happened to gain prominence in the Soviet navy. Apparently Kurkov had been chairman of the ship's committee earlier in the year, at the time of the July Crisis.

P. Kurkov, "Pervyi vystrel," *Nashi Dostizheniia* 11 (November 1934): 11–13.

66. I. G. Dykov, "Petrogradskii voenno-revoliutsionnyi komitet: boevoi bol'shevistskii shtab vooruzhennogo vosstaniia v oktiabre 1917 goda," *Voprosy Istorii*, 7 (July 1957): 32. I. I. Mints, a leading Soviet historian of the revolution, attributed the calling up of the *Aurora* to "the commissar of the Second Baltic Fleet Depot Troop." *Istoriia velikogo oktiabria* 2 (Moscow, 1968): 1064. Zakharov was the commissar and was in charge of clearing the bridges. A former shipmate of Dybenko's, he served in 1917 as a gunner on the island of Zerel; coming into sudden prominence in early October as the commissar-delegate of the Second Congress of the Baltic Fleet, he was sent to oversee the evacuation of the islands that were being invaded by the Germans. He was with a group of evacuees assigned temporarily to the depot troop in Petrograd. In his memoirs, however, he does not reveal any part that he may have played in moving the *Aurora*. V. Zakharov, "Reshaiushchie dni," in *Voennye moriaki*, pp. 435–43, 577–78.

67. Belyshev, "'Avrora' v dni oktiabria," pp. 370–71; A. B. Belyshev, "Doklad komissara kreisera 'Avrora,'" *Petrogradskaia Pravda*, no. 251 (5 November 1922); A. S. Nevolin, *Avrorovtsy* (Moscow, 1967), pp. 81–85.

68. Nikolai Nikitin, "Avrora," *Nashi Dostizheniia*, no. 11 (November 1934), pp. 6–7; Nevolin, *Avrorovtsy*, pp. 85–87.

69. Sivkov, *Kronshtadt*, pp. 316–18; Daniels, *Red October*, p. 173.

70. Flerovskii, "Kronshtadt v oktiabr'skoi revoliutsii," p. 139.

71. Ibid.; P. Mal'kov, "Shturmovye dni," in *Voennye moriaki*, pp. 461–63; and "V oktiabr'skie dni," *Znamia*, no. 11 (November 1956), pp. 137–39.

72. Flerovskii, "Kronshtadt v oktiabr'skoi revoliutsii," p. 140; A. A. Dorogov, "Vospominaniia matrosa Alekseia Antonovicha Dorogova o vziatii zimnego dvortsa," *Istoriia Proletariata SSSR*, no. 11 (1932), p. 105.

73. N. A. Khovrin, "V 1917 godu vo flote," *Krasnaia Letopis'* 20 (no. 5, 1926): 60; Dorogov, "Vospominaniia matrosa Alekseia Antonovicha Dorogova," p. 106.

74. B. A. Breslav, "Sed'moi osobyi," in *Petrograd v dni velikogo oktiabria*, pp. 363–66.

75. Dybenko, *Iz nedr tsarskogo flota*, p. 137; Sivkov, *Kronshtadt*, pp. 328–29. Cromie, who always seemed to be turning up at critical times, lunched with Razvozov on 25 October, obtaining rather inaccurate information: "I have never seen the C-in-C so depressed. Apparently the Central Committee of the Baltic Fleet sent three Norviks [*sic*] to Petrograd last night contrary to the orders of C-in-C and in response to a signal from

the Soviets for help, and this afternoon four trains of armed seamen are being sent as well. All leaves of officers and men is stopped, and things are very critical, the staff anticipating another outbreak." "Baltic Flotilla Report," 7 November 1917, PRO, ADM 137/1570.

76. Petrash, *Moriaki Baltiiskogo flota*, p. 253; *Baltiiskie moriaki v podgotovke*, pp. 376–77; Sivkov, *Kronshtadt*, p. 329. The commander of one of the torpedo boats, the *Metkii*, reports that Razvozov gave him oral permission to leave port. He adds that the officers of the ships remained in command up to the Neva; they knew that they were assisting a Bolshevik attempt to seize power, but, he claims, none thought that it would succeed. B. Ia. Il'vov, *Rokot moria* (Shanghai, 1935), pp. 93–98.

77. Kostiukov, "Kak my opozdali ko vziatiiu zimnego dvortsa," *Krasnyi Baltiets* 6 (1920) : 45–46.

78. Sivkov, *Kronshtadt*, pp. 330–33; Erykalov, *Oktiabr'skoe vooruzhennoe vosstanie*, pp. 425–34.

79. Khesin and Petrash agree on the figure of about 10,000 sailors in Petrograd on the night of the twenty-fifth, but Soviet scholars admit the difficulty of determining the exact numbers of sailors, workers, and soldiers that were actually involved. Erykalov faces the issue as well as anyone and finds that 7,000–8,000 soldiers, 5,000 Red Guards, and at least 6,000–7,000 sailors participated in the siege of the Winter Palace. Counting various detachments with other duties, such as the one under Khovrin in the Admiralty, and the standby crews on the ships, the number of Baltic sailors who were actually in the city surpasses 15,000, which is equivalent to more than a regular army division. Khesin, *Oktiabr'skaia revoliutsiia i flot*, p. 456; Petrash, *Moriaki Baltiiskogo flota*, pp. 258–59; Erykalov, *Oktiabr'skoi vooruzhennoe vosstanie*, p. 433; V. Nevskii, "V oktiabr'," *Katorga i Ssylka* 96–97 (nos. 11–12, 1932) : 35; M. Lur'e, "Vooruzhennoe vosstanie v Petrograde," *Istoricheskii Zhurnal* 7 (October 1937) : 50.

80. Sivkov, *Kronshtadt*, p. 330; Erykalov, *Oktiabr'skoe vooruzhennoe vosstanie*, pp. 435–39.

81. Nevolin, *Avrorovtsy*, pp. 87–88.

82. Daniels, *Red October*, p. 187.

83. *History of the Communist Party of the Soviet Union (Bolsheviks): Short Course*, edited by a commission of the Central Committee of the Communist Party of the Soviet Union (Moscow, 1951), p. 321.

84. Nevolin, *Avrorovtsy*, p. 89; Erykalov, *Oktiabr'skoe vooruzhennoe vosstanie*, p. 448. Many people at the time, both inside and outside of the palace, believed that the *Aurora* was actually firing live shells on the city. And some held to this belief years later: for example, Podvoi-

skii, "Lenin v 1917 godu (iz vospominanii)," *Oktiabr'* 34 (May 1957): 156.

85. A Western observer noted, "A good many of the shots were only gun-cotton, and the firing in all cases was so inaccurate that the Palace was only hit three times from the river side." Meriel Buchanan, *Petrograd, the City of Trouble, 1914–1918* (London, 1919), p. 194.

86. One of the best descriptions of the aftermath is in Melgunov, *Bolshevik Seizure of Power*, pp. 89–93. Several Baltic sailors were wounded during the attack, and apparently a few were killed, but none have been singled out by name and glorified for their sacrifice.

87. At least one early memoirist felt obliged to apologize for making the Bolshevik Revolution seem like a military operation. A. Tarasov-Rodionov, "Pervaia operatsiia," *Voennyi Vestnik* 42 (1924): 10.

CHAPTER 8

1. Leon Trotsky, *The History of the Russian Revolution*, vol. 3 (New York, 1934), p. 222.

2. S. P. Melgunov, *The Bolshevik Seizure of Power* (Santa Barbara, Calif., and Oxford, England, 1972), p. 65.

3. The phrase is attributed to Lenin, in a radiogram order of the Council of Peoples' Commissars to the cruiser *Admiral Makarov*, dated 30 October. The full sentence reads: "The Baltic fleet, truly devoted to the revolution, has come to the support of the rebelling people." E. P. Perovskii, *Vernyi dolgu revoliutsii* (Leningrad, 1964), p. 2; *Baltiiskie moriaki v podgotovke i provedenii velikoi oktiabr'skoi sotsialisticheskoi revoliutsii*, ed. by R. N. Mordvinov (Moscow-Leningrad, 1957), p. 316.

4. I. I. Vakhrameev, *Vo imia revoliutsii* (Moscow, 1957), p. 21; *Protokoly i postanovleniia tsentral'nogo komiteta Baltiiskogo flota* (Moscow-Leningrad, 1963), pp. 451–52 n.82. The sailor-delegates, representing all fleets and flotillas, were divided politically as follows: 47 Bolsheviks, 19 Left SRs, 5 Menshevik-Internationalists, 4 Right SRs, 2 Mensheviks, 2 anarchists, 6 nonparty, and 6 unknown. M. A. Stoliarenko, *V. I. Lenin i revoliutsionnye moriaki* (Moscow, 1970), pp. 122–23.

5. N. F. Izmailov, *Baltiiskii flot v oktiabr'skie dni* (Moscow, 1957), p. 43; F. F. Raskol'nikov, *Kronshtadt i Piter v 1917 godu* (Moscow-Leningrad, 1927), pp. 239–40; *Baltiiskie moriaki v podgotovke*, p. 295.

6. P. Z. Sivkov, *Kronshtadt* (Leningrad, 1972), pp. 339–40; *Baltiiskie moriaki v podgotovke*, pp. 303, 378.

7. Albert Rhys Williams, *Journey into Revolution: Petrograd, 1917–1918* (Chicago, 1969), pp. 139–43.

8. P. E. Dybenko, *Iz nedr tsarskogo flota k velikomu oktiabriu* (Moscow, 1958), pp. 147–52. Secondary sources vary widely with regard to the total number of sailors engaged on the "Gatchina front," from 3,000 (Melgunov, *Bolshevik Seizure of Power*, p. 148) to 10,000 (Sivkov, *Kronshtadt*, p. 343).

9. Melgunov, *Bolshevik Seizure of Power*, pp. 146–48; E. A. Giliarova, "V boiakh pod pulkovom," in *Petrograd v dni velikogo oktiabria* (Leningrad, 1967), pp. 456–60; Dybenko, *Iz nedr tsarskogo flota*, pp. 156–63. The surprisingly lenient terms allowed the Cossacks simply to go away if they promised that they would never fight against the revolution again and if they would turn over Kerensky for trial. On his part, Dybenko guaranteed that Lenin and Trotsky would not enter the new government until all charges (of being German spies) were proven false. But while this Baltic sailor pretended to exercise a plenipotentiary power, the former minister-president, Kerensky, abdicated his political influence and escaped, disguised as a sailor! Melgunov, *Bolshevik Seizure of Power*, pp. 154–55; Alexander Kerensky, *Russia and History's Turning Point* (New York, 1965), pp. 443–44.

10. Sivkov, *Kronshtadt*, p. 357. Details of the transit of these detachments is not available; it is quite possible that they were detained in Petrograd or were delayed en route.

11. I. Kolbin, in *Baltiiskie moriaki v podgotovke*, pp. 323–24; "Kak svodnyi morskoi otriad zakhvatil blindirovannyi poezd," *Armiia i Flot Rab. i Krest. Rossii*, no. 15 (8 December 1917); N. F. Izmailov and A. S. Pukhov, *Tsentrobalt* (Kaliningrad, 1967), pp. 215–16; A. F. Ilyin-Genevsky, *From the February Revolution to the October Revolution* (New York, 1931), pp. 121–22.

   Raskolnikov, who was the real organizer and commander of the expedition, is ignored in most Soviet versions because of his strong anti-Stalin statement as a defector in 1939. For an exception see A. P. Konstantinov, *F. F. Il'in-Raskol'nikov* (Leningrad, 1964), pp. 91–98, which was published during a brief period of rehabilitation.

12. A. S. Nevolin, *Avrorovtsy* (Moscow, 1967), pp. 100–101.

13. As quoted in R. V. Daniels, *Red October* (New York, 1967), p. 211.

14. Nevolin, *Avrorovtsy*, pp. 111–12; *Baltiiskie moriaki v bor'be za vlast' sovetov (noiabr' 1917–dekabr' 1918)*, ed. A. L. Fraiman et al. (Leningrad, 1968), pp. 46, 316.

15. Sivkov, *Kronshtadt*, p. 346.

16. Ibid., pp. 346–47, 356; *Baltiiskie moriaki v bor'be*, pp. 313–14 n.11.

17. Cromie, "Baltic Flotilla Report," 27 October/9 November 1917, PRO, ADM 137/1570.

18. Ivan Rengarten, "Oktiabr'skaia revoliutsiia v Baltiiskom flote," *Krasnyi Arkhiv* 25 (1927) : 53–54.
19. S. N. Timirev, *Vospominaniia morskogo ofitsera* (New York, 1961), pp. 143–49. Already, on 25 October, the commander of the battleship *Grazhdanin* had complained to Razvozov that because of the number of specialists who were leaving for Petrograd, it was impossible for his ship to fulfill any orders. Rengarten, "Oktiabr'skaia revoliutsiia," p. 50.
20. Timirev, *Vospominaniia morskogo ofitsera*, p. 143; NA and DID, in Buchanan to FO, 28 November 1917, PRO, FO 371/2999.
21. *Baltiiskie moriaki v bor'be*, pp. 312–13 n.2; I. I. Vakhrameev, *Vo imia revoliutsii* (Moscow, 1957), pp. 17–21.
22. Buchanan to FO, 19 November 1917, PRO, FO 371/2999.
23. Howard to FO, 12 November 1917, PRO, FO 371/2999.
24. Howard to FO, 15 November 1917, PRO, FO 371/2999.
25. Minute attached to Green to FO, 11 November, PRO, FO 371/2999.
26. Modest Ivanov, "Dve telegrammy," in *Voennye moriaki*, pp. 426–34. Dybenko had initiated the elevation of Ivanov before his departure from Helsingfors as Tsentrobalt's candidate for the proposed naval collegium. Radiogram journal, 25 July–31 December 1917, no. 602 (8:25, 27 October), SA, VK, 12034.
27. Tsentrobalt protocol no. 115 (8 November 1917), SA, VK, 3220.
28. Cromie, "Baltic Flotilla Report," 9/22 November, PRO, ADM 137/1570.
29. NA for DID, in Buchanan to FO, 28 November, PRO, FO 371/2999. The naval college was officially created by the Council of People's Commissars on 7 November. *Baltiiskie moriaki v bor'be*, p. 315 n.21.
30. SA, VK, 3220; published protocols in *Protokoly i postanovleniia*, pp. 254 ff.
31. *Protokoly i postanovleniia*, pp. 267–68.
32. Cromie, "Baltic Flotilla Report," 8/21 November 1917, PRO, ADM 137/1570.
33. Grove to FO, 9 November 1917, PRO, FO 371/3007. The British government refused to recognize the independence of Finland until the Constituent Assembly did so. Another consideration was that recognition would set a dangerous precedent for other parts of the Russian Empire. FO to Buchanan, 10 December 1917, and minute of Sir George Clerk attached, PRO, FO 371/3007.
34. Cromie, "Baltic Flotilla Report," 13 November 1917, PRO, ADM 137/1570.
35. Ibid., 18 November 1917.
36. *Sotsialist-Revoliutsioner*, no. 94 (9 November 1917). The closing of *Narodnaia Niva* by orders from Petrograd on 1 November and the

arrest of Sergei Tsion, its editor, also caused adverse reaction in Helsingfors toward the new government. *Narodnaia Niva*, no. 148 (1 November 1917—the last issue).

37. Cromie, "Baltic Flotilla Reports," 16 and 20 November, PRO, ADM 137/1570.

38. Protocol no. 121, 14 November 1917, SA, VK, 3220. Izmailov ignores this episode in his own history of Tsentrobalt. See Izmailov and Pukhov, *Tsentrobalt*, pp. 220–25.

39. *Protokoly i postanovleniia*, p. 247.

40. Ibid., pp. 274–80; SA, VK, 3220.

41. Kh. S. Marat, "Rabochie, soldaty i matrosy golosuiut za Lenina," *Voprosy Istorii KPSS*, no. 11 (November 1968), pp. 48–49. The main Western authority, Radkey, lists 62 percent of a total vote of 68,764 as Bolshevik, but his figures on the other parties make no sense. He notes, however, that the results from the Baltic fleet were not included in the two major published sources then available to him. See Oliver H. Radkey, *The Election to the Russian Constituent Assembly of 1917*, Harvard Historical Monographs no. 21 (Cambridge, Mass., 1950), pp. 12, 80.

The voting procedure was unique in the Baltic-fleet district, where each person was allowed to vote for two candidates by name: this explains the separate figures for Right and Left SRs. A breakdown for the Helsingfors region, including 97 of 100 precincts, is as follows: Bolsheviks—22,670 for Dybenko and 22,237 for Lenin; Left SRs—13,617 for Shishko and 12,906 for Proshian; Right SRs—7,620 for Maslov and 7,351 for Tsion; officers—855 for Demchinskii and 838 for Rengarten. *Armiia i Flot Rab. i Krest. Rossii*, no. 3 (23 November 1917). The fact that Dybenko, Shishko, and Maslov led their respective tickets is probably because all three were sailors, while Lenin, Proshian, and Tsion were not.

One might also suspect that there was some tampering with the results in Kronstadt, since an 84 percent vote for the Bolsheviks is out of line with their representation in the soviet. That the activities of the non-Bolshevik candidates had been confined to Helsingfors, whereas Dybenko and Lenin were well known in Kronstadt, may be part of the explanation. The large number that must have been absent at the time may have been recorded as voting with their rifles for the Bolsheviks.

42. Rengarten, "Oktiabr'skaia revoliutsiia," p. 64.

43. Marat, "Rabochie," p. 50.

44. Cromie, "Baltic Flotilla Report," 20 November/3 December, PRO, ADM 137/1570; Timirev, *Vospominaniia morskogo ofitsera*, pp. 155–59.

45. Protocol no. 125, 19 November 1917, SA, VK, 3220.
46. Rengarten, "Oktiabr'skaia revoliutsiia," pp. 66–74. Modest Ivanov revealed, in a letter written on 27 November that was published in reply to critics, his belief in the fundamental principle that officers and men must work together. *Baltiiskie moriaki v bor'be*, p. 45.
47. Stanley to Admiralty, 21 November 1917, PRO, ADM 137/1249.
48. "Memorandum for War Cabinet by First Sea Lord: Situation in the Baltic," 22 November 1917, PRO, CAB, 24/33.
49. Ibid.
50. "Withdrawal of Naval Forces from the Baltic," 29 November 1917, PRO, ADM 137/2706.
51. "Extract from War Cabinet Proceedings," 6 December 1917, PRO, FO 371/3018.
52. *Baltiiskie moriaki v bor'be*, pp. 315–16 n.26.
53. M. A. Stoliarenko, *V. I. Lenin i revoliutsionnye moriaki* (Moscow, 1970), pp. 133–35; *Armiia i Flot*, no. 6 (26 November 1917). The partial text of Lenin's speech is also in *Polnoe sobranie sochinenii*, 5th ed., vol. 34 (Moscow, 1962), pp. 112–18.
54. MA for DMI, in Buchanan to FO, 8 December 1917, PRO, FO 371/3017.
55. This was sometimes referred to as the "Council of Twenty." *Protokoly i postanovleniia*, pp. 452–53 n.89.
56. Of the 114 delegates, 82 were Bolsheviks, 29 were Left SRs, and 3 were nonparty. Aron Sheinman, the Helsingfors Soviet leader, became the new chairman, with Vladimir Nevsky and Torgushin (a Left SR) as assistants. *Sotsialist-Revoliutsioner*, no. 109 (28 November 1917).
57. Ibid., no. 101 (17 November 1917); no. 140 (12 January 1918). The proposal for funding that was submitted to Petrograd listed courses for twelve subjects in the following order: political economy, government organization, history of Russia, history of the revolutionary movement, history of the French Revolution, socialism, the agrarian question, the workers question, local self-government, the organization question, law, and programs of political parties. SA, VK, 3219. And the peasant soviet sponsored a separate agricultural school. *Sotsialist-Revoliutsioner*, no. 114 (3 December 1917).
58. MA for DMI, in Buchanan to FO, 12 December 1917, PRO, FO 371/3017.
59. Cromie, "Baltic Flotilla Report," 5/18 December 1917, PRO, ADM 137/1570; Rengarten, "Oktiabr'skaia revoliutsiia," pp. 75–77; Izmailov and Pukhov, *Tsentrobalt*, pp. 231–34; *Baltiiskie moriaki v bor'be*, pp. 57–58.
60. Nevolin, *Avrorovtsy*, pp. 115–17. The *Aurora* returned to Kronstadt

one week later, accompanied by three other cruisers, the *Rossiia*, the *Gromoboi*, and the *Diana*.

61. See Admiral Ruzhek's letter to Captain Graf, dated 5 December, in *Baltiiskie moriaki v bor'be*, pp. 56–57. See also H. Graf, *La Marine Russe dans la guerre et dans la révolution, 1914–1918* (Paris, 1928), pp. 307–9.
62. *Baltiiskie moriaki v bor'be*, pp. 52–54.
63. Ibid., p. 54.
64. Cromie, "Baltic Flotilla Report," 5/18 December 1917, PRO, ADM 137/1570.
65. *Protokoly i postanovleniia*, pp. 295–306 and passim. In May 1918, Balakin was involved in the protest of three destroyer crews over the organization of the defense of Petrograd. This action was considered counterrevolutionary, and he received a sentence of fifteen years of labor, which was later reduced to five years. *Baltiiskie moriaki v bor'be*, pp. 162–91, 238, 329–30.
66. *Protokoly i postanovleniia*, pp. 310–15; *Baltiiskie moriaki v bor'be*, no. 39, pp. 316–17.
67. Protocol, no. 4, 4 January 1918, *Protokoly i postanovleniia*, pp. 345–46; Dybenko, *Iz nedr tsarskogo flota*, pp. 172–75.
68. D. Fedotoff White, *Survival through War and Revolution in Russia* (Philadelphia, 1939), pp. 176–80.
69. Copy of the decree in *Baltiiskie moriaki v bor'be*, pp. 75–78.
70. Ibid., no. 52, p. 318; Izmailov and Pukhov, *Tsentrobalt*, pp. 247–51.
71. *Protokoly i postanovleniia*, pp. 395–413.
72. *Baltiiskie moriaki v bor'be*, pp. 104–6.
73. Ibid., p. 319 n.57; *Protokoly i postanovleniia*, p. 425; Izmailov and Pukhov, *Tsentrobalt*, pp. 270–71.
74. *Baltiiskie moriaki v bor'be*, pp. 106–10, 132.
75. Ibid., pp. 133–35.
76. Ibid., pp. 135–47, 321 n.76.
77. E. Dymman, "Na kanonerskoi lodke 'Groziashchii' v dni padeniia Gel'singforsa," *Krasnyi Flot*, no. 2 (1925), pp. 97–98.
78. The detailed report about the end of the British submarine squadron by the officer in charge, Lieutenant Downie, is in PRO, ADM 137/1570.
79. "Report on Fate of Russian Fleet," 9 December 1918, NA, RG 45, WA 6, box 612.
80. "State of Fleet on 12 February, 1919," NA, RG 45, WA 6, box 612.
81. U.S. naval attaché reports from Berlin, 27 October and 10 November 1922, NA, RG 38, 2151 (P-2-a).
82. G. Silin, "Iz zhizni matrosskikh kollektivov kommunistov," *Vooru-*

zhennyi Narod: Organ Voennyi Sektsii Petrogradskago Soveta, no. 62
(27 September 1918).

83. "Report of Swedish naval attaché in Petrograd, Commander Elliot,"
NA, RG 45, WA 6, box 606. The German fleet in the Gulf of Finland
was not faring much better. "The Russian officers who have seen and
mixed with the German sailors during the expedition in Finland have
witnessed changes in the discipline, and have found a great resemblance
between their state of mind and the Russians just before the revolution."
Naval intelligence report from Sweden, 23 September 1918, NA, RG 38,
10416 (C-10-g).

84. Konstantinov, *F. F. Il'in-Raskol'nikov*, pp. 147–49. For a detailed study
of the Kronstadt Revolt, see Paul Avrich, *Kronstadt, 1921* (Princeton,
N.J., 1970). The most complete published list of names of sailors involved is in *Pravda o Kronshtadte* (Prague, 1921).

BIBLIOGRAPHY

ARCHIVES, MUSEUMS, AND SPECIAL COLLECTIONS

British Museum, London
>   Manuscript Division: ADD. MSS. 51093 (Cecil Papers); ADD. MSS. 51105 (Foreign Office Memos).

Columbia University, New York
>   Archive of Russian and East European History and Culture: memoirs and papers of Dmitri Fedotoff White, Admiral Grigorovich, and other émigré officers and sailors.
>   Book and newspaper collections.

Hoover Institution, Stanford University, California
>   Golder collection; Veselago papers.

Library of Congress, Washington, D.C.
>   Manuscript Division: Root Collection.
>   Slavic Division.

National Archives, Washington, D.C.
>   Record Group 38: Operations Section, Office of Naval Intelligence; subgroup 98 (attaché reports).
>   Record Group 45: Naval Records Collection of the Office of Naval Records and Library, Subject File, 1911–27.
>   Record Group 165: Russia—Dispatch Entries (army attaché reports).
>   Microcopy 316, Records Relating to Internal Affairs of Russia and the Soviet Union, 1910–29.
>   Microcopy 367, roll 48: State Dept. Records Re World War I and Its Termination.

New York Public Library, New York
  Slavonic Division.
Public Record Office, London
  Foreign Office 371/2995–3021: dispatches pertaining to Russia.
  Foreign Office 800: Balfour and Bertie collections.
  Admiralty 1, 137, and 500, especially reports of Captain Cromie.
  Cabinet 24: War Cabinet papers.
Russian Imperial Naval Museum, Lakewood, New Jersey
Saltykov-Shchedrin State Public Library, Leningrad
  Newspaper and book collections.
Sota-Arkisto (War Archive), Helsinki
  Russian collection.
Sota-Museo (War Museum), Helsinki
  Photograph collection.
Suomen Kansallismuseo (National Museum of Finland), Helsinki
  Photograph collection.
Tsentral'nyi Voenno-Morskoi Muzei, Leningrad
Työväen-Arkisto (Labor Archive), Helsinki
  Newspaper and pamphlet collection.
University of Helsinki Library, Helsinki
  Slavonic collection.
  Newspaper collection.
Valtionarkisto (State Archive), Helsinki
  Archive of the War of Liberation.
  Newspaper collection.

NEWSPAPERS AND JOURNALS

1917

Armiia i Flot Rabochei i Krest'ianskoi Rossii [Army and navy of workers' and peasants' Russia]. Petrograd, government.

Armiia i Flot Svobodnoi Rossii [Army and navy of Free Russia]. Petrograd, government.

Delo Naroda [People's cause]. Petrograd, Socialist Revolutionary.

Golos Pravdy [Voice of truth]. Kronstadt, Bolshevik.

Golos Sotsial-Demokrata [Voice of social democracy]. Helsingfors, Menshevik.

Izvestiia Gel'singforsskago Soveta [News of the Helsingfors Soviet]. Helsingfors, Soviet.

Izvestiia Kronshtadtskago Soveta [News of the Kronstadt Soviet]. Kronstadt, Soviet.
Izvestiia Petrogradskago Soveta [News of the Petrograd Soviet]. Petrograd, Soviet.
Moriak [Sailor]. Helsingfors, Sailors Club.
Narodnaia Niva [People's field]. Helsingfors, Right SR.
Novaia Zhizn' [New life]. Petrograd, Socialist.
Novoe Vremia [New times]. Petrograd, Conservative.
Obshchee Delo [Common cause]. Helsingfors, Independent Socialist.
Pravda [Truth]. Petrograd, Bolshevik.
Priboi [Surf]. Helsingfors, Bolshevik.
Proletarskoe Delo [Proletarian cause]. Kronstadt, Bolshevik.
Rech' [Speech]. Petrograd, Kadet.
Sotsialist-Revoliutsioner [Socialist revolutionary]. Helsingfors, Left SR.
Svobodnyi Flot [Free navy]. Petrograd, government.
Volna [The Wave]. Helsingfors, Bolshevik.
Za Rossiiu [For Russia]. Helsingfors, Independent Socialist.

Post-1917

Chasovoi [Sentinel]. Paris, military.
Krasnaia Zvezda [Red star]. Moscow, military.
Krasnyi Flot [Red navy]. Petrograd-Leningrad.
Morskie Zapiski [Naval notes]. New York.
Morskoi Sbornik [Naval collection]. Petrograd-Leningrad.
Morskoi Zhurnal [Naval journal]. Prague.
Novoe Russkoe Slovo [New Russian word]. New York.
Novyi Zhurnal [New journal]. New York.
Petrogradskaia Pravda [Petrograd truth]. Petrograd.
Pravda [Truth]. Moscow.
Put' [The Way]. Helsingfors.
Russkii Golos [Russian voice]. Helsingfors.
Signal. Paris.
Voennaia Byl' [Military past]. Paris.
Vooruzhenoe [Arms]. Paris.
Zapiski Voenno-Morskago Istoricheskago Kruzhka [Notes of the Naval History Circle]. Paris and San Francisco.
Zarubezhnyi Morskoi Sbornik [Foreign naval collection]. Pilzen.

DOCUMENTARY AND REFERENCE SOURCES

Akhun, M. I., and Petrov, V. A. *1917 god v Petrograde: khronika sobytii i bibliografiia* [1917 in Petrograd: a chronicle of events and bibliography]. Leningrad, 1933.

"Baltflot v iiul'skie dni 1917 g." [The Baltic fleet in the July days of 1917], *Krasnyi Arkhiv* 46 (1931): 69–100.

Baltiiskie moriaki v bor'be za vlast' sovetov (noiabr' 1917–dekabr' 1918) [Baltic sailors in the struggle for the power of soviets, November 1917–December 1918]. Edited by A. L. Fraiman et al. Leningrad, 1968.

Baltiiskie moriaki v podgotovke i provedenii velikoi oktiabr'skoi sotsialisticheskoi revoliutsii [The Baltic sailors in the preparation and conduct of the Great October Socialist Revolution]. Edited by R. N. Mordvinov et al. Moscow-Leningrad, 1957.

"Baltiiskii flot ot iiulia k oktiabriu 1917 g." [The Baltic fleet from July to October 1917], *Krasnaia Letopis'* [Red chronicle] 32 (no. 5, 1929): 157–212.

Bol'shaia Sovetskaia Entsiklopediia [The great Soviet encyclopedia]. First edition. 65 vols. Moscow, 1925–31.

Documents of Russian History, 1914–1917. Edited by Frank A. Golder; translated by Emanuel Aronsberg. New York, 1927.

"Documents on British Relations with Russia, 1917–1918." Edited by David R. Jones. *Canadian American Slavic Studies* 7 (Summer 1973): 219–37; 7 (Fall 1973): 350–75; 7 (Winter 1973): 498–510.

Haupt, Georges, and Marie, Jean-Jacques. *Makers of the Russian Revolution: Biographies of Bolshevik Leaders.* Translated by C. I. P. Ferdinand. Ithaca, N.Y., 1974.

Krasnyi flot za svobodu i rodinu! (miting chernomortsev v Petrograde) [The Red navy for freedom and fatherland: the meeting of Black Sea sailors in Petrograd]. Petrograd, 1917.

"Kronshtadtskie moriaki v iiul'skom vystuplenii 1917 goda" [The Kronstadt sailors in the July uprising of 1917]. Edited by M. L. Lur'e. *Krasnaia Letopis'* 48 (no. 3, 1932): 76–105.

Lenin, V. I. *Polnoe sobranie sochinenii* [Complete collected works]. 55 vols. 5th ed. Moscow, 1958–65.

"Petrograd, 24–25 oktiabria 1917" [Petrograd, 24–25 October 1917]. *Novyi Mir* 33 (November 1957): 198–218.

Petrogradskii voenno-revoliutsionnyi komitet: dokumenty i materialy [The Petrograd Military Revolutionary Committee: documents and materials]. Edited by D. A. Chugaev et al. 3 vols. Moscow, 1966–67.

Protokoly i postanovleniia tsentral'nogo komiteta Baltiiskogo flota (1917–1918) [Protocols and declarations of the Central Committee of the Baltic fleet, 1917–1918]. Edited by D. A. Chugaev et al. Moscow-Leningrad, 1963.

Raionnye sovety Petrograda v 1917 godu [District Soviets of Petrograd in 1917]. Edited by S. H. Valk et al. 3 vols. Moscow, 1964.

Revoliutsionnoe dvizhenie v armii i na flote v gody pervoi mirovoi voiny 1914–fevral' 1917: sb. dokumentov [The revolutionary movement in the army and navy in the years of the First World War, 1914–February 1917: collection of documents]. Edited by A. L. Sidorov. Moscow, 1966.

The Russian Provisional Government, 1917: Documents. Selected and edited by Robert Paul Browder and Alexander F. Kerensky. 3 vols. Stanford, Calif., 1961.

The Russian Revolution and the Soviet State, 1917–1921: Documents. Selected and edited by Martin McCauley. London, 1975.

The Testimony of Kolchak and Other Siberian Materials. Edited by Elena Varneck and H. H. Fisher. Stanford University, Calif., 1935.

Velikaia oktiabr'skaia sotsialisticheskaia revoliutsiia: dokumenty i materialy [The Great October Socialist Revolution: documents and materials]: *Revoliutsionnoe dvizhenie v Rossii nakanune oktiabr'skogo vooruzhennogo vosstaniia* [The revolutionary movement in Russia on the eve of the October armed uprising]. Edited by D. A. Chugaev et al. Moscow, 1962.

Revoliutsionnoe dvizhenie v Rossii v aprele 1917 g.: aprel'skii krizis [The revolutionary movement in Russia in April 1917: The April Crisis]. Edited by L. S. Gaponenko et al. Moscow, 1958.

Revoliutsionnoe dvizhenie v Rossii v avguste 1917 g.: razgrom Kornilovskogo miatezha [The revolutionary movement in Russia in August 1917: the destruction of the Kornilov mutiny]. Edited by D. A. Chugaev et al. Moscow, 1959.

Revoliutsionnoe dvizhenie v Rossii v iiule 1917 g.: iiul'skii krizis [The revolutionary movement in Russia in July 1917: the July Crisis]. Edited by D. A. Chugaev et al. Moscow, 1959.

Voennye vosstaniia v Baltike v 1905–06 gg. [Military revolt on the Baltic in 1905–6]. Edited by A. K. Drezen. Moscow, 1933.

Vosstanie na bronenostse "Kniaz Potemkin Tavricheskii": vospominaniia, materialy i dokumenty [The revolt on the battleship *Prince Potemkin Tavricheskii*: memoirs, materials, and documents]. Edited by V. I. Nevskii. Moscow-Petrograd, 1924.

EYEWITNESS AND MEMOIR ACCOUNTS

BOLSHEVIK

Antonov-Ovseenko, Vladimir Alekseevich. "Baltflot v dni Kerenshchiny i krasnogo oktiabria" [The Baltic fleet during the reign of Kerensky and the Red October]. *Proletarskaia Revoliutsiia* 10 (October 1922): 118–29.

This former army officer was editor of the Bolshevik newspaper in Helsingfors in June and July 1917. Arrested in July and liberated in September, he served as tactical leader of the seizure of the Winter Palace in October. He was purged in 1937.

―――. *Stroitel'stvo Krasnoi Armii v revoliutsii* [The construction of the Red Army in the Revolution]. Moscow, 1923.
―――. *V revoliutsii* [In the Revolution]. Moscow, 1957.
―――. *V semnadtsatom godu* [In 1917]. Moscow, 1933.
Avtukhov, V. P. "Iiul'skie dni" [The July days]. *Morskoi Sbornik* 77 (no. 6, June 1924): 6–28.

A machinist on the *Amur*, Bolshevik since 1914.

―――. "Kornilovshchina" [The reign of Kornilov]. *Morskoi Sbornik* 77 (no. 8, August 1924): 1–16.
Baranov, Semen Nikandrovich. "Baltiitsy na iuge" [Baltic sailors in the South]. In *Voennye moriaki* (see below), pp. 378–98.

A member of Kronstadt Bolshevik committee in 1917; led propaganda effort in South Russia.

Belyshev, Aleksandr Viktorovich. " 'Avrora' v dni oktiabria" [The *Aurora* in the days of October]. In *Petrograd v dni velikogo oktiabria*, edited by V. E. Mushtukov, pp. 367–73. Leningrad, 1967.

A machinist of the *Aurora*, chairman of the ship's committee, and commissar of the cruiser in October. Still living in 1968.

―――. "Doklad commissara kreisera 'Avrora' " [Report of the commissar of the cruiser *Aurora*]. *Ogonek* 44 (October 1955): 15.
―――. "Vystrel 'Avrora' " [The shot of the *Aurora*]. In *Oktiabr'skoe vooruzhennoe vosstanie v Petrograde* [The October armed uprising in Petrograd], edited by S. P. Kniazev and A. P. Konstantinov, pp. 140–45. Leningrad, 1956.
Breslav, Boris Abramovich. "15 let tomu nazad" [15 years ago]. *Katorga i Ssylka* 96–97 (November–December 1932): 45–68.
―――. *Kanun oktiabria 1917 goda: s"ezd sovetov severnoi oblasti, 11–12 oktiabria 1917 g.* [On the eve of October 1917: the Congress of Soviets of the Northern Provinces, 11–12 October 1917]. Moscow, 1934.
―――. "Sed'moi osobyi" [The Seventh Detachment]. In *Petrograd v dni velikogo oktiabria* [Petrograd in the days of the Great October], pp. 356–66. Leningrad, 1967.
Dingel'shtedt, Fedor. "Vesna proletarskoi revoliutsii" [Spring of the Proletarian Revolution]. *Krasnaia Letopis'* 12 (no. 1, 1925): 192–214.

Bolshevik agitator at Kronstadt and Helsingfors.

Dorogov, Aleksei Antonovich. "Vospominaniia matrosa Alekseia Antono-vicha Dorogova o vziatii zimnogo dvortsa" [The memoirs of Sailor Aleksei Antonovich Dorogov about the taking of the Winter Palace]. *Istoriia Proletariata SSSR* 11 (1932): 104–8.

A sailor on the *Amur* and a member of the executive committee of the Kronstadt Soviet.

Duplitskii, D. "Baltiiskii flot v iiul'skie dni 1917 g." [The Baltic fleet in the July days of 1917]. *Krasnaia Letopis'* 2–3 (1922): 252–56.

A sailor at Helsingfors.

Dybenko, Pavel Efimovich. *Iz nedr tsarskogo flota k velikomu oktiabriu* [From the nadir of the Tsarist navy to the Great October]. Moscow, 1928. Edited and republished under the same title in 1958.

Bolshevik sailor from battleship *Imperator Pavel I (Respublika)*; chair-man of Tsentrobalt; arrested in July; returned to Helsingfors after the Kornilov affair; chairman of congresses of Baltic sailors in May and September; commissar of naval affairs after October; delegate to Con-stituent Assembly; rose to rank of general in Red Army and was purged in 1938.

———. "Moriaki Baltflota" [Sailors of the Baltic fleet]. In *V dni velikoi proletarskoi revoliutsii*, edited by E. Gorodetskii and E. Burdzhalov. Moscow, 1937.

———. *Oktiabr' na Baltike* [October on the Baltic]. Tashkent, 1934.

Egorov, Ivan Nikitich [Orlov]. "Matrosy Bol'sheviki nakanune 1917 goda" [The sailors of the Bolsheviks on the eve of 1917]. *Krasnaia Letopis'* 18 (no. 3, 1926): 6–30; 19 (no. 4, 1926): 68–92.

Professional revolutionary at Helsingfors in March and at Kronstadt from May to October.

Flerovskii, Ivan Petrovich. *Bol'shevistskii Kronshtadt v 1917 godu* [Bolshe-vik Kronstadt in 1917]. Leningrad, 1957.

A Bolshevik since 1905; member of the executive committee of the Kronstadt Soviet; member of Military Revolutionary Committee in 1917; served after October as commissar of the Baltic fleet; party work-er; died in 1960.

———. "Kronshtadskaia respublika" [The Kronstadt Republic]. *Proletar-skaia Revoliutsiia* 58 (November 1926): 29–55.

———. "Kronshtadtskii desant" [The Kronstadt landing]. *Ogonek* 45 (November 1956) : 2–3.

———. "Kronshtadt v oktiabr'skoi revoliutsii" [Kronstadt in the October Revolution]. *Proletarskaia Revoliutsiia* 10 (1922) : 130–50.

Gribakov, A. "Kronshtadttsy v Petrograde v iiul'skie dni" [Kronstadters in Petrograd in the July days]. *Petrogradskaia Pravda*, 13 July 1922.

Il'in-Zhenevskii, Aleksandr Fedorovich. "Bol'shevistskie gazety Kronshtadta i Gel'singforsa v 1917 g." [Bolshevik newspapers of Kronstadt and Helsingfors in 1917]. *Krasnaia Letopis'* 24 (no. 3, 1927) : 83–107.

Brother of Raskolnikov; fled abroad to escape arrest and studied at the University of Geneva; returned in Russia in 1914 and was commissioned an officer in a chemical battalion; wounded twice; led the founding of Bolshevik newspapers in Kronstadt and Helsingfors; purged and died in 1941.

———. "Iiul'skie dni 1917 goda v Petrograde" [The July days of 1917 in Petrograd]. *Krasnaia Letopis'* 18 (no. 3, 1926) : 43–57.

———. *Ot fevralia k zakhvatu vlasti* [From February to the seizure of power]. Leningrad, 1927.

[Ilyin-Genevsky, A. F.]. *From the February Revolution to the October Revolution, 1917.* New York, 1931. English translation of above.

Inge, Iu. "Avrora." In *V dni velikoi proletarskoi revoliutsii* [In the days of the Great Proletarian Revolution], pp. 160–64. Moscow, 1937.

Ivanov, Dmitrii. *Eto bylo na Baltike: vospominaniia matrosa* [This was on the Baltic: memoirs of a sailor]. L'vov, 1965.

Ivanov, Modest Vasil'evich. "Dve telegrammy" [Two telegrams]. In *Voennye moriaki* (see below), pp. 426–34.

Officer who sided with Bolsheviks in 1917.

Izmailov, Nikolai Fedorovich. *Baltiiskii flot v oktiabr'skie dni* [The Baltic fleet in the October days]. Moscow, 1957.

Sailor on *Afrika* at Kronstadt; petty-officer instructor; Bolshevik member of Tsentrobalt; chairman of Tsentrobalt from October to November 1917; chief commissar for Baltic fleet in 1918; still living in 1967.

———. "Vernye revoliutsii" [Loyal to the Revolution]. In *Petrograd v dni velikogo oktiabria*, pp. 149–53. Leningrad, 1967.

Khovrin, Nikolai Aleksandrovich. "Arest delegatsii moriakov" [The arrest of the delegation of sailors]. In *Oktiabr'skii shkval* [October storm], edited by S. P. Kudelli, pp. 87–89. Leningrad, 1927.

Sailor on the *Imperator Pavel I* (*Respublika*); a leading member of

Tsentrobalt; arrested in July; commissar in October; participant in 1957 and 1967 anniversary celebrations.

——. "1917-i god" [1917]. In *Voennye moriaki* (see below), pp. 243–75.

——. "V 1917 vo flote—vospominaniia moriaka" [In 1917 in the navy—memoirs of a sailor]. *Krasnaia Letopis'* 20 (no. 5, 1926) : 53–57.

Kolbin, Ivan Nikolaevich. "Baltiitsy v oktiabr'skie dni" [The Baltic sailors in the October days]. In *Oktiabr'skii shkval*, edited by S. P. Kudelli, pp. 118–23. Leningrad, 1927.

An instructor in the Student-Mine Detachment at Kronstadt; commissar of *Zaria Svobody* in October.

——. "Kronshtadt organizuetsia, gotovitsia k boiu" [Kronstadt organizes, prepares for battle]. In *Oktiabr'skii shkval*, pp. 23–50.

——. "Kronshtadt ot fevralia k Kornilovskikh dnei" [Kronstadt from February to the Kornilov days]. *Krasnaia Letopis'* 23 (no. 2, 1927) : 134–61.

——. "Kronshtadtsy ot fevralia k oktiabriu" [Kronstadters from February to October]. *Literaturnyi Sovremennik* 5 (May 1937) : 161–83.

——. *Kronshtadt v 1917 g.* [Kronstadt in 1917]. Leningrad, 1932.

Kondakov, Dmitrii Nikolaevich. "Krepost' revoliutsii (Kronshtadt ot fevralia k oktiabriu)" [Fortress of revolution: Kronstadt from February to October]. In *V ogne revoliutsionnykh boev (raiony Petrograda v dvukh revoliutsiiakh 1917 g.): sbornik vospominanii starykh bol'shevikov-pitertsev* [In the fire of revolutionary battles (districts of Petrograd in two revolutions of 1917): collection of memoirs of old Bolshevik-Petrograders], edited by E. R. Levitas et al., pp. 327–54. Moscow, 1967.

Sailor at Kronstadt; member of Bolshevik committee.

——. "V revoliutsionnom Kronshtadte" [In revolutionary Kronstadt]. In *Voennye moriaki* (see below), pp. 288–311.

Kurkov, P. "Kreiser 'Avrora'" [The cruiser *Aurora*]. *Bor'ba Klassov* 6–7 (1931) : 11–13.

Member of ship's committee of *Aurora*; arrested in July; commander of Soviet navy in 1930s; purged in 1938.

——. "1917 god na 'Avrora'" [1917 on the *Aurora*]. *Morskoi Sbornik* 80 (no. 10, October 1927) : 14–22.

——. "Pervyi vystrel" [First shot]. *Nashi Dostizheniia* 11 (November 1934) : 11–13.

Lamanov, Petr Nikolaevich. "V burnye dni" [In stormy days]. In *Oktiabr'skii shkval*, pp. 89–103. Leningrad, 1927.

Elected commander of naval forces at Kronstadt during 1917.

――――. "V Kronshtadte posle iiul'skikh dnei" [In Kronstadt after the July days]. *Krasnaia Letopis'* 24 (no. 3, 1927) : 23–34.
Lipko, S. A. "Matros z Kronshtadta—bil'shovits'kii agitator na Volini" [Sailor from Kronstadt—Bolshevik agitator in Volynia]. *Ukrains'kii Istorichnii Zhurnal* 11 (1966) : 116–18.
Liubovich, Artemii Moiseevich. "3–5 iiulia" [3–5 July]. *Leningradskaia Pravda,* 16 July 1925.
Ludri, Ivan Martynovich. "Sudovye komitety" [Ships' committees]. In *Oktiabr'skii shkval,* pp. 77–87. Leningrad, 1927.

Bolshevik leader at Kronstadt; commissar of Kexholm regiment in October; purged and died in 1939.

Lychev, Ivan Akimovich. *Potemkintsy* [Men of the *Potemkin*]. Moscow, 1965.

A participant in the *Potemkin* mutiny of 1905.

Mal'kov, Pavel Dmitrievich. "Shturmovye dni" [Stormy days]. In *Voennye moriaki* (see below), pp. 460–64.

Sailor on the cruiser *Diana*; member of Tsentrobalt and Tsentroflot; delegate to Second All-Russian Congress of Soviets; commandant of Smolny and of the Kremlin; died 1965.

――――. "V oktiabr'skie dni" [In the October days]. *Znamia* 11 (November 1956) : 132–46.
――――. *Zapiski komendanta Moskovskago kremlia* [Notes of the commandant of the Moscow Kremlin]. 3rd ed. Moscow, 1967.
Mokrousov, Aleksei Vasil'evich. "V noch' na 25 oktiabria" [In the night of 25 October]. In *Voennye moriaki* (see below), pp. 464–74.
Nevolin, A. S. *Avrorovtsy* [Men of the *Aurora*]. Moscow, 1967.

Bolshevik sailor on the *Aurora*.

Nevskii, Vladimir Ivanovich. "Voennaia organizatsiia i oktiabr'skaia revoliutsiia" [The military organization and the October Revolution]. *Krasnoarmeets—iubeleinyi nomer, 1917–1919* 10–15 (1919) : 34–44.

Party worker and historian; a leader of Battle Organization of the party and of the Military Revolutionary Committee in 1917.

――――. "V oktiabre" [In October]. *Katorga i Ssylka* 96–97 (nos. 11–12, 1932) : 27–45.

Bibliography

Nikitin, Nikolai. "Avrora" [*Aurora*]. *Nashi Dostizheniia* 11 (November 1934): 5–9.

Podvoiskii, Nikolai Il'ich. *God 1917* [The year 1917]. Moscow, 1958.

Leader of the Military Revolutionary Committee in October.

———. *Krasnaia gvardiia v oktiabr'skie dni* [The Red Guard in the October days]. Moscow, 1927. Earlier, unedited version of above.

———. "O voennoi deiatel'nosti V. I. Lenina" [About the military activities of V. I. Lenin]. *Kommunist* 1 (January 1957): 31–46.

Pronin, Aleksei Grigor'evich. "Burnye gody" [Stormy years]. *Oktiabr'* 34 (no. 8, August 1957): 144–56.

Sailor of Student-Mine Detachment at Kronstadt; leader of Kronstadt Soviet; Bolshevik liaison between Kronstadt and Smolny in October.

———. "Kronshtadttsy v oktiabr'skie dni 1917 goda" [Kronstadters in the October days of 1917]. In *Voennye moriaki* (see below), pp 270–81.

Raskol'nikov, Fedor Fedorovich [Il'in]. *Kronshtadt i Piter v 1917 godu* [Kronstadt and Petrograd in 1917]. Moscow, 1925. An edited version was published in 1964 under the title *Na boevykh postakh* [At the battle posts].

Student at St. Petersburg Polytechnic Institute; worker on *Pravda*; sublieutenant of Marine School; Kronstadt leader; arrested in July; commissar and commander of Baltic fleet in civil-war period; editor of *Morskoi Sbornik*; diplomatic service in 1930s; defected from post as minister to Bulgaria to avoid purge; died in France in 1939.

——— [Il'in, F.]. "Ob"ezd Kronshtadtskoi delegatsiei finskogo poberezh'ia v iiune 1917 goda" [The tour by the Kronstadt delegation of the Finnish shore in June 1917]. *Krasnaia Letopis'* 12 (no. 1, 1925): 216–38.

———. *Revoliutsionnyi flot* [Revolutionary navy]. Kronstadt, 1918.

———. "Revoliutsionnyi Kronshtadt" [Revolutionary Kronstadt]. *Morskoi Sbornik* 153 (nos. 2–3, February–March 1918): 45–57.

———. "Tov. Lenin i Kronshtadskaia 'respublika'" [Comrade Lenin and the Kronstadt Republic]. *Krasnaia Letopis'* 10 (no. 1, 1924): 45–49.

Revoliutsionnyi bronenosets: vozstanie v Chernomorskom flote [Revolutionary battleship: an uprising in the Black Sea fleet]. Geneva, 1905.

Roshal', Mikhail Grigor'evich. "Bol'sheviki Gel'singforsa" [Bolsheviks of Helsingfors]. In *Voennye moriaki* (see below), pp. 359–77.

Soldier, assigned to party work in Helsingfors; brother of Semen Roshal, Bolshevik leader at Kronstadt, who was killed in December 1917.

————. "K delu bol'shevikov" [In the cause of the Bolsheviks]. *Petrograd-skaia Pravda*, 5 November 1922.
Rovio, Gustav Semenovich. "Kak Lenin skryvalsia y Gel'singforsskogo 'politsmeistera'" [How Lenin hid at the Helsingfors' police chief's]. In *Lenin v 1917 godu: vospominaniia* [Lenin in 1917: recollections], compiled by A. P. Zhukov et al., pp. 148–56. Moscow, 1967.
Sadovskii, A. "Otnyne nachinaetsia novaia era" [Henceforth begins a new era]. *Zvezda* 11 (November 1967): 5–17.

A sailor on the *Aurora* in 1917.

Shliapnikov, Aleksandr Gavrilovich. *Semnadtsatyi god* [1917]. Moscow-Petrograd, 1923.

Valuable memoir of the leader of the Workers' Opposition.

Smirnov, P., et al. Review of F. F. Raskolnikov's *Kronshtadtsy: iz vospo-minanii bol'shevika* [Kronstadters: from the memoirs of a Bolshevik]. In *Krasnaia Letopis'* 50–51 (nos. 5–6, 1933): 214–15.
Smirnov, V. M. "Krasnaia osen' 1917 goda v Finliandii" [The Red autumn of 1917 in Finland]. *Krasnaia Letopis'* 50–51 (nos. 5–6, 1933): 45–83.
Taimi, Adolf. *Stranitsy perezhitogo* [Pages of a survivor]. 2d ed. Petro-zavodsk, 1955.

Worker at Helsingfors port; Finnish Communist leader.

Tarasov-Rodionov, A. "Pervaia operatsiia" [The first operation]. *Voennyi Vestnik* 4 (no. 42, 1924): 10–13.
Tochenyi, Naum Ivanovich. "Kronshtadttsy i vremennoe pravitel'stvo" [The Kronstadters and the Provisional Government]. In *Voennye moriaki* (see below), pp. 312–37.
Trotsky, Leon. *The History of the Russian Revolution.* Translated by Max Eastman. 3 vols. New York, 1932–34.
————. *My Life.* New York, 1960.
————. *1905.* Translated by Anya Bostock. New York, 1971.
Vakhrameev, Ivan Ivanovich. "My—baltiitsy" [We—the Baltic sailors]. In *Petrograd v dni velikogo oktiabria*, pp. 413–18. Leningrad, 1967.

Revolutionary from 1905; sailor from 1908; chairman of ship's committee of transport *Oland*; delegate to Second All-Russian Congress of Soviets; chairman of Navy Revolutionary Committee from October to December; died in 1965.

————. *Vo imia revoliutsii* [In the name of the Revolution]. Moscow, 1957.
Vishnevskii, Evgenii Ivanovich. "Matrosskaia fraktsiia Gel'singforsskogo

sovet: Tsentrobalt, organizatsiia matrosskikh mass" [The Sailors' Section of the Helsingfors Soviet: Tsentrobalt, the organization of the sailors]. In *Oktiabr'skii shkval*, pp. 50–77. Leningrad, 1927.

Leader of Sailors' Assembly of Helsingfors Soviet; one of founders of Sailors' University.

Voennye moriaki v bor'be za pobedu oktiabr'skoi revoliutsii [The sailors in the struggle for the victory of the October Revolution]. Edited by S. F. Naida. Moscow, 1958.

Volkov, Sergei Alekseevich. "Moriaki 'Samsona'" [Sailors of the *Samson*]. In *Petrograd v dni velikogo oktiabria*, pp. 351–56. Leningrad, 1967.

Sailor of *Samson* in Battle of Moon Sound and the October Revolution; civil-war commissar.

Zaitsev, P. "V Kronshtadte" [In Kronstadt]. *Novyi Mir* 33 (no. 7, July 1957): 166–72.

Zalezhskii, Vladimir Nikolaevich. *Iz vospominanii podpol'shchika* [From the memoirs of an underground revolutionary]. 2d ed. Kharkov, 1931.

Social Democrat from 1902; assigned as party worker to Helsingfors; died in 1957.

Zalutskii, Petr Antonovich. "V poslednye dni podpol'nogo Peterburgskogo komiteta bol'shevikov v nachale 1917 g." [During the last days of the underground Petersburg Committee of Bolsheviks at the beginning of 1917]. *Krasnaia Letopis'* 35 (no. 2, 1935): 34–37.

A leader of the Russian Bureau of the Central Committee in 1916–17.

Zinchenko, P. F. "My iz Kronshtadta" [We are from Kronstadt]. In *Oktiabrem rozhdennye* [October is born], edited by N. S. Gudkova, pp. 55–59. Moscow, 1967.

NON-BOLSHEVIK

Abramovitch, Raphael R. *The Soviet Revolution, 1917–1939.* New York, 1962.

A Menshevik leader.

Aprelev, Captain Boris. *Bryzgi moria* [Sea spray]. Prague, 1931.

Important for background; author not in Baltic in 1917.

———. *Nashei smene* [Those who take our place]. Shanghai, 1934.

Buchanan, Sir George. *My Mission to Russia and Other Diplomatic Memories.* 2 vols. London, 1923.

The British ambassador in Petrograd.

Buchanan, Meriel. *Petrograd, the City of Trouble, 1914–1918.* London, 1919.

The ambassador's daughter.

Chernov, V. M. *The Great Russian Revolution.* Translated and abridged by Philip E. Mosely. New Haven, Conn., 1936.

The Socialist Revolutionary leader; minister of agriculture in June and July 1917.

Crosley, Pauline S. *Intimate Letters from Petrograd.* New York, 1920.

Wife of the American naval attaché.

Fabritskii, S. S. *Iz proshlago (vospominaniia flagel'-ad'iutanta imperatora Nikolaia II)* [From the past: memoirs of the flag adjutant of Emperor Nicholas II]. Berlin, 1926.

Naval background; not in Baltic in 1917.

Fedotoff White, Dmitri. *Survival through War and Revolution in Russia.* Philadelphia, 1939.

Naval attaché in Washington in 1915; staff officer on destroyer in early 1917; assistant naval attaché in London; White Volga flotilla commander in 1918; captured by Bolsheviks; editor of *Morskoi Sbornik*; defected.

Graf, Garold Karlovich. *Na "Novike" (Baltiiskii flot v voinu i revoliutsiiu)* [On the *Novik*: the Baltic fleet in war and revolution]. Munich, 1922.

Destroyer commander of the Baltic fleet. Above also published in English translation as *The Russian Navy in War and Revolution from 1914 to 1918* (Munich, 1923) and in French, *La Marine russe dans la guerre et dans la révolution, 1914–1918* (Paris, 1928).

Guichard, Louis, and Novik, Dmitri. *Sous la croix de Saint-André.* Paris, 1929.

Iarchuk, Efim [Khaim Zakharovich]. *Kronshtadt v Russkoi revoliutsii* [Kronstadt in the Russian Revolution]. New York, 1923.

Anarchist leader at Kronstadt in 1917; supported Bolsheviks until March 1921.

Il'vov, B. Ia. *Rokot moria* [The roar of the sea]. Shanghai, 1935.

Commander of destroyer *Metkii* during the October Revolution.

Karpov, Captain. "Mysli o vozstaniia na flote" [Thoughts about revolt in the navy]. *Chasovoi* 77 (1 April 1932): 12–14; 78 (15 April 1932): 9–13.

Kerensky, Alexander F. *Russia and History's Turning Point.* New York, 1965.

Knox, Major General Sir Alfred. *With the Russian Army, 1914–17: Being Chiefly Extracts from the Diary of a Military Attaché.* 2 vols. London, 1921.

British military attaché in Russia during 1917.

Kryzhanovskii, N. "Vozstanie na kreisera 'Pamiat' Azova' v 1906 godu" [The revolt on the cruiser *Pamiat' Azova* in 1906]. *Morskie Zapiski* 6 nos. 3–4, December 1948): 3–17; 7 (no. 1, March 1949): 3–14; 7 (no. 2, June 1949): 16–32.

An officer on board the *Pamiat' Azova* in 1906.

Lebedev, Viktor [Vladimir Ivanovich]. *Souvenirs d'un volontaire russe dans l'armée française, 1914–1916.* Translated by P. F. Trogan and I. de Wyzewa. Paris, 1917.

Right Socialist Revolutionary and Kerensky supporter; assistant minister of war for naval affairs in July and August; later chief of staff for Kolchak during the civil war.

Lockhart, R. H. Bruce. *Memoirs of a British Agent: Being an Account of the Author's Early Life in Many Lands and of His Official Mission to Moscow in 1918.* London and New York, 1932.

British consul general in Moscow until August 1917.

Lukomskii, General A. S. *Vospominaniia.* 2 vols. Berlin, 1927.

Kornilov's chief of staff in 1917.

Mazurenko, K. K. *Na 'Slave' v Rizhkom zalive* [On the *Slava* in the Gulf of Riga]. Jordanville, N.Y., 1949.

Officer on battleship *Slava* in 1917.

Merkushov, Capt. V. "Otvergnutyi plan" [The rejected plan]. *Zarubezhnyi Morskoi Sbornik* 3 (January–March, 1929): 31–45.

Naval staff officer in Petrograd.

————. "Russkii flot i revoliutsiia" [The Russian navy and the Revolution]. *Chasovoi* 80 (15 May 1932): 15–18.

Monasterev, N., and Terestchenko, Serge. *Histoire de la marine russe.* Translated by Jean Perceau. Paris, 1932.

Price, M. Philips. *My Reminiscences of the Russian Revolution.* London, 1921.

British journalist in Russia; visited Kronstadt in June.

Reed, John. *Ten Days That Shook the World.* Vintage ed. New York, 1960.

Rengarten, I. I. "Baltiiskii flot nakanune oktiabria" [The Baltic fleet on the eve of October]. *Krasnyi Arkhiv* 35 (1929): 5–36.

Staff intelligence officer in 1917.

————. "Fevral'skaia revoliutsiia v Baltiiskom flote" [The February Revolution in the Baltic fleet]. *Krasnyi Arkhiv* 32 (1929): 88–124.

————. "Oktiabr'skaia revoliutsiia v Baltiiskom flote" [The October Revolution in the Baltic Fleet]. *Krasnyi Arkhiv* 25 (1927): 34–95.

Die Revolutionstäge in Helsingfors Februar bis Dezember 1917 von einem Russischen Militär. Berlin, 1919.

Anonymous anti-Bolshevik memoirs of revolution in fleet at Helsing-fors.

Scheer, Admiral Reinhard. *Germany's High Sea Fleet in the World War.* London, 1920.

Shteinberg, I. *Ot fevralia po oktiabr' 1917 g.* [From February through October 1917]. Berlin-Milan, 1919.

Memoirs of a leading Left Socialist Revolutionary.

Sukhanov, N. N. *The Russian Revolution: 1917.* Edited by Joel Carmichael. Torchbook ed. 2 vols. New York, 1962.

Valuable memoir of a Menshevik Internationalist.

Timirev, S. N. *Vospominaniia morskogo ofitsera: Baltiiskii flot vo vremia voiny i revoliutsii (1914–1918 gg.)* [Memoirs of a naval officer: the Baltic fleet during war and revolution, 1914–1918]. New York, 1961.

Commander of a cruiser in the Baltic in 1917; memoirs written in 1923.

Tschischwitz, Lieutenant General von. *The Army and Navy during the Conquest of the Baltic Islands in October, 1917: An Analytical Study Based on Actual Experiences.* Translated by Col. Henry Hossfield for the Army War College. Fort Leavenworth, Kans., 1933.

Commander of German invasion of the Baltic islands during September and October 1917.

Tsereteli, I. G. *Vospominaniia o fevral'skoi revoliutsii* [Memoirs of the February Revolution]. 2 vols. Paris, 1963.

Tsion, S. A. *Tri dnia vozstaniia v Sveaborge* [The three-day revolt in Sveaborg].

Memoirs of the 1906 revolt at the Sveaborg naval base by one of the leaders, who became a Socialist Revolutionary leader at Helsingfors during 1917.

Tsyvinskii, Admiral G. F. *50 let v imperatorskom flote.* [Fifty years in the Imperial Navy]. Riga, n.d.

Williams, Albert Rhys. *Journey into Revolution: Petrograd, 1917–1918.* Edited by Lucita Williams. Chicago, 1969.

An American journalist on the scene in October 1917.

Woytinsky, W. S. *Stormy Passage.* New York, 1961.

Menshevik supporter of Provisional Government.

SECONDARY SOURCES

SOVIET

Akhun, M. I., and Petrov, V. A. *Bol'sheviki i armiia v 1905–1917 gg.* [The Bolsheviks and the army in 1905–1917]. Leningrad, 1929.

Andreev, A. M. *Sovety rabochikh i soldatskikh deputatov nakanune oktiabria* [Soviets of Workers' and Soldiers' Deputies on the eve of October]. Moscow, 1967.

Astrakhan, Kh. M. *Bol'sheviki i ikh politicheskie protivniki v 1917 godu* [The Bolsheviks and their political opponents in 1917]. Leningrad, 1973.

Avrekh, A. Ia. *Stolypin i tret'ia duma* [Stolypin and the Third Duma]. Moscow, 1968.

Belli, V. A. "Dni fevral'skoi revoliutsii v minnoi divizii Baltiiskogo flota v Revele" [The days of the February Revolution in the Mine Division of the Baltic fleet at Revel]. In *Sbornik dokladov voenno-istoricheskoi sektsii,* vol. 2, Leningradskii dom uchenykh im. M. Gor'kogo Akademiia Nauk SSSR, pp. 40–42. Moscow-Leningrad, 1959.

Beskrovnyi, L. G. *Ocherki voennoi istoriografii Rossii* [Essays on Russian military historiography]. Moscow, 1962.

————. *Russkaia armiia i flot v XIX veke: voenno-ekonomicheskii potential Rossii* [The Russian army and navy in the nineteenth century: the military-economic potential of Russia]. Moscow, 1973.

Blinov, A. "Matrosskie komitety Baltiiskogo flota v 1917 godu" [Sailors' Committees of the Baltic Fleet in 1917]. *Voenno-Istoricheskii Zhurnal* 11 (November 1967): 110–15.

Bogdanov, A. V. *Moriaki-baltiitsy v 1917 g.* [Sailors in the Baltic in 1917]. Moscow, 1955.

Bor'ba bol'shevikov za armiiu v trekh revoliutsiiakh [The struggle of the Bolsheviks for the army in three revolutions]. Edited by L. G. Beskrovnyi, L. S. Gaponenko, and S. V. Tiutiukin. Moscow, 1969.

Burdzhalov, E. N. *Vtoraia russkaia revoliutsiia: Moskva; front; periferiia* [The second Russian Revolution: Moscow; the front; the periphery]. Moscow, 1971.

————. *Vtoraia russkaia revoliutsiia: vosstanie v Petrograde* [The second Russian Revolution: the uprising in Petrograd]. Moscow, 1967.

D'Or, O. L. *Krasnyi chasovoi Kronshtadt* [The Red Guard Kronstadt]. Moscow, 1920.

Drezen, A. K. "Baltiiskii flot v godu pod"ema (1910–1913)" [The Baltic fleet in the years of ascent, 1910–1913]. *Krasnaia Letopis'* 3 (1930): 124–63.

Dykov, I. G. *Pobeda oktiabr'skogo vooruzhennogo vosstaniia v Petrograde v 1917 godu* [The victory of the October armed uprising in Petrograd in 1917]. Moscow, 1957.

Egorov, Al. *Baltflot v gody reaktsii, 1909–1913* [The Baltic fleet in the years of reaction, 1909–1913]. Moscow, 1928.

Eideman, R., and Melikov, V. *Armiia v 1917 g.* [The army in 1917]. Moscow-Leningrad, 1927.

Erykalov, E. F. *Oktiabr'skoe vooruzhennoe vosstanie v Petrograde* [The October armed uprising in Petrograd]. Leningrad, 1966.

Gaponenko, L. S. *Velikaia oktiabr'skaia sotsialisticheskaia revoliutsiia* [The great October socialist revolution]. Moscow, 1957.

Garkavenko, D. A. "Sotsial'nyi sostav matrosov russkogo flota v epokhu imperializma" [The social strata of the sailors of the Russian navy in the epoch of imperialism]. *Istoriia SSSR* 5 (May 1968): 36–42.

Gerbach, V. V., et al. *Rabochii-baltiitsy v trekh revoliutsiiakh* [Workers of the Baltic Works in three revolutions]. Leningrad, 1959.

Golub, P. A. *Partiia, armiia i revoliutsiia: otvoevanie partiei bol'shevikov armii na storonu revoliutsii (mart 1917–fevral' 1918)* [The party, the army, and the Revolution: the winning of the army to the side of the

Revolution by the Bolshevik party, March 1917–February 1918]. Moscow, 1967.

Guseinov, F. A. "O bol'shevistskikh fraktsiiakh v sovetakh v 1917 g." [About the Bolshevik factions in the soviets in 1917]. *Voprosy Istorii KPSS* 10 (October 1968): 114–20.

Gusev, K. V., and Eritsian, Kh. A. *Ot soglashatel'stva k kontrrevoliutsii (ocherki istorii politicheskogo bankrotstva i gibeli partii sotsialistov-revoliutsionerov)* [From reformism to counterrevolution: essays on the history of political bankruptcy and ruin of the party of the Socialist Revolutionaries]. Moscow, 1968.

Hubatsch, Walther. *Kaiserliche Marine: Aufgaben und Leistungen*. Munich, 1975.

Ignat'ev, A. V. *Vneshniaia politika vremennogo pravitel'stva* [The foreign policy of the Provisional Government]. Moscow, 1974.

Il'ina, I. V. *Bor'ba partii bol'shevikov protiv proiavlenii "levizny" v period podgotovki oktiabr'skoi revoliutsii* [The struggle of the Bolshevik party against the manifestation of "Leftism" in the period of preparation for the October Revolution]. Moscow, 1967.

Iunga, E. S. *Bessmertnyi korabl'* [Immortal ship]. Moscow, 1957.

Ivanov, N. Ia. *Kornilovshchina i ee razgrom* [The reign of Kornilov and its destruction]. Leningrad, 1965.

———. *Velikii oktiabr' v Petrograde* [The great October in Petrograd]. Leningrad, 1957.

Izmailov, N. F., and Pukhov, A. S. *Tsentrobalt*. 2d rev. ed. Kaliningrad, 1967.

Kapustin, M. I. *Soldaty severnogo fronta v bor'be na vlast' sovetov* [Soldiers of the Northern Front in the struggle for Soviet power]. Moscow, 1957.

———. *Zagovor generalov (iz istorii Kornilovshchiny i ee razgroma)* [The conspiracy of generals: from the history of the Kornilov Affair and its failure]. Moscow, 1968.

Khesin, S. S. "Lichnyi sostav russkogo flota v 1917 godu" [The personnel of the Russian navy in 1917]. *Voenno-Istoricheskii Zhurnal* 11 (November 1965): 99–104.

———. *Matrosy revoliutsii* [Sailors of the Revolution]. Moscow, 1958.

———. *Oktiabr'skaia revoliutsiia i flot* [The October Revolution in the navy]. Moscow, 1971.

———. "Tsentrobalt (k 50 letiiu sozdaniia)" [Tsentrobalt: toward the fiftieth anniversary]. *Voenno-Istoricheskii Zhurnal* 4 (April 1967): 120–25.

———. *Voennye moriaki v bor'be za vlast' sovetov, oktiabr' 1917 g.–mart 1918 g.* [The sailors in the struggle for Soviet power, October 1917–March 1918]. Moscow, 1953.

Kitanina, T. M. *Voenno-infliatsionnye kontserny v Rossii 1914-1917 gg.* [War inflation effects on factories in Russia, 1914-1917]. Leningrad, 1969.

Kiuru, M. Kh. *Boevoi rezerv revoliutsionnogo Petrograda v 1917 g.: iz istorii russkikh bol'shevistskikh organizatsii v Finliandii* [The battle reserves of revolutionary Petrograd in 1917: from the history of the Russian Bolshevik organizations in Finland]. Petrozavodsk, 1965.

Klopotov, B. E. "K 250-letiiu sudostroeniia v Leningrade" [On the two hundred and fiftieth anniversary of shipbuilding in Leningrad]. *Sudostroenie* 1 (1960) : 81-83.

Konstantinov, A. P. *F. F. Il'in-Raskol'nikov.* Leningrad, 1964.

Kornatovskii, N. *Partiia i oktiabr'skoe vosstanie v Petrograde* [The party and the October uprising in Petrograd]. Leningrad, 1933.

Krymov, A. "Iz fevral'skikh tumanov—k ogniam oktiabria, moriaki v fevral'skoi revoliutsii" [From the February mists—to the Fires of October: the sailors in the February Revolution]. *Krasnyi Flot* 3 (1925) : 17-24.

Lebedev, V. V. *Mezhdunarodnoe polozhenie Rossii nakanune oktiabr'skoi Revoliutsii* [The international position of Russia on the eve of the October Revolution]. Moscow, 1967.

Lur'e, M. "Vooruzhennoe vosstanie v Petrograde" [The armed uprising in Petrograd]. *Istoricheskii Zhurnal* 7 (no. 10, October 1937) : 46-64.

Marat, Kh. S. "Rabochie, soldaty, i matrosy golosuiut za Lenina" [Workers, soldiers, and sailors vote for Lenin]. *Voprosy Istorii KPSS* 11 (November 1968) : 42-52.

Medvedev, V. K. "Kronshtadt v iiul'skie dni 1917 goda" [Kronstadt in the July days of 1917]. *Istoricheskie Zapiski* 42 (1953) : 262-75.

Miller, V. I. "Petrogradskii granizon v fevral'skie dni 1917 godu" [The Petrograd garrison in the February days of 1917]. *Voenno-Istoricheskii Zhurnal* 2 (1967) : 117-24.

————. *Soldatskie komitety russkoi armii v 1917 g.* [Soldiers' committees of the Russian army in 1917]. Moscow, 1974.

Mints, I. I. *Istoriia velikogo oktiabria* [History of the great October]. 2 vols. Moscow, 1967-68.

Mitel'man, M. *Oktiabr'skoe vooruzhennoe vosstanie v Petrograde v 1917 g.* [The October armed uprising in Petrograd in 1917]. Moscow, 1938.

Muratov, Kh. I. *Revoliutsionnoe dvizhenie v Russkoi armii v 1917 godu* [The revolutionary movement in the Russian army in 1917]. Moscow, 1958.

Naida, S. F. *Revoliutsionnoe dvizhenie v tsarskom flote, 1825-1917* [The revolutionary movement in the Tsarist navy, 1825-1917). Moscow, 1948.

Nazarov, A. F. *Nikolai Markin.* Moscow, 1964.

Nelaev, V. "Matros-bol'shevik Timofei Ul'iantsev" [Sailor-Bolshevik Timofei Uliantsev]. *Voenno-Istoricheskii Zhurnal* 10 (October 1968): 106–9.

Okun', S. B., ed. *Putilovets v trekh revoliutsiiakh: sbornik materialov po istorii putilovskogo zavoda* [The men of Putilov in three revolutions: collection of materials on the history of the Putilov Works]. Moscow, 1933.

———. "Vosstanie na kreisere 'Pamiat' Azova' v 1906 godu" [The revolt on the cruiser *Pamiat' Azova* in 1906]. *Krasnaia Letopis'* 39 (no. 6, 1930): 65–95.

Ozolin, Ia. "Narastanie i khod oktiabr'skikh sobytii" [The escalation and course of the October events]. *Morskoi Sbornik* 11 (November 1932): 54–58.

Pavlovich, N. B., ed. *Flot v pervoi mirovoi voine* [The navy in the First World War]. 2 vols. Moscow, 1964.

Perovskii, E. P. *Vernyi dolgu revoliutsii* [A loyal duty to the Revolution]. Leningrad, 1964.

Petrash, V. V. *Moriaki Baltiiskogo flota v bor'be za pobedu oktiabria* [Sailors of the Baltic fleet in the struggle for the victory of October]. Moscow-Leningrad, 1966.

Pointkovskii, S. *Oktiabr' 1917 g.* [October 1917]. Moscow-Leningrad, 1927.

Pokrovskii, M. N., ed. *Ocherki po istorii oktiabr'skoi revoliutsii* [Essays on the history of the October Revolution]. 2 vols. Moscow-Leningrad, 1927.

Pukhov, A. S. *Moonzundskoe srazhenie* [The Battle of Moon Sound]. Moscow, 1957.

———. "Petrogradskii garnizon i Baltiiskii flot v dni fevral'skoi revoliutsii" [The Petrograd garrison and the Baltic fleet in the days of the February Revolution]. In *Sbornik dokladov voenno-istoricheskoi sektsii*, vol. 2, pp. 5–20. Moscow-Leningrad, 1959.

———. See Izmailov, above.

Rabinovich, S. E. *Vserossiiskaia voennaia konferentsiia bol'shevikov 1917 goda* [The All-Russian Military Conference of Bolsheviks of 1917]. Moscow, 1931.

Semenov, K. T. "Rost i ukreplenie bol'shevistskikh partiinykh organizatsii v marte–aprele 1917 goda" [The growth and strengthening of Bolshevik party organizations in March–April 1917]. *Voprosy Istorii KPSS* 2 (1957): 142–53.

Senchakova, L. T. *Revoliutsionnoe dvizhenie v russkoi armii i flote: v kontse XIX–nachale XX v.* [The revolutionary movement in the Russian army and navy: at the end of the nineteenth century–beginning of the twentieth century]. Moscow, 1972.

Shalaginova, L. M. "Esery-internatsionalisty v gody pervoi mirovoi voiny" [The SR-Internationalists in the years of the First World War]. In *Pervaia miovaia voina, 1914–1918*, edited by A. L. Sidorov et al. Moscow, 1968.

Shatsillo, K. F. *Russkii imperializm i razvitie flota nakanune pervoi mirovoi voiny (1906–1914 gg.)* [Russian imperialism and the development of the navy on the eve of the First World War, 1906–1914). Moscow, 1968.

Shigalin, G. I. *Voennaia ekonomika v pervuiu miovuiu voinu (1914–1918 gg.)* [War economy in the First World War, 1914–1918]. Moscow, 1956.

Shishkin, V. F. "Kronshtadtskii intsident v mae 1917 goda" [The Kronstadt incident in May 1917]. *Uchenye zapiski, Leningradskii gosudarstvennyi pedagogicheskii institut imeni A. N. Gertsena* 152 (1958): 3–27.

Sidorov, A. L. *Ekonomicheskoe polozhenie Rossii v gody pervoi mirovoi voiny* [The economic position of Russia in the years of the First World War]. Moscow, 1973.

Sivkov, P. Z. *Kronshtadt: stranitsy revoliutsionnoi istorii* [Kronstadt: pages of revolutionary history]. Leningrad, 1972.

Sobolev, G. L. *Revoliutsionnoe soznanie rabochikh i soldat Petrograda v 1917 godu* [The revolutionary consciousness of workers and soldiers of Petrograd in 1917]. Leningrad, 1973.

Soboleva, P. I. *Oktiabr'skaia revoliutsiia i krakh sotsial-soglashatelei* [The October Revolution and the failure of the social-compromisers]. Moscow, 1968.

Startsev, V. I. *Ocherki po istorii Petrogradskoi krasnoi gvardii i rabochei militsii* [Essays on the history of the Petrograd Red Guard and Workers Militia]. Moscow-Leningrad, 1965.

Stoliarenko, M. A. *Syny partii—baltiitsy* [Sons of the party—sailors of the Baltic]. Leningrad, 1969.

———. *V. I. Lenin i revoliutsionnye moriaki (V. I. Lenin i rabota partii bol'shevikov v voenno-morskom flote 1903–1917 gg.)* [V. I. Lenin and the revolutionary sailors: V. I. Lenin and the work of the Bolshevik party in the navy, 1903–1917]. Moscow, 1970.

Tsypkin, G. A. *Krasnaia gvardiia v bor'be za vlast' sovetov* [The Red Guard in the struggle for the power of soviets]. Moscow, 1967.

Vladimirova, Vera. *Kontr-revoliutsiia v 1917 g. (Kornilovshchina)* [Counter-revolution in 1917: the Kornilov Affair]. Moscow, 1924.

Zakova, A. "Armiia i flot nakanune velikoi sotsialistichskoi revoliutsii" [The army and navy on the eve of the Great Socialist Revolution]. *Istoricheskii Zhurnal* 7 (no. 9, September 1937): 25–31.

Zlokazov, G. I. *Petrogradskii sovet rabochikh i soldatskikh deputatov v period mirnogo razvitiia revoliutsii (fevral'–iiun' 1917 g.)* [The Petrograd Soviet of Workers' and Soldiers' Deputies in the period of the peaceful development of the Revolution, February–June 1917]. Moscow, 1969.

Znamenskii, O. N. *Iiul'skii krizis 1917 goda* [The July Crisis of 1917]. Moscow-Leningrad, 1964.

NON-SOVIET

Anweiler, Oskar. *The Soviets: The Russian Workers, Peasants, and Soldiers Councils, 1905–1921.* Translated by Ruth Hein. New York, 1974.

Arendt, Hannah. *On Revolution.* New York, 1963.

Asher, Harvey. "The Korniloff Affair: A Reinterpretation." *Russian Review* 29 (no. 3, July 1970): 286–300.

Avrich, Paul. *Kronstadt, 1921.* Princeton, N.J., 1970.

———. *The Russian Anarchists.* Princeton, N.J., 1967.

Carr, E. H. *The Bolshevik Revolution, 1917–1923.* 3 vols. New York, 1951–53.

Chamberlin, W. H. *The Russian Revolution, 1917–1921.* 2 vols. New York, 1935.

Coates, W. P., and Coates, Zelda K. *Russia, Finland and the Baltic.* London, 1940.

Coper, Rudolf. *Failure of a Revolution: Germany in 1918–1919.* Cambridge, England, 1955.

Daniels, Robert V. *The Conscience of the Revolution.* Cambridge, Mass., 1960.

———. *Red October: The Bolshevik Revolution of 1917.* New York and London, 1967.

Deutscher, Isaac. *The Prophet Armed: Trotsky, 1879–1921.* New York, 1954.

———. *The Unfinished Revolution: Russia, 1917–1967.* London, 1967.

Dunn, John M. *Modern Revolutions: An Introduction to the Analysis of a Political Phenomenon.* Cambridge, England, 1972.

Ferro, Marc. *The Russian Revolution of February 1917.* London, 1972.

Florinsky, Michael T. *The End of the Russian Empire.* New York, 1961.

———. *Russia: A History and an Interpretation.* 2 vols. New York, 1953.

Futrell, Michael. *Northern Underground: Episodes of Russian Revolutionary Transport and Communications through Scandinavia and Finland, 1863–1917.* London, 1963.

Ganzen, A. V., and Zhitkov, K. G. *Rossiiskii imperatorskii flot* [The Russian imperial navy]. Petrograd, 1916.

Golovin, N. N. *The Russian Army in the World War.* New Haven, Conn., 1931.

Greger, René. *The Russian Fleet, 1914–1917*. London, 1972.

Haimson, Leopold. "The Problem of Social Stability in Urban Russia, 1905–1917." *Slavic Review* 23 (no. 4, 1964): 619–42; 24 (no. 1, 1965): 1–22.

Harmaja, Leo. *Effects of the War on Economic and Social Life in Finland*. Carnegie Endowment for International Peace, Division of Economics and History. New Haven, Conn., 1933.

Horn, Daniel. *The German Naval Mutinies of World War I*. New Brunswick, N.J., 1969.

Katkov, George. *Russia 1917: The February Revolution*. London, 1967.

———. "The Russian Navy and the Revolution: (a) 1905 to 1921." In *The Soviet Navy*, edited by Commander M. G. Saunders, pp. 84–92. London, 1958.

Kirby, David. "The Finnish Social Democratic Party and the Bolsheviks." *Journal of Contemporary History* 7 (January–April 1972): 181–98.

———. "A Navy in Revolution: The Russian Baltic Fleet in 1917." *European Studies Review* 4 (October 1974): 345–58.

Krohn, Aarni. *Tsaarin Helsinki: idyllista itsenaisyyteen* [Tsarist Helsinki: an ideal autonomy]. Helsinki, 1967.

Liebman, Marcel. *The Russian Revolution*. Translated by Arnold J. Pomerans. New York, 1970.

Longley, David A. "Officers and Men: A Study of the Development of Political Attitudes among the Sailors of the Baltic Fleet in 1917." *Soviet Studies* 25 (1973): 29–50.

———. "Some Historiographical Problems of Bolshevik Party History (The Kronstadt Bolsheviks in March 1917)." *Jahrbücher für Geschichte Osteuropas*, n.s. 27 (no. 4, 1974): 494–514.

Melgunov, S. P. *The Bolshevik Seizure of Power*. Edited and abridged by Sergei G. Pushkarev. Santa Barbara, Calif., 1972.

———. *Martovskie dni 1917 goda* [The March days of 1917]. Paris, 1961.

Mitchell, Donald W. *A History of Russian and Soviet Sea Power*. New York, 1974.

Morris, L. P. "The Russians, the Allies and the War, February–July 1917." *Slavonic and East European Review* 50 (no. 118, January 1972): 29–48.

Pethybridge, Roger. *The Spread of the Russian Revolution: Essays on 1917*. London, 1972.

Pinchuk, Ben-Cion. *The Octobrists in the Third Duma, 1907–1912*. Seattle, Wash., and London, 1974.

Pipes, Richard, ed. *Revolutionary Russia: A Symposium*. New York, 1968.

Polvinen, Tuomo. *Venäjän vallankumous ja Suomi, 1917–1920* [The Russian Revolution and Finland, 1917–1920]. Vol. 1: *Helmikuu 1917–toukokuu 1918* [February 1917–May 1918]. Porvoo and Helsinki, 1967.

Rabinowitch, Alexander. *The Bolsheviks Come to Power: The Revolution of 1917 in Petrograd.* New York, 1976.

———. *Prelude to Revolution: The Petrograd Bolsheviks and the July 1917 Uprising.* Bloomington, Ind., and London, 1968.

Radkey, Oliver H. *The Agrarian Foes of Bolshevism.* New York, 1958.

———. *The Election to the Russian Constituent Assembly of 1917.* Cambridge, Mass., 1950.

Rohwer, Jürgen. "The Russians as Naval Opponents in Two World Wars." In *The Soviet Navy,* edited by Commander M. G. Saunders, pp. 44–74. London, 1958.

Rosenberg, William G. *Liberals in the Russian Revolution: The Constitutional Democratic Party, 1917–1921.* Princeton, N.J., 1974.

Schapiro, Leonard. *The Communist Party of the Soviet Union.* 2d ed., rev. and enl. New York, 1971.

———. *The Origin of the Communist Autocracy: Political Opposition in the Soviet State: First Phase, 1917–1922.* New York, 1961.

Seton-Watson, Hugh. *The Russian Empire, 1801–1917.* London, 1967.

Smith, C. Jay, Jr. *Finland and the Russian Revolution, 1917–1922.* Athens,

Stone, Norman. *The Eastern Front, 1914–1917.* New York, 1975.
  Ga., 1958.

Ulam, Adam B. *The Bolsheviks.* New York, 1965.

Ullman, Richard H. *Anglo-Soviet Relations, 1917–1921.* Vol. 1: *Intervention and the War.* Princeton, N.J., 1961.

Von Laue, Theodore H. *Why Lenin? Why Stalin?* Rev. ed. Philadelphia, 1971.

Wade, Rex A. *The Russian Search for Peace: February–October 1917.* Stanford, Calif., 1969.

Warth, Robert D. *The Allies and the Russian Revolution.* Durham, N.C., 1954.

Wettig, G. *Die Rolle der russischen Armee in revolutionären Machtkampf 1917* (Forschungen zur osteuropäischen Geschichte, 12). Berlin, 1967.

DISSERTATIONS

Hartgrove, Joseph D. "Red Tide: The Kronstadters in the Russian Revolutionary Movement, 1901–1917. University of North Carolina, 1975.

Mawdsley, Evan. "The Baltic Fleet in the Russian Revolution, 1917–1921." University of London, 1972.

Medlin, Virgil D. "The Reluctant Revolutionaries: The Petrograd Soviet of Workers' and Soldiers' Deputies 1917." University of Oklahoma, 1974.

INDEX

Åbo (Turku), Åbo-Åland area, 19, 41, 77, 85, 94, 139, 148, 203, 228 n.25, 235 n.52, 244 n.103
Admiral Makarov (cruiser), 32, 98, 124, 134, 212
Admiralty (building), 123, 125, 189, 192, 199, 263 n.79
Admiralty shipyards, 8
Afanasev, A. M., 229 n.35
Afrika (training ship), 186
Aleambarov, Capt. M. N., 49
Aleksandr II (training mineship), 55
Alekseev, Gen. Mikhail, 49
Alexander II, 2, 20
Alexander III, 20–21
Alexandra (empress), 61
Alexandria, 33
Allies (Entente), 44, 163, 174–75, 199, 204, 206, 258 n.34
All-Russian Congress of Workers' and Soldiers' Deputies. *See* First All-Russian Congress of Soviets; Second All-Russian Congress of Soviets
Alnichenkov, Ivan (Menshevik), 244 n.103
Altfater, Capt. Vasilii, 47–48, 72, 208

Amur (minelayer), 185–86
Anarchists, 111, 134, 164; in July 1917, 115–16, 118–19, 244 n.108, 245 n.4, 246 n.10; after October Revolution, 202–3
Anchor Square (Kronstadt), 26, 68–69, 88, 119
Andrei Pervosvannyi (battleship), 74–75, 78, 83, 103, 109, 239 n.46
Anisimov, V. A., 243 n.96
Antonov-Ovseenko, Vladimir: as Helsingfors Bolshevik leader, 95, 112, 157, 164–67, 169, 219; arrest of, 130, 132, 141; in October Revolution, 178–79, 181–86 passim, 189–90, 193–94; in Soviet government, 198, 214
Ariadne (hospital ship), 40
Arkhangelsk, 42–43, 166, 175
Armiia i Flot Svobodnoi Rossii, 131
Artamanov, Capt. L. K., 128–29, 144
Arturus (steamer), 32
Astoria, Hotel, 42, 63, 145
Aurora (cruiser), 11, 18–19, 33, 142, 144, 162, 229 n.28; in February–March Revolution, 64–67, 73–75; during July Crisis, 120, 132; in October 1917, 181–90, 261 n.65,

Index

Index

Port Arthur, 3
Potemkin (battleship), mutiny on, 3, 6, 12, 23–25, 30–31
Pozharov, Nikolai (Bolshevik, Kronstadt), 144
Pravda (newspaper, Petrograd), 34, 102–4, 129
Preobrazhinsky Regiment, 26, 83
Preparliament (Democratic Council of the Republic), 167–68, 185
Priboi (newspaper, Helsingfors), 130, 169
Price, M. Philips, 112
Progressive Bloc, 60, 231 n.5
Proletarskoe Delo (newspaper, Kronstadt), 127
Pronin, Aleksei (Bolshevik, Kronstadt), 68, 94, 145, 181, 183, 193, 198, 214
Pronskii, Konstantin, 229 n.35
Proshian, Prosh (Left SR, Helsingfors), 112, 116, 130, 132, 141, 177, 201, 245 n.2, 267 n.41
Protopopov, A. D. (minister of interior), 62
Provisional Government: foreign policy of, 62, 105–6, 180; formation of, 63, 70, 73, 77; fleet support for, 73, 146–48; attempts by, to control fleet, 75, 80, 86, 130–34; naval policies of, 86, 90; internal policies of, 105, 157; fleet opposition to, 105, 115–25 passim, 137, 152, 165–66, 181, and passim, 203; war efforts, 117, 168; dilemmas of, 168, 217; fall of, 181–92
Pskov, 196
Pulkovo Heights, 193–95
Purishkevich, V. M., 6
Putilov Works, 8–9, 19, 60, 63, 120
Pyshkin, Genadii (SR, Kronstadt), 244 n.103

Rabochii Put (newspaper, Petrograd), 180

Raimo, Pavel, 176
Raskolnikov, Fedor (Bolshevik), 40, 100, 109–10, 113, 132, 146, 164, 240 n.63; in Kronstadt Soviet, 106–8, 244 n.103; during 1917 July Crisis, 119, 121–22, 127–28, 246 n.15, 247 n.16, 247 n.19; in October 1917, 167, 178, 193, 195, 198, 260 n.51; after October Revolution, 209–10, 213–14, 219, 265 n.11
Rasputin, Gregory, 61–62
Rastorguev, Ilia *(Poltava)*, 93
Razvozov, Capt.-Adm. Aleksandr, 126, 130, 135, 140, 151, 153–54, 159, 187, 197, 202–3, 207–8, 262 n.75, 263 n.76, 266 n.19
Recruitment, for navy, 16–17, 39, 224 n.31
Red Army, 212
Red Guards, 178–79, 181, 188, 193–94, 201, 261 n.60, 263 n.79
Reed, John, 193
Remnev, Afanasii (Bolshevik, Kronstadt), 119, 127–28, 132
Rengarten, Capt. Ivan (staff, *Krechet*), 48-49, 72, 93, 96, 141, 153, 177, 228 n.15, 267 n.41
Resanov, F. E., 230 n.51
Respublika (battleship), 83, 102, 124, 126, 189, 196, 213, 239 n.46, 246 n.7. See also *Imperator Pavel I*
Retivyi (mine sweeper), 77
Revel: as base, 7, 19, 26, 51, 126, 140, 157, 166, 176; revolutionary activity in, before 1917, 29–31, 33–34; in March 1917, 67, 71–72, 238 n.36, 239 n.37
Revel Soviet: formation of, 93–94, 238 n.36; party strength in, 95, 134
Revolutionary Committee (Helsingfors), 146–48, 154, 256 n.4
Revolution of 1905, 1, 14, 24–28
Riazanov, David, 196
Riga, 7, 19, 143, 157

DATE DUE

22 Feb 84			
GAYLORD			PRINTED IN U.S.A.